THE SPIRIT OF THE PSALMS

RHETORICAL ANALYSIS, AFFECTIVITY,
AND PENTECOSTAL SPIRITUALITY

לַמְנַצֵּחַ יַחַלְּעֻזֹּ וְדִיֹרֶךָ הוֹשִׁיעָה יְמִינְךָ וַעֲנֵנוּ
אֱלֹהִים דִּבֶּר בְּקָדְשׁוֹ אֶעְלֹזָה אֲחַלְּקָה
שְׁכֶם וְעֵמֶק סֻכּוֹת אֲמַדֵּד לִי גִלְעָד
וְלִי מְנַשֶּׁה וְאֶפְרַיִם מָעוֹז רֹאשִׁי יְהוּדָה
מְחֹקְקִי מוֹאָב סִיר רַחְצִי עַל אֱדוֹם
אַשְׁלִיךְ נַעֲלִי עָלַי פְּלֶשֶׁת הִתְרוֹעָעִי
מִי יֹבִלֵנִי עִיר מָצוֹר מִי נָחַנִי עַד אֱדוֹם הֲלֹא
אַתָּה אֱלֹהִים זְנַחְתָּנוּ וְלֹא אֵתָצֵא אֱלֹהִים
בְּצִבְאוֹתֵינוּ הָבָה לָנוּ עֶזְרָת מִצָּר
וְשָׁוְא תְּשׁוּעַת אָדָם
בֵּאלֹהִים נַעֲשֶׂה חָיִל וְהוּא יָבוּס צָרֵינוּ

לַמְנַצֵּחַ עַל נְגִינַת לְדָוִד
שִׁמְעָה אֱלֹהִים רִנָּתִי הַקְשִׁיבָה תְּפִלָּתִי מִקְצֵה הָאָרֶץ
אֵלֶיךָ אֶקְרָא בַּעֲטֹף לִבִּי בְּצוּר יָרוּם מִמֶּנִּי
תַנְחֵנִי כִּי הָיִיתָ מַחְסֶה לִי מִגְדָּל עֹז מִפְּנֵי
אוֹיֵב אָגוּרָה בְאָהָלְךָ עוֹלָמִים
אֶחֱסֶה בְסֵתֶר כְּנָפֶיךָ סֶּלָה כִּי אַתָּה אֱלֹהִים
שָׁמַעְתָּ לִנְדָרָי נָתַתָּ יְרֻשַּׁת יִרְאֵי שְׁמֶךָ
יָמִים עַל יְמֵי מֶלֶךְ תּוֹסִיף שְׁנוֹתָיו
כְּמוֹ דֹר וָדֹר יֵשֵׁב עוֹלָם לִפְנֵי אֱלֹהִים חֶסֶד
וֶאֱמֶת מַן יִנְצְרֻהוּ כֵּן אֲזַמְּרָה שִׁמְךָ
לָעַד לְשַׁלְּמִי נְדָרַי יוֹם יוֹם

לַמְנַצֵּחַ עַל יְדוּתוּן מִזְמוֹר לְדָוִד אַךְ
אֶל אֱלֹהִים דּוּמִיָּה נַפְשִׁי מִמֶּנּוּ יְשׁוּעָתִי
אַךְ הוּא צוּרִי וִישׁוּעָתִי מִשְׂגַּבִּי לֹא אֶמּוֹט

רַבָּה צַר אַתָּה הִתְחוֹלַתָּנוּ עַל אִישׁ תְּרָצֶּחוּ
כֻּלְּכֶם כְּקִיר נָטוּי גָּדֵר הַדְּחוּיָה אַךְ
מִשְּׂאֵתוֹ יָעֲצוּ לְהַדִּיחַ יִרְצוּ כָזָב בְּפִיו
יְבָרֵכוּ וּבְקִרְבָּם יְקַלְלוּ סֶלָה אַךְ לֵאלֹהִים
דּוֹמִּי נַפְשִׁי כִּי מִמֶּנּוּ תִּקְוָתִי אַךְ
הוּא צוּרִי וִישׁוּעָתִי מִשְׂגַּבִּי לֹא
אֶמּוֹט עַל אֱלֹהִים יִשְׁעִי וּכְבוֹדִי צוּר עֻזִּי
מַחְסִי בֵּאלֹהִים בִּטְחוּ בוֹ בְכָל עֵת
עָם שִׁפְכוּ לְפָנָיו לְבַבְכֶם אֱלֹהִים מַחֲסֶה
לָּנוּ סֶלָה אַךְ הֶבֶל בְּנֵי אָדָם כָּזָב בְּנֵי אִישׁ
בְּמֹאזְנַיִם לַעֲלוֹת הֵמָּה מֵהֶבֶל יָחַד
אַל תִּבְטְחוּ בְעֹשֶׁק וּבְגָזֵל אַל תֶּהְבָּלוּ
חַיִל כִּי יָנוּב אַל תָּשִׁיתוּ לֵב אַחַת דִּבֶּר
אֱלֹהִים שְׁתַּיִם זוּ שָׁמָעְתִּי עֹז לֵאלֹהִים
וּלְךָ אֲדֹנָי חָסֶד כִּי אַתָּה
תְשַׁלֵּם לְאִישׁ כְּמַעֲשֵׂהוּ

מִזְמוֹר לְדָוִד בִּהְיוֹתוֹ בְּמִדְבַּר יְהוּדָה
אֱלֹהִים אֵלִי אַתָּה אֲשַׁחֲרֶךָּ צָמְאָה
לְךָ נַפְשִׁי כָּמַהּ לְךָ בְשָׂרִי בְּאֶרֶץ צִיָּה וְעָיֵף
בְּלִי מָיִם כֵּן בַּקֹּדֶשׁ חֲזִיתִךָ לִרְאוֹת
עֻזְּךָ וּכְבוֹדֶךָ כִּי טוֹב חַסְדְּךָ מֵחַיִּים
שְׂפָתַי יְשַׁבְּחוּנְךָ כֵּן אֲבָרֶכְךָ בְחַיָּי בְּשִׁמְךָ
אֶשָּׂא כַפָּי כְּמוֹ חֵלֶב וָדֶשֶׁן תִּשְׂבַּע
נַפְשִׁי וְשִׂפְתֵי רְנָנוֹת יְהַלֶּל פִּי אִם
זְכַרְתִּיךָ עַל יְצוּעָי בְּאַשְׁמֻרוֹת אֶהְגֶּה בָּךְ
כִּי הָיִיתָ עֶזְרָתָה לִּי וּבְצֵל כְּנָפֶיךָ אֲרַנֵּן

Psalms 60-63 Codex Leningrad

THE SPIRIT
OF THE PSALMS

RHETORICAL ANALYSIS, AFFECTIVITY,
AND PENTECOSTAL SPIRITUALITY

Lee Roy Martin

CPT

CPT Press
Cleveland, Tennessee

The Spirit of the Psalms
Rhetorical Analysis, Affectivity, and Pentecostal Spirituality

Published by CPT Press
900 Walker ST NE
Cleveland, TN 37311
USA
email: cptpress@pentecostaltheology.org
website: www.cptpress.com

Library of Congress Control Number: 2018903477

ISBN-13: 978-1-935931-70-6

The cover art is from a stained glass window in the Notre Dame Cathedral in Paris, France.

Citations of Scripture are translations of the author unless specified otherwise.

This QR Code links to Prof. Martin's presentation on Psalm 130, the 2018 'Clarence J. Abbott Lecture in Biblical Studies' at the Pentecostal Theological Seminary, Cleveland, TN, USA.

Dedicated to
Darryl, Angela, and Mary
My siblings who have made my life richer

As a deer longs for flowing streams,
so my soul longs for you, O God.
(Ps. 42.1 NRSV)

CONTENTS

ACKNOWLEDGMENTS

The completion of this long-term project would not have been possible without the support and assistance of family, friends, colleagues, the academic community, and Grace Community Church. I am deeply grateful for the input, encouragement, and feedback that I have received from these groups with which I enjoy valuable relationships.

The academic community has given important feedback regarding my work. Three of the chapters in this book were presented first at annual meetings of the Society for Biblical Literature, and three were presented at annual meetings of the Society for Pentecostal Studies. I have profited greatly from my participation in these academic societies, where important discussions have taken place both in the formal sessions and around the table.

The writing of this monograph has spanned three administrations at the Pentecostal Theological Seminary (where I teach), and each of the Presidents (Steven Land, Lamar Vest, and Michael Baker) have encouraged my work and provided the time and space to conduct my research and writing. David Han, VP for Academics, has diligently supported faculty development and has been an advocate for the faculty. The continued support of the Seminary administration and Board of Trustees – even during the difficult challenges that are facing seminaries today – is greatly appreciated.

I owe a great debt to colleagues and students at the Seminary, who have shared my passion for the difficult task of integrating academics and spirituality. I have benefited from ongoing dialogue with the entire faculty and with each of my students. Special thanks is due to John Christopher Thomas, seminary professor *par excellence*, with whom I have shared untold hours discussing the biblical text. Chris has been a colleague, a dependable friend, and a partner in publications. His devotion to excellence and attention to detail have improved my presentation at many points.

As always, I express my appreciation to my family. Karen, my wife, has been my companion in life and constant supporter. Stephen, Michael, and Kendra, our children, have motivated me to excellence in scholarship. My daughter-in-law Marilyn has encouraged me continually; and my grandsons Caleb and Joshua have provided for me times of refreshing, whether exploring the forest, riding roller coasters, playing baseball, or reading the Bible.

Finally, I would be the first to admit that mine is only one of many valid perspectives on the book of Psalms. I trust that my study of Psalms will contribute to biblical scholarship, encourage the church, and please God.

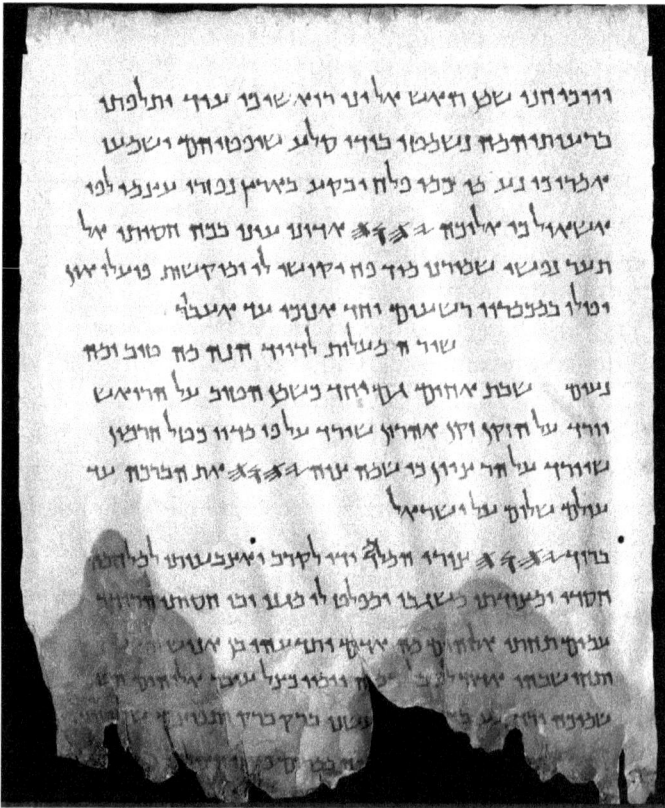

Psalms 141, 133, and 144 DSS 11Q5

PREFACE

The studies in this volume represent my attempt to hear the message of the book of Psalms through rhetorical analysis, which includes examination of the figures of speech, the emotive language, and the poetic forms (both in terms of genre and verse structure). This hearing of the book of Psalms takes place from within my Pentecostal community and in light of my Pentecostal spirituality. In the past, the study of rhetoric has served as a means of recovering the so-called original intent of the author. I am concerned, however, with the impact of the rhetoric – how it affects the hearer of the text. When we read a psalm, how are we affected? What is our response? How does it make us feel? How does the psalm impact our spirituality and our spiritual practices? Furthermore, how do our passions influence our interpretation of the text?

My academic interest in the Psalms began in 1993, when I was called upon by Lee University to teach a course on the book of Psalms. As part of my preparation for the course, I read Claus Westermann's work on the Psalms,[1] which led me to conclude that more work was needed to explicate the passionate emotive content of the Psalms. At that time, I developed the outline for a book on the Psalms and recorded the outline in the front of my Bible.

My idea for writing on the Psalms was put on hold when I began to teach at the seminary, and I found myself working day and night while pastoring a church, teaching at the seminary, writing a doctoral thesis, and raising a family. Reflecting back on my choices, though, I cannot explain why I never considered the Psalms as a doctoral project. All I can say is that there is a time and a season for all things, and apparently, 1993 was not the time for me to write on the Psalms.

---

[1] Claus Westermann, *The Living Psalms* (Grand Rapids, MI: Eerdmans, 1989); *idem, Praise and Lament in the Psalms* (Atlanta, GA: John Knox Press, 1981); *idem, The Praise of God in the Psalms* (Richmond: John Knox Press, 1965); *idem, The Psalms: Structure, Content & Message* (Minneapolis, MN: Augsburg Pub. House, 1980).

My interest in the Psalms was renewed in 2010, when I re-read Walter Brueggemann's article, 'Bounded by Obedience and Praise', in which he argued that Psalm 1 calls for dutiful and obedient adherence to the demands of the torah, a view that I had myself taught and preached.[2] As I re-read the psalm, however, a word in v. 2 leaped out at me – the word was 'delight'. The verse reads, 'His delight is in the torah of Yahweh, and in his torah he meditates day and night'. At that moment, I realized that I was hearing something different from what Brueggemann had heard. Affected by the word 'delight', I saw the torah as a source of joy rather than as a duty. Instead of a demand for obedience, I saw Psalm 1 as an invitation to a life of blessing. My hearing of v. 2 prompted me to develop a journal article that expounded my affective interpretation of the first Psalm.[3]

Although I did not originally foresee a series of articles on the Psalms, a series did indeed form in my mind gradually over the next few years. I added to the first article with studies on Psalms 63, 107, 105, 106, 91, 150, and 130 (in that order).[4] I also presented conference papers on the early Pentecostal reception history of the Psalms, on worship in the Psalms, and on the poor in the Psalms. Consequently, what I had intended as a one-off article on the Psalms evolved into a series of works on the affective dimension of the

---

[2] Walter Brueggemann, 'Bounded by Obedience and Praise: The Psalms as Canon', *JSOT* 50 (1991), pp. 63-92.

[3] Lee Roy Martin, 'Delight in the Torah: The Affective Dimension of Psalm 1', *OTE* 23.3 (2010).

[4] Lee Roy Martin, 'Longing for God: Psalm 63 and Pentecostal Spirituality', *JPT* 22.1 (2013); *idem*, Martin, Lee Roy, '"Oh Give Thanks to the Lord for He Is Good": Affective Hermeneutics, Psalm 107, and Pentecostal Spirituality', *PNEUMA* 36.3 (Fall 2014), pp. 1-24; *idem*, '"Bless the Lord, O my soul": Psalm 103 and Pentecostal Spirituality' (Annual Meeting of the Society for Pentecostal Studies, Lakeland, FL, Mar 2015); *idem*, 'Israel's Story and Our Story: Hearing the Whole Story from Psalms 105 and 106' (Annual Meeting of the Society for Pentecostal Studies, San Demas, CA, 2016); *idem*, 'Psalm 91 and Pentecostal Spirituality: Dwelling in the Secret Place of the Most High' (Annual Meeting of the Society of Biblical Literature, San Antonio, TX, Nov 2016); *idem*, 'Psalm 150 and Pentecostal Spirituality' (Annual Meeting of the Society of Biblical Literature, Boston, MA, Nov 2017); and *idem*, 'Psalm 130: The Hopeful Cry of Lament' (16th Annual Clarence J. Abbott Lecture in Biblical Studies; Pentecostal Theological Seminary, Feb 2018). I also published the following works on the Psalms: 'The Book of Psalms and Pentecostal Worship', in Lee Roy Martin (ed.) *Toward a Pentecostal Theology of Worship* (Cleveland, TN: CPT Press, 2016), pp. 47-88. 'The Use and Interpretation of the Psalms in Early Pentecostalism as Reflected in the Apostolic Faith from 1906 through 1915', *OTE* 30.3 (2017).

Psalms that eventually revived my long-buried plan for a book. Three of these chapters are published here for the first time.

The psalms that are included were chosen for a variety of reasons: for their importance in the structure of the Psalter, for their representation of form-critical categories, for their historical significance to the Pentecostal movement, and for their connection to the central affective categories of love, compassion, joy, gratitude, courage, and hope. Therefore, I began with Psalm 1 because of its role as an introduction to the Psalter. Psalm 63 is included because it represents the passionate pursuit of God that underlies much of the Psalter and which is fundamental to pietistic and mystical spirituality. Psalm 91, a psalm of trust, has been a favorite of Pentecostals from the beginning of the tradition. Psalms 105 and 106 represent the category of historical recital, and they are suggestive for the development of a theology of 'testimony'. Psalm 107 is a personal favorite and connects to the affection of 'gratitude'. Psalm 130 represents the laments; and, finally, Psalm 150 is the climax of the Psalter – it also reflects the goal of the life of faith; and it expresses the quintessence of Pentecostal worship.

In addition to the studies of individual psalms, I have also included a chapter that explores the theology of worship in the Psalms and a chapter that examines early Pentecostal reception history of the Psalms. The examination of Pentecostal testimonies, sermons, songs, and essays contributes to the overall project in a number of ways. First, the *Wirkungsgeschichtliche* study of the early Pentecostal literature aims to correct any previously held misconceptions about the Pentecostal interpretation of the Psalms. Second, the act of engaging with the early literature furthers the researcher's formation as a Pentecostal interpreter as it instills the Pentecostal affections. Third, early Pentecostal approaches to the Psalms can contribute to the ongoing construction of contemporary Pentecostal hermeneutics.

I have written this work as a contribution both to the academy and to the global Christian community, and I offer it in the Spirit of the psalmist, who urged his hearers, 'Magnify the LORD with me, and let us exalt his name together' (Ps. 34.3 [4]).

ABBREVIATIONS

Early Pentecostal Periodicals

AF	*The Apostolic Faith*, Los Angeles, CA
AFO	*The Apostolic Faith*, Portland, OR
AGH	*Assemblies of God Heritage*
TBC	*The Bridal Call*
TBM	*The Bridegroom's Messenger*
CGE	*The Church of God Evangel*
FCr	*Foursquare Crusader*
HG	*The Household of God*
LRE	*The Latter Rain Evangel*
PE	*The Pentecostal Evangel/The Christian Evangel*
PH	*Pentecostal Herald*
PHA	*The Pentecostal Holiness Advocate*
PT	*Pentecostal Testimony*
TP	*The Pentecost*
WE	*Weekly Evangel*
TWT	*The Whole Truth*
WW	*Word and Witness*

Other

AB	*Anchor Bible*
AJPS	*Asian Journal of Pentecostal Studies*
ANF	*The Ante-Nicene Fathers*
ASV	American Standard Version (1901)
BCOTWP	Baker Commentary on the Old Testament Wisdom and Psalms
BDB	Francis Brown, *et al.*, *The New Brown, Driver, Briggs, Gesenius Hebrew and English Lexicon: With an Appendix Containing the Biblical Aramaic* (trans. E. Robinson; Peabody, MA: Hendrickson, 1979).
Bib	*Biblica*
BW	*The Biblical World*
BZ	*Biblische Zeitschrift*
CC	*The Christian Century*

CBQ	*Catholic Biblical Quarterly*
CDCH	David J.A. Clines (ed.), *The Concise Dictionary of Classical Hebrew* (Sheffield, UK: Sheffield Phoenix Press, 2009).
CEB	Common English Bible
CHALOT	W.L. Holladay and L. Köhler, *A Concise Hebrew and Aramaic Lexicon of the Old Testament* (Leiden: Brill, 2000).
CQ	*Communication Quarterly*
CSB	Holman Christian Standard Bible (2004)
CSR	*Christian Scholar's Review*
CTJ	*Calvin Theological Journal*
DCH	David J.A. Clines, *Dictionary of Classical Hebrew* (8 vols.; Sheffield: Sheffield Academic Press, 1993).
NNACMS	Centre for Pentecostal Theology Native North American Contextual Movement Series
DRA	Douay-Rheims Version (1899 American edn)
ECC	Eerdmans Critical Commentary
EJT	*European Journal of Theology*
EP	*Ekklesiastikos Pharos*
ESV	English Standard Version (2001)
ETR	*Études théologiques et religieuses*
FC	Ewald, Marie L. (ed.), *Fathers of the Church: A New Translation* (Washington, DC: Catholic University of America Press, 1964-66).
FOTL	Forms of the Old Testament Literature
GKC	W. Gesenius, E. Kautzsch, and A.E. Cowley, *Gesenius' Hebrew Grammar* (Oxford: The Clarendon Press, 2nd English edn, 1910).
HALOT	L. Köhler and W. Baumgartner, *The Hebrew and Aramaic Lexicon of the Old Testament* (2 vols.; Leiden: Brill, Study edn, 2001).
HTR	*Harvard Theological Review*
HTS	*Hervormde Teologiese Studies*
ICC	International Critical Commentary
IJPT	*International Journal of Practical Theology*
Int	*Interpretation*
JBL	*Journal of Biblical Literature*
JEPTA	*Journal of the European Pentecostal Theological Association*
JETS	*Journal of the Evangelical Theological Society*
JPS	Jewish Publication Society Holy Scriptures (1917)
JPT	*Journal of Pentecostal Theology*
JPTSup	Journal of Pentecostal Theology Supplement Series
JRA	*Journal of Religion in Africa*

JRE	*Journal of Religious Ethics*
JSem	*Journal for Semitics*
JSOT	*Journal for the Study of the Old Testament*
JSOTSup	Journal for the Study of the Old Testament Supplement Series
KJV	Authorized King James Version (1769 ed.)
LA	*Liber Annuus: Annual of the Studium Biblicum Franciscanum Jerusalem*
LXX	Rahlfs, *Septuaginta* (1935)
NAB	New American Bible (1991)
NASB	New American Standard Bible (1977)
NAU	New American Standard Bible (1995)
NCBC	New Century Bible Commentary
NIBC	New International Biblical Commentary
NICOT	New International Commentary on the Old Testament
NIDOTTE	Willem Van Gemeren (ed.), *New International Dictionary of Old Testament Theology and Exegesis* (5 vols.; Grand Rapids, MI: Zondervan, 1997).
NIV	New International Version (1984)
NJB	New Jerusalem Bible (1985)
NKJV	New King James Version (1982)
NPNF	P. Schaff and H. Wace (eds.), *A Select Library of Nicene and Post-Nicene Fathers of the Christian Church. Second Series* (14 vols. Grand Rapids, MI: Eerdmans, 1952).
NRSV	New Revised Standard Version (1989)
NRV	La Sacra Bibbia Nuova Riveduta (1994)
NSKAT	Nuer Stuttgarter Kommentar Altes Testament
OTE	*Old Testament Essays*
PG	J.P. Migne (ed.), *Patrologiae Cursus Completus ... : Series Graeca* (161 vols.; Paris: Garnier, 1857-1886).
PL	J.P. Migne (ed.), *Patrologiae Cursus Completus ... : Series Latina* (221 vols.; Paris: Apud Garnier Fratres, 1844).
PNEUMA	*PNEUMA: The Journal of the Society for Pentecostal Studies*
PTM	Paternoster Theological Monographs
QJS	*Quarterly Journal of Speech*
ResQ	*Restoration Quarterly*
RSV	Revised Standard Version (1973)
RV	English Revised Version (1885)
SBET	*Scottish Bulletin of Evangelical Theology*
TDOT	Botterweck *et al.* (eds.), *Theological Dictionary of the Old Testament* (15 vols.; Grand Rapids, MI: Eerdmans, 1974-).
THOTC	Two Horizons Old Testament Commentary
ThT	*Theology Today*

TLOT	E. Jenni and C. Westermann (eds.), *Theological Lexicon of the Old Testament* (3 vols.; Peabody, MA: Hendrickson Publishers, 1997).
TNK	Jewish Publication Society TANAKH (1985)
TS	*Theological Studies*
TWOT	R.L. Harris, G.L. Archer, and B.K. Waltke (eds.), *Theological Wordbook of the Old Testament* (Chicago: Moody Press, 1999).
USQR	*Union Seminary Quarterly Review*
VE	*Verbum et Ecclesia*
VT	*Vetus Testamentum*
VTSup	Vetus Testamentum Supplement Series
VUL	Latin Vulgate (Weber edn, 1983)
WBC	Word Biblical Commentary
WTJ	*Wesleyan Theological Journal*

Ad te dñe leuaui animã meã.

DTEDÑE
leuaui animam
meam : dñs ms̄ inte
confido ñerubescã.
Neq̃ irrideant
me inimici mei :
& enim uniusi
q̄ sustinent te
ñ confundent.
Confundant
oms̄ iniqua
agentes : super uacue.
Vias tuas dñe demonstra michi :
& semitas tuas edoce me.
Dirige me inueritate tua &doce me :
quia tu es deus saluator meus :
& te sustinui tota die.
Reminiscere miserationũ tuarũ dñe :
& misericordiarum tuarũ que a sc̄lo sc̄.
Delicta iuuentutis mee :
& ignorancias meas ne memineris.

Psalm 25 [24] Medieval Illuminated MS in Latin

1

PSALM 1: ENTERING THE PSALTER WITH DELIGHT

Introduction

Recent studies of the Psalms have continued to include generous attention to the canonical shape of the Psalter, and Psalm 1 figures prominently in those discussions.[1] It is generally agreed that the editors of the Psalter selected and placed Psalm 1 as an introduction to the collection of psalms.[2]

---

[1] The most recent studies include Steven Shawn Tuell, 'Psalm 1', *Int* 63.3 (2009), pp. 278-80; Bernd Janowski, 'Wie Ein Baum an Wasserkanälen: Psalm 1 Als Tor Zum Psalter', in F. Hartenstein and M. Pietsch (eds.), *'Sieben Augen Auf Einem Stein' (Sach 3,9)* (Neukirchen-Vluyn: Neukirchener Verlag, 2007), pp. 121-40; Bruce K. Waltke, 'Preface to the Psalter: Two Ways', *Crux* 43.3 (2007), pp. 2-9; C. John Collins, 'Psalm 1: Structure and Rhetoric', *Presbyterion* 31.1 (2005), pp. 37-48; Peter W. Flint *et al.*, *The Book of Psalms: Composition and Reception* (VTSup 99; Boston: Brill, 2005); and Michael LeFebvre, 'Torah-Meditation and the Psalms: The Invitation of Psalm 1', in P.S. Johnston and D. Firth (eds.), *Interpreting the Psalms: Issues and Approaches* (Downers Grove, IL: IVP Academic, 2005), pp. 213-25.

[2] This view of Psalm 1 apparently goes back as far as Origen (*'Exegetica in Psalmos'*, *PG*, 12.1099). Cf. the comments of Kemper Fullerton, 'Studies in the Hebrew Psalter', *BW* 36 (1910), p. 323. Jerome suggests that the first psalm's lack of a title indicates its role as a preface. He writes, 'Quidam dicunt hunc psalmum quasi praefationem esse Spiritus sancti, et ideo titulum non habere' (*PL* 26.823). Cf. other pre-critical writers: John Calvin, *Commentary on the Book of Psalms* (trans. James Anderson; Grand Rapids, MI: Eerdmans, 1949), I, p. 1; Matthew Poole, *A Commentary on the Holy Bible* (3 vols.; London: The Banner of Truth Trust, 1962), II, p. 1; Adam Clarke, *The Holy Bible Containing the Old and New Testaments: ... With a Commentary and Critical Notes* (6 vols.; New York: Abingdon-Cokesbury, A new edn, 1883), III, p. 219; and critical scholars Charles A. Briggs and Emilie Grace Briggs, *A Critical and Exegetical Commentary on the Book of Psalms* (ICC; 2 vols.; Edinburgh:

One of the most helpful and influential articles in the debate about the macrostructure of the Psalter is Walter Brueggemann's innovative piece, 'Bounded by Obedience and Praise: The Psalms as Canon'.[3] Brueggemann argues that shape of the Psalter registers a theological and experiential progression that begins with the 'duty' of 'obedience'[4] and concludes with 'glad, unconditional praise'.[5] Between Psalms 1 and 150, a drama unfolds – the drama of the life of faith. He proposes further that Psalm 1 presents a coherent theology in which obedience produces a life of blessedness and well-being. This settled theology, however, is quickly shattered by the psalms of lament, which demonstrate that suffering comes even to those who are faithful. Psalm 73, found at the center of the Psalter, is the 'threshold'[6] in the movement from obedience to praise. Psalm 73 is comprehensive in its scope, including a restatement of the theology of Psalm 1, coupled with protests against God and statements of confidence in the goodness of God. At the end of the journey from coherent theology through protest and confidence lies the goal of complete praise. Psalm 150 exemplifies this ultimate goal – 'the joyous self-abandonment'[7] of pure praise.

Brueggemann's article has been cited widely and has met with near universal approval,[8] and it is with much appreciation that I propose

---

T. & T. Clark, 1969), I, p. 3; Artur Weiser, *The Psalms: A Commentary* (Philadelphia: Westminster, 1962), p. 102; Robert Henry Pfeiffer, *Introduction to the Old Testament* (New York: Harper, 1948), pp. 619-20; Hans-Joachim Kraus, *Psalms 1-59* (trans. H.C. Oswald; Continental Commentaries; Minneapolis, MN: Augsburg Pub. House, 1988), pp. 113-14; and Gerald H. Wilson, 'The Shape of the Book of Psalms', *Int* 46.2 (1992), pp. 129-42.

I would maintain (in agreement with other scholars) that Psalm 2 is also prefatory, and that Psalms 1 and 2 combine to form the introduction to the Psalter.

[3] Walter Brueggemann, 'Bounded by Obedience and Praise: The Psalms as Canon', *JSOT* 50 (1991), pp. 63-92, reprinted in Walter Brueggemann, *The Psalms and the Life of Faith* (ed. Patrick D. Miller; Minneapolis, MN: Fortress Press, 1995), pp. 189-213.

[4] Brueggemann, *The Psalms and the Life of Faith*, pp. 190-92.

[5] Brueggemann, *The Psalms and the Life of Faith*, p. 193.

[6] Brueggemann, *The Psalms and the Life of Faith*, p. 204. See also Walter Brueggemann and Patrick D. Miller, 'Psalm 73 as a Canonical Marker', *JSOT* 72 (1996), pp. 45-56.

[7] Brueggemann, *The Psalms and the Life of Faith*, p. 212.

[8] E.g. Wilson, 'The Shape of the Book of Psalms', pp. 34-35; R.N. Whybray, *Reading the Psalms as a Book* (JSOTSup 222; Sheffield, UK: Sheffield Academic Press, 1996), p. 85; Nancy L. DeClaissé-Walford, *Reading from the Beginning: The Shaping of the Hebrew Psalter* (Macon, GA: Mercer University Press, 1997), p. 43; M.A. Vincent, 'The Shape of the Psalter: An Eschatological Dimension?', in P.J. Harland and

to engage and build upon Brueggemann's groundbreaking work. When I came back to his article during my recent study of the Psalms, I found myself struggling over his use of the word 'obedience' as the characteristic descriptor for Psalm 1. My hearing of the psalm suggests that while obedience may lie in the background, it is not in the foreground.[9] I will argue in this chapter, therefore, that Psalm 1 does not teach the duty of obedience so much as it evokes affection for the torah.[10] In Psalm 1, the righteous are not those who obey the torah but are those who 'delight in the torah' (v. 2).

A Translation of Psalm 1

We will begin with a brief look at the whole Psalm; it reads as follows:

[1] Oh, the blessedness of the man who
    has not walked in the counsel of the wicked,
    and in the pathway of sinners he has not stood,
    and in the seat of the scorner he has not sat.
[2] Rather, his delight is in the torah of Yahweh,
    and in his torah he will meditate day and night.

C.T.R. Hayward (eds.), *New Heaven and New Earth – Prophecy and the Millennium: Essays in Honour of Anthony Gelston* (Leiden: Brill, 1999), p. 69; J. Kenneth Kuntz, 'Wisdom Psalms and the Shaping of the Hebrew Psalter', in Randal A. Argall, Beverly A. Bow, and Rodney A. Werline (eds.), *For a Later Generation* (Harrisburg, PA: Trinity Press International, 2000), p. 151; John Goldingay, *Psalms* (BCOTWP; 3 vols.; Grand Rapids, MI: Baker Academic, 2006), I, p. 58. Questions have been raised by Wilson, 'The Shape of the Book of Psalms', p. 136, n. 26, who writes, 'While Brueggemann's treatment will probably influence how I personally read and appropriate the Psalter in the future, it has thus far left me with a vague sense of incompleteness in understanding the final form of the Psalter'. Other disapproving responses include those offered by Jerome F.D. Creach, *Yahweh as Refuge and the Editing of the Hebrew Psalter* (JSOTSup 217; Sheffield, UK: Sheffield Academic Press, 1996), p. 17 and LeFebvre, 'Torah-Meditation and the Psalms', p. 216.

[9] Instead of the commonly used term 'reading', I prefer the term 'hearing' because (1) it is a biblical term; (2) it reflects the orality of biblical and Pentecostal contexts; (3) it is relational, presupposing an external voice who is speaking; (4) it suggests faithful obedience since 'hearing' often means 'obeying'; (5) it implies transformation, since faithful hearing transforms; (6) unlike the process of 'reading' Scripture, 'hearing' implies submission to the authority of the text. See Lee Roy Martin, *The Unheard Voice of God: A Pentecostal Hearing of the Book of Judges* (JPTSup 32; Blandford Forum, UK: Deo Publishing, 2008), pp. 52-79.

[10] I would normally capitalize 'torah' (תורה) when referring to the five books of Moses; but I am using lower case throughout this article because 'torah of Yahweh' in Ps. 1.2 is ambiguous – it may or may not signify the books of Moses. See the discussion of 'torah' on pp. 14-16.

³ He will be like a tree planted beside channels of water,
  which gives its fruit in its season
 and its leaf will not wither,
  and everything it does will thrive.

⁴ Not so are the wicked.
  Rather, they are like the husk which the wind drives.
⁵ Therefore, the wicked will not stand in the judgment,
  nor sinners in the congregation of the righteous;
⁶ because Yahweh knows the way of the righteous,
  but the way of the wicked will perish.[11]

Structure and Overview of Psalm 1

The structure of the psalm is debated, and each proposed structure will yield its own nuances of meaning; nevertheless, my thesis remains valid no matter which structure one chooses to follow.[12] I have chosen to arrange the psalm in two parts:

1. *The blessedness of the righteous* (vv. 1-3). The theme of the psalm, announced in v. 1, is the 'blessedness' or 'happiness' of the person who is not influenced by evil and does not practice evil but instead is moved by the torah of Yahweh and practices meditation in it. Three descriptive names are given to the evil person ('wicked', 'sinner', 'scorner'), but the happy person is not yet identified by any titles. The person who delights in the torah is like a flourishing and productive tree.

2. *The ruination of the wicked* (vv. 4-6). The wicked, in contrast to the righteous, are like worthless husks of grain. The wicked do not

---

[11] Unless otherwise stated, quotations from Scripture are the translations of the author.

[12] Cf. Goldingay, *Psalms*, I, pp. 81-88, who outlines the psalm in three parts: (1) vv. 1-3, (2) vv. 4-5, and (3) v. 6. See also Collins, 'Psalm 1: Structure and Rhetoric', pp. 37-48; Pierre Auffret, 'Comme Un Arbre ... Étude Structurelle du Psaume 1', *BZ* 45.2 (2001), pp. 256-64; Walter Vogels, 'A Structural Analysis of Ps 1', *Bib* 60 (1979), pp. 410-16; and Remi Lack, 'Le Psaume 1 – Une Analyse Structurale', *Bib* 57 (1976), pp. 154-67. I suggest that Psalm 1 may be chiastic in the broad sense of the term: A-blessed state of the righteous contra 'the way' of the wicked, B-success of the righteous, B'-failure of the wicked, A'-Yahweh's care of the righteous contra the end of 'the way' of the wicked. Cf. Rolf A. Jacobson, 'Psalm 1', in Nancy L. DeClaissé-Walford, Rolf A. Jacobson, and Beth LaNeel Tanner, *The Book of Psalms* (NICOT; Grand Rapids, MI: Eerdmans, 2014), p. 58.

flourish and have no status among God's people. They have no standing at the place of judgment and no place in the congregation of the
righteous. In v. 5, the happy person is identified at last, though in the
plural – 'righteous ones'. It is finally revealed to the hearer that the
psalm is describing the blessedness of the *righteous* (heretofore un-
named) in contrast to the ruination of the *wicked*. The move from the
singular ('the man') to the plural ('righteous ones') is grammatically
necessary in v. 5 because a 'congregation' requires more than one person, but in v. 6 'the way of the righteous ones' could just as easily
have been framed in the singular. The plural may be a way of sum-
marizing and of giving the psalm a general application. The Psalm's
overall theme of the blessedness of the righteous (expressed through
the contrast between the righteous and the wicked) is confirmed and
sharpened in the final verse – 'Yahweh knows (ידע) the way of the
righteous, but the way of the wicked will perish (אבד)'. It is Yahweh's
providence that guarantees the blessedness of the righteous and the
destruction of the wicked.

Brueggemann is correct in saying that Psalm 1 'presents a morally
coherent world' with no 'ambiguity or slippage'.[13] The righteous are
blessed and the wicked are doomed. Brueggemann, however, unjus-
tifiably equates righteousness with 'obedience' and torah with 'duty'
and 'command'.[14] Moreover, his emphasis upon obedience creates an
excessive dialectical tension between Psalm 1 and Psalm 150. He
writes, 'Though *obedience* is the beginning point of the Psalter and *insisted* upon with great *severity*, by Psalm 150 the *rigors* of *obedience* have
all been put behind the praising community … As Israel moves from
commandment to communion, the *weight of duty* is overridden by the
delight of lyrical community with God'.[15] While I agree that a dialectic exists between the two psalms, I do not perceive the tension to be
as deep as Brueggemann proposes. Of the happy person Ps. 1.2 declares, 'His delight is in the torah of Yahweh, and in his torah he
meditates day and night'. Consequently, I do not perceive an 'insistence'; rather I discern an invitation. I do not detect 'severity'; I hear
congratulations. Instead of the 'rigors of obedience', I sense the joy

---

[13] Brueggemann, *The Psalms and the Life of Faith*, p. 191.
[14] Brueggemann, *The Psalms and the Life of Faith*. 'Obedience' is used throughout
the piece; 'duty' is found on pp. 193, 195, 196, and 197; and 'command' is found
on pp. 191, 194, 196, and 197.
[15] Brueggemann, *The Psalms and the Life of Faith*, p. 195 (emphasis added).

of discovering God's revelation. Instead of the 'weight of duty', I observe the delight of communion with God. Instead of 'commandment', I understand torah to be the entire story of Israel's life in covenant with Yahweh.

Blessedness of the Righteous

I have chosen Brueggemann's article as my point of entry because he exceeds all others in his stress upon obedience. However, he is not the first nor the last to argue that Psalm 1 presents the demand for obedience. Other interpreters offer less forceful but concordant interpretations. Origen argues that meditation upon the torah includes the requirement of producing 'consistent works' (τὰ κατάλληλα ἔργα), and he posits that meditation results in 'living perfectly according to the law' (κατὰ τὸν νόμον τελείως βιοῦντι).[16] Jerome concludes that delighting in the torah is an expression of 'wholehearted obedience'.[17] According to Calvin, Ps. 1.2 teaches 'that God is only rightly served when his law is obeyed'.[18] Adam Clarke understands the torah to be the 'rule' of life, the 'holy standard', which is not to be heard only but is to be performed.[19] Many recent interpreters adopt a similar stance.[20]

---

[16] Origen, '*Exegetica in Psalmos*', *PG* 12:1088. Cf. Hilary of Poitiers who claims that meditation in the torah consists in 'pious performance of its injunctions' and in 'fulfilment of the Law by the works we do' ('Homilies on the Psalms', *NPNF* 2.9, p. 239).

[17] Jerome, 'Homily on Psalm 1' (*FC* 48, p. 6).

[18] Calvin, *Psalms*, p. 4.

[19] Clarke, *Commentary*, III, p. 220. Cf. Poole, *Commentary*, II, p. 1.

[20] DeClaissé-Walford, *Reading from the Beginning*, p. 38, equates righteousness with 'individual obedience'. Cf. Vincent, 'Shape of the Psalter', p. 65; Denise Dombkowski Hopkins, *Journey through the Psalms: A Path to Wholeness* (New York: United Church Press, 1990), p. 3; Patrick D. Miller, *Israelite Religion and Biblical Theology: Collected Essays* (JSOTSup 267; Sheffield, UK: Sheffield Academic Press, 2000), p. 280; and Samuel L. Terrien, *The Psalms: Strophic Structure and Theological Commentary* (ECC; Grand Rapids, MI: Eerdmans, 2003), p. 60. Erich Zenger, 'Psalm 1', in Frank-Lothar Hossfeld and Erich Zenger, *Die Psalmen I, Psalm 1-50* (Die Neue Echter Bibel Kommentar Zum Alten Testament Mit Der Einheitsübersetzung; Würzburg: Echter Verlag, 1993), p. 47, states that meditation on the torah leads to a life of success in the 'fear of God' ('*Gottesfurcht*'). Cf. Erhard Gerstenberger, *Psalms: Part 1, with an Introduction to Cultic Poetry* (Grand Rapids, MI: Eerdmans, 1988), p. 42, who admits that the psalm has no direct 'admonition', insists on describing the message as one of 'strong exhortative discourse'.

Despite the long history of viewing Psalm 1 as a call to obedience, I would argue that such an interpretation does not accurately reflect the wording of the text. The psalm itself does not use 'obedience', rather it describes the happy person by means of a broader term – 'righteous' (צדיקים, vv. 5-6). The righteous are depicted in two ways: first, the psalm reveals what the righteous are *not*; and second, it reveals what they *are*. The righteous are *not* like the wicked (רשעים); rather they *are* lovers of the torah. Throughout the psalm, the righteous person stands in contrast to the wicked (vv. 1, 4-6). The righteous person has not been influenced by the habits and dispositions of the 'wicked', the 'sinner', and the 'scorner' (v. 1). The 'way of the righteous' (v. 6) represents the thriving Israelite's whole manner of being, lived faithfully in covenant with Yahweh. It is opposite to the 'way of the wicked' (v. 6), which perishes. Viewed positively, the righteous are those who take delight in the torah and meditate (הגה) in it always (v. 2).

On the one hand, the contrast between the wicked and the righteous implies that the righteous are obedient; but on the other hand, righteousness must not be limited to or equated with obedience. Obedience is only one aspect of righteousness. When the psalm comes to the positive portrayal of the righteous (v. 2), the terminology shifts unexpectedly away from behavior and toward the affections.[21] The righteous are not like the wicked; instead, the righteous delight in the torah. Surprisingly, the entire psalm includes no commands or injunctions, and it includes no language that falls within the semantic range of 'obey'. The language is that of affirmation ('Blessed is the man'), which evokes a desire for righteousness by means of the indirect and subtle effect of the poem's inviting and hopeful mood. The hearer of Psalm 1 is told that the person who delights in the torah will flourish like a well-watered tree. The psalm, therefore, is 'warmly encouraging a godly lifestyle'.[22]

The language of obedience permeates the Hebrew Bible and would be expected in a text like Psalm 1, in which the blessedness of

---

[21] LeFebvre, 'Torah-Meditation and the Psalms', p. 216, suggests that the misconstrual of Ps. 1 as a call of obedience is due to its common association with Pss. 19 and 119, two Psalms that do emphasize obedience. He argues that the 'dialectic behind 1:1-2 is not "sinning vs obeying", but "delight-in-sinful-counsel vs delight-in-torah"' (p. 216, n. 11).

[22] Geoffrey Grogan, *Psalms* (THOTC; Grand Rapids, MI: Eerdmans, 2008), p. 42.

the righteous is emphasized. Commentators have rightly pointed to the similarities between Psalm 1, Deut. 17.18-19, and Josh. 1.8.[23] According to the Deuteronomic instructions to Israel's king, he must keep a copy of the torah, and 'he shall read (קרא) therein all the days of his life, that he may learn to fear Yahweh his God, to keep (שמר) all the words of this instruction (תורה) and these statutes, to do (עשה) them' (Deut. 17.19). Likewise, Yahweh's mandate to Joshua reads, 'Do not let this book of the torah depart from your mouth; but you shall meditate (הגה) in it day and night, so that you may be careful (שמר) to do (עשה) everything written in it because then you will make your way prosperous (צלח) and then you will succeed (שכל)'.

While the similarities between the three texts are obvious, the differences are striking. Both Deut. 17.19 and Josh. 1.8 include clear demands for obedience, using the terms 'keep' (שמר) and 'do' (עשה). Surprisingly, these terms (and similar ones) are absent from the parallel text in Psalm 1. The unique phrasing of Ps. 1.2 challenges any preconceived interpretation that might be assumed from the association with other texts. Charles A. Briggs, noting the variation, argues, 'the Ps. substitutes for the external, "depart out of thy mouth," the first clause of Jos. 1.8, the internal "delight in," indicating a later and more matured conception'.[24]

Psalm 1 stands apart from parallel texts by placing the idea of obedience in the background while the affections are in the foreground. Obedience would have been in the foreground if Ps. 1.2 had read, 'He *keeps* (שמר) the torah of Yahweh' (cf. 1 Chron. 22.12); 'He *performs* (עשה) the torah' (cf. Ezra 7.10); 'He *walks* (הלך) in the torah' (cf. Ps. 119.1; Jer. 44.10); or 'He *obeys* (שמע) the torah' (cf. Isa. 30.9). However, to 'delight' in the torah pushes into a different semantic domain. Delighting in the torah does not exclude obedience, but it moves the emphasis to the realm of the affections.

Moreover, the word 'torah' would have registered 'duty' or 'command' if the second line of v. 2 had included the word 'commandment' (מצוה, cf. Prov. 3.1), 'statute' (חק, cf. Amos 2.4), or 'judgment'

---

[23] E.g. Poole, *Commentary*, II, p. 1; Briggs and Briggs, *Psalms*, I, pp. 4, 5; Peter C. Craigie, *Psalms 1-50* (WBC 19; Waco, TX: Word, 1983), p. 60; James L. Mays, *Psalms* (Interpretation; Louisville, KY: John Knox Press, 1994), p. 41; and Grogan, *Psalms*, p. 42.

[24] Briggs and Briggs, *Psalms*, I, p. 4.

(מִשְׁפָּט, cf. 2 Kgs 17.34) as a parallel to 'torah'.[25] If torah were regarded here as equivalent to commandments that call for obedience, the writer could have stated as much through the use of parallelism, but instead he uses 'torah' in both lines. The word 'torah' (תּוֹרָה) is found 36 times in the Psalms, but only here does it stand in parallel to itself. In Psalm 1, therefore, we find no evidence that obedience is in the foreground.

Delight in the Torah

Overstating the demand for obedience may lead hearers to ignore the important affective dimension of the psalm that is expressed in v. 2: 'His delight is in the torah of Yahweh'.[26] That the word 'delight' (חֵפֶץ) has reference to the affections is discerned from its usage and is confirmed by the lexica, which define the Hebrew word as 'joy, delight',[27] 'delight, pleasure'.[28] It denotes 'the direction of one's heart or passion',[29] a pleasurable emotional attraction.[30] Outside the Psalter, 'delight' (חֵפֶץ) can denote the attraction between a man and a woman – we read that the son of Hamor 'delighted in Jacob's daughter' (Gen. 34.19). Also, חֵפֶץ can refer to God's pleasure in his people and their actions – the Israelites are hopeful that Yahweh 'delights' in them (Num. 14.8), and Samuel insists that Yahweh has greater 'delight' in Saul's obedience than in his sacrifices (1 Sam. 15.22).

Within the Psalter, it is said that God does not 'delight in wickedness' (5.4),[31] rather his people are his 'delight' (16.3, cf. 37.23). The psalmist claims, '[Yahweh] delivered me because he delighted in me' (18.19, cf. 35.27). We learn of the wicked, however, that 'they delight in lies' (62.40). The unrighteous nations 'delight in war' (68.30), but

---

[25] Psalm 119, for example, utilizes a variety of terms interchangeably.

[26] Ironically, Brueggemann uses the word 'delight' not in reference to Psalm 1 but in reference to Psalm 150, although neither 'delight' nor any of its synonyms is found in Psalm 150; see Brueggemann, *The Psalms and the Life of Faith*, pp. 193, 95, 96.

[27] *HALOT*, I, p. 340. Cf. *DCH*, p. 127.

[28] *BDB*, p. 343. G.J. Botterweck, חָפֵץ, *TDOT*, V, p. 93, states that 'emotional overtones predominate … "have pleasure in." As a substantive, this yields "pleasure" and the "treasure" in which one has pleasure.'

[29] *NIDOTTE*, II, p. 231.

[30] *TWOT*, I, pp. 310-11.

[31] Where English versification differs from the Hebrew, the English will be used.

the 'meek … delight themselves in the abundance of peace' (37.11). God's people are enjoined, 'Delight yourself also in Yahweh, And he will give you the desires of your heart' (37.4).

In light of the texts mentioned above, 'delight' (חפץ) should be understood as an affective term, and its prominence in Psalm 1 testifies to the importance of the affections in the life of the righteous.[32] Psalm 1.2, however, is not alone in its affirmation that the righteous are those who take 'delight' (חפץ) in the torah of Yahweh. A similar sentiment is echoed four times in Psalm 119 (vv. 70, 77, 92, and 174). Furthermore, the Psalter calls for not only a delight in the 'torah' but also a delight in the Lord's 'statutes' (119.16), his 'testimonies' (119.24), and his 'commandments' (112.1; 119.47). Affection for the torah might even correspond to a desire for 'God himself'.[33] The psalmist confesses, 'Whom do I have in heaven but you? And besides you, I desire (חפץ) nothing on earth' (Ps. 73.25).

The perspective of the Psalms is somewhat different from that of the wisdom literature, where we read, 'Happy (אשרי) is the man who finds wisdom' (Prov. 3.13). In Proverbs, the righteous are encouraged to desire and seek wisdom above all things (e.g. Prov. 2.10; 3.15; 4.6-8), but in the Psalms they are urged to pursue the torah.

Affection for the torah, which Psalm 1 evokes, is not out of character with the theology of other psalms; and the word 'delight' (חפץ) is not the only term that suggests the importance of affection for the torah. The writer of Psalm 119 declares, 'Oh, how I love (אהב) your torah! It is my contemplation (שיחה) all the day' (v. 97, cf. vv. 113, 127, 140, 163, and 165). Psalm 19 praises God's 'law', 'testimony', 'precepts', 'commandments', and 'judgments', saying, 'They are more desirable (חמד) than gold, yes, than much fine gold: sweeter also than honey and the honeycomb' (v. 10, cf. Ps. 119.72, 103). Through the use of other affective terms the hearer of the Psalms is encouraged to put the torah 'in his heart' (לב) (37.31; 40.8), to 'rejoice' (שוש) in the torah (119.14, 111, 162), to 'long for' (תאב) Yahweh's precepts (119.40), to 'rejoice' (שמח) in his statutes (19.8), to 'desire' (יאב) his commandments (119.131), to 'run' (רוץ) toward them (119.32), and to make them his 'songs' (זמר, 119.54) and his 'desire' (שעשע). The hearer is enjoined to 'rejoice' (שמח) and 'be glad' (גיל) because of

---

Yahweh's judgments (48.11; 97.8). The psalmist pleads longingly, 'Open my eyes, that I may see wondrous things (פלא) out of your torah' (119.18, cf. v. 129). The tenor of the Psalms is similar to that of Jeremiah who exclaims, 'Your word was for me the joy (ששׂון) and rejoicing (שׂמחה) of my heart' (Jer. 15.16).

The above texts demonstrate a common interest in the affective dimension of torah devotion. To delight in the torah is an affective inclination, a passionate disposition. To delight in the torah is to rejoice in it, to love it, to long for it, to desire it more than gold, and to enjoy it more than honey. The words of the torah, declares Terrien, 'penetrate the heart, stir the emotions, warn the intellect, and energize the volition'.[34] The emphasis of Psalm 1 is not upon deeds but delight, not on duty but desire, not on obedience but on affections that are rightly oriented towards God. 'The righteous man, who rejects the influence of the ungodly, finds his physical and mental vigor in the delights afforded by the Law of Yahweh'.[35] Torah obedience is vital to the Hebrew tradition, but Psalm 1 registers another theme, namely, the inner life of the heart that longs to hear God's voice and that welcomes the torah 'with affection and joy'.[36] John Calvin writes, 'from this love of the law proceeds constant meditation upon it … all who are truly actuated by love to the law must feel pleasure in the diligent study of it'.[37] Psalm 1 promotes 'delight-nurturing meditation on torah'.[38]

Passion in the Psalms and the Passions of the Hearing Community

Biblical scholarship has given little attention to the affective dimension of biblical poetry in general and of the Psalms in particular. The modern approach to scholarship emphasizes historical questions and

---

[34] Terrien, *The Psalms*, p. 73. Cf. Jaroslav Pelikan *et al.* (eds.), *Luther's Works* (55 vols.; Saint Louis, MO: Concordia Pub. House, 1955), where Luther writes that psalmist uses the word 'delight' as a way of saying, 'Thy law is not in the outer edges and skin of my heart, but in the inside, in innermost and complete dedication' (X, p. 14).

[35] Terrien, *The Psalms*, p. 72.

[36] Konrad Schaefer, *Psalms* (Berit Olam; Collegeville, MN: Liturgical Press, 2001), p. 4.

[37] Calvin, *Psalms*, p. 5.

[38] LeFebvre, 'Torah-Meditation and the Psalms', p. 217.

values objective analysis; therefore, it is not surprising that the academy would neglect the poetic passions. Modern study of the Psalms centers on questions of authorship, *Sitz im Leben*, compositional history, literary genre, poetic structure, ancient Near Eastern parallels, grammar, and semantics. I would argue that the function of poetry is to evoke the affections and provoke the passions. Therefore, poetry cannot be understood at a distance; it requires that the hearer enter its world of imagery and emotion. The apprehension and appreciation of poetry requires first that we experience it and only secondarily that we analyze it. Terrien declares, 'Such a *Credo* must be sung, not signed. Doxology is the key to theology ... The protophilosophical thinking of sapiential reflection is necessary, but it must remain ancillary'.[39] This chapter attempts to stimulate awareness of the affective dimension of the Psalms and to awaken the hearer to the advantages of a passionate involvement with the text. I echo the sentiments of Rickie D. Moore who wants to show 'the prominent presence of passion in the biblical writings themselves, a presence which has been long overlooked or dismissed by the *dispassionate* modes of scholarship which have until recently monopolized modern biblical study'.[40]

It is perhaps my interpretive location within the Pentecostal community that has made me aware of the affective impact of Ps. 1.2. Steven J. Land has shown that Pentecostal spirituality, which is often

---

[39] Terrien, *The Psalms*, p. 60.

[40] Rick D. Moore, *The Spirit of the Old Testament* (JPTSup 35; Blandford Forum, UK: Deo Publishing, 2011), pp. 102-103 (emphasis original). Moore finds support in Robert O. Baker, 'Pentecostal Bible Reading: Toward a Model of Reading for the Formation of the Affections', in Lee Roy Martin (ed.) *Pentecostal Hermeneutics: A Reader* (Leiden: Brill, 2013), pp. 95-108; W. Dow Edgerton, *The Passion of Interpretation* (Literary Currents in Biblical Interpretation; Louisville, KY: Westminster/John Knox Press, 1992); Walter Brueggemann, *Abiding Astonishment: Psalms, Modernity, and the Making of History* (Louisville, KY: Westminster/John Knox Press, 1st edn, 1991); Abraham Joshua Heschel, *The Prophets* (2 vols.; New York: Harper & Row, 1962); and Jeffrey Lloyd Staley, *Reading with a Passion: Rhetoric, Autobiography, and the American West in the Gospel of John* (New York: Continuum, 1995). A recent edited volume, F. Scott Spencer (ed.), *Mixed Feelings and Vexed Passions: Exploring Emotions in Biblical Literature* (Resources for Biblical Study 90; Atlanta: SBL Press, 2017), is a significant move toward recognizing the passions found *in the text*, but the writers fail to acknowledge the influence of the passions found *in the interpreter*. An example of the kind of interpretation that appreciates the passions of the text and the passions of the interpreter is Larry R. McQueen, *Joel and the Spirit: The Cry of a Prophetic Hermeneutic* (JPTSup 8; Sheffield: Sheffield Academic Press, 1995). I will cite the CPT Press edition (Cleveland, TN: CPT Press, 2009).

caricatured as 'emotionalism', is generated by the transforming power of the Holy Spirit, who infuses the believer with apocalyptic passions in anticipation of the coming kingdom. These renewed affections (orthopathy) serve as integrating center for a Spirit-filled life that orients also the mind (orthodoxy) and actions (orthopraxy).[41] Moreover, the passionate and participative worship of Pentecostals appeals to the heart more than it appeals to the intellect.[42] I find that the psalmist's encouragement to 'delight in the torah' is consistent with Pentecostal spirituality and that the passionate pleas and the exuberant praises that we find in the Psalms are consistent with Pentecostal worship. Like the psalmist, the Pentecostal community seeks to 'serve the Lord with joy' (Ps. 100.2) and to confess, 'I rejoiced when they said unto me, Let us go into the house of the Lord' (Ps. 122.1; cf. 26.8; 27.4; 84.10).[43]

Given the fact that Pentecostalism emerged from the holiness movement, it might be expected that I would be drawn to Brueggemann's interpretation of Psalm 1 as a demand for obedience. While it is true that obedience is central to the Pentecostal tradition, it is also true that obedience which is not generated by Godly affections is no more than legalism.[44] Jesus insisted that all behavior is governed by the affections of the heart (Mt. 5.17-48) and that all of God's commandments can be summarized in the command to love (Lk. 10.27).[45] John Wesley, the grandfather of Pentecostalism, argued

---

[41] Steven J. Land, *Pentecostal Spirituality: A Passion for the Kingdom* (JPTSup 1; Sheffield, UK: Sheffield Academic Press, 1993). I will cite from the CPT Press version (Cleveland, TN: CPT Press, 2010), pp. 31-57. See also pp. 120-36 for Land's further explication of the role of the affections.

[42] For a sound assessment of the formative role of Pentecostal worship, see R. Jerome Boone, 'Community and Worship: The Key Components of Pentecostal Christian Formation', *JPT* 8 (1996), pp. 129-42.

[43] On the importance of the affections in Christian formation and worship, see also James K.A. Smith, *Desiring the Kingdom: Worship, Worldview, and Cultural Formation* (Cultural Liturgies, 1; Grand Rapids, MI: Baker Academic, 2009).

[44] Cf. Weiser, *The Psalms*, p. 104, who insists, 'The psalmist does not therefore stop at the external aspect of a godliness based upon the law … the law is here not regarded as an irksome burden but as a source of joy'. Similarly, Manfred Oeming, *Das Buch Der Psalmen: Psalm 1-41* (NSKAT; Stuttgart: Verlag Katholisches Bibelwerk, 2000), p. 55, writes that 'the righteous person has joy (*'Freude'*) in the instruction of the Lord and meditates upon it by day and by night … Torah, however, is not understood as an oppressive burden (*'Last'*), as a weight of petty prohibitions … but as a way to live, as a way of life in the presence of God.'

[45] Luther writes insightfully, 'what is held without love and delight is not held for long' (Pelikan *et al.* (eds.), *Luther's Works*, X, p. 14).

that holiness is a matter of 'heart and life', showing that all behavior is an expression of the affections. He writes, '[Christian perfection is] love governing the heart and life, running through all our tempers, words, and actions'; and 'pure love reigning alone in the heart and life, this is the whole of Christian perfection'.[46] Genuine righteousness, therefore, does not flow out of a sense of duty and obligation but out of love for God and his torah. Schaefer observes, 'An individual is formed by what one loves and reflects on continually. What delights us invades us'.[47]

Brueggemann suggests that the normal trajectory of Christian formation is the 'move from duty to delight',[48] but I would argue that for those who are converted as adults, the opposite is true. God's act of salvation produces in those who are saved a deep gratitude and affection, which in turn generates heartfelt obedience. The exodus produces a song of praise, and only afterwards does Israel commit to obedience through the covenant. I would admit, however, that affection may wane and require rediscovery. The prophet Isaiah calls Israel to that process of rediscovery when he writes, 'This people has drawn near to me with its mouth and honored me with its lips, but its heart is far from me; and its worship of me has been a commandment of men, learned by rote' (Isa. 29.13). Unfortunately, Israel's affections were not rekindled until they experienced anew the saving acts of God in the form of the exodus from exile.[49]

The Meaning of 'Torah' (תורה) in Ps. 1.2

The object of delight for the righteous is the 'torah of Yahweh', a phrase (תורה יהוה) that occurs 19 times in the Hebrew Bible.[50] The 'torah' can denote either the five books of Moses, the larger written canon (in whole or in part), or the more general 'teaching' of

---

[46] John Wesley, *A Plain Account of Christian Perfection* (New York: G. Lane & P.P. Sanford, 1844), pp. 17, 21.

[47] Schaefer, *Psalms*, p. 6.

[48] Brueggemann, *The Psalms and the Life of Faith*, p. 195, n. 16.

[49] I would suggest that this post-exilic passion can be discerned from the psalms of the period, though the post-exilic prophets register Israel's continuing struggle to reach the place of joyous, heartfelt service to Yahweh.

[50] Exodus 13.9; 2 Kgs 10.31; Isa. 5.24; 30.9; Jer. 8.8; Amos 2.4; Pss. 1.2; 19.8; 119.1; 1 Chron. 16.40; 22.12; 2 Chron. 12.1; 17.9; 31.3, 4; 34.14; 35.26; Ezra 7.10; and Neh. 9.3.

Yahweh, which may include both written and oral traditions.[51] In most cases the exact meaning of 'torah' is difficult to determine, but in seven out of the 19 occurrences, the 'torah of Yahweh' refers to a written document. It can be a book (ספר, 2 Chron. 17.9; 34.14; Neh. 9.3); it can be something written (כתוב, 1 Chron. 16.40; 2 Chron. 31.3; 35.26); and it can be the work of the pen (עט, Jer. 8.8). John Calvin contends that 'torah' in Psalm 1 refers to the 'whole of Scripture', including the Psalms.[52] Briggs, on the other hand, limits 'torah' to the books of Moses, the 'Pentateuch'.[53] Because of the similarities between Ps. 1.2, Deut. 17.19, and Josh. 1.8, Psalm 1 could be directed toward Israel's king, and the 'torah' might refer to a written copy of the law. However, the lack of any reference to the king and the use of the plural 'righteous ones' (Ps. 1.5, 6) as the subject of the psalm indicate a more general audience, an audience that would not have daily access to a written copy of the torah. McCann argues that 'torah' fundamentally means 'instruction', and that it here refers not only to written scriptures but also to 'the whole sacred tradition of God's revelation'. He points out that Psalm 1, in contrast to parallel texts (Deut. 17.18-19 and Josh. 1.8), contains 'no mention of a book or a copy of the law'.[54] Approaching the question from the perspective of Jewish tradition, Schaefer argues that torah consists of two parts: (1) the 'story of God's actions' with Israel and (2) the 'precepts and guidelines that shape' its life. These two parts can be described as 'narration and obligation' (הגדה and הלכה), and together they represent the totality of 'God's will or design for the chosen people'.[55] I conclude, therefore, that the phrase 'torah of Yahweh' in Ps. 1.2 signifies any and all of Yahweh's teaching,[56] both narratives and commands, both written and oral.

---

51 Terrien, *The Psalms*, p. 72.
52 Calvin, *Psalms*, p. 4.
53 Briggs and Briggs, *Psalms*, I, p. 5.
54 J. Clinton McCann, Jr., 'Psalms', in *The New Interpreter's Bible* (Nashville, TN: Abingdon Press, 1996), IV, p. 684. Cf. Kraus, *Psalms 1-59*, p. 116; and Jacobson, 'Psalm 1', p. 59.
55 Schaefer, *Psalms*, p. 3.
56 Cf. the JPS TANAKH (1985), which translates Ps. 1.2a, 'the teaching of the LORD is his delight'.

Theologically, torah signifies the narrative ethos that forms the Israelite faith community.[57] The torah stands in contrast to the way of the wicked, the path of the sinner, and the seat of the scorner, which are destructive influences that deform character and destroy community. The righteous, therefore, delight in the torah because, as Kraus writes, 'it is no fixed, static entity, but a power that is creative and life-giving'; it is a personal word 'that goes forth from Yahweh's person'; and as a 'spoken purposive word' it contains 'healing, saving, creative powers'.[58]

The Meaning of 'meditate' (הגה) in Ps. 1.2

The righteous person delights in the torah, and that delight is manifested through continual reflection upon it. The meaning of the Hebrew הגה, translated here 'meditate', is not entirely clear. What is clear, however, is that it does not correspond exactly to the English 'meditate', which means 'to exercise the mind in thought or reflection'.[59] While 'meditate' often denotes a silent activity, the Hebrew הגה seems in most cases to signify some sort of audible, vocal utterance. It has been defined as 'moan, growl, utter, speak, muse',[60] and 'utter, mutter, moan (mourn, KJV), meditate, devise, plot';[61] and it may be an example of onomatopoeia.[62] The word carries a variety of meanings depending upon its syntactical role. Used intransitively, the verb הגה can mean 'moan' (Isa. 16.7), 'growl' (Isa. 31.4), 'coo' (Isa. 38.14), or 'mutter' (Isa. 8.19). When followed by an object, it can mean 'speak' (Psa. 37.30, parallel to דבר) or possibly 'devise, plot' (Ps. 2.1, Prov. 24.2). In one case, הגה is followed by an infinitive where it apparently signifies 'ponder, consider': 'The heart of the righteous ponders how to answer, but the mouth of the wicked pours forth evil' (Prov. 15.28). However, given that in other contexts הגה is

---

[57] The theological function of torah is explored by Walter Brueggemann, *The Creative Word: Canon as a Model for Biblical Education* (Philadelphia: Fortress Press, 1982), pp. 14-39.

[58] Hans-Joachim Kraus, *Theology of the Psalms* (trans. K.R. Crim; Minneapolis, MN: Augsburg Pub. House, 1986), p. 34.

[59] John Simpson and Edmund Weiner (eds.), *Oxford English Dictionary* (Oxford: Oxford University Press, 2nd edn, 1989).

[60] *BDB*, p. 211.

[61] *TWOT*, I, p. 468.

[62] My friend Kevin Spawn reminded me of this fact.

expressed through utterance, the contrast here might be between the loud and thoughtless speech of the wicked and the quieter, more deliberate speech of the righteous.[63]

In Ps. 1.2 the verb הגה is followed by the preposition 'in' (ב), a usage that represents still another syntactical variation. The same construction is found in the following texts:

(1) 'This book of the torah shall not depart out of your mouth; you shall meditate (הגה) in it day and night' (Josh. 1.8).
(2) 'My mouth will praise you with joyful lips. When I remember you on my bed, I meditate (הגה) on you in the night watches' (Ps. 63.5b-6).
(3) 'I remember my song in the night ... I will meditate (הגה) on all your work, and muse (שיח) on your mighty deeds' (Ps. 77.6-12).
(4) 'I remember the days of old; I meditate (הגה) on all your works; I muse (שיח) on the work of your hands' (Ps. 143.5).

In light of the fact that the torah is to be in Joshua's 'mouth', it seems likely that his meditation would include some form of utterance. Also, two of the three examples from Psalms include parallels to the word שיח (Ps. 77.12 and 143.5), which may signify 'rehearsing' a matter[64] and most often includes speech (Ps. 55.2, 18; 64.2; 69.13; 102.1; 105.2; 142.3). Furthermore, the context of singing is evident in Psalm 63 and 77, which leads Ringgren to conclude that in these texts 'meditation is expressed in a song of praise'.[65]

The verb הגה, therefore, likely denotes a thoughtful, deliberate utterance, which is usually spoken softly or even unintelligibly. Translating הגה precisely has proven to be difficult, and almost all translations have settled on 'meditate' in Ps. 1.2.[66] Luther, however, in choosing '*redet*' ('speaks') emphasizes the vocal sense, as does the *New Jerusalem Bible* in their choice of the word 'murmur'. The intellectual

---

[63] At one point, Rolf Jacobson states that הגה signifies 'study'; but, later, he writes, 'It properly denotes verbalized rumination' ('Psalm 1', p. 61).

[64] *TWOT*, II, p. 875.

[65] A. Negoiță and H. Ringgren, 'הגה', in *TDOT*, III, p. 323.

[66] For example, see LXX, Vulgate, ASV, CJB, CSB, DRA, ERV, ESV, Geneva, JPS, KJV, NASB, NAU, NIV, NKJ, NLT, NRSV, RSV, Louis Segond (French, 1910), Reina-Valera (Spanish, 1960), and NVB (Italian, 1996).

aspect is stressed in the *New American Bible* and the JPS *TANAKH* (1985) who render הגה as 'study'.

Meditation on the torah might be accomplished through the reading of the written text, as in the case of Josh. 1.8. Or for those who do not have access to the written torah, meditation could be in the form of recitation from memory or in rehearsing the traditional narratives. Meditation might also signify the 'audible murmuring'[67] of one whose thoughts are occupied in deep reflection upon God's words and deeds. The possibilities are open because the verb הגה does not specify an exact method or type of oral activity; rather it denotes the 'quality' of that utterance.[68] Negoită contents that הגה 'is sometimes used to express the feelings of the human soul. With *siach* [שׂיח] in particular, *haghah* [הגה] means that a man "is lost in his religion," that he is filled with thoughts of God's deeds or his will'.[69] In Ps. 1.2, the verb הגה 'highlights that the speaker's wholehearted sentiments are being revealed … It is an expression of innermost delight in torah'.[70] Therefore, the emotive connotations of הגה make it a fitting parallel to חפץ ('delight'), thus carrying forward the affective import of Ps. 1.2.[71]

The significance of the affective dimension of הגה, which is barely noted in discussions of Psalm 1, becomes conspicuous when we observe the connections between הגה and singing. LeFebvre, going beyond Ringgren's aforementioned comment that הגה can signify the utterance of a song, argues convincingly that the meditation of Ps. 1.2 can include the singing of psalms as one of its modes of expression. LeFebvre points to Psalms 63 and 77 (mentioned above) as examples where הגה has reference to singing; and he adds a third text, which reads, 'My lips shall rejoice greatly when I sing unto thee … My tongue will utter (הגה) your righteousness all the day' (Ps. 71.23-

---

[67] Negoită and Ringgren, 'הגה', p. 323. Zenger, 'Psalm 1', p. 47, understands הגה signify the 'hallowed recitation' ('*halblaute Rezitieren*') of the torah; and Allen P. Ross, *A Commentary on the Psalms* (Kregel Exegetical Library; 3 vols.; Grand Rapids, MI: Kregel Academic & Professional, 2011), I, p. 189, states that the meaning of הגה includes 'memorization of divine instruction'.

[68] LeFebvre, 'Torah-Meditation and the Psalms', p. 219.

[69] Negoită and Ringgren, 'הגה', p. 323.

[70] LeFebvre, 'Torah-Meditation and the Psalms', p. 219.

[71] During discussions at the meeting of the Society of Biblical Literature, Pentecostal New Testament scholar Blaine Charette suggested that Paul's reference to 'groanings' of the Holy Spirit (Rom. 8.26) may be an echo of the Hebrew הגה.

24).[72] Another connection between meditation and singing, noted by Terrien, is the noun הגיון (derived from הגה) which 'is a sung soliloquy, whispered with a susurration of the lips, the arrhythmic and melodic exteriorization of an inner reflection' (see Pss. 9.16 and 92.3).[73] LeFebvre shows still another connection between torah and song, observing that Moses wrote both the book of the law and a commemorative song (Deut. 31.22-24). The song is taught to the people, and the book of the law is handed over to the Levites and elders. Thus, 'Deut. 31–32 identifies law-contemplation with worshipful song-singing. It is the song which will be forever known by the people (Deut. 31:21), while the book is not accessible to them'.[74] Consequently, although reading the torah, reciting oral tradition, and reflecting on torah may be possible modes of expressing meditation (הגה), the worshipful singing of psalms may be the form of meditation that is most appropriate to the context of Ps. 1.2; and it may be the clearest manifestation of the affective import of the verb 'meditate' (הגה).

Finally, it should not be overlooked that the commendation to meditate in the torah appears within a psalm, suggesting perhaps that 'Ps. 1 itself becomes a demonstration of what is envisioned in 1:2'.[75] Therefore, as an introduction to the Psalter, Ps. 1.2 may not conceive of the Psalms as a part *of* the torah,[76] but as passionate meditations *on* the torah. The content of the Psalter could certainly support such a conclusion since numerous explicit references and allusions to elements of the torah are found throughout the Psalms.[77] For example, Ps. 19.1-6 is a delight-filled meditation on the torah's claim that God is creator: 'The heavens declare the glory of God, and the firmament shows his handiwork' (v. 1). Psalm 44.1-3 is a passionate meditation on the conquest story: 'You drove out the nations with your hand' (v.

---

[72] LeFebvre, 'Torah-Meditation and the Psalms', p. 218-25; contra Gerald H. Wilson, *The Editing of the Hebrew Psalter* (SBL Dissertation Series 76; Chico, CA: Scholars Press, 1985), p. 207, who goes so far as to say that Psalm 1 'indicates that [the Psalter] is a collection to be read rather than performed'.

[73] Terrien, *The Psalms*, p. 73.

[74] LeFebvre, 'Torah-Meditation and the Psalms', p. 222.

[75] LeFebvre, 'Torah-Meditation and the Psalms', p. 224.

[76] Contra Brevard S. Childs, *Introduction to the Old Testament as Scripture* (Philadelphia: Fortress Press, 1st American edn, 1979), p. 513, and Craig C. Broyles, *Psalms* (NIBC; Peabody, MA: Hendrickson, 1999), p. 42.

[77] Cf. E.W. Hengstenberg, *Commentary on the Psalms* (3 vols.; Cherry Hill, NJ: Mack Publishing Co., 1972), I, p. 11.

2a).[78] The psalms of lament often appeal to the justice that is demanded by the torah. Psalm 78 delights in Yahweh's mercy from the time of Jacob to David. Psalm 105 meditates on the Abrahamic covenant (vv. 9-22) and delights in the salvation of exodus (vv. 23-45). Furthermore, the fivefold division of the Psalter may support my contention that the entire collection is to be viewed in part as worshipful reflection upon the five books of the torah. Perhaps the singing of the Psalms is not the only way of taking delight in the torah, but it is one way. It follows that the promise of 'blessedness' (Ps. 1.1) accrues to the person who reads, recites, and sings the Psalms with delight.[79]

Conclusion

I have shown that the common interpretation of Psalm 1 as a call for obedience, a view exemplified by Walter Brueggemann's influential article, 'Bounded by Obedience and Praise: The Psalms as Canon', does not quite capture the emphasis of the text. Psalm one sets up an opposition between the righteous and the wicked – the righteous are 'blessed' and the wicked 'perish'. The righteous are identified by their resistance to the lure of wicked counsel and by their affection for the torah of Yahweh. While it is true that Psalm 1 announces Yahweh's approval of the 'righteous', righteousness is not limited to or equated with 'obedience'. Instead, the psalm points to the affections rather than to behavior as the key element of the righteous person – 'his delight is in the torah of Yahweh and in his torah he meditates day and night' (Ps. 1.2). Instead of calling for obedience to the torah, Psalm 1 evokes affection for the torah. 'The blessed one is thus identified not by social status or by mere behavior but by attitude'.[80] Psalm 1.2 suggests that delight in the torah 'is the determining and effective disposition of the truly happy life'.[81]

---

[78] If 'torah' consists of the larger tradition, as I have argued above, then the conquest would be a part of that 'teaching'.

[79] See Creach, *Yahweh as Refuge and the Editing of the Hebrew Psalter*, who ties together the ideas of meditating in the torah and 'seeking refuge in Yahweh' (pp. 69-73). He suggests that meditating upon the torah perhaps became a 'means of protecting oneself spiritually from enemies' (p. 79).

[80] Broyles, *Psalms*, p. 42.

[81] Kraus, *Psalms 1-59*, p. 117.

In its role as an introduction to the Psalter, Psalm 1 sets the tone for encountering the Psalms, identifying the affective disposition that is necessary to enter the Psalter. Psalm 1 suggests that right worship begins with rightly oriented affections. When Psalm 1 invites meditation on the torah as a response to God's self-revelation, it becomes its own example. It offers itself as a model of torah meditation, a model which is picked up and expanded by the psalms that follow. The psalms, therefore, serve as exemplars of what it means to delight in the torah of the Lord.

The psalm's accentuation of the affections suggests that the study of biblical poetry in general and of the Psalms in particular can benefit from an approach that is attuned to the passions that are inherent in the text and the passions that are brought to the text by the interpreter. Moreover, the invitation to a passionate engagement with the text has implications beyond the study of the poetic literature. Perhaps the time has come that all biblical interpreters confess not only their intellectual presuppositions but also their affective inclinations and dispositions. This affective approach to the text is evident in the writings of Martin Luther, whose comments on Ps. 1.2 register his own passionate affection for the torah of the Lord:

> [This affection] is the pure desire of the heart … it is not only the love of the Law but also a loving delight in the Law which the world and the prince of the world can destroy and defeat neither by prosperity nor by adversity. Yet through need, ignominy, the cross, death, and hell this 'desire' breaks through to victory.[82]

---

[82] Pelikan *et al.* (eds.), *Luther's Works*, XIV, p. 295.

Psalm 1 Medieval Illuminated Manuscript

2

PSALM 63: LONGING FOR GOD

Introduction

In my first semester at Bible college, I began reading through the entire Bible. As might be expected, a number of Scripture passages made a deep impression upon me, and one of those was Psalm 63, particularly the first two verses: 'my soul is thirsty for you; my flesh longs for you … thus I have seen you in the sanctuary, beholding your power and your glory'. I heard in Psalm 63 a passionate prayer, an articulation of deep spiritual inclinations. I heard an expression of the psalmist's intense desire to encounter God and to experience God's presence. I also recognized the psalmist's commitment to seek after God and to respond to God's gracious acts with praise and with constant loyalty. Because of the content of the psalm and its passionate tone of expression, I memorized the psalm and began to recite it regularly as a part of my own prayers.

The longing for God expressed in Psalm 63 gave voice to the passion for God that was generated by my own Pentecostal spirituality, a spirituality that Steven Jack Land has characterized as 'a passion for the kingdom', which is 'ultimately a passion for God'.[1] I suggest in this study that Psalm 63 can function as an individual and/or communal prayer that voices the passionate aspects of Pentecostal spirituality. Furthermore, in its function as Holy Scripture, this psalm can

---

[1] Land, *Pentecostal Spirituality*, pp. 2, 97, 120, 73-80, 212, 219. Cf. Mark J. Cartledge, 'Affective Theological Praxis: Understanding the Direct Object of Practical Theology', *IJPT* 8.1 (2004), p. 36.

guide Pentecostals in their pursuit of an encounter with God and in their longing for God's presence.[2]

In this constructive and integrative study, I examine Psalm 63 through the lens of Pentecostal spirituality; however, before examining Psalm 63, I will describe what I am calling an 'affective approach' to the biblical text. The affective approach calls for the hearer to attend to the affective tones that are present in the text and to allow the affections of the hearer to be shaped by the text. Once I have described the affective approach, I will present an affective Pentecostal hearing of Psalm 63 that emerges from my location within the Pentecostal community. Then I will suggest ways in which Psalm 63 can contribute to the affective formation of the Pentecostal church of today. On the one hand, therefore, my hearing of Psalm 63 is informed by and shaped by my own Pentecostal experience. On the other hand, my Pentecostal spirituality and experience is influenced by my engagement with Psalm 63.

Before proceeding to the study, I would offer five explanatory comments: 1) My work on the Psalms is not an attempt to create a new method for biblical study. However, it is an attempt to utilize contemporary methods that are conducive to the Pentecostal ethos, theology, and spirituality. 2) Although my work is generated by my Pentecostal spirituality and is aimed at the Pentecostal tradition, I recognize that affective engagement is common to all humans.[3] Therefore, all readers of Scripture are invited to 'listen in' to the conversation in hope that they too may find this study beneficial. 3) The Pentecostal movement is a global, diverse, and multifaceted tradition;

---

[2] Pentecostal spirituality identifies closely with the prayers of the Psalter; therefore, I find it difficult to accept the argument of James L. Mays, 'A Question of Identity: The Threefold Hermeneutic of Psalmody', *Asbury Theological Journal* 46.1 (1991), pp. 87-94 (88), who states the following regarding the Psalms:

> It is, however, a fact that these prayers have become difficult and strange for contemporary Christians. Where our predecessors in prayer received and used this language with a sense of recognition, discovery and illumination, it has become problematic for many in our time … This pilgrim that must make a way as if through a dark valley surrounded by foes to trust and obedience. This human whose desire will not be satisfied by anything less than the experience of God. This individual in the prayer psalms has come to be different, a stranger, sometimes embarrassing.

Mays' assertion could not be farther from the truth for 600 million Pentecostals and Charismatics around the world.

[3] Smith, *Desiring the Kingdom*, argues convincingly that human life is shaped largely by the affections.

therefore, I do not claim to speak for all Pentecostals. 4) Biblical exegesis and hermeneutics demand the utilization of a variety of methods and approaches. Therefore, within a holistic biblical hermeneutic, the affective dimension of Scripture is only one of the many dimensions of the text that should be investigated as a part of sound exegesis. I would argue, however, that the affective dimension has been overlooked and underutilized in the academic study of Scripture. 5) This chapter is a provisional proposal that I submit to the community of faith for their discerning response. I hope that it will generate further conversation about creative engagement with the biblical text.

An Affective Approach to Interpretation

The development of my affective approach to the Psalter takes into consideration Walter Brueggemann's insightful critique of both the precritical and critical approaches to the study of the Psalms. He argues on the one hand that the 'devotional tradition of piety is surely weakened by disregarding the perspectives and insights of scholarship' and on the other hand that the critical tradition 'is frequently arid, because it lingers excessively on formal questions, with inability or reluctance to bring its insights and methods to substantive matters of exposition'.[4] Brueggemann's proposal for a postcritical 'functional' approach,[5] in which the critical and pietistic traditions inform and correct each other, places the Psalms within the journey of faith and recognizes their value as prayers for the ancient Hebrews and for subsequent faith communities.[6]

Brueggemann's functional approach in its broad parameters makes room for scholarly consideration of the emotive quality of the

---

[4] Walter Brueggemann, *The Message of the Psalms: A Theological Commentary* (Augsburg Old Testament Studies; Minneapolis, MN: Augsburg Pub. House, 1984), p. 16.

[5] Brueggemann, *The Psalms and the Life of Faith*, pp. 3-32.

[6] Brueggemann, *The Psalms and the Life of Faith*, pp. 33-66. My approach should not be confused with the resurgent mystical, spiritual, or allegorical approach presented by David C. Steinmetz, 'The Superiority of Pre-Critical Exegesis', *ThT* 37 (1980), pp. 27-38, or Celia Kourie, 'Reading Scripture through a Mystical Lens', *Acta Theologica* 15/Suppl. (2011), pp. 132-53. While I appreciate Steinmetz's critique of historical criticism, I have argued that returning to allegory or the medieval mystics is not an option. See Lee Roy Martin, 'Pre-Critical Exegesis of the Book of Judges and the Construction of a Post-Critical Hermeneutic', *EP* 88 (2006), pp. 338-53.

Psalms. It might be argued that the affective dimension is too 'subjective' to be included in academic study. Expecting objections to the affective approach, Daniel C. Mcguire remarks, 'It is not for nothing that the rationalist is upset by the inclusion of affectivity … Affectivity imports mystery and depth. We can feel more than we can see or say'.[7] For this reason, biblical scholarship has given little attention to this affective dimension of biblical poetry in general and of the Psalms in particular. Yet I would argue that the function of poetry is to evoke (and provoke) the passions and to form the affections. The study of the Psalms, therefore, can benefit from a hermeneutic that appreciates the affective dimensions of the text and that takes full advantage of the passions that are brought to the text by the interpreter.

It is well known that the affections played a significant role in the spirituality of Jonathan Edwards[8] and John Wesley.[9] Deep affective currents have been observed also in the Eastern Orthodox tradition, a tradition that influenced both Edwards and Wesley.[10] Recently, B.I.

---

[7] Daniel C. Maguire, '*Ratio Practica* and the Intellectualistic Fallacy', *JRE* 10.1 (1982), p. 23.

[8] See, for example, Jonathan Edwards, *Religious Affections* (Works of Jonathan Edwards; New Haven: Yale Univ Pr, 1959); Timothy Hessel-Robinson, 'Jonathan Edwards (1703-1758): A Treatise Concerning Religious Affections', in *Christian Spirituality* (London: Routledge, 2010), pp. 269-80; John E. Smith, 'Testing the Spirits: Jonathan Edwards and the Religious Affections', *USQR* 37.1-2 (1982), pp. 27-37; Roger Ward, 'The Philosophical Structure of Jonathan Edward's Religious Affections', *CSR* 29.4 (2000), pp. 745-68; Wayne L. Proudfoot, 'From Theology to a Science of Religions: Jonathan Edwards and William James on Religious Affections', *HTR* 82.2 (1989), pp. 149-68, and Iain D. Campbell, 'Jonathan Edwards' Religious Affections as a Paradigm for Evangelical Spirituality', *SBET* 21.2 (2003), pp. 166-86.

[9] See Gregory S. Clapper, 'John Wesley's Abridgement of Isaac Watts' the Doctrine of the Passions Explained and Improved', *WTJ* 43.2 (2008), pp. 28-32; *idem, John Wesley on Religious Affections: His Views on Experience and Emotion and Their Role in the Christian Life and Theology* (Pietist and Wesleyan Studies; Metuchen, NJ: Scarecrow Pr, 1989); Kenneth J. Collins, 'John Wesley's Topography of the Heart: Dispositions, Tempers, and Affections', *Methodist History* 36.3 (1998), pp. 162-75; and Randy L. Maddox, 'A Change of Affections: The Development, Dynamics, and Dethronement of John Wesley's Heart Religion', in *'Heart Religion' in the Methodist Tradition and Related Movements* (Lanham, MD: Scarecrow Press, 2001), pp. 3-31.

[10] Cf. Edmund J. Rybarczyk, 'Spiritualities Old and New: Similarities between Eastern Orthodoxy & Classical Pentecostalism', *PNEUMA* 24.1 (2002), pp. 7-25, who argues that the Orthodox, like Pentecostals, insist firmly that 'knowledge of God is not limited to the intellectual domain of human existence, but that the believer can sense and hear God in visceral and profound ways' (p. 10). See also *idem,*

McGroarty has argued that it was the view of the 14th-Century English mystic Hilton that human wholeness ('health') cannot be attained outside of an affective engagement with God.[11] Dale Coulter has expounded upon the affective dimension in Catherine of Siena,[12] Bernard of Clairvaux, Richard of St. Victor, Catherine of Genoa, and Martin Luther, concluding that their common theology of 'encounter centers upon affectivity as the point of contact between the divine and human'.[13] And Jeffrey Gros points out the importance of the Franciscan movement's 'concern for direct human experience of Christ'.[14] These studies, among many others, have shown that the concern for the formation of the affections is present not only in Pentecostalism but also in a wide variety of traditions.

As mentioned in Chapter 1, Steven Land observes that while Pentecostals accept the necessity of orthodoxy (right doctrine) and orthopraxy (right practice), they see orthopathy (right affections) as the integrating center for both orthodoxy and orthopraxy.[15] Consequently, a Pentecostal approach would recognize the Psalms not only as a witness to right theology and practice, but also as an important

---

Beyond Salvation: Eastern Orthodoxy and Classical Pentecostalism on Becoming Like Christ (PTM; Carlisle, UK: Paternoster Press, 2004). In the Orthodox writers, the affective dimension of spirituality is usually couched in the language of encountering the presence and mystery of God. See Ecumenical Patriarch Bartholomew, *Encountering the Mystery: Understanding Orthodox Christianity Today* (New York: Doubleday, 1st edn, 2008); Vladimir Lossky, *The Mystical Theology of the Eastern Church* (London: J. Clarke, 1st edn, 1957), and Alexander Schmemann, *The Historical Road of Eastern Orthodoxy* (Chicago: H. Regnery, 1966). On the influence of Orthodox theology on Edwards and Wesley, see, for example, Michael James McClymond and Gerald R. McDermott, *The Theology of Jonathan Edwards* (New York: Oxford University Press, 2012), and S.T. Kimbrough, *Orthodox and Wesleyan Spirituality* (Crestwood, NY: St. Vladimir's Seminary Press, 2002).

[11] Brendan Ignatius McGroarty, 'Humility, Contemplation and Affect Theory', *Journal of Religion and Health* 45.1 (2006), pp. 57-72.

[12] Catherine of Siena, *The Dialogue* 13 (trans. and intro. Suzanne Noffke, OP; New York, NY: Paulist Press, 1980), p. 48; cited in Dale Coulter, 'Pentecostals and Monasticism: A Common Spirituality?', *AGH* 30 (2010), p. 45.

[13] Dale M. Coulter, 'The Spirit and the Bride Revisited: Pentecostalism, Renewal, and the Sense of History', *JPT* 21.2 (2012), pp. 298-319.

[14] Jeffrey Gros, 'Ecumenical Connections across Time: Medieval Franciscans as a Proto-Pentecostal Movement?', *PNEUMA* 34.1 (2012), p. 75. Gros calls for 'a robust appreciation of spiritual experience' (p. 91).

[15] Land, *Pentecostal Spirituality*, pp. 21, 34, 127-59. See also Cartledge, 'Affective Theological Praxis', p. 36; and Wolfgang Vondey, *Pentecostal Theology: Living the Full Gospel* (Systematic Pentecostal and Charismatic Theology; New York: Bloomsbury T&T Clark, 2017), pp. 24-27.

contributor to the formation of the affections. The affections, not to be confused with transitory feelings or emotions, are the abiding dispositions and passions of the heart that characterize a person's deepest desires.[16] The Psalms, therefore, teach us not only what to think (orthodoxy) and what to do (orthopraxy) but also what to desire (orthopathy). To say it another way, the Psalms contribute to both intellectual and affective learning: 'Intellectual learning aims at learning facts and their relation and at rational analysis … In affective learning, on the other hand, feelings and emotions are predominant. With affective learning one aims to develop emotional and moral sensitivities and to achieve a deep commitment to certain values'.[17] Mark Cartledge adds, 'Indeed, one could argue that the affections inform not only believing and action but also the imagination as well, without which significant advances in understanding would be impossible'.[18]

The process of affective interpretation requires at least four cooperative moves on the part of the hearer. First, the hearer of the psalm must identify and acknowledge the affective dimensions of the text, an acknowledgement that is by no means automatic or common for scholars, who tend to concentrate their attention upon historical critical concerns. Every psalm includes an affective dimension, which may involve hope or despair, love or hate, trust or fear, admiration or scorn, pride or shame, joy or despondency, to mention but a few examples. The poetic genre demands that the hearer give attention to its emotive content.

Second, the hearer of the psalm must acknowledge his or her own passions that are brought to the interpretive process. It is important that the hearer of the text recognize when his or her affections correspond to the affections of the psalmist and when they do not correspond, because the passions of the hearer can dramatically impact the resulting interpretation.

Third, the hearer of the psalm must be open to the emotive impact of the text. Before the hearer can experience the affective dimension of the text, he or she may be required to enter the world of

---

[16] Land, *Pentecostal Spirituality*, p. 34. Cf. Thomas Ryan, 'Revisiting Affective Knowledge and Connaturality in Aquinas', *TS* 66.1 (2005), pp. 55-58, 63. The affections, of course, play a key role in the creation of feelings and emotions.

[17] Richard Ognibene and Richard Penaskovic, 'Teaching Theology: Some Affective Strategies', *Horizons* 8.1 (1981), p. 98.

[18] Cartledge, 'Affective Theological Praxis', p. 38. Cf. Smith, *Desiring the Kingdom*, pp. 135, 52.

the psalmist and to enter the emotive flow of the textual stream. Robert O. Baker argues that the reading of the biblical text involves both the mind and the affections of the reader. He insists that 'reading the Bible is not just a cognitive experience, but an affective one as well'.[19] He argues further that seeking

> to understand the ideational/rational content of a text without also seeking to experience and reflect upon its emotive effect is to skew the text's message … By committing to read the text objectively from a critical distance, the professional reader subverts the text's evocative power or is at least unable to express the feeling that the text evokes in him or her.[20]

Fourth, the hearer must allow himself or herself to be transformed by the affective experiencing of the psalm. As the hearer engages the biblical text, his or her affections are shaped by that engagement. 'The affective capacity of the person can be modified and hence grow in sensitivity, intensity, and scope'.[21] In its canonical role as Scripture, the book of Psalms makes a significant contribution toward a theology of worship, and part of the message of the Psalms is that right worship begins with rightly oriented affections. Thus, through the hearing of the Psalms the desires of the heart are transformed and redirected toward God so that the affections of gratitude, trust, and love (affections that foster worship) are generated and nourished.

Although I would insist that the third and fourth moves are essential to an affective engagement with the text, I would admit that they are difficult (if not impossible) to accomplish within a written document. They are experiences that may be validated by testimony and description (as in my own testimony that began this chapter), but the transformative experience itself is outside the bounds of written

---

[19] Baker, 'Pentecostal Bible Reading', p. 107. Cf. Martin, *The Unheard Voice of God*, pp. 70-71. See also Edgerton, *The Passion of Interpretation*, who agrees that every interpretation involves the passions of the interpreter. See also Cartledge, 'Affective Theological Praxis', pp. 42, 51, and Kenneth J. Archer, *A Pentecostal Hermeneutic for the 21ˢᵗ Century: Spirit, Scripture and Community* (JPTSup 28; London: T&T Clark, 2004). I will cite from the CPT Press version, *A Pentecostal Hermeneutic: Spirit, Scripture and Community* (Cleveland, TN: CPT Press, 2009), p. 234.

[20] Baker, 'Pentecostal Bible Reading', p. 95.

[21] Ryan, 'Revisiting Affective Knowledge', p. 57.

discourse. Consequently, the bulk of my study will give attention to the first two movements of the affective hermeneutical process.

In what follows, I will offer an affective hearing of Psalm 63. My interpretive location within the Pentecostal community has caused me to appreciate the affective dimension of the Psalms, and I find Psalm 63 to be particularly suited to an affective interpretation. The psalmist's yearning to encounter God's power and glory is consistent with aspirations of many Christians, and the passionate prayers and exuberant praises that we find in Psalm 63 are consistent with the ethos of emerging forms of worship.

As stated above, appreciation for the affective dimension of the text is only one aspect of a holistic hermeneutic. The affective elements become clearer and more precise when they emerge from sound exegesis. Therefore, as a foundation for the study, we will overview the text of Psalm 63 and examine its structure and genre.

A Translation of Psalm 63

¹ A psalm of David when he was in the wilderness of Judah

² God, you are my God; I will seek you earnestly.
    My soul thirsts for you;
My flesh longs for you
    In a dry and weary land without water.
³ Thus in the sanctuary I have seen you,
    Beholding your power and your glory.

⁴ Because your covenant loyalty is better than life,
    My lips will praise you.
⁵ Thus I shall bless you during my life;
    In your name I shall lift up my hands.
⁶ Like marrow and fatness my soul will be satisfied,
    And my mouth will offer praise with joyful lips.

⁷ Whenever I remembered you on my bed,
    In the night watches I would meditate on you,
⁸ Because you were my help,
    In the shadow of your wings I would shout for joy.
⁹ My soul has stuck close behind you;
    Your right hand has upheld me.

¹⁰ As for them who will seek to ruin my life,
  They will go into the depths of the earth.
¹¹ They will be delivered over to the power of the sword;
  They will be a prey for foxes.
¹² But as for the king, he will rejoice in God;
  Everyone who swears by him will glory,
  Because the mouth of those speaking deception will be
  stopped.

Structure and Genre of Psalm 63

The structure of Psalm 63 is unclear,²² and scholars have divided the
psalm in a variety of ways.²³ I suggest a four-part structure, beginning
after the superscription (v. 1):²⁴

1. Longing for God's Presence (vv. 2-3).
Verses 2-3 hold together as an introduction that establishes the overall topic of the psalm as the psalmist's intention to passionately and
habitually pursue the presence of God.

2. Praise for God's Covenant Loyalty (vv. 4-6).
The second section, like the first, includes an affirmation that is expressed syntactically with a verbless clause ('you are my God' and
'your kindness is better than life'). The verbless clauses are followed
by statements of future intent ('I will seek you' and 'my lips will praise
you'). The first two sections each include verses held together by the
conjunction 'thus' (כֵּן). The first section begins with seeking God and
ends with seeing God. The second section both begins and ends with

²² Cf. Michael Wilcock, *The Message of Psalms 1–72: Songs for the People of God*
(Downers Grove, IL: InterVarsity Press, 2001), I, p. 222, and Marvin E. Tate, *Psalms
51-100* (WBC 20; Dallas, TX: Word Books, 1990), p. 125.
²³ James Limburg, *Psalms* (Louisville, KY: Westminister John Knox Press, 1st
edn, 2000), pp. 208-10, divides the psalm into three parts: vv. 1-4, body and soul;
vv. 5-8, remembering; and vv. 9-11, rejoicing. J.P. Fokkelman, *The Psalms in Form:
The Hebrew Psalter in Its Poetic Shape* (Leiden: Deo Publishing, 2002), p. 71, finds six
divisions made up of the following verses: 2-3, 4-5, 6-7, 8-9, 10-11, 12.
²⁴ I will follow the Hebrew versification. Each of the four sections consists of
three bicola except for the final verse, which concludes emphatically with a tricola.
Cf. Terrien, *The Psalms*, pp. 460-61, and Hans-Joachim Kraus, *Psalms 60-150* (trans.
H.C. Oswald; Continental Commentaries; Minneapolis, MN: Augsburg, 1989), p.
18. See also J.W. Rogerson and John W. McKay, *Psalms* (3 vols.; Cambridge:
Cambridge University Press, 1977), II, pp. 64-65, who find the same structure, except that they separate the final verse as another section.

the mention of praise, and each of its verses (4-6) mentions praise either literally or figuratively. Each verb in this section is a *yiqtol* and should be translated as future tense.

3. Remembrance of God's Faithfulness (vv. 7-9).
The third section (vv. 7-9) is held together by a focus upon remembrance of God's actions in the past.[25] Verses 7-8 consist of two compound sentences, each of which begins with a *qatal* verb and is followed by a habitual *yiqtol*.[26] Verse 9 is made up of two sentences that utilize *qatal* verbs.

4. Rejoicing in God's Covenant Protection (vv. 10-12).[27]
The fourth section turns to the eventual downfall of the psalmist's enemies, and all of the verbs are *yiqtols* that should be translated as future tense.

The four sections of Psalm 63 are held together by two parallel threads that span the entire psalm. The first thread is the psalmist's affirmations about God that are either stated directly or are implied by the passive voice: God is his God (v. 2); God's covenant kindness is greater than life (v. 3); God will satisfy the psalmist's desires (v. 5); God has been the psalmist's help (v. 7) and support (v. 8); God will destroy the psalmist's enemies (vv. 9, 10, 11). The second thread consists of statements that describe the psalmist's response to God. These responses can be summarized in two categories: seeking God (v. 2) and praising God (vv. 3, 4, 5, 7, 11). We may also infer that the psalmist's past actions are appropriate for the present and future. These past responses are remembering God (v. 6), meditating upon God (v. 6), and sticking close to God (v. 8).

Like the laments, Psalm 63 begins with a direct address to God (v. 2), and it includes other elements that are common to the laments: a mention of enemies (v. 9), a promise to praise God (v. 11), and a statement of trust (v. 7). Consequently, a number of scholars have

---

[25] Cf. Susanne Gillmayr-Bucher, 'David, Ich und der König: Fortschreibung und Relecture in Psalm 63', in Josef M. Oesch, Andreas Vonach, and Georg Fischer (eds.), *Horizonte biblischer Texte: Festschrift für Josef M. Oesch zum 60. Geburtstag* (Göttingen: Vandenhoeck & Ruprecht, 2003), pp. 71-89 (76); and Briggs and Briggs, *Psalms*, II, p. 74, and in ref. to v. 8 as past tense, see Kraus, *Psalms 60-150*, p. 17.

[26] Cf. Gillmayr-Bucher, 'David, Ich und der König', p. 74.

[27] Gillmayr-Bucher, 'David, Ich und der König', p. 76, agrees that vv. 10-12 hold together as a unit.

classified Psalm 63 as an individual lament.[28] However, the direct address to God, though common to the laments, is not confined to them (e.g. Pss. 8.1; 9.1; 18.1; 21.1; 30.1; 65.1; 84.1; 101.1; 104.1; 115.1; 138.1; 145.1), and therefore is not a defining feature of the lament. Moreover, the laments function as a voice of protest and complaint to God, and Psalm 63 does not contain a protest or complaint,[29] neither does it contain any of the usual indicators of complaint, such as the questions 'Why…?' and 'How long…?'. Enemies are mentioned, but they are not presented as a direct and immediate threat. Instead, they exist as a constant political reality, an everyday obstacle to the king. Furthermore, the lament psalms function as petitions to God for his immediate intervention, but Psalm 63 contains no such plea. Some commentators would translate the verbs in vv. 10-11 as petitions, but I suspect that they do so because they are predisposed to classifying the psalm as a lament.[30]

The laments normally emerge from the perception that God is absent, distant, and unresponsive. The absence of God is perceived through the presence of troubles, such as enemies or sickness, that plague the psalmist. In the lament psalm, the plea for God's return and for God's presence is associated with a petition for deliverance. When God returns to the psalmist, he will intervene to answer the psalmist's petitions. Psalm 63, however, is different from the lament in that it expresses a plea for God's presence quite apart from a specific petition for deliverance. The plea for God's presence is not associated with any other petition. The presence of God is an end in itself. Enemies may be present and will soon be vanquished, but still the petition is focused more directly upon a yearning for God himself.

In light of the above considerations, John Goldingay, along with other scholars, has identified Psalm 63 as a song of trust.[31] The songs

---

[28] Nancy L. DeClaissé-Walford, *Introduction to the Psalms: A Song from Ancient Israel* (St. Louis, MO: Chalice Press, 2004), p. 147; C. Hassell Bullock, *Encountering the Book of Psalms: A Literary and Theological Introduction* (Grand Rapids, MI: Baker Academic, 2001), p. 144.

[29] Bullock, *Encountering the Book of Psalms*, classifies the psalm as a lament even though he admits that it contains no complaint or petition (p. 44).

[30] On the difficulties involved in interpreting Hebrew verb tense in poetry, see Alviero Niccacci, 'Analysing Biblical Hebrew Poetry', *JSOT* 74 (1997), pp. 77-93, especially p. 91.

[31] Goldingay, *Psalms*, II, p. 255. Westermann, *The Living Psalms*, classifies it as a song of trust (p. 57), but for him the song of trust is a subcategory of the lament

of trust or 'songs of confidence', as Brueggemann describes them, may have developed as an expansion of the statement of trust that is commonly found in the laments. Within Brueggemann's typology, these songs function to express a 'new orientation' similar to the perspective conveyed by the songs of thanksgiving. The songs of confidence, however, are more 'generalized' and 'more distanced from the crisis and more reflective' than the songs of thanksgiving.[32] Offering a new orientation to living in covenant with God, Psalm 63 reflects upon God's past faithfulness, expresses the psalmist's deep longing for God's presence, and affirms the psalmist's lifelong commitment to seek God and to praise God.

Rhetorical/Affective Analysis of Psalm 63

Our overview of the text, structure, and genre of Psalm 63 reveals a number of affective components that intersect with Christian spirituality. In the first section of the psalm (vv. 2-3), the supplicant expresses an unquenchable longing for God's presence. A mood of joy and thankfulness permeates the second section (vv. 4-6). The third section (vv. 7-9) expresses thankfulness, but it is a thankfulness that leads to expressions of deep trust and commitment to God. The final section of the psalm (vv. 10-12) registers a mood of confident hope for the future.

Longing for God's Presence (vv. 2-3)
A passion for God is evident in the first words of the psalmist: 'God, you are my God'.[33] The entire psalm, therefore, is grounded upon the certainty of the divine human relationship;[34] 'the emphatic "my God"

(p. 58). Tate, *Psalms 51-100*, p. 125, insists that 'the affirmative, testimony-like statements in vv. 4-5, 6-8, 9 indicate clearly that this is a psalm of confidence'.

[32] Brueggemann, *Message of the Psalms*, p. 152.

[33] Kraus, *Psalms 60-150*, p. 17, argues that אלהים אלי אתה אשחרך should be rendered, 'God, my God, you – I seek you', so that אתה functions to add emphasis (Cf. Gen. 49.8). However, it is clear that in its four other occurrences (Pss. 22.11; 118.28; 140.7; cf. also Ps. 31.15, אלהי אתה), the phrase אלי אתה should be translated 'you are my God', and I would argue that it carries the same meaning here. Cf. Franz Delitzsch, *Biblical Commentary on the Psalms* (trans. Francis Bolton; 3 vols.; Grand Rapids, MI: Eerdmans, 1867). In any case, the personal claim ('my God') is clear and striking.

[34] Briggs and Briggs, *Psalms*, II, p. 72.

expresses the covenantal bond with all its assurances'.[35] God had said to Israel, 'I will be your God and you will be my people' (Lev. 26.12). The relationship is one of covenant. However, the psalm is written from a complex context, one in which the relationship with God is assumed but in which the presence of God is not perceived. The psalmist is hungry and thirsty, wandering in a dry and thirsty land.

Because God is his God, the psalmist determines that he will seek God 'earnestly' (שׁחר). Rather than use the more formal בקשׁ[36] the psalmist chooses a denominative verb from the word that means 'dawn' and that 'connotes to seek with one's whole heart',[37] to 'seek longingly, wholeheartedly, desperately'.[38] Thus, the psalmist 'expresses a powerful, longing desire for the near presence of God'.[39]

The longing for God is made more concrete through the metaphorical, yearning cry, 'My soul is thirsty for you, my flesh longs for you'.[40] The language of hunger and thirst 'voices the intensity of emotional intimacy between the psalmist and God'.[41] Combination of 'soul' and 'flesh' signifies that the whole person is involved in the longing.[42] The longing of body and soul speaks of 'a religion that is satisfied with nothing less than God himself and is prepared to wait and wait for him'.[43]

---

[35] John Eaton, *The Psalms: A Historical and Spiritual Commentary with an Introduction and New Translation* (London: T & T Clark International, 2003), p. 235.

[36] A.A. Anderson, *The Book of Psalms: Based on the Revised Standard Version* (NCBC; 2 vols.; Grand Rapids, MI: Eerdmans, 1981), I, p. 456.

[37] Mitchell J. Dahood, *Psalms* (AB; 3 vols.; Garden City, NY: Doubleday, 1966), p. 96.

[38] *CDCH*, p. 456.

[39] Tate, *Psalms 51-100*, p. 127.

[40] The verb כמה is a *hapax legomenon* whose meaning, 'long, yearn for', is deduced from Semitic cognates and from the context. See *CDCH*, p. 178.

[41] James L. Crenshaw, *The Psalms: An Introduction* (Grand Rapids, MI: Eerdmans, 2001), p. 15. It is likely that צמא in the perfect signifies a state of thirst that began in the past and continues into the present (cf. Judg. 4.19).

[42] Briggs and Briggs, *Psalms*, II, p. 73.

[43] John W. McKay, 'The Experiences of Dereliction and of God's Presence in the Psalms: An Exercise in Old Testament Exegesis in the Light of Renewal Theology', in Paul Elbert (ed.) *Faces of Renewal: Studies in Honor of Stanley M. Horton Presented on His 70th Birthday* (Peabody, MA: Hendrickson Publishers, 1988), p. 10. In his study of the Psalms, McKay proposes to 'look for a moment beneath the skin of (reconstructed) rituals in an attempt to tap the heartbeat of religious experience in many psalms of lamentation that speak of dereliction and longing for the presence of God'.

The psalmist's level of yearning is equal to that of 'a dry and weary land without water'. Although the reference to the 'dry and weary land' is probably metaphorical,[44] it nevertheless provides a vivid image that would be readily identifiable to the original Palestinian hearers of the psalm. It recalls a similar statement found earlier in the Psalter: 'As the deer pants for the water brooks, so my soul pants for you, O God. My soul thirsts for God, for the living God' (Ps. 42.1-2).

The psalmist longs, body and soul, for his God. He longs deeply and passionately for God's presence, a presence that he has experienced in the past. The absence of God is even more painful given the memory of previous joyful times in the 'sanctuary', among the people of God.[45] In God's holy place, recounts the psalmist, 'I have seen you, beholding your power and your glory'. 'Thus' (כֵּן), 'as his soul thus thirsted for God and longed for him, he was allowed to behold him'.[46] The psalmist's longing to encounter God in the sanctuary finds echoes in other psalmic texts: 'My soul longed and even yearned for the courts of the Lord' (Ps. 84.2); 'I will dwell in the house of the Lord forever' (Ps. 23.6); and 'that I may dwell in the house of the Lord all the days of my life, to behold the beauty of the Lord (Ps. 27.4).

The psalmist testifies to having 'seen' (חזה) God.[47] Kraus suggests that the verb probably refers to a theophany,[48] but Anderson counters that although חזה is 'used as a technical term for receiving prophetic visions … the allusion in v. 2 need not be to a theophany or vision'.[49] Attempting to describe the psalmist's encounter, Tate writes, 'The visionary experience of the verb חזה ("to see/have a

---

[44] Weiser, *The Psalms*, p. 454. Cf. Tate, *Psalms 51-100*, p. 127, and Crenshaw, *Psalms*, p. 16. G.F. Hasel, 'יעף', in *TDOT*, VI, pp. 148-54 (54).

[45] Weiser, *The Psalms*, p. 454, claims that the setting for the whole psalm is the sanctuary. Cf. Hengstenberg, *Commentary on the Psalms*, II, p. 303. I would argue, however, that nothing in the psalm suggests that the psalmist is in the sanctuary. Instead, he is away from the sanctuary, and he 'describes his former times of worship in the sanctuary' (Stephen J. Lennox, *Psalms: A Bible Commentary in the Wesleyan Tradition* [Indianapolis, IN: Wesleyan Pub. House, 1999], p. 197).

[46] Weiser, *The Psalms*, pp. 454-55.

[47] *CDCH*, p. 111, indicates that the word means 'see, perceive'.

[48] Kraus, *Psalms 60-150*, p. 19. On the significance of 'seeing' as a metaphor for encountering the divine, see A. Rebecca Basdeo Hill, *Visions of God in Ezekiel: Pentecostal Explorations of the Glory and Holiness of Yahweh* (Cleveland, TN: CPT Press, 2018).

[49] Anderson, *The Book of Psalms*, I, p. 456.

vision") is not described in detail, and doubtless differed in form and degree among worshipers'. The psalmist's vision of God may have involved physical rituals and it may have included the 'verbal and mental, combined with the rich symbolism of the temple'.[50]

Whatever form the vision took, it is described here as a manifestation of God's 'power and glory'. The two lines of v. 3 stand in parallel to each other with the second line refining the first. The phrase, 'I have seen you', is restated as 'beholding your power and your glory'.[51] God's 'power' is his sovereign capacity to choose, to act, and to intervene in the world (for both judgment and salvation). His 'glory' is the display of his weightiness, his awesomeness, his majesty, and his holiness. The seeing of God and the beholding of God's power and glory refer to an encounter with God, an experience of God's presence which he had enjoyed on earlier occasions and 'for which the psalmist's heart thirsts'.[52] Kraus concludes, 'This profound high esteem of the communion with God forms the actual center of the profound psalm'.[53]

Gratitude (vv. 4-6)

Following upon the moving articulation of his unquenchable longing for God's presence, the psalmist breaks forth in joyous praise. 'I will praise you', he declares to God, 'because your kindness (חסד) is better than life'. Before Psalm 63, human life in its fullness, enjoyed in covenant with God, was understood as the ultimate benefit of God's covenant loyalty (חסד).[54] Now, however, the psalmist suggests that God's kindness and human life might be envisioned as two separate spheres. Kraus insists that this 'discrimination between lovingkindness and life was something wholly new'.[55] Eaton surmises that the psalmist is striving 'to express the inexpressible wonder of one who

---

[50] Tate, *Psalms 51-100*, p. 127.

[51] The infinitive construct here is epexegetical or circumstantial. See *GKC*, §114o; Bruce K. Waltke and Michael Patrick O'Connor, *An Introduction to Biblical Hebrew Syntax* (Winona Lake, IN: Eisenbrauns, 1990), §36.2.3e; Paul Joüon and T. Muraoka, *A Grammar of Biblical Hebrew* (Subsidia Biblica 14; Rome: Pontifical Biblical Institute, 1991), §124o. Cf. the RSV.

[52] Rogerson and McKay, *Psalms*, II, p. 65.

[53] Kraus, *Psalms 60-150*, p. 21.

[54] *CDCH*, p. 126, defines חסד as 'loyalty, faithfulness, kindness, love, mercy', a quite broad definition.

[55] Kraus, *Psalms 60-150*, p. 20.

experiences' God's covenant loyalty.[56] In agreement with Eaton, Terrien asserts, 'No other psalmist expresses with such ambiguous and yet convincing overtones his apprehension of the divine embrace'.[57]

In celebration of God's faithful love, the psalmist pledges to 'praise' God, to 'bless' God, and to 'lift up' his hands to God in worship. Lifting up the hands is the 'customary attitude of the worshipper in prayer … a sign of an expectant trust that one's empty hands will be "filled" with divine blessings'.[58] This elaborate praise will not be offered briefly or intermittently; it will continue throughout the psalmist's 'life'. He promises to bless the Lord 'in perpetual worship'.[59]

The mood of exuberant jubilation is reinforced with the statement, 'Like marrow and fatness my soul will be satisfied'. 'Marrow and fatness' may 'form a hendiadys meaning "very rich food"',[60] or the expression may refer to 'the sacrificial feasts which characterised seasons of rejoicing before God in the worship of the temple'.[61] Either way, the psalmist anticipates a great feast, but not literally; he is instead contemplating a kind of satisfaction that will be 'like' the satisfaction of a great feast. Thus, the psalmist again imagines the blessings of God to be distinct from the material world. The covenant loyalty of God is like a sumptuous feast that quenches the thirst and satisfies the hunger. Because of God's kindness, the psalmist can look forward to a full and joyous life; and because he is blessed, his 'mouth will offer praise with joyful lips'.

Trust and Commitment (vv. 7-9)

The third section of Psalm 63 continues to express thankfulness, but the tone transitions to a mood of deep trust and commitment to God. While vv. 4-6 declare the present and future value of God's immeasurable kindness, vv. 7-9 recall the past benefits of the psalmist's relationship to God. The psalmist asserts that just as God has been faithful to him, he has been faithful to God by remembering (זכר) God and meditating (הגה) upon God, two activities that signal deep devotion and commitment.

---

56 Eaton, *The Psalms*, p. 235.
57 Terrien, *The Psalms*, p. 462.
58 Anderson, *The Book of Psalms*, I, p. 457.
59 Briggs and Briggs, *Psalms*, II, p. 73.
60 Tate, *Psalms 51-100*, p. 124. Cf. Anderson, *The Book of Psalms*, I, p. 458.
61 Briggs and Briggs, *Psalms*, II, p. 73.

The psalmist remembers that, with God as his 'help', he shouted for joy underneath the covering of God's 'wings', which represent God's 'protection'.[62] He remembers further that he 'stuck close' to God and that God supported him. The phrase 'stuck close' is difficult to translate into English. The verb דבק means 'to cling, to cleave, to stick to' (cf. Gen. 2.24), but in combination with אחרי, it apparently means to 'pursue or follow very closely behind'.[63] Metaphorically, it signifies 'loyalty, affection, etc.'[64] Israel is commanded to 'cling' to Yahweh (Deut. 10.20; 13.5; Josh. 23.8; Ps. 119.31). While the psalmist 'stuck close' to God, God 'upheld' him with his powerful 'right hand'. 'With all the strength of his will he clings to God, to whom he owes his outward and inward support'.[65] This reciprocal relationship 'is almost a definition in personalized language of the *ḥesed* relationship between God and his people in the covenant'.[66] Calvin comments that the psalmist would 'follow with unwearied constancy, long as the way might be, and full of hardships, and beset with obstacles'.[67]

Confident Hope (vv. 10-12)

This final section of the psalm registers a mood of confident hope for the future. The section unfolds through a contrast between the psalmist's enemies and 'the king'. The enemies, who seek 'to ruin'[68] the psalmist, will 'go into the depths of the earth', and they will become the 'prey of foxes'.[69] The king, however, will rejoice in God, along with all those who swear allegiance to God, because the mouths of the deceivers 'will be stopped'.

The psalmist is confident that justice will prevail, that evil will be punished, and that God's people 'will glory' in their covenant relationship with God. Wicked enemies, struck down by 'the sword', 'will most certainly receive their due punishment ... their dead bodies will

---

[62] Anderson, *The Book of Psalms*, I, p. 458.

[63] *HALOT*, I, p. 209.

[64] *BDB*, p. 179. Cf. Tate, *Psalms 51-100*, p. 128.

[65] Weiser, *The Psalms*, p. 455.

[66] Rogerson and McKay, *Psalms*, p. 67. Cf. Lennox, *Psalms: A Bible Commentary in the Wesleyan Tradition*, p. 198.

[67] Calvin, *Psalms*, p. 383.

[68] The Hebrew for 'ruin' is actually a noun, prefixed with a preposition that suggests purpose: 'They seek my life for the purpose of ruin'. See *DCH*, p. 450, and *HALOT*, II, p. 1427.

[69] *HALOT*, II, 1445, define שׁועל as 'fox'. So *BDB*, but they add, 'perhaps also jackal' (p. 1048).

be desecrated' by wild animals.[70] Deprived of a proper burial,[71] they will cast down to the 'underworld' of the dead.[72] In the end, those who seek to ruin God's people will themselves be ruined.

The king,[73] however, will 'rejoice in God', and those who swear allegiance to 'him' will glory. In the phrase 'swear by him', the antecedent of the pronoun 'him' is God.[74] All who swear by him is the psalmist's way of connecting the psalm to the community of faith.[75] It 'is a poetic description of the Israelites',[76] and the combined reference to the king and all who 'swear' by God's name is 'probably a comprehensive phrase denoting the whole community of the faithful with the king as its head'.[77] Thus, the king is 'representative or exemplary of the person who seeks God'.[78]

The last section of Psalm 63 is a fitting conclusion to this psalm of reorientation. The psalmist has admitted his sense of separation from God's presence (v. 2) and his need to be satisfied by God's kindness (v. 6). He has remembered (v. 7) times when he needed God's help (v. 8) and God came to his aid. In this final strophe, he acknowledges the ongoing presence of dangerous enemies who threaten his safety. Nevertheless, his past experiences of God's presence (v. 3), God's covenant loyalty (v. 4), and God's tender care (v. 9) have generated a renewed confidence in God's faithfulness. The psalmist is convinced that God's people will prevail in the end.

Acknowledging the Passions of the Hearer

Psalm 63 is a passionate expression of the psalmist's spiritual longings after God. These longings are suggestive of the affective component of Christian spirituality in general and Pentecostal spirituality

---

[70] Anderson, *The Book of Psalms*, I, p. 459.

[71] Lennox, *Psalms: A Bible Commentary in the Wesleyan Tradition*, p. 198.

[72] Kraus, *Psalms 60-150*, p. 20.

[73] Anderson, *The Book of Psalms*, I, p. 459. Contra Eaton, *The Psalms*, p. 235, and Hengstenberg, *Commentary on the Psalms*, II, p. 301, who argues that the reference to the king does not necessarily mean that the psalmist must be the king or that this is a royal psalm.

[74] Tate, *Psalms 51-100*, p. 128; cf. Terrien, *The Psalms*, p. 464; contra Anderson, *The Book of Psalms*, I, p. 459.

[75] Tate, *Psalms 51-100*, p. 128.

[76] Weiser, *The Psalms*, p. 456.

[77] Rogerson and McKay, *Psalms*, p. 67.

[78] McCann, 'Psalms', IV, p. 928.

in particular. I find that the psalmist's 'hunger' and 'thirst' for God is consistent with Pentecostals' passion for God and that the desire to encounter God in the sanctuary is consistent with the goals of Pentecostal worship.

Psalm 63 is a hopeful song, but it is uttered from a place of emptiness and longing. Like the psalmist, Pentecostals sometimes find themselves in a 'dry and weary land without water', where God's presence is not apparent. In those times of spiritual drought, laments and cries for help are commonly heard; and the goal of those cries is the renewed manifestation of God's presence.[79]

Chris Green insists that 'Pentecostal spirituality is nothing if not a *personal* engagement' with God.[80] Although I am most familiar with North American Pentecostalism and do not claim to speak for all Pentecostals, my associations with Pentecostals in Latin America, Africa, Australia, Asia, Europe, and the UK lead me to conclude that a passionate affective spirituality is common to all Pentecostals.[81] Like the psalmist, the Pentecostal community is hungry and thirsty for God and seeks to behold God's power and glory, to lift up their hands in adoration, to testify of past blessings, to praise God with joyful lips, to shout for joy, to stick close to God, to rejoice in God, and to live in hope of the coming reign of God. Daniel Castelo argues that this experiential element of Pentecostal spirituality places Pentecostalism within the Christian mystical tradition.[82] Orthodox theologian Alexander Schmemann acknowledges the value of

---

[79] The absence of God is expressed most deeply in Psalm 88. See Chris E.W. Green, "'I am Finished'", *PNEUMA* 40.1-2 (2018), pp. 150-66. However, even this dark lament that never makes the turn toward praise is founded on the psalmist's assurance that Yahweh is his God (Ps. 88.1).

[80] Chris E.W. Green, *Toward a Pentecostal Theology of the Lord's Supper: Foretasting the Kingdom* (Cleveland, TN: CPT Press, 2012), p. 289 (emphasis original).

[81] Regarding Korean spirituality, see Julie C. Ma, 'Korean Pentecostal Spirituality: A Case Study of Jashil Choi', *AJPS* 5.2 (2002), pp. 235-54, and Myung Soo Park, 'Korean Pentecostal Spirituality as Manifested in the Testimonies of Believers of the Yoido Full Gospel Church', *AJPS* 7.1 (2004), pp. 40-41, 44-48, 55. For African spirituality, see David J. Maxwell, 'The Durawall of Faith: Pentecostal Spirituality in Neo-Liberal Zimbabwe', *JRA* 35.1 (2005), pp. 5-6, 21. This commonality extends also to Charismatics; see James H.S. Steven, 'The Spirit in Contemporary Charismatic Worship', in T. Berger and B.D. Spinks (eds.), *Spirit in Worship—Worship in the Spirit* (Collegeville, MN: Liturgical Press, 2009), pp. 245-59 (249-53).

[82] Daniel Castelo, *Pentecostalism as a Christian Mystical Tradition* (Grand Rapids, MI: Eerdmans, 2017).

mystical encounter when he writes that 'all genuine theology is mystical at the root, since it is primarily evidence of religious experience'.[83]

The psalmist's longing for the manifestation of God's 'power and glory' can be compared to Pentecostalism's 'holy desire for God Himself'.[84] This longing for God is described repeatedly in early Pentecostal literature. For example, Alice Flower writes, 'All I seemed to sense was a deep craving for the overflowing of His love in my heart. At that moment it seemed I wanted Jesus more than anything in all the world'.[85] Reflecting on her passion for God, Zelma E. Argue recalls, 'my whole heart seemed to just one big vacuum craving and crying for God'.[86] Echoing the words of Ps. 63.6, Alice E. Luce affirms, 'the Lord is our portion. We have had a real taste of the Lord and found out that he is a satisfying portion'.[87]

The Pentecostal longing for God can be described partly as the desire for a personal encounter with God. Albrecht argues that for 'Pentecostals, the entire ritual field and the drama that emerges within the ritual matrix is aimed toward an *encounter*'.[88] Jaichandran and Madhav agree:

> It cannot be denied that the most important value that governs Pentecostal spirituality is the locus of individual experience. Viewed positively, this means that the Pentecostal is not satisfied until he or she has had an experience with God … A person is not satisfied by hearing about someone else's experience with God; they must experience God themselves.[89]

---

[83] Schmemann, *The Historical Road of Eastern Orthodoxy*, p. 235.

[84] Daniel Castelo, 'Tarrying on the Lord: Affections, Virtues and Theological Ethics in Pentecostal Perspective', *JPT* 13.1 (2004), p. 53.

[85] Alice Reynolds Flower, 'My Pentecost', *AGH* 20 (Winter 1997-98), p. 18; excerpted from her *Grace for Grace: Some Highlights of God's Grace in the Daily Life of the Flower Family* (Springfield, MO: privately published, 1961).

[86] Cited by Edith Waldvogel Blumhofer, *'Pentecost in My Soul': Explorations in the Meaning of Pentecostal Experience in the Assemblies of God* (Springfield, MO: Gospel Pub. House, 1989), p. 159.

[87] Cited by Blumhofer, *'Pentecost in My Soul'*, p. 136.

[88] Daniel E. Albrecht, 'Pentecostal Spirituality: Looking through the Lens of Ritual', *PNEUMA* 14.2 (1992), pp. 107-25 (110) (emphasis original).

[89] Rebecca Jaichandran and B.D. Madhav, 'Pentecostal Spirituality in a Postmodern World', *AJPS* 6.1 (2003), p. 55.

Of course, as with other revivalist movements, Pentecostalism has generated unwelcomed excesses and unbiblical experiences.[90] The psalmist's longing for God, however, is not a longing for an experience for experience's sake, but it is a longing for God in relation, in covenant; and it is a longing that Pentecostals seek to imitate.[91]

The psalmist's experience of 'seeing' God and 'beholding' the power and glory of God are signs to the Pentecostal that God is open to human encounter. Keith Warrington writes, 'Two pertinent words when referring to Pentecostal spirituality are "expectancy" and "encounter". Pentecostals expect to encounter God. It undergirds much of their worship and theology and may even be identified as another way of defining worship'.[92] From Azusa Street until now, Pentecostals everywhere have insisted upon the present reality of God's presence to save, sanctify, fill with the Holy Spirit, heal, and reign as coming king.[93]

Conclusions and Implications for the Church

In his article on 'Community and Worship', Jerome Boone argues that the 'single most important goal of any Pentecostal worship service is a personal encounter with the Spirit of God'.[94] This encounter will often include the manifestation of spiritual gifts and the

---

[90] Jaichandran and Madhav, 'Pentecostal Spirituality in a Postmodern World', pp. 57, 59.

[91] Cf. Cecil M. Robeck, Jr., 'The Nature of Pentecostal Spirituality', *PNEUMA* 14.2 (1992), p. 105, and Veli-Matti Kärkkäinen, '"Encountering Christ in the Full Gospel Way": An Incarnational Pentecostal Spirituality', *JEPTA* 27.1 (2007), pp. 11-12. Kärkkäinen explicates Pentecostal worship as the 'longing for meeting with the Lord' (pp. 17-20). Cf. Darlene Zschech, 'The Role of the Holy Spirit in Worship: An Introduction to the Hillsong Church, Sydney, Australia', in T. Berger and B.D. Spinks (eds.), *Spirit in Worship—Worship in the Spirit* (Collegeville, MN: Liturgical Press, 2009), pp. 285-92 (86-89).

[92] Keith Warrington, *Pentecostal Theology: A Theology of Encounter* (New York: T & T Clark, 2008), p. 219. Cf. Daniel E. Albrecht, *Rites in the Spirit: A Ritual Approach to Pentecostal/Charismatic Spirituality* (JPTSup 17; Sheffield, UK: Sheffield Academic Press, 1999), pp. 226, 38-39.

[93] *AF* 1.1 (Sept. 1906), p. 1 and *passim*. Writing in the first issue of *PNEUMA*, William MacDonald, 'Temple Theology', *PNEUMA* 1.1 (Spring 1979), insists, 'Unless we dare claim that Christianity was fossilized in the first century, we must contend that the Spirit is still speaking to the churches' (p. 48). Cf. Cecil M. Robeck, *The Azusa Street Mission and Revival: The Birth of the Global Pentecostal Movement* (Nashville, TN: Nelson Reference & Electronic, 2006), p. 132.

[94] Boone, 'Community and Worship', p. 137.

worshipers will experience 'the Spirit as transformational power'.[95] He points to the importance of prayer as a 'divine-human encounter in which burdens are relinquished' to God, who cares and who has the power to eliminate those burdens.[96] Furthermore, Boone observes the value of personal testimony as a means of honoring God and of forming the faith of the listeners. Boone warns, however, that the Pentecostal movement is in danger of losing its distinctive Pentecostal spirituality. Perhaps we should ask, 'Has Pentecostalism left its "first love" (Rev. 2.4)?'[97]

If the Pentecostal movement is to maintain its vitality from generation to generation, it must periodically reclaim the spiritual passion that we find demonstrated in Psalm 63. The biblical text functions as a vehicle of spiritual formation that can inform Pentecostal spirituality and practice. I would suggest the following ways in which Psalm 63 can help to shape the spirituality of the Pentecostal movement both now and in the future. These implications are only suggestive, and they (along with the chapter in its entirety) are meant to promote dialogue and creative engagement with the biblical text.

1. Spiritual formation should include the nurture and development of the affect. Opportunities for affective engagement and expression should be offered. These opportunities include affective expressions through worship, prayer, testimony, and waiting upon God.

In a recent article, Johnathan Alvarado elaborates on the distinctive characteristics of Pentecostal worship. He writes, 'Spirit-filled worship is marked and characterized by a vivid awareness of the presence of God and the activity of the Holy Spirit within the lives of the saints and within the context of the worship experience'.[98] Alvarado argues that Spirit-filled leadership in worship requires three things: 1) the 'skillful handling of the biblical text' as the Word of God, 2) 'an understanding of the Spirit's presence' and influence, and 3) 'the intentional involvement of the congregation'.[99] After looking at Psalm 63, I would suggest a fourth requirement (perhaps as an

---

[95] Boone, 'Community and Worship', p. 138.

[96] Boone, 'Community and Worship', p. 130.

[97] Cf. Zschech, 'The Role of the Holy Spirit in Worship', p. 287, who laments that the Western church prefers comfortable worship over passionate worship.

[98] Johnathan E. Alvarado, 'Worship in the Spirit: Pentecostal Perspectives on Liturgical Theology and Praxis', *JPT* 21.1 (2012), p. 143.

[99] Alvarado, 'Worship in the Spirit', pp. 146-47.

expansion of number 2): the worship leader must possess a deep longing to encounter God through the Holy Spirit and to lead others into that encounter. Worship leaders must conceive of their ministry as formative, for 'in worshipping God we come to behold the object that orients and disposes us properly. One learns to love God by beholding Him and communing with Him'.[100]

2. Churches must provide frequent and open-ended opportunities for prayer. Psalm 63.2-9 is a sustained direct address to God, in which the psalmist uses the second person address, 'you', 18 times. The spiritual life cannot be nurtured without times of deep communion with God in prayer. Pentecostal spirituality is formed and expressed through regular and intensive times of prayer and fasting.[101] Christian formation cannot be accomplished quickly and without struggle. Discipleship consists of more than just right thinking, right teaching, and right doctrine; it must include right 'feeling', that is, rightly oriented affections.

When we read Psalm 63, we are overhearing the prayers of the psalmist, and in so doing we are being shaped to follow the psalmist's example. Similarly, our prayers should be overheard by others,[102] who will learn from us that honest expressions of pain and struggle are acceptable to God and that a passion for God's presence is commendable.

3. In our practice of the Pentecostal life and ministry, we must become hungry and thirsty for God, desperate for God's presence. The psalmist expresses dependence upon God as a 'help' and as a 'support'. The psalmist feels that he will die of hunger and thirst unless God appears with his refreshing presence. In many cases, however, our desperation for God's presence and help has been supplanted by structures of our own invention, substitutes for the power and glory of God. We can do 'church' without God. Consequently, prayers of desperation are rarely heard because we have back up plans, safety nets, and formal structures that can exist without God's help.

4. The Church must reaffirm its eschatological hope. I observe that vv. 10-12 point to the future and could even be considered

---

[100] Castelo, 'Tarrying on the Lord', p. 38.
[101] Ma, 'Korean Pentecostal Spirituality', p. 238 and *passim*.
[102] Gerald T. Sheppard, 'Theology and the Book of Psalms', *Int* 46 (1992), p. 143.

eschatological in focus: The wicked will be punished; those who are faithful to God will rejoice in God's protection; and the kingdom of God will manifest itself as a kingdom of justice and righteousness.

5. Pentecostals face the danger of seeking out experiences rather than seeking God for God's sake. In the past, Pentecostals called this kind of shallow emotionalism 'wild fire'. On the one hand, it is all too easy for worship to become no more than entertainment or self-gratification. On the other hand, genuine encounter with God results in a dramatic experience. It is an experience that cannot be manipulated by ministers and worship leaders who prompt and prod the congregation until they are worked up into a frenzy. The disciples' encounter with God through the Holy Spirit in Acts 2 was powerful and moving, but it did not occur as a result of their own artificial efforts. In response to their prayer, their worship, and their waiting, the Holy Spirit came upon them as an external force sent from heaven. Similarly, the focus of Psalm 63 is upon the relational quality of the encounter between the psalmist and God.

6. The Christian community must recover the practice of testimony. Psalm 63 is directed to God, but it is a song that is meant to be heard by the congregation, and as such, it functions as testimony. The psalmist testifies to the experience of seeing God's glory in the sanctuary, and to the many times when God has been a help and a support. This testimony includes aspects of the psalmist's spiritual journey, such as times of praise, meditation, and sticking close to God. The recounting of the psalmist's own longing for God is an implicit challenge to the hearer to pursue God with the same fervent intensity and with the same unreserved yearning.

3

PSALM 91: DWELLING IN THE SECRET PLACE OF THE MOST HIGH

Introduction

I had not originally intended to include Psalm 91 in this project, but when I shared with a friend from Guatemala my plan for a book on the Psalms, he remarked, 'Of course you will write about Psalm 91'. His comment caused me to investigate the popularity of the psalm among Pentecostals, and I discovered that it is cited frequently in the early periodical literature. A search of Pentecostal periodicals reveals 140 citations of Psalm 91 between the years 1906 and 1945, making it the fourth most popular psalm among Pentecostal writers during that period (following Psalms 119, 103, and 37).[1] The extensive use of the psalm in the Pentecostal–Charismatic tradition (and its misuse in connection to the health-and-prosperity gospel) has compelled me to include it among these studies.

My hermeneutical strategy for the Psalms is an integrated approach that appreciates both the original context of the psalm and the function of the psalm in the Christian context. I begin with the hearing of the psalm as a way of experiencing the text and entering into the world of the text. The hearing is followed by a close reading of the text that examines the psalm's structure, themes, and rhetorical devices. The next step is to identify the affective dimensions of the

---

[1] I conducted a full-text search of the periodicals that are found online at the Consortium of Pentecostal Archives (https://pentecostalarchives.org/) and at the Flower Pentecostal Heritage Center (https://ifphc.org/).

psalm and to relate those to corresponding elements of Pentecostal theology, spirituality, and worship.

This methodology attempts to incorporate developments in Pentecostal biblical hermeneutics that give priority to literary features, rhetorical analysis, canonical shaping, biblical diversity (and unity), the experiential grid of the fivefold gospel, and the formation of meaning through the triad of Scripture, the Spirit, and interpretive community.[2] Recent Pentecostal forays into hermeneutics have expanded on the role of the community to include the effective history (*Wirkungsgeschichte*) of early Pentecostalism;[3] therefore, I have chosen to widen my approach by utilizing history of effects in this study of Psalm 91. The history of effects is viewed somewhat like a 'testimony' of past experiences with the text. As testimony, the examples from effective history are placed into conversation with the text and with contemporary interpreters. The effective history does not govern the contemporary interpretation, but it serves as one voice – 'a great cloud of witnesses' (Heb. 12.1) – within the larger Pentecostal community of faith. In this chapter, I will listen to the witness of early Pentecostals regarding Psalm 91 as one element of my interpretation of the psalm.

Inasmuch as the first decade of the Pentecostal movement (1906-1915) represents the theological 'heart' of the tradition,[4] the effective history from that period is the primary witness to a Pentecostal

---

[2] For an overview of the development of Pentecostal biblical hermeneutics, see John Christopher Thomas, '"Where the Spirit Leads": The Development of Pentecostal Hermeneutics', *Journal of Beliefs & Values: Studies in Religion & Education* 30.3 (2009), pp. 289-302. A number of significant works on Pentecostal hermeneutics are collected in Martin (ed.), *Pentecostal Hermeneutics: A Reader*; and the most comprehensive study is Archer, *A Pentecostal Hermeneutic*.

[3] Regarding the Pentecostal utilization of *Wirkungsgeschichte*, see John Christopher Thomas, 'The Spirit, the Text, and Early Pentecostal Reception' (48th Annual Meeting of the Society for Pentecostal Studies, College Park, MD, 2019); Martin W. Mittelstadt, 'Receiving Luke–Acts: The Rise of Reception History and a Call to Pentecostal Scholars', *PNEUMA* 40.3 (2018), pp. 367-88; Green, *Toward a Pentecostal Theology of the Lord's Supper*, pp. 74-181; Melissa L. Archer, *'I Was in the Spirit on the Lord's Day': A Pentecostal Engagement with Worship in the Apocalypse* (Cleveland, TN: CPT Press, 2014), pp. 68-118; and David R. Johnson, *Pneumatic Discernment in the Apocalypse: An Intertextual and Pentecostal Exploration* (Cleveland, TN: CPT Press, 2018), pp. 101-92.

[4] Land, *Pentecostal Spirituality*, p. 1; Walter J. Hollenweger, *The Pentecostals* (trans. R.A. Wilson; Minneapolis, MN: Augsburg Pub. House, 1st USA edn, 1972), p. 551.

approach to Scripture.[5] That is not to say that contemporary constructive theology should follow the exact lines of the early tradition;
on the contrary, as a living tradition, Pentecostalism must not be fossilized. However, if Pentecostal theology is to remain genuinely Pentecostal, any new paths that are constructed must remain faithful to
the heart of the Pentecostal tradition.

A Translation of Psalm 91

[1] He who dwells in the secret place of the Most High
   Will spend the night[6] under the shadow of the Almighty.[7]
[2] I will say to Yahweh, 'My refuge and my fortress,
   My God' – I will trust in him.

[3] Indeed, he, himself, will snatch you from the trap of the hunter,[8]
   And from the deadly pestilence.
[4] With his feathers[9] he will cover[10] you,
   And under his wings you shall take refuge:

---

[5] See Chapter 9 for a study of the effective history of the Psalms in the *Apostolic Faith* (1906-1915), the periodical that was published by William Seymour and the Azusa St. Mission.

[6] E.B. Oikonomou, 'לין', *TDOT*, VII, pp. 543-46, points out that the use of לין presupposes a journey, thus introducing the theme of protection during travel, which is explored later in the psalm.

[7] A number of interpreters have suggested that the difficult syntax of vv. 1-2 should be smoothed out by emending v. 2. Samuel Rosenblatt, 'Notes on the Psalter', *JBL* 50.4 (1931), pp. 308-10, argues that the imperfect אמר should be a participle אמר so that the syntax of v. 2 would be parallel to that of v. 1 (which begins with the participle ישב. Kraus, *Psalms 60-150*, p. 219, appealing to the LXX (ἐρεῖ) makes the verb 3rd person (יאמר). However, Erich Zenger, 'Psalm 91', in Frank-Lothar Hossfeld and Erich Zenger, *Psalms 2: A Commentary on Psalms 51-100* (trans. Linda M. Maloney; Hermeneia; Minneapolis, MN: Fortress Press, 2005), p. 426, points out that an emendation 'destroys the pragmatism of the psalm'. For other examples of a substantive participle followed by a finite verb, see *GKC*, §116x.

[8] Although פח יקוש is usually translated 'snare of the fowler', the terms can refer more generically to any kind of trap and any kind of hunter. Therefore, *DCH*, defines פח as 'trap, snare, of any kind' (VI, p. 672) and יקוש as '(game) hunter' (IV, p. 273). Cf. *NIDOTTE*, III, p. 595.

[9] The word 'feathers' (אברה), often translated 'pinions', is construct singular in the Hebrew. Always used in parallel to 'wings' (כנף), אברה appears to function here as a collective; therefore, the English rendering should be plural (cf. Deut. 32.11). See *DCH*, I, p. 115; and Tate, *Psalms 51–100*, p. 448.

[10] The jussive form (יָסֶךְ) is here used on 'rhythmical grounds' but with the meaning of the ordinary imperfect (*GKC* §109k).

His faithfulness is a shield and fortress.[11]

⁵You shall not be afraid of the terror by night;
    Of the arrow that flies by day;
⁶Of the pestilence that walks in darkness;
    Of the destruction that ravages at noon.
⁷A thousand may fall at your side,
    And ten thousand at your right hand –
    It will not come near you.
⁸Only with your eyes you shall behold,
    And the recompense of the wicked you will see.

⁹Because you have made Yahweh, who is my refuge,
    Even the Most High, your habitation;
¹⁰No harm will come to you,
    And no plague will come near your tent.
¹¹Because he will command his angels concerning you,[12]
    To guard you in all your ways.
¹²Upon their hands they will carry you,
    Lest you strike your foot against a stone.
¹³Upon the lion and the viper you will tread;
    You will trample the young lion and the serpent.[13]

¹⁴Because he set his affection on me, I will rescue him:

---

[11] The Hebrew סחרה is a hapax legomenon with uncertain meaning. A.A. Mac-Intosh, 'Psalm 91.4 and the Root סחר', *VT* 23 (1973), pp. 56-62 (61), proposes the translation '(supernatural) protection'. His argument, though appealing, does not convince, because it removes סחרה from the realm of metaphor, making the phrase out of place within a passage that consistently relies on metaphor.

[12] Regarding the *dagesh* in לך, see *GKC* §20.c.

[13] Contra Zenger 'Psalm 91', p. 431 and n. 12, תנין is not a sea serpent or dragon. Real animals (lion, cobra, young lion, serpent), not mythical ones, are the perceived threat in v. 13. Cf. Exod. 7.9, 10, 12; and Deut. 32.33, where תנין clearly refers to a land snake. See also *HALOT*, p. 1764; *BDB*, p. 1072; and *DCH*, VIII, pp. 654-55. Ancient Christian writers have viewed the 'serpent' as a symbol of Satan. For example, Jerome (FC 57, p. 87) writes,

> That to the just and the beloved of God is given, moreover, the power to tread upon that ancient, contemptible snake and to crush his whole army under their heel, we shall find stated very clearly in the Gospel, for the Lord says to the apostles: 'Behold, I have given you power to tread upon serpents and scorpions.' Lk. 10.19.

I will set him on high,[14] because he knows my name.
[15] He will call upon me, and I will answer him:
  I will be with him in trouble;
  I will liberate him,[15] and I will honor him.
[16] With long life[16] will I satisfy him,
  And I will show him my salvation.

Genre of Psalm 91

Psalm 91 is a song of trust,[17] and the theme of trust is named explicitly in v. 2: 'I will trust (בטח) in him'. We find in the psalm neither an utterance of prayer nor a voicing of praise. Instead, prayer lies under the surface as an implication of a life totally committed to God, and praise awaits as a next step that must follow after the psalmist's proclamation of God's faithfulness. It is surprising that in a psalm devoted to Yahweh's commitment to the one who trusts in him, there is no mention of Yahweh's covenant loyalty (חסד) which is praised frequently in the Psalms. Instead, the psalmist acknowledges Yahweh's 'faithfulness' (אמת, v. 4),[18] a term that overlaps in meaning with חסד and which is often used in parallel with חסד (Gen. 24.27; 32.11; Exod. 34.6; Pss. 40.11; 57.4, 11; 61.8; 86.15; 89.2, 14; 108.5; 117.2; Isa. 16.5; Micah 7.20).

The form-critical emphasis upon distinct *Gattungen* has had the unfortunate (and probably unintended) consequence of 'ghettoizing' the psalms that do not fit into one of the major forms. However, some of the most loved and appreciated psalms fall outside of Gunkel's major categories. These include Psalm 91 and other psalms of trust. Despite their lack of defining 'form', I would argue that the psalms of trust are central to the overall message of the Psalter and

---

[14] The *piel* of שגב means to 'make high, inaccessible', and by extension, to 'protect'. See *HALOT*, pp. 1305-1306, and *DCH*, VIII, p. 111.

[15] *DCH*, III, p. 239, defines חלץ as 'loosen', 'deliver'.

[16] The Hebrew idiom for 'long life' is 'length of days' (ארך ימים).

[17] Other songs of trust include Psalms 23, 27, 46, 63, and 103. In his, *Message of the Psalms*, Brueggemann uses the term 'songs of confidence' and places them in the category of songs of 'new orientation' (p. 152).

[18] It is interesting, however, to note the similarity in sounds between the Hebrew for 'covenant loyalty' (חסד) and 'seek refuge' (חסה), which is used here in parallel with 'faithfulness' (אמת, v. 4).

to the theology of the Old Testament. They encourage the people of God to adopt a 'new orientation' to the life of faith, an orientation based on unqualified trust in Yahweh.[19] The psalms of trust project a way of life in which the people of God rely upon Yahweh at all times.

Canonical Placement of Psalm 91

Brueggemann states that Psalms 90-92 'focus on the theme of God's refuge in response to the crisis of the fall of the Davidic kingdom portrayed in Psalm 89'.[20] Coming immediately after the Prayer of Moses (Psalm 90), Psalm 91 might be expected to exhibit a number of lexical parallels with its predecessor. We find only two explicit parallels, but they are significant ones. Both psalms declare that Yahweh is a מעון, a 'dwelling place' or 'habitation' (90.1; 91.9), and both psalms use the word 'satisfy' (שבע) as a term descriptive of God's blessings (90.14; 91.16). In addition to these *linguistic* similarities, there appear to be extensive *thematic* similarities. Gerald H. Wilson has observed that Psalms 90-106 (Book IV of the Psalter) share a common interest in Moses;[21] and Psalm 91 may have been placed after Psalm 90 as a response to the prayer of Moses.[22] Moses laments the brevity of human life (90.3-10), and he prays, 'Oh, satisfy us with your covenant loyalty' (90.14). Yahweh answers, 'With long life I will satisfy him' (91.16).

If Psalm 91 is viewed through the lens of the exodus tradition, other connections to Moses become apparent. The references to plague and pestilence might be compared to the plagues that were unleashed against the Egyptians, but which caused no harm to the Israelites. God's promise, 'A thousand may fall at your side, and ten thousand at your right hand – it will not come near you' (91.7), may remind the hearer of the death of Egypt's firstborn. Leonard Knight imagines that the psalmist 'has in mind the devastating retribution

---

[19] Brueggemann, *Message of the Psalms*, p. 152.

[20] Walter Brueggemann and W.H. Bellinger, *Psalms* (New Cambridge Bible Commentary; New York: Cambridge University Press, 2014), p. 395.

[21] Wilson, *The Editing of the Hebrew Psalter*, pp. 214-19. Cf. Erich Zenger, 'The God of Israel's Reign over the World (Psalm 90-106)', in Norbert Lohfink and Erich Zenger, *The God of Israel and the Nations: Studies in Isaiah and the Psalms* (trans. E.R. Kalin; Collegeville, MN: Liturgical Press, 2000), pp. 161-90 (186).

[22] Brueggemann and Bellinger, *Psalms*, p. 395.

that was poured out upon the firstborn of Egypt when the death angel passed and upon the armies of Pharaoh when the Red Sea closed upon them'.[23] Other dangers that are named in Psalm 91 might allude to the perils that Israel faced during the wilderness wanderings. Moses reminded Israel, '[Yahweh] led you through that great and terrible wilderness, in which were fiery serpents and scorpions' (Deut. 8.15). The reference to Yahweh's wings (91.4) could represent the wings of the cherubim on the ark of the covenant,[24] and it might also remind the hearer of Exod. 19.4, which states, 'You have seen what I did to the Egyptians, and how I carried you on eagles' wings, and brought you to myself'. After they entered Canaan, Israel lived in houses; but during Israel's journey with Moses, the people lived in tents, and Ps. 91.10 promises, 'no plague will come near your tent'. Psalm 91's reference to angelic protection reminds the hearer of the same kind of angelic guidance that had been provided to the Israelites as they traveled through the dangerous wilderness (Exod. 14.19; 23.20; 33.2). The Hebrew word חשׁק, indicating strong affection, is used only 16 times in the Hebrew Bible, yet it is found twice in reference to the exodus (Deut. 7.7; 10.15) and once in Psalm 91 (v. 14). In Exod. 3.13-15, Moses learns Yahweh's name, and in Ps. 91.14, Yahweh promises to protect the person who knows Yahweh's name. Finally, the promise of 'salvation' (Ps. 91.16) is a reminder of Israel's deliverance from Egyptian bondage. At the Red Sea, Moses encouraged them saying, 'Do not fear; stand still and see the salvation of Yahweh' (Exod. 14.13).

Structure of Psalm 91

This richly imaginative and deeply moving psalm has a clear movement from beginning to end, but its elements are arranged so ingeniously that the structure has been described in a number of ways. On one extreme is Jan Fokkelman, who divides the structure into seven strophes, the first five having two verses each and the sixth and seventh having three verses each.[25] On the opposite extreme is Walter

---

[23] Leonard C. Knight, 'I Will Show Him My Salvation: The Experience of Anxiety in the Meaning of Psalm 91', *ResQ* 43.4 (2001), pp. 280-92 (283).

[24] Weiser, *The Psalms*, p. 607.

[25] Fokkelman, *The Psalms in Form*, pp. 101, 167.

Brueggemann, who divides the psalm into only two equal sections, vv. 1-8 and 9-16.[26]

The psalm begins with the psalmist's confession of trust (vv. 1-2), which introduces the main theme. The verses in next large section (vv. 3-13) stand together because they all speak to an anonymous person who is addressed as 'you'. That large section can be divided after v. 8, which is followed by a 'rhetorical pause'.[27] A new subsection begins with v. 9, which seems to recall v. 1 in its repetition of the words 'refuge' and 'Most High'. Verses 9-13 feature the repetition of 'because' (כִּי), and vv. 12 and 13 each begin with 'upon' (עַל). The final section (vv. 14-16) is direct speech from Yahweh, who promises salvation to the hearer of the psalm. Therefore, the psalm might be outlined as follows:

    I. Confession of Trust (vv. 1-2)

    II. Promise of Protection (vv. 3-13)

       A. Rescue from Dangers (vv. 3-8)

       B. Guarded and Protected (vv. 9-13)

    III. Yahweh's Promise of Salvation (vv. 14-16)

Rhetorical Features of Psalm 91

The most obvious rhetorical device in Psalm 91 is the arrangement of speaker and hearer. The psalm begins by speaking about the hearer in the third person singular, 'the one who dwells in the secret place' (v. 1); and it ends in the same manner, 'I will show him my salvation' (v. 16). Between the beginning and end of the psalm, the psalmist addresses the hearer in the second person ('you'), and God is spoken of in the third person ('he'). Furthermore, the speech about God and the hearer alternates back and forth. In two places, the psalmist speaks in the first person. Verse 2 states, 'I will say to the Lord' (v. 2), and v. 9 includes the words, 'Yahweh, my refuge'. At both of these

---

[26] Brueggemann, *Message of the Psalms*, p. 156. A thorough examination of the structure is provided by Pierre Auffret, 'L' Étude Structurelle des Psaumes Réponses et Compléments I (Pss. 51, 57, 63, 64, 65, 86, 90, 91, 95)', *Science et Esprit* 48.1 (1996), pp. 45-60. Auffret argues that v. 3 should be distinguished from v. 4, because v. 3 speaks of dangers from which God delivers, but v. 4 states protections that God gives. He joins vv. 5-8 as one unit, and he separates v. 13 from vv. 11-12 (p. 53).

[27] Brueggemann, *Message of the Psalms*, p. 156.

points we find reference to the key vocabulary of 'refuge' and 'dwelling place'.[28]

Other effective rhetorical features include the placement of 'the wicked', the wide use of synonyms, and the repetition of themes. The sudden (and somewhat unexpected) appearance of the 'wicked ones' at the center of the psalm (v. 8) creates an implied contrast between those who trust God and those who do not trust God. The psalmist's naming of God with four different terms (El Elyon, Shaddai, Elohim, and Yahweh) is described by Fokkelman as 'a virtuoso variation'[29] that skillfully depicts the majesty of God and generates awe in the hearer. A plethora of overlapping terms symbolize the hearer's location. The hearer, who lives in a 'tent' (אהל) is invited to dwell in the 'secret place' and in the 'shadow of the Almighty'. Yahweh is the hearer's 'refuge', 'fortress', 'shield', and 'habitation'. Verbs that describe abiding and dwelling include ישׁב ('to dwell') לין, ('to remain/to lodge'), and חסה ('to seek refuge'). In addition to the general terms, 'harm' (רעה) and 'trouble' (צרה), 12 specific dangers are named: 'the trap of the hunter',[30] 'the deadly pestilence',[31] 'the terror by night', 'the arrow that flies by day',[32] 'the pestilence that walks in darkness', 'the destruction that ravages at noon', the 'plague', the striking of one's 'foot against a stone', 'the lion', 'the viper', 'the young lion', and 'the serpent'. Although for some people these dangers are metaphorical, for others they are very real and present threats to life and health.[33]

---

[28] Fook Kong Wong, 'Use of Overarching Metaphors in Psalms 91 and 42/43', *Sino-Christian Studies* 9 (2010), pp. 7-27, argues that the 'overarching metaphor' of Psalm 91 is that Yahweh is a refuge.

[29] Fokkelman, *The Psalms in Form*, p. 167.

[30] Theodoret, *Theodoret of Cyrus: Commentary on the Psalms, 73-150* (ed. R.C. Hill; Washington, DC: Catholic University of America Press, 2001), p. 103, writes that the 'trap' refers 'not only to obvious enemies but also to those who lie in wait, watching and hatching secret schemes, by snare suggesting the furtive scheme'.

[31] Zenger, 'Psalm 91', p. 430, argues that דבר might be translated as 'thorn' rather than 'pestilence'. The 'thorn of destruction', then, would refer to a thorn-tipped arrow for killing birds. He suggests that such a translation keeps the parallelism of vv. 3-4 within the 'avian world'. However, Zenger's proposal is not necessary, given that דבר as 'pestilence' is used in reference to animals as well as to humans (Exod. 9.3; Jer 21.6; Ps. 78.50). Cf. *DCH*, II, p. 411.

[32] Knight, 'I Will Show Him My Salvation', p. 282, writes, 'The focus is not so much on the weakness of the wayfarer as it is on those who are hostile to his success'.

[33] Brueggemann, *Message of the Psalms*, p. 156.

The most impressive rhetorical feature of Psalm 91 may be its conclusion, which consists of direct speech from Yahweh. If the testimony of the psalmist does not persuade the hearer to trust in Yahweh, then Yahweh's own statement of commitment should be sufficient confirmation of the psalmist's claims. The bold series of eight affirmations is Yahweh's personal assurance to the person who trusts in Yahweh.[34] Regarding the person who is committed to Yahweh, Yahweh promises:

I will rescue him
I will set him on high
I will answer him
I will be with him
I will liberate him
I will honor him
I satisfy him
I will show him my salvation.[35]

The wide vocabulary and the careful repetition make the message of the psalm vivid, moving, and appealing to virtually any audience, of any occupation, in any situation, and of any age. Even a child has bruised her foot on a stone. The creative rhetoric and 'lively inner rhythm'[36] also draws in the hearer and makes real the world of the psalm.

From beginning to end, Psalm 91 displays affective, emotive language. It begins with hopeful anticipation and concludes with confident assurance. The theme trust and confidence in God is evident throughout. John E. Kuizenga observes,

This old familiar Psalm is full of the premonition of danger; but more remarkable is the fact that in every verse it speaks also of the Deliverer. The Psalm is not a dirge of calamity; it is a song of assurance, of courage, of a faith that does not falter ... In this

[34] Meghan D. Musy, 'Hearing Voices: Exploring Psalmic Multivocality as Lyric Poetry' (PhD diss., McMaster Divinity College, 2018), pp. 106-16.
[35] Four different terms in Psalm 91 signify some form of deliverance: 'snatch out' (נצל), 'rescue' (פלט), 'liberate' (חלץ), and 'salvation' (ישע).
[36] Weiser, *The Psalms*, p. 605.

passage the conviction of the power and faithfulness of God is greater than the fear of calamity.[37]

There is an affective tension, however, that moves the hearers emotions through a series suspenseful scenarios. The naming of real, life-threatening dangers is unsettling and produces uncertainty and apprehension. Those negative emotions, however, are quickly quelled by the onslaught of positive images. We may step in a trap, but God will snatch us out of it. Epidemics may rage, but they will not approach our tent. In the night, in the day, in darkness, and at noon, we will not fear, because it is only the wicked who will fall. Angels have been sent as our bodyguards, and with their help we can walk over evil beasts. If we find ourselves in trouble, Yahweh will be with us.

We know that the promises of Psalm 91 are not always fulfilled literally in the real world where pain is prevalent, where good people grieve, and where the faithful suffer. We also know, however, that in the real world a child is pulled to safety from the rubble of an earthquake, a young man returns from war unscathed, a teenager walks away from a car accident, and a mother survives cancer. We know both the bad and the good, and we prefer to hold them together in tension; but the Psalms often focus on one extreme or the other.[38] Therefore, the psalmist is either 'dancing' (30.11) or 'in anguish' (55.4), either crying 'from the depths' (130.1) or shouting 'for joy' (35.27). In order to be convincing, the psalm must be intense; it must rhetorically drive home its point without qualification. Psalm 91 declares the trustworthiness of Yahweh without compromise and without exception. Weiser writes, 'By virtue of the soaring energy of its

---

[37] John E. Kuizenga, 'The Shadow of the Almighty', *Theology Today* 4.1 (1947), pp. 17-18 (17).

[38] Westermann, *The Living Psalms*, p. 15, argues that life can be compared to a pendulum that swings from the extreme of pain to the extreme of joy, and these two extremes in life are represented in the Psalms by psalms of lament and psalms of praise. In 'The Bible and the Life of Faith: A Personal Reflection', *Word & World* 13.4 (1993), p. 340, Westermann recalls that his upbringing in the Lutheran liturgical tradition had not prepared him to see prayer as anything more than a religious act. However, while incarcerated in a WWI Russian POW camp, his view of prayer and his view of the Psalms changed. He writes,

Under the influence of my wartime experiences, I realized that the people who had written and prayed the psalms understood prayer differently than we do. Prayer was closer to life, closer to the reality in which they lived … in the Psalter, crying to God grows out of life itself; it is a reaction to the experiences of life, a cry from the heart.

trust in God it leaves behind every earthly fear, every human doubt and all inhibiting considerations, and lifts [the hearer] up above the depressing realities of life to the hopeful certitude of a faith which is able to endure life and to master it'.[39]

The final section of the psalm, Yahweh's personal address to the one who trusts, contains especially potent affective terms. Each of the eight promises that are found in vv. 14-16 causes the hearer to experience hope, courage, gratitude, and joy. 'In this psalm the last word belongs to Yahweh, and the last word is caring protection.'[40]

In a rare statement that reflects Yahweh's own desire to be loved, Yahweh declares, 'Because he set his affection (חשק) on me, I will rescue him' (v. 14). The verb חשק suggests deep desire and affection, coupled with strong attachment and devotion.[41] 'It concerns cleaving and yearning and desiring. It is that which binds Yahweh to this psalmist.'[42] It signifies 'affective love',[43] and it is used in the torah to describe Yahweh's commitment to Israel. Moses declares, 'Yahweh set his affection (חשק) on your fathers, to love them; and he chose their descendants after them, you above all peoples, as it is today' (Deut. 10.15). In the same way that Yahweh yearns for Israel, Israel must yearn for Yahweh. Yahweh desires and expects to receive more than trust – Yahweh desires to receive devoted affection.

Pentecostal Effective History of Psalm 91

Psalm 91 has been used in a variety of settings throughout history by both Jews and Christians. At times it has served as a magical talisman to ward off evil,[44] and it was inscribed on amulets and buildings. Both

---

[39] Weiser, *The Psalms*, p. 613.
[40] Brueggemann, *Message of the Psalms*, p. 157.
[41] *HALOT*, p. 362; *DCH*, III p. 333; and *BDB*, pp. 365-66.
[42] Brueggemann, *Message of the Psalms*, p. 157.
[43] Zenger, 'Psalm 91', p. 431.
[44] Cf. J. de Fraine, 'Le Démon du Midi: Ps 91', *Biblica* 40.2 (1959), pp. 372-83. The LXX, Latin, and Targums all translate ישוד in Ps. 91.6 as a reference to evil spirits, apparently on account of its similarity to שד ('demon'). All of the Hebrew versions, however, including the Qumran MSS, have the verb ישוד ('destroys'). Jerome delivered two homilies on Psalm 91, and in the first, he quotes v. 6 as 'attack of the noonday demon' (FC 48, p. 159); but, in the second, he translates the same phrase as 'the devastating plague at noon' (FC 57, p. 84). The first homily is apparently based on the Old Latin, which Jerome mentions at the beginning. In the

Jews and Christians have used it as an aid to exorcism. Churches in Africa and Asia have recited Psalm 91 as a means of warding off both spiritual and physical threats such as evil spirits, civil wars, and natural disasters.[45] Psalm 91 has been called the 'Soldier's Psalm', and during the WWI, it was known as the 'Trench Psalm'.[46] Frederick Gaiser identifies the dangers of using Psalm 91 as a magical talisman, and he states, 'There is great confidence in this vision but, alas, no magic, and no immediate indemnity from the terrible realities of mortality and human strife; but this is only because God chooses to be with us in the world that is rather than to promise a world of make-believe that is not'.[47]

Like other traditions before it, Pentecostals have loved Psalm 91; they have used it; and, at times, they have abused it. This review of the effective history will provide an opportunity for discerning re-flection on the Pentecostal appropriation of the hopeful message of Psalm 91. The material will be grouped topically according to the writers' approaches to Psalm 91.[48]

Psalm 91 is an Encouragement to Piety and Service.
In a letter to the *Bridegroom's Messenger*, dated Dec. 19, 1907, William J. Seymour encourages the readers to be 'saved and sanctified and filled with the Almighty Holy Spirit'. He closes his inspirational mes-sage with the following benediction: 'I hope the Lord will keep you humble and even under the shadow of His wing and in the secret of the Most High. Hallelujah to His name!'[49] Seymour takes the meta-phors of Psalm 91 as references to private spirituality.

Personal piety is also a concern of Aimee Semple McPherson, founder of the Church of the Foursquare Gospel, who writes that intimacy with God

---

second homily, however, he appeals twice to the Hebrew text, suggesting that he developed the homily from the Hebrew, not from the Latin.

[45] Philip Jenkins, 'The Travels of Psalm 91', *CC* 135.2 (2018), pp. 36-37. Cf. F.H. Welshman, 'Psalm 91 in Relation to Malawian Cultural Background', *Journal of Theology for Southern Africa* 8 (Sept 1974), pp. 24-30.

[46] Knight, 'I Will Show Him My Salvation', p. 284.

[47] Frederick J. Gaiser, '"It Shall Not Reach You": Talisman or Vocation? Read-ing Psalm 91 in Time of War', *Word & World* 25.2 (2005), pp. 191-202 (199).

[48] Studies of early Pentecostal periodicals have often organized their discus-sions by separating the holiness stream from the finished work stream of the tra-dition. In the interpretation of Psalm 91, however, the literature shows little differ-ence between the two streams.

[49] W.J. Seymour, 'Letter from Bro. Seymore [sic]', *TBM* 1.5 (Jan 1, 1908), p. 2.

is the outcome of consistently dwelling in God's presence. 'He that dwelleth in the secret place of the Most High shall abide under the shadow of the Almighty' (Psalm 91:1). First, personal communing with God; then joint communion in fellowship with other disciples. Both Old and New Testaments are filled with accounts of united meetings of worship, praise, and prayer.[50]

Writing from Macao, China, missionary T.J. McIntosh reports both the opposition and the success that he had experienced in his ministry. He urges the readers to 'abide' in Christ and trust wholly in him. Only then will fruit come. He adds,

> We plainly see, then, the way to have miracle working power is by abiding in the true vine, Christ Jesus, and having Him abide in us. Reader, the writer is seeking a continual abiding place in Christ, where he will forever dwell in the shadow of the Almighty. Outside of Christ we cannot bear fruit for 'without Me ye can do nothing'.[51]

Similarly, Elizabeth A. Sexton, editor of *The Bridegroom's Messenger*, extends greetings for the new year. She reads Psalm 91 as an encouragement to faithful service, but she does not read it as an exemption from all trouble:

> The new year has dawned. Shall we not purpose in our hearts to give Him better service this year, if He tarries, than ever in the past? We do not know the joys or the sorrows that may overtake us. It is enough to know that Jesus is coming soon. This hope will keep us looking up beyond all bitter disappointments of this life to the perennial delights of being in His holy presence forever. Oh, let us keep hid away under the shadow of the Almighty.
>
> 'He shall cover thee with His feathers and under His wing shalt thou hide. His truth shall be thy shield and thy buckler.' God bless and keep you till He comes.[52]

A.J. Tomlinson, leader of the Church of God (Cleveland, TN) and editor of the *Church of God Evangel*, laments the war (WWI), stating

---

[50] Aimee Semple McPherson, 'Song of Praise', *FCr* 6.38 (July 6, 1932), p. 7. Cf. H.W. Cooksey, 'Secret Place of the Most High', *FCr* 12.46 (May 10, 1939), p. 5.

[51] T.J. McIntosh, 'Letter from Brother McIntosh', *TTBM* 1.15 (June 1, 1908), p. 4.

[52] Elizabeth A. Sexton, 'Editorial', *TTBM* 9.178 (Jan 1, 1916), p. 1.

that 'The awful war devil is still slaying his millions. His greed and
thirst for blood is never satisfied'. After a lengthy critique of the war,
Tomlinson turns his attention to the role of the Church in the world.
He declares that the Church's warfare against evil is more important
and more lasting that the war against Germany. 'Our first duty is to
the church', he writes, not to the 'stars and stripes'. Therefore, he calls
every member of the Church to a deeper dedication to the Lord's
service. He writes,

> Just now I feel our people need to hide away a little deeper under
> the shadow of the Almighty. Psalm 91:1. There is a sense in which
> we can hide away with Christ in God (Col. 3:3) and still be in full
> warfare with the devil and his forces. A deeper and more vivid
> consecration to God will be necessary for every child of God this
> year. Don't think of trying to bridge over this year on flowery beds
> of ease. There is no time for ease now. The tensions of the nations
> are tightened almost to the highest pitch. As our work is more
> important, more urgent, we must tighten our tensions up to the
> very highest pitch and plunge in to win or die, and win if we do
> die.[53]

Like Sexton, Tomlinson sees Psalm 91 as an invitation to a deeper
spiritual life and to a full engagement in ministry to the world. God's
promises do not enable the Church to avoid spiritual battle; instead,
they enable the Church to trust God while in the midst of spiritual
battle.

Missionaries were involved in the type of ministry that Tomlinson
demanded. For example, Mrs. G.C. Legge was a missionary to China,
and she gives an account of her experiences on the field. In a short
section with the heading, 'The Lord Careth for Us', she writes,

> We are now beginning our fifth year in China. We can truly say we
> have met with many hills and valleys along the way, literal hills and
> spiritual hills … As we spent the closing moments of the year in
> 1933 on our knees I asked the Lord for a verse for this year. He
> spoke to me, 'Dwell in the secret place,' (taken from Psalm 91:1),
> not just go to the Secret Place occasionally, but stay there. It means

---

[53] A.J. Tomlinson, 'The Awful World War', *CGE* 8.8 (Feb 24, 1917), p. 1.

that is we are to be ready for the coming of Jesus; it means that if we are to be able to stand in the battle.[54]

Psalm 91 is Protection against Violence.

After hearing news of political tensions in Hong Kong that threatened the lives of several missionaries, Elizabeth Sexton calls on readers to trust God's promise of protection:

> The letter from our missionaries at Hong Kong, in this issue, gives us something of the situation in China and the unrest prevailing, particularly in South China. There will be danger of further outbreaks. Let us pray for the protection of our dear missionaries, and claim together for them the promise that 'Because thou hast made the Lord, which is my refuge, even the Most High, thine inhabitation, there shall no evil befall thee, neither shall any plague come nigh thy dwelling.'[55]

Ralph Williams and two young men arrived in Tacuba, El Salvador, hoping to travel over the mountain the next day to a newly established church. During the night, a group of armed rebels took over the town; and when Williams was alerted of the sudden development, he and his friends began to pray. He wrote the following account:

> knowing their ruthless methods of killing and sharing the spoils, also their little tolerance of all opposition we reassured ourselves of His promises, reading Psalm 91, and committed ourselves into His care having great assurance that though the weapons of our warfare are not carnal yet they are mighty in God.

After lying low for a couple of days, they attempted an escape from the town, but they were captured by the armed rebels. Williams writes, 'However we had not forgotten Psalm 91 and were looking for the Lord to deliver us in one way or another.' They were soon released by the rebels and returned to their church, thanking God for his intervention.[56]

---

[54] Mrs. G.C. Legge, 'We Stand Upon the Verge of the Unknown', *PHA* (Mar 29, 1934), p. 5.

[55] Elizabeth A. Sexton, 'Editorial', *TTBM* 4.88 (June 15, 1911), p. 1.

[56] Ralph Williams, 'Violence and Bloodshed in El Salvador', *PE* 939 (Mar 12, 1932), pp. 8-9. Many stories from soldiers were published during and after WWI. E.g, 'It Shall not Come Nigh Thee', *PE* 179 (Mar 3, 1917), p. 16.

Psalm 91 is a Promise of Immunity against Disease.

The promise of good health is the most common theme in the early Pentecostal reception history of Psalm 91. The psalm is often understood as a guarantee of immunity against any and all diseases and plagues. However, if a believer should become ill, then the psalm becomes a promise of miraculous healing.[57] Some writers seem to view Psalm 91 almost as a magical text, while others hold a more nuanced interpretation. Moreover, the readers are strongly encouraged to appropriate the promises by faith, because a lack of faith can make the promise ineffective.[58]

Lillian Denney, a missionary in India writes, 'We have been having an epidemic of cholera, and many deaths ... I had no fear for our people. We have the promise, "there shall no plague come nigh thy dwelling."'[59] Having a view similar to that of Denney, H.W. Mitchell, remarks on 'the benefits of consecration':

> When you are fully consecrated and altogether on God's side He brings you into a place of safety. If you are altogether His, then you are under the shelter of the 91st Psalm, in the place where 'no plague shall come nigh your dwelling;' though there be destruction and pestilence all around yet you are safe.[60]

J.H. King, leader of the International Pentecostal Holiness Church, expresses a somewhat different view regarding the promises of Psalm 91. According to King, one should pray and trust in God,

---

[57] See Lilian B. Yeomans, 'Thy Children like Olive Plants', *PE* 673 (Nov 20, 1926), p. 17, who testifies to a healing and cites Ps. 91.10; Sybil Scott, 'By Faith We Were Healed!', *BC* 12.2 (Feb 1928), pp. 13-14, testifies to being healed of tuberculosis after enduring nine months of suffering. Her healing came when she remembered Psalm 91. See also G. Sigwalt, 'My Testimony of Divine Healing', *PHA* 8.23 (Oct 2, 1924), pp. 12-14 (12).

[58] Disobedience can also invalidate the promises. See Mrs. C.B. Leftwich, 'Tithing', *TTBM* 26.288 (Dec 1932), p. 6; and 'The Blessings of Obeying God's Word', *PHA* (Dec 8, 1932), pp. 5-6.

[59] Lillian Denney, 'From India', *TTBM* 11.206 (Oct 1, 1918), p. 3.

[60] H.W. Mitchell, 'The Ear-Marks of a Consecrated Life', *LRE* (June 1921), pp. 6-9 (8). Cf. missionary Flora H. James, 'A Fruitful Field in Hong Kong, China', *PE* 197 (July 7, 1917), p. 12, who expresses trust in the promises of Psalm 91 and asks for prayer during the 'season when plague is prevalent'. See also H.W. Mitchell, 'The Keeping Power of God', *LRE* (Feb 1919), p. 9, who professes trust in God during the influenza epidemic; and missionary W.J. Taylor, 'From Kobe, Japan', *TTBM* 9.182 (May 1, 1916), p. 4.

but even the most holy believer may contract disease as a test of their faith. Regarding the influenza epidemic of 1918, King explains,

> It is due to God's mercies that I have been exempt from this terrible plague. I prayed earnestly that I might escape, and God assured me that I should not have it. I praise Him for deliverance thus far ... I was blessed in going to pray for others afflicted with influenza and pneumonia ... The assurance that I would be preserved from the contagion by the power of God was sweet and comforting. Christ as refuge was made real and more precious in the midst of death riding on every breeze. When He is our habitation we can rest in the assurance that He will suffer no plague to come nigh our dwelling. But this requires an extra degree of faith or a claiming the protection of the covenant. Holy people have sickness. It may be they do not enter fully into their privileges in Christ. However, it is wise to conclude that God may allow those that abide in Christ to be sorely tested through sickness, even those who are said to be most holy. God has a right to subject us to test as He sees proper, and if it comes through physical suffering as the chosen channel this is quite legitimate.[61]

Unlike King, Mrs. James Hare, was not protected from the 'fevers' that raged through Sierra Leone, West Africa, where she served as a missionary. She testifies that when she first came to Africa, God gave her the promises of Psalm 91; however, she soon became ill. She writes,

> Although the fever reached me and God permitted the enemy to bring me down to death's door with it, yet all the time there was that faith of God in me that He would raise me up, and that the sickness was for His glory because the people watched me ... and saw how God triumphed.[62]

---

[61] J.H. King, 'Monthly Letter', *PHA* 2.33-34 (Dec 19-26, 1918), p. 6. Others who conclude that perfect health is not guaranteed by Psalm 91 include H. Steil, 'Naomi, the Woman of Sorrows', *PE* 1261 (July 9, 1938), p. 6, 11 (6), who writes, 'It is a mistake to think that trouble is a sign that God has forsaken us. God has promised, "I will be with him in trouble. I will deliver him and honor him." Psalm 91:15.' See also, 'Question Box', *PHA* 2.33-34 (Dec 19-26, 1918), p. 16.

[62] Mrs. James Hare, 'Divinely Used and Protected', *LRE* 3.7 (Apr 1911), p. 22.

Psalm 91 is Protection against False Teaching.

In a lead article for the *Church of God Evangel*, A.J. Tomlinson observes that the Church is continually challenged by false teachers who seek to deceive believers with new and diverse errors. He understands the 'snare' of Ps. 91.3 as a metaphor that stands for the trickery of false teachers. He writes,

> Quite recently an article came for the paper … In the article in more than one place mention was made of the Lord showing him certain things contained therein. I knew the Lord had not shown him, because the Lord does not lead people to accept error, but I knew he was sincere and could bear with him, and be loving and tender with him. I trust the Lord will deliver him (Psalm 91:3) from the snare of the fowler that was laid for him.[63]

In an article entitled 'Foursquare Gospel! Forward March!', Aimee Semple McPherson unpacks the metaphors of Psalm 91 even more than Tomlinson had done. She declares that her church is in a battle for the truth of the gospel. The Foursquare army is 'confronted by the hordes of Satan … Attacked by the Legions of Formalism' as it defends the 'Word of God against the demolishing scissors of the Higher Critic'. In her eloquent, colorful, and impassioned argument, McPherson cites only two biblical texts: Acts 2.4 and Ps. 91.7. She observes that every previous revival movement had faced severe resistance. She writes that the Foursquare Gospel has experienced divine manifestations; but, like in earlier movements, those blessings of the Spirit have been accompanied by intense persecution. In the face of this opposition, McPherson proclaims triumphantly,

> A thousand may fall at our side under the fire of the guns of evolution and unbelief; and ten thousand at our right hand (Ps 91:7) by the shrapnel of false religion and modernism. Satan my set his machine gun nests of persecution on the surrounding hills. But we are marching in the center of the Foursquare box barrage of God's protecting care … It is only when we leave the charmed

---

[63] A.J. Tomlinson, 'Warnings against Strange Doctrines', *CGE* (July 10, 1920), p. 1. Cf. G. Krieger, 'A Sanctified Mind', *TTBM* 2.29 (Jan 1, 1909), p. 4, who infers from Psalm 91 that a sanctified mind is needed for correct interpretation of Scripture.

circle of His blessed will that we lay ourselves open to the fire of the enemy.[64]

McPherson's paraphrase of Ps. 91.7 and its direct application to her contemporary circumstances is a result of several hermeneutical moves on her part: 1. Psalm 91 is not taken literally; that is, the thousands who fall are not casualties of real war but are victims of spiritual battle. 2. The promise of protection is conditioned upon obedience, a point that is inferred from v. 8 of the psalm itself, a verse that may describe the fallen as 'the wicked'. 3. The situation of the original hearers is analogous to McPherson's hearers, in that both are faced with a variety of threats and both are encouraged to trust in divine protection.

Psalm 91 is a Safeguard against Heated Conflicts.

A writer identified only as J.H.J. provides an unusual symbolic reading of the phrase 'under the shadow of the Almighty' (Ps. 91.1).

> In the shadow of the Almighty, we are sheltered from all destructive heat – the heat of fretfulness, and every other form of unholy fire which so often destroys the delicate treasures of the soul. The shadow of the Almighty will keep us cool and collected, and all our powers will do their work in quietness. Every day we encounter friction in some mode or another, and friction always tends to engender a dangerous heat … Now, in all these inflammatory perils our safety is to turn into 'the shadow of the Almighty'.[65]

Apparently, J.H.J. believes that the coolness of the shade symbolizes the inner calm of the believer who does not allow conflicts to produce anger.

Psalm 91 Reveals God as Mother.

Another surprising interpretation is offered by Lillian L. Stokes. Evangelist Stokes reflects on five terms that describe God: Father, Mother, Friend, Lover, and Bridegroom. She admits that although the picture of God as Mother has limited biblical support, the metaphor can be found 'in a number of places'. She writes,

> In Psalm 91:1, 'He that dwelleth in the secret place of the Most High shall abide under the shadow of the Almighty.' A beautiful

---

[64] Aimee Semple McPherson, *BC* 12.4 (Sept 1928), pp. 14-15, 32-33 (33).
[65] J.H.J., 'The Cooling Shadow', *PHA* 11.43 (Mar 1, 1928), p. 6.

picture of a mother sheltering her children with her wings. Ah, how we all remember being protected 'neath the loving arms of our mother. God's eye doth ever behold His righteous children.[66]

Psalm 91 Produces Inner Peace.
M.G. Swarts, a student at the Church of God Bible Training School, offers a brief article on Psalm 91, in which he declares that the 'secret place' (Ps. 91.1) is a place of peace and tranquility. He tells the story of John Wesley's journey from England to America. During the trip across the Atlantic, the ship encountered a great storm, and Wesley was terrified. A group of Moravian Christians, however, were joyfully singing praises to God. Swarts continues:

> Wesley asked how it was that they could do this in such a storm. One of them replied, 'Have you never heard, "Perfect love casteth out fear?"' They were in the secret place of God. We, too, can lodge in the secret place of God where the storms and trials will not disturb our hearts.[67]

Apostolic leader Andrew Urshan informs the readers of *Word and Witness* of the many persecutions that accompanied his missionary work in Europe. He was imprisoned for five months; his home was looted; his clothes were stolen; he was 'many times in the jaws of death'; and three of his fellow workers were 'shot as martyrs'. Still, while bedfast from sickness, he testifies the following:

> … the sweet peace of God has flooded my soul. Glory. Many thousands have fallen on our sides but we have kept under His wings. Surely Psalm 91 has been fulfilled in our lives. My soul magnifies the great Jehovah!
>
> In this terrible condition God has given us many souls. Some were killed and went home to heaven. Others passed away by hot fever by which thousands are dying. The rest are praising and blessing God with us…[68]

---

[66] Lillian L. Stokes, 'A Bible Picture of God', *TBM* 29.306 (Apr 1936), p. 5.

[67] M.G. Swarts, 'God's Secret Place', *CGE* 29.11 (May 14, 1938), p. 7. See also C.W. Goforth, 'To the Discouraged', *CGE* 30.18 (July 1, 1939), p. 15, who writes, '… Psalm 91:2. The only perfect refuge is in the Lord'.

[68] 'Brother Urshan Heard From', *WW* 12.8 (Aug 1915), p. 6. Cf. Sister Nary, 'My Times are in His Hand', *BC* 1.10 (Mar 1918), p. 6, who writes of her many sufferings, while claiming to live 'in the secret place of the Most High' and to abide 'under the shadow of the Almighty' (Ps. 91.1).

Psalm 91 Refers to Life in the Millennium

Writing in the *Latter Rain Evangel*, D. Wesley Myland enumerates seven 'facts or conditions' that will come to pass during the millennial reign of Christ on earth. The sixth of these facts is that the righteous will be blessed with long life. Myland insists, 'Psalm 91, which is the Millennial Psalm, will be literally fulfilled'; and, 'Then we will be "under the shadow of the Almighty," hiding in God. "With long life shall I satisfy him and show him My salvation."'[69]

Conclusion

The effective history of Psalm 91 in early Pentecostal periodicals provides a brief glimpse into the world view, hermeneutics, and spirituality of the Pentecostal tradition. The testimonies, sermons, and articles reviewed here demonstrate that early Pentecostals identified with the message of Psalm 91 and appropriated it in many contexts and situations. Although a few of the examples reveal unusual or fanciful interpretations, most of the writers view the psalm in ways that are consistent with the ancient Jewish context. That is, Psalm 91 is a declaration of God's promises to care for his people, to protect them from harm, and to be with them in times of trouble. The psalm generates faith, hope, confidence, and gratitude in the hearer. However, the hearer knows that Psalm 91 is a confession of faith, not a theological treatise. The promises of God are genuine, but they are not 'absolutes'. The paradox is stated well by Pentecostal pastor Joseph Tunmore. In a 'message' to the Assemblies of God General Council, Tunmore set forth the believer's responsibility to 'appropriate' the promises of God. Tunmore states that although God 'has promised that no plague shall come nigh our dwelling', God 'may bring you down to death, and you ought to be just as willing to die as to live, if He can thereby be glorified'.[70]

---

[69] D. Wesley Myland, 'The Book of Revelation of Jesus Christ: Eleventh Lecture – Christ Coming in Glory', *LRE* 4.5 (Feb 1912), p. 11. Aimee Semple McPherson apparently agrees with Myland. See *FC* 2.48 (Sept 16, 1931), p. 7.

[70] Joseph Tunmore, 'The Essentials to Pentecost', *PE* (Nov 2, 1918), p. 3.

4

PSALMS 105 AND 106: TELLING THE WHOLE STORY

Introduction

Psalms 105 and 106 recount portions of Israel's story. As such, they share the characteristics of other psalms of historical recital, such as Psalms 78, 135, and 136.[1] Observing that Psalms 105 and 106 stand side-by-side, Charles and Emily Briggs argued they were originally one psalm, and Walther Zimmerli called them 'twin psalms'.[2] Taken separately, Psalms 105 and 106 offer a variety of historical, theological, and spiritual treasures. However, the juxtaposition of these two psalms within the Psalter yields much fruit that might have been ignored if they had been placed in separate locations. By placing these two texts side-by-side, the editors of the Psalter virtually ensure that neither voice will be heard alone.

Both Psalms 105 and 106 tell the familiar story of Israel, emphasizing the exodus narrative and the ensuing covenant with Yahweh. The two narratives, however, present contrasting versions of Israel's

---

[1] Cf. Leslie C. Allen, *Psalms 101-150* (WBC Vol. 21; Waco, TX: Word Books, rev. edn, 2002), p. 67. According to Anja Klein, 'Fathers and Sons: Family Ties in the Historical Psalms', in M.S. Pajunen and J. Penner (eds.), *Functions of the Psalms and Prayers in the Late Second Temple Period* (Berlin: Walter de Gruyter, 2017), p. 320, the nature and number of historical psalms continues to be debated, but there is some agreement that Psalms 78, 105, 106, 135, and 136 'make up the core' of the historical psalms.

[2] Briggs and Briggs, *Psalms*, II, p. 342; Walther Zimmerli, 'Zwillingspsalmen', in *idem, Studien zur alttestamentlichen Theologie und Prophetie: Gesammelte Aufsätze Band II*, Theologische Bücherei 51 (Munich: Kaiser, 1974), pp. 261-71.

relationship to Yahweh. In Psalm 105, the history of Israel is made up of a series of continual victories; but in Psalm 106, the same history consists of repeated episodes of Israel's disobedience. Because of their differing perspectives on Israel's history, it seems reasonable to assume that the two psalms are responses to two different contexts. Psalm 105 calls for celebration, but Psalm 106 demands confession and repentance. My thesis is that the juxtaposition of these variant narratives functions as a corrective to an unhealthy one-sided version of the story.

Listening to the students in my recent course on the book of Judges has reminded me that Christians prefer stories in which the characters are clearly defined as either good or evil and in which the events in the narrative have a simple cause-and-effect relationship. We find it difficult to negotiate the tensions in the biblical text that are created by complex characters and ambiguous situations. Pentecostals have been exposed to their fair share of this simplicity in the form of either triumphalism or fatalism. We have heard the stories of healings, miracles, deliverances, and successes (and so we should), but we rarely hear about the deep struggles and multiple failures that also make up the lives of Pentecostal leaders and believers. Much like the story of Israel, our corporate Pentecostal story and our individual stories are complex and multi-layered. For the sake of our future, we must tell the whole story!

In this chapter I will offer a brief study of each psalm and suggest contexts in which their messages might be helpful, then I will suggest ways in which the canonical juxtaposition of the two psalms creates a theological tension that must not be alleviated.

A Translation of Psalm 105

[1] Give thanks to Yahweh, call upon his name;
    Make known among the peoples his deeds.
[2] Sing to him, make music to him;
    Shout out all his wonders.
[3] Exult in his holy name;
    Let the hearts of those who seek Yahweh rejoice.
[4] Seek Yahweh and his strength;
    Seek his face always.
[5] Remember his wonders which he has done,

his marvels, and the judgments from his mouth,
⁶ Offspring of Abraham, his servant,
    Sons of Jacob, his chosen ones.
⁷ He is Yahweh our God;
    His judgments are in all the earth.
⁸ He has remembered his covenant forever,
    The word which he commanded to a thousand generations,
⁹ The covenant which he made with Abraham,
    And his oath to Isaac.
¹⁰ And he confirmed it to Jacob for a statute,
    To Israel as an everlasting covenant,
¹¹ Saying, To you I will give the land of Canaan
    Your allotted inheritance,
¹² When they were only a few men in number,
    Very few, and strangers in it.
¹³ And they wandered from nation to nation,
    From one kingdom to another people.
¹⁴ He permitted no one to oppress them,
    And he rebuked kings for their sakes:
¹⁵ Do not touch my anointed ones,
    And do not harm my prophets.
¹⁶ And he called for a famine in the land;
    He broke the whole support of bread.
¹⁷ He sent a man before them,
    Joseph, who was sold as a slave.
¹⁸ They afflicted his feet with fetters,
    With an iron collar his neck;
¹⁹ Until the time that his word came to pass,
    The word of Yahweh tested him.
²⁰ The king sent and released him,
    The ruler of peoples, and set him free.
²¹ He made him lord of his household,
    And ruler over all his possessions,
²² To imprison his princes at will,
    That he might teach his elders wisdom.
²³ And Israel came to Egypt;
    And Jacob sojourned in the land of Ham.
²⁴ And he made his people very fruitful,
    And made them stronger than their enemies.

²⁵ He turned their hearts to hate his people,
　To deal craftily with his servants.
²⁶ He sent Moses his servant,
　And Aaron whom he had chosen.
²⁷ They performed his signs among them,
　And miracles in the land of Ham.
²⁸ He sent darkness and made it dark;
　And they did not rebel against his words.
²⁹ He turned their waters into blood,
　And caused their fish to die.
³⁰ Their land teemed with frogs
　In the chambers of their kings.
³¹ He spoke, and flies came
　Gnats in all their territory.
³² He gave them hail for rain,
　And flaming fire in their land.
³³ He struck down their vines and their fig trees,
　And he shattered the trees of their territory.
³⁴ He spoke, and locusts came,
　And grasshoppers, without number,
³⁵ And ate up all vegetation in their land,
　And ate up the fruit of their land.
³⁶ And he struck down all the firstborn in their land,
　The first fruits of all their vigor.
³⁷ And he brought them out with silver and gold;
　And among his tribes there was not one who stumbled.
³⁸ Egypt celebrated when they left;
　For the dread of them had fallen upon them.
³⁹ He spread a cloud for a covering,
　And fire to give light by night.
⁴⁰ They asked, and he brought quail,
　And with bread from heaven he satisfied them.
⁴¹ He opened the rock, and water gushed out;
　A river ran in the dry places.
⁴² For he remembered his holy word
　To Abraham his servant;
⁴³ And he brought out his people with rejoicing,
　His chosen ones with a joyful shout.
⁴⁴ And he gave them the lands of nations,

And they possessed what the peoples had toiled for,
[45] So that they might keep his statutes,
   And observe his laws,
Praise Yah!

The Structure of Psalm 105

Psalm 105 divides quite easily into three main sections:[3]

   I. Call to worship (vv. 1-6)
   II. Recital of Israel's Story (vv. 7-45a)
          a. Covenant with Abraham (vv. 7-11)
          b. Patriarchal sojourn in Canaan (vv. 12-15)
          d. Joseph's story and Israel's entry into Egypt (vv. 16-23)
          e. Israel's Time in Egypt (vv. 24-38)
          f. Miracles in the Wilderness (vv. 39-41)
          g. Reflection on God's faithfulness (vv. 42-43)
   III. Renewed Call to worship (v. 45b)

The first section (vv. 1-6) consists of a series of ten imperatives and one jussive that make up an introductory call to worship. Apart from Psalm 150, Psalm 105 contains the longest call to worship in the entire Psalter (in Psalm 150, the verb הלל ('praise') is found 12 times in the imperative and once in the jussive).[4] Israel is invited to give thanks,[5] call, make known, sing, sing, talk, glory, rejoice, seek, seek, remember. These imperatives are addressed to the 'seed of

---

[3] Cf. Erhard Gerstenberger, *Psalms, Part 2, and Lamentations* (FOTL 15; Grand Rapids, MI: Eerdmans, 2001), p. 230. My outline agrees with Hossfeld, except that Hossfeld views vv. 1-3 as a unit and vv. 4-7 as a second unit. See Frank-Lothar Hossfeld, 'Psalm 105', in Frank-Lothar Hossfeld and Erich Zenger, *Psalms 3: A Commentary on Psalms 101-150* (ed. K. Baltzer; trans. L.M. Maloney; Hermeneia; Minneapolis, MN: Fortress Press, 2011), p. 66. I would argue that the change of subject from 'you' to 'he' in v. 7 suggests that v. 7 starts a new unit that belongs with vv. 8-11. Cf. Terrien, *The Psalms*, p. 723; Rolf A. Jacobson, 'Psalm 105', in DeClaissé-Walford, Jacobson, and Tanner, *The Book of Psalms*, p. 783; and Allen, *Psalms 101-150*, p. 53.

[4] In Psalm 150, the verb הלל is found 12 times in the imperative and once in the jussive.

[5] G. Mayer, 'ידה III. Usage', *TDOT*, V, pp. 431-42, points to dual meanings, 'praise' and 'confess', that merge together in the usage of ידה.

Abraham', the 'children of Jacob, [Yahweh's] chosen ones'.[6] Rolf Jacobson points out that all of the imperatives are in the plural, 'meaning that the entire congregation is to become those who *testify* about
God's actions. That is, the congregation is to become a corporate
witness to what God has done and to the character of the Lord as a
faithful God.'[7] The emphasis here is on Israel's testimony within the
context of worship. Israel is called upon to glorify Yahweh on account of Yahweh's deeds, wonders, holy name, signs, and judgments
that have been manifested within the story of Israel.[8]

The second section (vv. 7-45a) is a chronological recital of Israel's
story, beginning with Yahweh's covenant with Abraham, which was
subsequently confirmed to Isaac and Jacob. Yahweh promised the
land of Canaan to the patriarchs and protected them in their nomadic
wanderings throughout the Promised Land. Leslie Allen observes
that to this small patriarchal group, the promise of obtaining the land
'must have seemed an unattainable dream'.[9] The story continues with
descriptions of Yahweh's faithful care of Joseph and Yahweh's resolve to save Israel through the mission of Moses. The plagues upon
Egypt are recounted in detail, and Israel's departure from Egypt is
celebrated with great relish.[10] The wilderness wanderings are described in terms of Yahweh's wondrous protection and his miraculous provision of quail, bread from heaven, and water from the rock.
This middle section concludes with the assurance that all of Yahweh's
works were based upon his faithful remembrance of the covenant
with Abraham. Consequently, the covenant (or 'promise', v. 42) is fulfilled by Israel's inheritance of the land (v. 44). While the first section
focuses almost entirely on Israel's praise of God, this second section
supplies the motive for that praise. In 35 verses, we find 30 verbs with
Yahweh as the subject of the action, a fact that suggests Yahweh's
saving activity as the dominant theme of the narrative.

---

[6] Cf. Marty E. Stevens, 'Psalm 105', *Int* 57.2 (2003) p. 188. Allen, *Psalms 101-
150*, points out that the term 'chosen' had 'postexilic associations with the promise
of the land, in the light of Isa. 65.9-10' (p. 57).

[7] Jacobson, 'Psalm 105', p. 787 (emphasis original).

[8] Cf. Robert L. Cate, 'Psalm 105: The Mighty Acts of God', *The Theological
Educator* 29 (1984) p. 56.

[9] Allen, *Psalms 101-150*, p. 58.

[10] Regarding the number of the plagues here, see B. Margulis, 'Plagues Tradition
in Ps 105', *Bib* 50.4 (1969), pp. 491-96; Samuel E. Loewenstamm, 'Number of
Plagues in Psalm 105', *Bib* 52.1 (1971), pp. 34-38; and W. Dennis Tucker, Jr.,
'Revisiting the Plagues in Psalm CV', *VT* 55.3 (2005), pp. 401-11.

The third and final section (v. 45b) consists only in the brief exhortation, 'Praise Yah!'.

Although the narrative in vv. 8-44 is laid out in chronological fashion, the structure also includes chiastic elements. Robert Alden suggests the following A B A' pattern:

A – Giving thanks to the Lord for remembering his covenant
　　with Abraham (vv. 1-11)
　B – Narrative of the exodus (vv. 12-41)
A' – Praising the Lord for remembering his word to Abraham
　　(vv. 42-45).[11]

Joachim Vette expands the chiasm from two levels to three:

A – 'Praise and thanks' ('*Lob und Dank*', vv. 1-7)
　B – 'Covenant' ('*Bund*', vv. 8-11)
　　C – 'History' ('*Geschichte*', vv. 12-43)
　B' – 'Covenant' ('*Bund*', vv. 44-45a)
A' – 'Praise and thanks' ('*Lob und Dank*', v. 45b).[12]

The chiasm that I propose corresponds to the structures discerned by Alden and Vette but includes more levels:

A – Call to worship הלל (vv. 1-4)
　B – His chosen ones בחר (v. 6)
　　C – Covenant with Abraham דבר (v. 8)
　　　D – Wandering in Canaan הלך (vv. 12-15)
　　　　E – Yahweh sent Joseph שלח vv. 16-22)
　　　　　F – Israel enters Egypt יעקב/ישׂראל (v. 23)
　　　　　　G – Yahweh made his people stronger than
　　　　　　　　their enemies (v. 24)
　　　　　F' – Israel oppressed עבדיו/עמו (v. 25)
　　　　E' – Yahweh sent Moses שלח (vv. 26-36)
　　　D' – Returning toward Canaan הלך (vv. 37-41)
　　C' – Holy Word to Abraham דבר (v. 42)
　B' – His chosen ones בחר (v. 43)
A' – Call to worship הלל (v. 45b)

---

[11] Robert L. Alden, 'Chiastic Psalms (III): A Study in the Mechanics of Semitic Poetry in Psalms 101-150', *JETS* 21.3 (1978), pp. 201-202.

[12] Joachim Vette, 'Psalm 105', in Manfred Oeming and JoachimVette, *Das Buch der Psalmen: Psalm 90-151* (Stuttgart: Verlag Katholisches Bibelwerk, 2016), p. 99.

Several of the elements of my chiasm are named by Alden as repetitions. For example, he notices the repetition of 'Abraham' (vv. 6,
9, 42), 'remember' (vv. 8, 42), 'word' (vv. 8, 42), 'people' (vv. 1, 43),
and 'earth' (vv. 7, 44); but he does not recognize how these repetitions
fit within a chiastic pattern.[13]

Vette argues that although the term 'covenant' is not mentioned
at the end of the psalm, the reference to 'statutes' and 'laws' referred
to in v. 45 is an allusion to the covenant.[14] Vette is correct to see how
the reference to 'statutes' and 'laws' points to the Sinai covenant.
However, the covenant that is in view in vv. 6-11 is not the Sinai covenant; it is the Abrahamic covenant. Moreover, the emphasis of this
Psalm is on the word of God as promise not as law. In fact, the entire
Sinai narrative is missing from the Psalm. Therefore, v. 45a is not
strictly parallel with vv. 8-11; rather, v. 42 (which mentions Abraham)
should be paired with vv. 8-9 as it is in my chiastic structure. Nevertheless, the unexpected call for obedience to 'statutes' and 'laws' provides a powerful conclusion to the psalm, and it creates a bridge to
Psalm 106 (which emphasizes obedience).

Although Alden's and Vette's observations are helpful, the chiastic
structure can be expanded even further by taking note of other lexical parallels. It will be observed that the chiastic structure corresponds quite closely to the chronological structure given earlier.
However, the key Hebrew terms that are displayed in the chiasm
point the hearer to elements of the story that might have been overlooked previously. For example, the call to worship stands out prominently no matter which structure is employed; however, the chiasm
draws attention to the people of God as the 'chosen ones' and to the
covenant as God's 'word'. The repetition of the word 'going' (הלך)
suggests that Israel's life with Yahweh is a journey, and the use of
'sent' (שׁלח) in relation to both Joseph and Moses underlines Yahweh's purposeful activity in guiding, preserving, and saving Israel. In
the case of Joseph especially, the 'path to glory lay through suffering',
a fact that would not be insignificant to those who suffered in the
exile.[15] The middle verses (23-25) do not have precise lexical parallels,
but the terms 'Israel' and 'Jacob' function as synonymous parallels to

---

[13] Alden, 'Chiastic Psalms (III)', p. 201.
[14] Vette, 'Psalm 105', p. 99.
[15] Allen, *Psalms 101-150*, p. 58. Cf. Gerstenberger, *Psalms, Part 2*, p. 230.

'his people' and 'his servants'.[16] The center of the chiasm states, '[Yahweh] made his people very fruitful, and he made them mightier than their adversaries' (v. 24), thus drawing attention to Yahweh's power to prosper his people even when they are surrounded by foes who would attempt to destroy them.

Rhetorical Analysis of Psalm 105

Psalm 105 is a joyful celebration of the mighty acts of Yahweh that demonstrate Yahweh's faithful commitment to the covenant with Israel.[17] This psalm generates in the hearer a number of related responses that are based upon prominent elements of the psalm, which include Yahweh's faithfulness, commitment, care, purposefulness, power, and resolve. In response to Yahweh's character and actions, the hearer is moved toward the affections of gratitude, love, trust, courage, awe, and joy.[18]

The story of Israel as narrated in Psalm 105 is the story of Yahweh's mighty work on behalf of Israel, which includes Yahweh's choosing, covenanting, guiding, protecting, saving, giving, and remembering. Yahweh performs 'wonders' that both *'subvert our knowledge,* our epistemology, our ways of knowing', and they also *'subvert our political-economic power arrangements',* thus 'displacing our certitude' and leaving us in a state of amazement.[19] The remembrance of God's miraculous acts is an important feature of Pentecostal testimony.

Everything revolves around Yahweh's faithful devotion to the covenant with Abraham.[20] In Psalm 105, the actions of Israel have little impact on the story – Israel's role is to follow Yahweh's lead. Even though Israel suffers at the hands of their Egyptian oppressors, the tone of the psalm is one of confident hope in Yahweh's commitment to Israel. The original hearers, therefore, would be moved to trust in Yahweh's ability and resolve to deliver Israel from her enemies. 'The emphasis is placed on Yahweh's power and dominance

---

[16] Regarding the significance of the terms 'chosen' and 'servant', see Jacobson, 'Psalm 105', p. 794.

[17] Cf. Jacobson, 'Psalm 105', pp. 782, 788, 789.

[18] Cf. Phillip McMillion, 'Psalm 105: History with a Purpose', *ResQ* 52.3 (2010) p. 179.

[19] Brueggemann, *The Psalms and the Life of Faith*, p. 41 (emphasis original).

[20] Cf. Hossfeld, 'Psalm 105', p. 70. Cf. Gerstenberger, *Psalms, Part 2*, p. 231.

over the Egyptian empire'.[21] The trust and hope that is generated by Psalm 105 would be particularly beneficial to those hearers who were suffering in the exile or in postexilic contexts.[22]

The lengthy series of imperatives (vv. 1-5) invites Israel to remember Yahweh's saving works and to praise Yahweh with singing. This text, therefore, calls upon the people of God to rejoice in God's mighty works and faithful character and to praise God for those attributes and actions. Psalm 105, therefore, would be appropriate within any context that calls for the celebration of God as savior, protector, provider, and guide. 'Recounting and remembering God's wondrous deeds in our history leads to reliance on God's faithfulness and response in our own lives.'[23]

A Translation of Psalm 106

[1] Praise Yah!
>Give thanks to Yahweh, for he is good!
>For his covenant loyalty is everlasting.

[2] Who can utter the mighty acts of Yahweh?
>Who can proclaim all his praise?

[3] Blessed are those who keep justice,
>The one doing righteousness at all times.

[4] Remember me, Yahweh, with the favor of your people;
>Visit me with your salvation,

[5] That I may see the good of your chosen ones,
>That I may rejoice in the gladness of your nation,
>That I may glory with your inheritance.

[6] We have sinned with our fathers;
>We have done wrong;
>We have acted wickedly.

[7] Our ancestors in Egypt did not understand your wonders;
>They did not remember the multitude of your mercies,
>And they rebelled by the sea -- the Red Sea.

[8] But he saved them for his name's sake,
>To make known his might.

---

[21] Scott A. Ellington, 'The Reciprocal Reshaping of History and Experience in the Psalms: Interactions with Pentecostal Testimony', *JPT* 16.1 (2007), p. 25.

[22] Cf. Brueggemann and Bellinger, *Psalms*, p. 454.

[23] Stevens, 'Psalm 105', p. 189.

⁹ And he rebuked the Red Sea, and it dried up;
So he led them through the depths, like the wilderness.
¹⁰ He saved them from the hand of the hater,
And redeemed them from the hand of the enemy.
¹¹ The waters covered their adversaries;
Not one of them was left.
¹² And they believed his words;
They sang his praise.
¹³ They hurried, they forgot his works;
They did not wait for his counsel,
¹⁴ But craved exceedingly in the wilderness,
And they tested God in the desert.
¹⁵ And he gave them their request,
But sent leanness into their soul.
¹⁶ And they envied Moses in the camp,
And Aaron the holy one of Yahweh,
¹⁷ The earth opened up and swallowed Dathan,
And covered the company of Abiram.
¹⁸ A fire was kindled in their company;
The flame burned up the wicked.
¹⁹ They made a calf in Horeb,
And they worshiped the molded image.
²⁰ Thus they changed their glory
Into the image of an ox that eats grass.
²¹ They forgot God their savior,
Who had done great things in Egypt,
²² Wonders in the land of Ham,
Awesome things by the Red Sea.
²³ And he said he would destroy them,
Had not Moses his chosen one stood in the breach
before him,
To turn away his wrath, lest he destroy them.
²⁴ Then they despised the pleasant land;
They did not believe his word,
²⁵ But they murmured in their tents,
And did not heed the voice of Yahweh.
²⁶ And swore an oath against them,
To overthrow them in the wilderness,
²⁷ To cast down their descendants among the nations,

And to scatter them in the lands.
²⁸ And they joined themselves to Baal-Peor,
And they ate sacrifices for the dead.
²⁹ And they provoked him to anger with their deeds,
And the plague broke out among them.
³⁰ Then Phinehas stood up and intervened,
And the plague was stopped.
³¹ And that was accounted to him for righteousness
To all generations forevermore.
³² They angered him also at the waters of strife,
So that it went ill with Moses on account of them;
³³ Because they rebelled against his Spirit,
So that he spoke rashly with his lips.
³⁴ They did not destroy the peoples,
Concerning whom Yahweh had commanded them,
³⁵ But they mingled with the nations
And learned their works;
³⁶ They served their idols,
Which became a snare to them.
³⁷ They even sacrificed their sons
And their daughters to demons,
³⁸ And shed innocent blood,
The blood of their sons and daughters,
Whom they sacrificed to the idols of Canaan;
And the land was polluted with blood.
³⁹ Thus they were defiled by their own works,
And played the harlot by their own deeds.
⁴⁰ The wrath of Yahweh was kindled against his people,
So that he abhorred his own inheritance.
⁴¹ And he gave them into the hand of the nations,
And those who hated them ruled over them.
⁴² Their enemies also oppressed them,
And they were subjected under their hand.
⁴³ Many times he delivered them;
But they rebelled in their counsel,
And were brought low for their iniquity.
⁴⁴ Nevertheless he regarded their affliction,
When he heard their cry;
⁴⁵ And for their sake he remembered his covenant,

And relented according to the multitude of his mercies.
[46] He also made them to be pitied
By all those who carried them away captive.
[47] Save us, Yahweh our God,
And gather us from among the nations,
To give thanks to your holy name,
To triumph in your praise.
[48] Blessed be Yahweh, God of Israel
From everlasting to everlasting!
And let all the people say, 'Amen!'
Praise Yah!

Structure of Psalm 106

Although Hossfeld proposes only a three-part structure to Psalm 106, consisting of vv. 1-5, 6-46, and 47-48,[24] I would argue for five distinct sections, with 'Praise Yah' being a call to worship that serves as an inclusio to the psalm, as it does in several hymns of descriptive praise (cf. Psalms 113, 115, 117, 135, and 146-150).[25] The major difference in our outlines, however, is the location of vv. 4-5. Hossfeld places these two verses outside the main body of the song, but the fact that the prayer for salvation (v. 4) is repeated in v. 47 convinces me that vv. 4-5 belong with the main body. I would outline the psalm as follows:

I. Call to worship – 'Praise Yah!' (v. 1a)
II. Thanksgiving, and a blessing on the righteous (vv. 1b-3)
III. Prayer for salvation based upon Israel's story (vv. 4-47)
    A. Opening prayer for forgiveness of sin (vv. 4-6)
    B. Israel's story of sin and forgiveness (vv. 7-46)
        1. Wonders of Egypt – yet Israel rebelled (vv. 7-12)
        2. In the wilderness, Israel tempted God (vv. 13-15)
        3. In the wilderness, Dathan swallowed up (vv. 16-18)
        4. The Golden Calf (vv. 19-23)
        5. Refusal to enter Canaan (vv. 24-27) (cf. Numbers 13-14)

---

[24] Frank-Lothar Hossfeld, 'Psalm 106', in Hossfeld and Zenger, *Psalms* 3, pp. 86-87. Allen, *Psalms 101-150*, provides an overview of the various proposals regarding structure (pp. 68-70). The variations from one commentator to another are not significant.

[25] Oddly, Ross, *A Commentary on the Psalms*, places the first 'Hallelujah' inside the body of the poem, but the concluding 'Hallelujah' he puts outside the poem as an 'Epilogue' (p. 283).

6. Sin and plague at Baal-Peor (vv. 28-31)
7. Moses' striking of the rock (vv. 32-33)
8. Israel's idolatry in Canaan 34-39)
9. The cycles of the Judges (vv. 40-46)
C. A prayer for salvation from exile (47)
IV. Closing word of praise (48a)
V. Renewed call to worship – 'Praise Yah!' (48b)[26]

The first and last sections form an inclusio consisting only of 'Praise Yah', which is the call to worship. The opening, therefore, suggests a hymn of praise, but the core of the psalm is instead a prayer of confession.[27] Richard J. Clifford classifies Psalm 106 as a lament,[28] but Erhard Gerstenberger views it as a combination of 'Communal Confession' and 'Hymnic Instruction'.[29] Leslie Allen argues that the combination of hymn and lament in Psalm 106 illustrates the 'limitations of the form-critical method',[30] but Walter Beyerlin insists that this new form makes sense in light of religious tensions that were present after 587 BCE, when the praise of God was difficult and needed to be renewed through the use of confession and historical recital.[31] The second section continues the call to worship and expands upon it by affirming Yahweh's covenant loyalty (חסד, v. 1b) and mighty works (v. 2). Verse three pronounces a blessing upon those who 'guard justice and perform righteousness at all times', a pronouncement that later becomes prominent by virtue of the righteousness of Phinehas (v. 31).

---

[26] It should be pointed out that v. 48 functions as a concluding doxology to Book IV of the Psalter.
[27] Cf. Brueggemann and Bellinger, *Psalms*, p. 458. The combination of hymn and lament in Psalm 106 illustrates the 'limitations of the form-critical method' (Allen, *Psalms 101-150*, p. 65).
[28] Richard J. Clifford, *Psalms 73-150* (Abingdon Old Testament Commentaries; Nashville: Abingdon, 2003), p. 156.
[29] Gerstenberger, *Psalms, Part 2*, p. 244.
[30] Allen, *Psalms 101-150*, p. 65.
[31] Walter Beyerlin, 'Der nervus rerum in Psalm 106', *ZAW* 86.1 (1974), pp. 50-64. Beyerlin's key statement (p. 62), which is paraphrased above, reads,
Sie tut dies, indem sie an Hand der Vätergeschichte gegenwärtige Sündenschuld beichtet und als Lob-Hindernis abbaut. Sie tut es überdies, indem sie der akuten Bedrängnis, die verbittert und stumm gemacht hatte, Anstöße zur Einsicht und Umkehr entnimmt. Und sie versucht es auch damit, daß sie der Geschichtstradition das Zeugnis sich durchhaltender Gotteshuld sowie den Aufschluß abringt, huldvolle Hilfe intendiere letztendlich Jahwes Lobpreisung.

The third and central section both begins and ends with a prayer for forgiveness and salvation (vv. 4-6 and 47).[32] The psalmist moves from 'me' (vv. 4-5) to 'we' (v. 6), 'a remarkable testimony of solidarity between the individual and nation',[33] indicating the importance of confession not only for the individual but also for the community as a whole. The opening and closing prayers 'frame' the narrative of Yahweh's previous saving activity in Israel's history, which functions as the grounds of confidence upon which the prayer for salvation rests.[34] The narration of Israel's story (vv. 7-46) includes nine episodes of rebellion, beginning with the exodus and extending to Judges. Common to all episodes is the fact that the people turn away from God or revolt against the God-appointed leaders.[35] However, these narratives illustrate Yahweh's generous forgiveness, which is based in the covenant and, more particularly, in his covenant loyalty (חסד). 'The theme throughout the psalm is clear. Israel has been chronically unfaithful … nonetheless God has repeatedly forgiven her and shown mercy.'[36] Therefore, Vette can argue that the fate of Israel does not depend upon their merit, but upon God's grace. Repentance happens after, and in response to, the gift of salvation. It is not that repentance leads to redemption but that redemption leads to repentance. Therefore, praise and repentance are not opposites, but are a two-fold appropriate response to the great deeds of God.[37]

Psalm 106 is a chronological narrative from v. 7 to v. 46; but, like Psalm 105, the structure can also be viewed chiastically. Robert Alden observes the following A B A' pattern:

A – 'Exhortation to praise' (1-5)

   B – 'Review of exodus rebellions' (6-46)

---

[32] The prayer (occurring as it does within a hymn) is 'quite exceptional' (Terrien, *The Psalms*, p. 731).

[33] Schaefer, *Psalms*, p. 262.

[34] Cf. Hossfeld, 'Psalm 106', pp. 88, 93.

[35] Joachim Vette, 'Psalm 106', in Oeming and, *Das Buch der Psalmen: Psalm 90-151*, p. 104.

[36] Schaefer, *Psalms*, p. 264.

[37] Vette, 'Psalm 106', p. 105, writes,

Gottes Heilsgeschichte mit Israel ist die Konsequenz seiner Bundesbeziehung mit seinem Volk. Es ist nicht das Verdienst des Volkes, dass sich sein Schicksal wendet; es ist allein Gottes Besinnung auf seine Gnade, die die Strafe enden lässt. Israels Buße geschieht nach dieser Erlösungstat als Reaktion auf die geschenkte Errettung. Nicht Buße führt zur Erlösung, sondern Erlösung führt zur Buße.

A' – 'Prayer and benediction' (47-48).

Alden also observes the repetition of a number of key words, such as 'salvation', 'Hallelujah', 'nation', 'give thanks', 'praise', 'forever', and 'people'; but he does not arrange the repetitions into a chiastic pattern.[38] Similarly, J.P. Fokkelman notes that the 'opening and closing stanzas form a clear inclusion'.[39]

Using explicit lexical parallels found in the psalm, I propose the following chiastic structure:

A – Praise Yah הללויה (v. 1)
  B – Forever לעולם (v. 1)
    C – Praise תהלה (v. 2)
      D – Prayer for salvation ישע (v. 4)
        E – They did not remember (זכר) God's רב חסד (v. 7)
          F – Rebellion by Red Sea מרה (v. 7)
            G – Enemies איב (vv. 8-12)
              H – They forgot God's works מעשה (vv. 13-15)
                I – Their jealousy of Moses משה (vv. 16-18)
                  J – Moses stood up עמד (vv. 19-23)
                    K – Despised pleasant land ארץ (v. 24)
                      L – Grumbling in their tents
                        באהליהם (v. 25)
                      L' – Falling in the wilderness
                        במדבר (v. 26)
                    K' – Scattered to other lands ארץ (v. 27)
                  J' – Phinehas stood up עמד (vv. 28-31)
                I' – They provoked Moses משה (vv. 32-33)
              H' – Learned Canaanite works מעשה (vv. 34-40)
            G' – Enemies איב (vv. 41-42)
          F' – Rebellion in Judges מרה (v. 43)
        E' – God remembered (זכר) covenant and רב חסד (v. 45)
      D' – Prayer for salvation ישע (v. 47)
    C' – Praise תהלה (v. 47)
  B' – Forever לעולם (v. 48)
A' – Praise Yah הללו־יה (v. 48).

---

[38] Alden, 'Chiastic Psalms (III)', pp. 201-202.
[39] Jan P. Fokkelman, *Major Poems of the Hebrew Bible: At the Interface of Hermeneutics and Structural Analysis* (Studia Semitica Neerlandica 37; Assen, The Netherlands: Van Gorcum, 1998), p. 270.

My proposal for a chiastic structure bears some similarity to the outlines of both Pierre Auffret and Joachim Vette. Auffret proposes the following similar chiasm:

A – (vv. 1-5)
   B – (vv. 6-12)
      C – (vv. 13-15)
         D – (vv. 16-18)
            E – (vv. 19-23)
               F – (vv. 24-26)
            E' – (vv. 28-31)
         D' – (vv. 32-33)
      C' – (vv. 34-42)
   B' – (vv. 43-46)
A' – (vv. 47-48).[40]

Vette's understanding of the structure is very close to that of Auffret. Vette proposes the following outline:

vv. 1-5:   Call for praise and thanks
vv. 6-12:   Rescued from their enemies
vv. 13-15:   Disobedience in the wilderness
vv. 16-18:   Rebellion in the wilderness camp
vv. 19-22:   Idolatry at Horeb
v. 23:   Intercession by Moses
vv. 24-27:   Refusal of the Promised Land
vv. 28-29:   Iniquity at Baal-Peor
vv. 30-31:   Intercession by Phinehas
vv. 32-33:   Provocation in Meriba
vv. 34-39:   Disobedience in the taking of the land
vv. 40-42:   Punishment from God
vv. 43-46:   Punishment and confirmation of the covenant
v. 47:   Final doxology of the Psalm
v. 48:   Final doxology of Book IV of Psalms.[41]

Although Vette does not present his outline in the form of a chiasm, it clearly bears the marks of a chiasm, as may be seen in this slightly

---

[40] Pierre Auffret, "'Afin que nous rendions grâce à ton nom'": Étude structurelle du Psaume 106', *Studi Epigrafici e Linguitici* 11 (1994), pp. 75-96.
[41] Vette, 'Psalm 106', p. 104.

modified version of his structure that closely resembles Auffret's outline and my own proposed chiastic structure:

> A – Call for praise and thanks (vv. 1-5)
>> B – Rescued from their enemies (vv. 6-12)
>>> C – Disobedience in the desert (vv. 13-15)
>>>> D – Rebellion against Moses (vv. 16-18)
>>>>> E – Intercession by Moses (vv. 19-23)
>>>>>> F – Refusal of the Promised Land (vv. 24-27)
>>>>> E' – Intercession by Phinehas (vv. 28-31)
>>>> D' – Provocation of Moses (vv. 32-33)
>>> C' – Disobedience in the taking of the land (vv. 34-40)
>> B' – Turned over to their enemies (vv. 41-46)
> A' – Doxology (vv. 47-48)

Although similar to both Auffret's and Vette's outlines, my proposal is more detailed and relies on the parallels of specific Hebrew vocabulary. The lexical parallels in the chiastic structure of Psalm 106 highlight a number of key elements that can easily get lost in the lengthy story of Israel's failures. As was the case with Psalm 105, the chiastic structure of Psalm 106 highlights a number of key elements that can easily get lost in the lengthy story of Israel's failures.

For example, the prayers for salvation (D and D' in my proposed structure) are based upon Yahweh's חסד (E and E'), which might be translated as 'mercy', 'loyalty', or 'covenant commitment'.[42] The theological paradigm is the exodus, which emphasizes Yahweh's attentive response to Israel's cries. Although the exodus itself is not mentioned at the end of Psalm 106, the language of vv. 44-45 recalls the exodus motif: Yahweh 'saw'; Yahweh 'heard'; and Yahweh 'remembered his covenant' (Exod. 2.24-25). Richard Nysse writes,

> The psalmist places the reader at the pivot of Exod 2:23-25. Only now, this is not just past narration. There is a direct move to the present, coming in the form of a petition: 'Save us, O LORD our God, and gather us from among the nations' (106:47). In a sense, Ps 106 calls for a new exodus.[43]

---

[42] Goldingay, *Psalms*, III, p. 219, translates חסד simply as 'commitment'. For a helpful discussion of חסד, see Kraus, *Theology of the Psalms*, p. 44.
[43] Richard William Nysse, 'Retelling the Exodus', *Word & World* 33.2 (2013), p. 165.

Within the section that details Israel's unfaithfulness during the time of the judges (vv. 34-40), Auffret has uncovered still another overlapping layer of chiastic structure:[44]

> A – Yahweh (v. 34)
>   B – their deeds (v. 35)
>   C – idols (v. 36)
>   D – they sacrificed (v. 37)
>   E – sons and daughters (v. 37)
>   F – blood (v. 38)
>   F' – blood (v. 38)
>   E' – sons and daughters (v. 38)
>   D' – sacrificed (v. 38)
>   C' – idols (v. 38)
>   B' – their deeds (v. 39)
> A' – Yahweh (v. 40)

As Allen points out, the chiasm in vv. 34-40 'accentuates the Canaanization of Israel' as a decisive element in Yahweh's choice to punish Israel with exile.[45]

Returning to my chiastic outline, we observe that the sins of Israel are characterized as 'rebellion' (מרה) (F and F'), which 'implies a conscious and willful attitude, [and] calls attention to the active, subjective participation of the person in his/her position'.[46] Even though Israel is rebellious throughout the narrative, both Moses and Phinehas perform heroic actions by 'standing up' against the evil (J and J').[47] The metaphor of 'standing up' (עמד) pictures Moses and Phinehas entering the breach 'like a brave soldier defending a town from an enemy who wishes to penetrate through an opening in the wall'.[48] Psalm 106, therefore,

---

[44] Auffret, 'Étude structurelle du Psaume 106', pp. 75-96.

[45] Allen, *Psalms 101-150*, p. 68.

[46] *TLOT*, I, p. 687. Dahood, *Psalms*, III, p. 75, unwisely repoints the verb, changing its root from מרה to מרר and translates it as 'hardened'.

[47] Rolf Jacobson, 'Psalm 106', in DeClaissé-Walford, Jacobson, and Tanner, *The Book of Psalms*, p. 803, observes that the psalm 'introduces a new theme here, the theme of the importance of the agency of the ancestral leaders'.

[48] Gili Kugler, 'The Dual Role of Historiography in Psalm 106: Justifying the Present Distress and Demonstrating the Individual's Potential Contribution', *ZAW* 126.4 (2014), p. 550.

gives the office of the intercessor a significant place in God's relation to his sinful people. God answers when he hears the cry that that they lift up on behalf of sinners (v. 44). The psalm itself in its closing petition is such a cry of an intercessor on behalf of his congregation and people.[49]

Kugler suggests that the psalm may be calling for intercessors who will, like Moses and Phinehas, stand up to exilic challenges and bring salvation to Israel.[50]

The role of Moses is emphasized in the chiasm, inasmuch as two episodes of the story center on either jealousy towards Moses or the provocation of Moses (I and I'). Inasmuch as Book IV begins with a psalm attributed to Moses (90) and ends with a psalm that highlights Moses, the Mosaic emphasis of Book IV stands out. Therefore, Erich Zenger has argued that Psalms 90-106 have a Pentateuchal orientation, emphasizing the role of Moses over David within Israel's story.[51]

Yahweh's punishment of Israel in the form of the exile comes into focus by the reference to Israel's rejection of the 'pleasant land' and by the reference to Israel's being scattered to foreign lands (K and K'). At the center of the chiasm we find further expansion on the reason for the punishment of Israel (both in the wilderness and in the exile) in their refusal to obey God and enter the promised land (Numbers 13-14), a decision that marked the turning point in the book of Numbers (cf. Deut. 1.26-27). Because of Israel's unbelief there, Yahweh swore 'to make them fall in the wilderness' and 'scatter them' among the nations (vv. 26-27). Gili Kugler argues, therefore, that the psalmist views the rebellion in the wilderness as the reason

---

[49] Mays, *Psalms*, p. 343.

[50] Kugler, 'The Dual Role of Historiography in Psalm 106', p. 552.

[51] Zenger, 'The God of Israel's Reign', pp. 165, 186. A similar argument is presented by Gerald H. Wilson, 'Shaping the Psalter: A Consideration of Editorial Linkage in the Book of Psalms', in J. Clinton McCann, Jr (ed.), *Shape and Shaping of the Psalter* (JSOTSup 159; Sheffield: JSOT Press, 1993), pp. 72-80 (75-76). See also Jerome F.D. Creach, 'The Shape of Book Four of the Psalter and the Shape of Second Isaiah', *JSOT* 80 (1998), p. 65; and Krista Mournet, 'Moses and the Psalms: The Significance of Psalms 90 and 106 within Book IV of the Masoretic Psalter', *Conversations with the Biblical World* 31 (2011), pp. 66-79. For a critique of Zenger and Wilson, see Lindsay Wilson, 'On Psalms 103–106 as a Closure to Book IV of the Psalter', in E. Zenger (ed.), *Composition of the Book of Psalms* (Bibliotheca Ephemeridum Theologicarum Lovaniensium 238; Leuven: Uitgeverij Peeters, 2010), pp. 755-68.

for the 40 years of wandering and as a nascent cause for the later Babylonian exile.[52]

As is shown above, the idolatry of the Judges period contributes to Israel's downfall (vv. 34-44), but the sins that characterized the monarchy, reported throughout 1 and 2 Kings, are not mentioned in Psalm 106. In fact, the monarchy is not mentioned at all in the psalm.[53] The failure to mention the monarchic period may suggest that an early version of the psalm existed, perhaps, in the Davidic period but was later adapted to speak to the exilic audience.

Hearing Psalm 106

Based upon Yahweh's covenant faithfulness in the past, Israel is given the courage and faith to plead for forgiveness in their present context, which appears to be the Babylonian exile (v. 47). This version of Israel's story is filled with their repeated violations of their covenant commitment to Yahweh; but despite Israel's continued rebellion, Yahweh's covenant loyalty endures and Israel is saved time and again. Thus, Judith Gärtner writes, 'On the basis of his חסד JHWH turns to his people again and again like at the Red Sea and thereby allows for a continuation of Israel's history'.[54] Therefore, Psalm 106 is 'a testimony to the fidelity of the Lord in being forgiving, merciful, and faithful to the covenant in spite of Israel's persistent sin'.[55] As in Psalm 105, Yahweh's saving action is initiated when Yahweh remembers 'his covenant' (v. 45). Scott Ellington remarks, 'The function of this historical recital, then, was to motivate God to forgive in the present based on his long track record as a forgiving God'.[56]

Normally, prayers for repentance take the form that we call lament, but not here. Although Psalm 106 does not take the form of a lament, it functions in much the same way as a lament. Thus, there

---

[52] Kugler, 'The Dual Role of Historiography in Psalm 106', p. 547. Kugler (p. 548) argues further that Ezekiel predates Psalm 106 and that the psalmist copied from Ezek. 20.23, which reads, 'Nevertheless, I lifted my hand in the desert that I would scatter them among the nations and disperse them throughout the lands'.

[53] Goldingay, however, views the repeated cycles of rebellion (v. 43) as having reference to 'Judges, Kings and Chronicles' (*Psalms*, III, p. 237).

[54] Judith Gärtner, 'The Torah in Psalm 106: Interpretations of JHWH's Saving Act at the Red Sea', in Zenger (ed.), *Composition of the Book of Psalms*, pp. 479-88 (485).

[55] Jacobson, 'Psalm 106', p. 796.

[56] Ellington, 'The Reciprocal Reshaping of History and Experience in the Psalms', p. 25.

are different ways to pray for mercy. It is clear that the community is suffering on account of their disobedience. This version of Israel's story creates an entirely different mood from the joyous version that is found in the previous psalm. From the more somber tone of Psalm 106, the hearer would be expected to experience feelings of grief and sorrow over Israel's past transgressions. Also, the hearer might be moved toward personal humility toward God and might experience deep gratitude for God's gifts of grace and mercy. A community that hears Psalm 106 would be reminded of its own story, which undoubtedly would include times of failure that, in turn, would demand repentance.

Psalm 106 is a valuable resource for both the individual and the community of faith and should be read whenever there is a need for God's mercy and salvation. Leslie Allen writes, 'There is a Lenten feel about this psalm for Christian readers, who look back to the cross as a signpost both to the dark reality of human sin and to the saving love of the Father and Son'.[57] John Goldingay suggests that 'the declining church in the United States' should 'consider the implications of these earlier stories, which illustrate the pattern Ps. 106 finds in Israel's story'.[58] This psalm moves the heart toward confession and repentance; and those who hear Psalm 106 are confident that God will forgive, inasmuch as it portrays God as one who in the past has been longsuffering, kind, and merciful to a rebellious people.[59]

The Value of Story

To some degree, the entire Psalter functions as Israel's testimony to the character and acts of God.[60] Two types of psalms, however, are more explicitly testimonial in nature: 1. the thanksgiving psalms and 2. the psalms of historical recital. The thanksgiving psalms recount specific occasions when God intervened in the life of the psalmist to

---

[57] Allen, *Psalms 101-150*, p. 74.

[58] Goldingay, *Psalms*, III, p. 240.

[59] Cf. Hossfeld, 'Psalm 106', p. 95, who writes, 'The psalm carries confidence of rescue from the end of the psalm to its beginning'.

[60] In his Old Testament theology, Walter Brueggemann presents the entire OT as a collection of testimonies regarding Yahweh. The testimonies are generated by what are commonly called the various 'traditions'. See Walter Brueggemann, *Theology of the Old Testament: Testimony, Dispute, Advocacy* (Minneapolis, MN: Fortress Press, 1997).

bring help to either the individual or to the community.[61] Normally, this divine intervention was in response to the psalmist's cry for help as found in the psalms of lament. The psalms of historical recital, however, give more attention to Israel's corporate story and testify to God's saving activity in the history of Israel. This type of psalm bears close similarities to what we call the hymns and may even be classified as a hymn or as an expansion of the hymn type. Like Psalms 105 and 106, the hymns normally begin with a call to worship and end with a renewed call to worship. An important implication of the calls to worship in Psalms 105 and 106 is that these testimonies (like others in the Psalter) are performed in the context of worship.[62]

The themes of the hymns and the psalms of historical recital are similar and may include creation, God's sovereignty, the exodus, and God's care for the needy. In the hymns, therefore, the motive for praise often includes a reference to the exodus, but the psalms of historical recital are presented as a broader narrative that may reach back to the creation (cf. Psalm 136) and may extend forward into the monarchy (cf. Psalm 78).

Like the prose narratives of the Old Testament, the psalms of historical recital are articulations of Israel's theology,[63] but the psalms are narrative theology set forth in the literary form of lyric poetry. The Psalms, therefore, are sung theology. Thus, Goldingay can write of Psalm 105, 'It is thus teaching; but it is also worship'.[64] The psalms of historical recital teach us that theological truth can be learned, taught, handed down, and understood in light of experience. Robert Cate argues that revelation is transmitted through the singing of Psalms 105 and 106 because 'The mighty acts of God reveal the God of the mighty acts'.[65] Knowledge of God is more than propositional truth; it is relational truth. Scott Ellington adds, 'Testimony in the

---

[61] Scott A. Ellington, 'The Costly Loss of Testimony', *JPT* 16 (2000), pp. 48-59, explores the kinds of testimony offered in the psalms of thanksgiving. Ellington argues that thanksgiving (i.e. testimony) and lament are 'two sides of the same coin' (pp. 50-51). See also Ellington, 'The Reciprocal Reshaping of History and Experience in the Psalms', pp. 28-31, in which Ellington elaborates on the nature of Scripture as testimony.

[62] Scott A. Ellington, '"Can I Get a Witness": The Myth of Pentecostal Orality and the Process of Traditioning in the Psalms', *JPT* 20.1 (2011), pp. 9-14.

[63] Goldingay, *Psalms*, III, p. 217, states that Psalm 105 'does on a small scale what the great OT narrative works do on a large scale'.

[64] Goldingay, *Psalms*, III, p. 203.

[65] Cate, 'Psalm 105: The Mighty Acts of God', p. 50.

Psalms is an act of traditioning in which Israel's story is brought into the present, experienced anew, and projected into the future'.[66] The God of Psalms 105 and 106 is a God who is deeply invested in the life of his people and who responds to their prayers, their cries, their praises, and their worship. God intervenes with signs and wonders, and God intervenes with forgiveness and healing. In the same way that Psalms 105 and 106 display Hebrew theology, our own testimonies will reveal our theology.

Hearing Early Pentecostal Testimonies

The periodical literature demonstrates that early Pentecostals were not averse to sharing testimonies that resembled both Psalm 105 and Psalm 106. I will share brief excerpts from testimonies that fall into each category. In a testimony entitled 'Pentecost in Spokane, Wash', M.L. Ryan celebrates the advent of revival:

> God began to work in Pentecostal power. Souls were saved and sanctified and baptized with the Holy Ghost, and healed in body … Over one hundred souls have been saved, cleansed, and baptized with the Holy Ghost and fire, and the work has passed beyond all bounds or keeping track of same.[67]

In 'Further News from Nyack, New York', A.W. Vian reports on the Annual Council of the Christian and Missionary Alliance and testifies to the following: '[We witnessed] the marvelous workings of the Holy Ghost as never seen here … Meetings ran on day and night for nearly a week without human leadership, no thought of time, trains, meals, sleep, etc.'[68] Hundreds of other examples of celebratory testimony could be cited from the periodical literature.

Early Pentecostal writers also spoke of their struggles and their failures. The troubling experience of early Pentecostal leader G.B. Cashwell is well known. Cashwell testifies to his process of 'crucifixion' that prepared him to overcome his racism and submit to the leadership of William Seymour, the African-American pastor at the Azusa St. Mission. Cashwell writes,

---

[66] Ellington, 'The Reciprocal Reshaping of History and Experience in the Psalms', p. 28.

[67] *AF* 1.7 (Apr. 1907), p. 4.

[68] *HG* 3.11, p. 6.

As soon as I reached Azusa Mission, a new crucifixion began in my life and I had to die to many things, but God gave me the victory. The first altar call I went forward in earnest for my Pentecost. I struggled from Sunday till Thursday. While seeking in an upstairs room in the Mission, the Lord opened up the windows of heaven in the light of God began to flow over me in such a power as never before.[69]

A testimony attributed to 'A Worker' described the following struggle under the heading, 'Arrested for Jesus' Sake':

I came from Frisco to Los Angeles five days after the earthquake and heard about these Pentecostal people … At first I opposed and openly fought them and said it was the devil. The result was I backslid altogether and had to go back and ask forgiveness and do my first works over again, even down to having the devils cast out of me. Afterward I received pardon and the cleansing blood again through fasting and prayer and much study of the word.[70]

Early Pentecostal self-revelatory testimonies confirm the value of seeing Psalms 105 and 106 as models for Pentecostal testimony. For the sake of our children and for the sake of the Pentecostal movement, we must be willing to tell the whole story.

Hearing Psalms 105 and 106 Together

Psalms 105 and 106 tell the same story from very different perspectives. Psalm 105 includes no consideration of a rebellious Israel; but Psalm 106 considers little else. Jacobson writes that 'whereas Psalm 105 *accentuates* the positive … Psalm 106 *eliminates* the positive'.[71] Terrien argues that Psalms 105 and 106 'contradict and yet complete each other in the dialectic of sin and grace'.[72] I would state it differently and suggest that each of these two psalms is one-sided, telling the story from a single vantage point. Psalm 105 is the story of powerful miracles and great victories, but Psalm 106 is the story of miserable failures and deep disappointments. Each psalm has its purpose, and each can speak to the Church within certain situations.

---

[69] *AF* 1.4 (Dec. 1906), p. 2.
[70] *AF* 1.4 (Dec. 1906), p. 3.
[71] Jacobson, 'Psalm 106', p. 796 (emphasis original).
[72] Terrien, *The Psalms*, p. 733.

The juxtaposition of the two psalms creates a theological tension that we might be inclined to alleviate through an artificial blending of the two perspectives into one, more 'balanced' theology. However, the tension should be maintained because there are occasions that benefit from one perspective.[73]

What do we learn from seeing these two stories side-by-side? First, Psalms 105 and 106 offer two kinds of testimony for two different contexts. Psalm 105 is a celebration of Yahweh's mighty works, and Psalm 106 is a prayer for Yahweh's mercy. We need to hear the optimistic testimony of Psalm 105, especially when we are facing challenges and difficulties.[74] Nevertheless, when we are living well, it is dangerous only to focus on the positive to the exclusion of our own failings. Therefore, we need both Psalm 105 and 106. There are dangers in singing Psalm 105 alone: 1. It can produce unrealistic and unbelievable expectations. 2. It does not prepare the Church for God's discipline. 3. It can lead to false sense of security. 4. It invites self-confident boasting. 5. It can produce triumphalism and spiritual elitism ('We are the chosen'). 6. It can create an environment that invites disastrous failure and subsequent denial.[75] Our children and new converts need to know the whole truth or else they will develop a false view of the Christian life and will eventually become discouraged because they cannot live up to that illusion.

These dangers can be avoided by occasionally singing Psalm 106, a psalm that mocks our triumphalism and crushes our self-confidence.[76] However, if we sing only Psalm 106, we open ourselves to a different but still unhealthy version of the faith. By itself and in the wrong context, Psalm 106 might lead us to believe that obedience is

---

[73] Goldingay, *Psalms*, III, p. 203, observes the incompleteness of the narrative in Psalm 105, inasmuch as there is no reference to Sinai or the wilderness wanderings: 'the people go straight from Egypt to Canaan'. Goldingay adds that the psalm is 'oriented to meet the worshippers' needs in a particular context'. Cf. Richard William Nysse, 'Retelling the Exodus', *Word & World* 33.2 (2013), 165.

[74] For example, Goldingay, *Psalms*, III, p. 218, suggests that Psalm 105 would be a liberating message 'in the time of Ezra or Nehemiah'.

[75] Terrien, *The Psalms*, p. 725, asserts that Psalm 105 may represent the 'pious nationalism' and self-assuredness of Jeremiah's enemies. Jacobson, 'Psalm 106', p. 807, adds that 'the history of God's people must never become a glorious narrative of triumph'.

[76] Cf. Terrien, *The Psalms*, p. 733, who writes, 'Unlike Psalm 105, this psalm rejects nationalism as a caricature of patriotism that hides collective guilt. The psalmist has been nourished by the realism and honest of the great prophets, from Amos and Hosea to Isaiah and Micah, and above all from Jeremiah.'

impossible, holiness can be attained only in heaven, continual failure is inevitable, and living under the cloud of God's judgment is our unavoidable destiny – a fatalistic and depressing version of Christianity indeed.

Second, despite their differences, Psalms 105 and 106 share an underlying theology. To put it in the words of Hossfeld, they 'draw on the same strand'.[77] In addition to the common narrative content regarding the patriarchs, the exodus, and the conquest of Canaan, they contain a number of other lexical parallels. Both psalms refer to Israel as Yahweh's 'chosen' (105.6, 43; 106.5), and both psalms ground Yahweh's saving activity in the 'covenant' with Abraham, which Yahweh 'remembered' (105.8, 9, 10, 42; 106.45). Furthermore, in both psalms the acts of Yahweh are described as 'wonders' (105.2, 5; 106.7, 22). Based upon these similarities, Walther Zimmerli states,

> [I]n the praise of God the two statements are profoundly joined: the magnifying of the unshakable covenant loyalty of YHWH and the public confession of the sinfulness of the history of the people of God, in which its individual members also know themselves to be involved. This sinfulness leads to a depth out of which only the miracle of God's faithfulness toward his covenant promise can save. The one does not wish to be heard without the other.[78]

Third, Psalms 105 and 106 reflect something about the nature of Scripture. The Bible presents the one story of God and the world (the unity of Scripture) in a variety of ways (the diversity of Scripture) in order to speak a message to believers in different contexts and situations (the ongoing dynamic of the Spirit-Word).

Fourth, these psalms are a reminder that every story is told from a certain perspective and with a certain agenda.[79] Whether the narrative is found in the Bible, a Church history textbook, a personal journal, a denominational publication, a Church bulletin, or an oral testimony, the story will represent a certain perspective that determines what is included and what is omitted.

---

[77] Hossfeld, 'Psalm 106', p. 95.

[78] Zimmerli, 'Zwillingspsalmen', pp. 261-71. Cited in Hossfeld, 'Psalm 106', p. 75.

[79] On the ideological motivations for the shaping of Israel's historical narratives, see Ellington, 'The Reciprocal Reshaping of History and Experience in the Psalms', pp. 18-31. Nysse, 'Retelling the Exodus', p. 157, applies this point to the book of Exodus, arguing that Exodus, too, is a biased account of the exodus.

Fifth, these psalms suggest a way forward when reflecting upon the complex history of Christianity in general and the Pentecostal movement more specifically. On the one hand, our critics are eager to expose our weaknesses and display the skeletons from our closets; but, on the other hand, we may be tempted to sanitize our history and deny that any failures ever existed. Whenever a tradition makes claims to being the 'true' Church, it must then guard its reputation and issue denials regarding any questionable practices or behavior. Israel claims to have been chosen by God as his own special possession, yet their scriptures include not only their successes but also their failures. Similarly, the failures of any Christian tradition do not necessarily disqualify that tradition from participation in God's kingdom.

Sadly, many of our own scholars, pastors, and laity have succumbed to the criticisms of the Pentecostal movement and have abandoned the tradition. They discard the 'undesirable' elements of Pentecostalism, but in doing so, they have often discarded the heart and soul of Pentecostal theology and spirituality as well. Wade Phillips' new history of the Church of God uncovers a number of embarrassing moments in the Pentecostal story, but I believe that the whole story should be told.[80] May God forgive our transgressions just as he forgave Israel's transgressions.

Finally, the canonical placement of Psalms 105 and 106 highlights links to the surrounding psalms. Psalm 104 speaks of God's mighty works in creation, a subject that leads naturally to Psalm 105, which relates God's mighty works in the exodus. Psalms 105, 106, and 107 all begin with 'Praise the LORD', and both Psalms 106 and 107 add, '... for he is good; his covenant loyalty is everlasting'. Moreover, as will be noted in the next chapter's discussion, Psalm 107.3 ('gathered from the lands') answers the prayer of Ps. 106.47 ('gather us from among the nations'). Thus, Psalms 105-107 speak powerfully to the exiles and to all who are landless.

---

[80] Wade H. Phillips, *Quest to Restore God's House: A Theological History of the Church of God (Cleveland, Tennessee), Vol. I 1886-1923, R.G. Spurling to A.J. Tomlinson, Formation-Transformation-Reformation* (Cleveland, TN: CPT Press, 2015).

5

PSALM 107: THE GRATITUDE OF THE REDEEMED[1]

Introduction

The last public speech of Martin Luther King Jr demonstrated his consummate skill as a communicator. King's masterful rhetoric captivated multitudes and changed the course of history. From the pulpit of Mason Temple in Memphis, TN, Dr King concluded his remarks with the following declaration:

> … somewhere I read of the freedom of assembly. Somewhere I read of the freedom of speech. Somewhere I read of the freedom of press. Somewhere I read that the greatness of America is the right to protest for rights. So just as I say we aren't going to let any dogs or water hoses turn us around, we aren't going to let any injunction turn us around.
>
> Well I don't know what will happen now. We've got some difficult days ahead. But it really doesn't matter to me now because I've been to the mountaintop. And I don't mind. Like anybody, I would like to live a long life, longevity has its place. But I'm not concerned about that now. I just want to do God's will. And he's allowed me to go up to the mountain, and I've looked over, and I've seen the promised land. I may not get there with you, but I want you to know tonight that we as a people will get to the

---

[1] This chapter was my Presidential Address to the Society for Pentecostal Studies, delivered at the society's annual meeting in Springfield, MO, 2014.

promised land. So I'm happy tonight; I'm not worried about anything; I'm not fearing any man. 'Mine eyes have seen the glory of the coming of the Lord.'[2]

Although Dr. King is not the subject of this chapter, his speeches and writings illustrate the fact that the shaping of a community's worldview, ethics, opinions, and theology is influenced by both logical reasoning and affective desire. King illustrates this point because a significant component of his speeches and writings is the affective dimension of his argument – his appeal to the hearts and passions of the hearers. The genius of King's approach lies in his unequalled ability to address both the mind and the heart as he alternates between impeccable logic and emotional appeal. As shown in Chapter 9 of this monograph, early Pentecostals also appealed to both reason and to the affections in their use of the Psalms, an approach that is consistent with the rhetoric of the Psalms themselves, which combine both logical and affective argumentation.

King was not the first, and he was not the last, to combine appeals to both reason and affection in order to create a holistic argument. I might have used an excerpt from a political campaign speech, a beer commercial, or a clip from cable news. All of these means of communication take advantage of the human tendency to choose and act according to desire rather than reason. The basic affections of humanity, love, gratitude, hope, hate, fear, belonging, intimacy, purpose, are instruments used in the media to produce a change of attitude, will, or behavior in their audience. Advertisements, for example, create desire. Apple CEO Steve Jobs remarked that 'people don't know what they want until you show it to them'.[3]

---

[2] This excerpt from Martin Luther King's speech can be viewed here: http://youtu.be/YB4bV34G17g or here: http://youtu.be/bvQEhAhjUnA. A better example of King's approach to rhetoric (but not available on video) is his 'Letter from Birmingham Jail', which is perhaps his finest literary achievement and most profound defense of his nonviolent program. Its full text is included in Martin Luther King, *Why We Can't Wait* (New York: Harper & Row, 1964), pp. 64-84. See my literary study of the 'Letter': Lee Roy Martin, 'Letter from Birmingham Jail', in Laurence W. Mazzeno (ed.), *Masterplots II: Christian Literature* (12 Vols., Pasadena, CA: Salem Press, 4th edn, 2010), VI, pp. 3200-3202, available at http://www.leeroymartin.com/CPT/LRM_Writings.html.

[3] Steve Jobs and George W. Beahm, *I, Steve: Steve Jobs, in His Own Words* (Chicago, IL: Agate, 2011), p. 1997.

I could have chosen examples from ancient writers such as Demosthenes, Cicero, Gorgias,[4] or Aristotle,[5] who made use of affective language in their speeches. I could have cited modern leaders who used affective appeal as a key component of their arguments – people like Theodore Roosevelt, Winston Churchill, Indira Ghandi, John F. Kennedy, Nelson Mandela, Shirley Chisholm, and, on the negative front, Adolf Hitler. The biblical writers, like other authors before them and after them, combined both logical and affective argumentation.

When I speak of the affections, I mean more than 'emotions'.[6] Emotions are temporary responses to surrounding stimuli, but affections are lasting dispositions, our deepest desires. Pentecostal theologian Dale Coulter writes, 'As innate dispositions, the affections are movements that arise from human nature and also form it in particular ways as persons habituate themselves to this or that set of objects'.[7] However, emotions and affections are vitally connected – the affections often generate emotions; emotions can be indicators of the affections; and the affections can be stirred by emotional appeals.[8] Steven Jack Land, in his ground-breaking work, *Pentecostal Spirituality*, argued that the affections of 'gratitude as praise-thanksgiving, compassion as love-longing, and courage as confidence-hope'[9] form the

---

[4] The Greek rhetorician Gorgias (c. 485-380 BCE) argued that 'the function of an orator is not logical demonstration so much as emotional presentation that will stir the audience's will to believe' (George Alexander Kennedy, *Classical Rhetoric & Its Christian & Secular Tradition from Ancient to Modern Times* [Chapel Hill: University of North Carolina Press, 1999], p. 36).

[5] Cf. Eugene Garver, *Aristotle's Rhetoric: An Art of Character* (Chicago: University of Chicago Press, 1994), pp. 104-38.

[6] See the discussions above on pp. 12-13 and 25-30.

[7] Dale M. Coulter, 'The Whole Gospel for the Whole Person: Ontology, Affectivity, and Sacramentality', *PNEUMA* 35.2 (2013), p. 157.

[8] Theologians, scientists, and psychologists have not agreed upon the definitions of 'emotion' and 'affections', and they have not determined the exact connection between the two. My approach is stated above; however, my argument does not require a precise formulation of this connection. See Thomas Dixon, *From Passions to Emotions: The Creation of a Secular Psychological Category* (Cambridge: Cambridge University Press, 2003); Monica Greco and Paul Stenner, *Emotions: A Social Science Reader* (New York: Routledge, 2008); and Gregory S. Clapper, 'Affections', in Joel B. Green (ed.), *Dictionary of Scripture and Ethics* (Grand Rapids, MI: Baker Academic, 2011), pp. 44-45.

[9] Land, *Pentecostal Spirituality*, p. 47.

'integrating center' of Pentecostal spirituality.[10] John Christopher Thomas names five affections that correspond broadly to the elements of the Fivefold Gospel: Salvation/Gratitude, Sanctification/Compassion, Spirit Baptism/Courage, Healing/Joy, Return of Jesus/Hope. He writes,

> While it is possible to construe the relationship between the elements of the five-fold and the transformation of the affections differently, these should serve to illustrate the point that the Pentecostal interpreter's formation within the worshipping Pentecostal community, not only opens one up to interpretive possibilities based on his or her experience, but also has a deeply transforming impact upon the interpreter's affections, which itself orients the interpretive process for the Pentecostal interpreter.[11]

Consequently, according to Wolfgang Vondey, 'Pentecostal scholarship arises from the affections rather than intellectual ability. The emphasis on love, passion, desire, feeling, or emotion rejects the sole rule of the intellect while attempting to integrate the right affections' with the right thinking and the right practices.[12]

Recognizing the complex argumentation found in the biblical text, James Muilenburg challenged biblical scholars to move beyond the methodology of form criticism and to pursue rhetorical criticism.[13] Rhetoric, according to Aristotle, 'may be defined as a faculty of

---

[10] Land, *Pentecostal Spirituality*, pp. 50, 52, 63. See also, Steven J. Land, 'A Passion for the Kingdom: Revisioning Pentecostal Spirituality', *JPT* 1 (1992), pp. 34-35.

[11] John Christopher Thomas, '"What the Spirit Is Saying to the Church": The Testimony of a Pentecostal in New Testament Studies', in Kevin L. Spawn and Archie T. Wright (eds.), *Spirit and Scripture: Exploring a Pneumatic Hermeneutic* (New York: T & T Clark, 2012), p. 117. For more on a theological approach to the affections, see Gregory S. Clapper, *John Wesley on Religious Affections: His Views on Experience and Emotion and Their Role in the Christian Life and Theology* (Metuchen, NJ: Scarecrow Press, 1989), and Daniel Castelo, 'Tarrying on the Lord: Affections, Virtues and Theological Ethics in Pentecostal Perspective', *JPT* 13.1 (2004), pp. 31-56.

[12] Wolfgang Vondey, *Pentecostalism: A Guide for the Perplexed* (New York: T & T Clark, 2013), p. 139. He adds,

> ... arising from the pursuit of affective knowledge, Pentecostal scholarship is dominated by the imagination rather than reason ... The imagination stands in contrast to the dominance of reason and order; it is more improvisational, more playful than the productivity, performance, and instrumentality demanded by the established institutions, disciplines, languages, and methodologies of the modern academy (p. 139).

[13] James Muilenburg, 'Form Criticism and Beyond', *JBL* 88 (1969), pp. 1-18.

discovering all the possible means of persuasion on any subject', and those means include both *logos* (the rational) and *pathos* (the affective).[14] Similarly, rhetorical criticism as practiced by biblical scholars examines 'the literary artistry of a biblical book or biblical passage and ... the techniques that they used to manipulate their readers, to argue their case, and to persuade their audience of the validity of their argument'.[15]

Rhetorical criticism (sometimes called literary criticism) grew quickly in its appeal and is now recognized widely in the academy as a valuable approach to biblical studies.[16] However, despite the contemporary plethora of rhetorical studies, the affective argument of the text, what Aristotle called *pathos*, continues to be undervalued and generally avoided. I argue that the biblical writers adopted a rhetorical approach that took advantage of what they knew to be true about human dependence upon the affect as a constituent of the decision making process. Therefore, the affective dimension of biblical rhetoric, which has been viewed by critical biblical scholars as peripheral at best, should be taken seriously as a necessary ingredient of a complete exegetical and hermeneutical approach to the biblical text.

At this point I would offer two points of clarification. First, when biblical scholars encounter the word 'affective', they equate it with spiritualizing, preaching, subjectivism, confessional readings, allegory, and any variety of non-academic ways of approaching the Bible. My proposal, however, is not an affirmation of non-critical approaches, nor is it a move to create a new interpretational method, but it is limited to the argument that no matter what methods are used, an examination of the affective component of the text must be included as a part of the holistic interpretational process.

Second, although it is helpful (for the sake of argument) to distinguish between rational proofs and affective proofs, that distinction must not become absolute. Reason always includes an element of emotion and the affect is in part rational. Coulter explains,

> Affections are also movements of the rational soul and therefore have a cognitive dimension. Desire, joy, anger, fear, and other affective movements all relate to some object ... to view affections

---

[14] Aristotle and J.E.C. Welldon, *The Rhetoric of Aristotle* (London: Macmillan, 1886), p. 10.
[15] Eryl W. Davies, *Biblical Criticism* (London: T & T Clark, 2013), p. 108.
[16] Cf. Davies, *Biblical Criticism*, pp. 107-12.

in this way is to get back behind the view of emotions as involuntary, irrational feelings that emerged and then became dominant in the late 18th and 19th centuries …[17]

The Affective Nature of Humanity

Biblical scholarship has operated under the false assumption that humans are primarily rational creatures, but recent studies have demonstrated the contrary. Jonathan Haidt, after many years of clinical psychological research, argues that the affections, not reason, rule the human decision-making process. He insists that 'The worship of reason, which is sometimes found in philosophical and scientific circles, is a delusion'.[18] James K.A. Smith offers a similar assessment from a philosophical and theological perspective. Smith argues that humans are fundamentally affective rather than rational creatures, and that human behavior is ruled by the affections rather than by the mind.[19] He argues convincingly that the way humans 'inhabit the world is not primarily as thinkers, or even believers, but as more affective, embodied creatures'.[20]

The conclusions of Haidt and Smith suggest that the biblical writers would be expected to present their arguments in a holistic fashion that included both logical and affective proofs. Observation demonstrates that every biblical text includes an affective dimension, which may involve hope or despair, love or hate, trust or fear, admiration or scorn, pride or shame, to mention but a few examples, although the affective aspect varies in prominence from one text to another. The study of biblical literature, therefore, can benefit from an exegetical approach that appreciates the affective dimensions of the text. Takamitsu Muraoka insists that 'one ought not to dissociate form from

---

[17] Coulter, 'The Whole Gospel', p. 158. Closely related to the discussion of affectivity and deserving of an entire study, is the interpretation of biblical literature as art. Wayne C. Booth, *Modern Dogma and the Rhetoric of Assent* (Notre Dame, IN: University of Notre Dame Press, 1974), argues that art 'is of fundamental importance in making and changing our minds' (p. 168). He writes, 'We are what we have consumed; we take in whatever takes us in, and we are forever altered' (p. 167).

[18] Jonathan Haidt, *The Righteous Mind: Why Good People Are Divided by Politics and Religion* (New York: Pantheon Books, 2012), p. 107, cf. 34, 103. My thanks to Walter Brueggemann for pointing me to Haidt's book.

[19] Smith, *Desiring the Kingdom*.

[20] Smith, *Desiring the Kingdom*, p. 47.

meaning, for literary and rhetorical devices constitute part of the meaning and message'.[21]

Until now, scholars have attended to the rational approach, but newer approaches such as socio-linguistics, speech act theory, *Wirkungsgeschicte*, narrative criticism, and reader-oriented approaches all beg for something more than a hermeneutic focused on rational, logical ideas. My point is that no matter what critical method is used, whether it be historical-grammatical exegesis, sociological interpretation, ideological approaches, feminist approaches, contextual approaches, or ideological approaches, every aspect of the text should be considered, and the affective dimension is one aspect of the text.

An Opportunity for Pentecostal Scholars

Although the study of affective language is not a uniquely Pentecostal approach, Pentecostal scholars are in a good position to utilize their insights in this area, as has been demonstrated by Rickie D. Moore,[22] Larry McQueen,[23] and others.[24] The affective spirituality of Pentecostalism means that we come to the text with an openness and sensitivity to elements of text that other scholars may not perceive. Nevertheless, I recognize the dangers in advocating for an affective approach. Pentecostals are already caricatured as 'emotional', 'experience centered', and lacking in critical skills. It is likely that any appeal to affectivity will only add fuel to the fire. I respond to this objection with three assertions.

First, we should acknowledge God's gifts to us, and our scholarship should take full advantage of those gifts. It might be argued that

---

[21] T. Muraoka, 'Foreward', in L.J. de Regt *et al.*, *Literary Structure and Rhetorical Strategies in the Hebrew Bible* (Assen, The Netherlands: Van Gorcum, 1996), p. x.

[22] In his review of Rickie Moore's *The Spirit of the Old Testament*, Richard Israel observes, 'Perhaps the most significant aspect of the book is the consistent sensitivity to the affective dimension of the texts'. Richard D. Israel, 'Rickie D. Moore, *The Spirit of the Old Testament* (JPTSup 35; Blandford Forum, Uk: Deo Publishing, 2011)', *PNEUMA* 35.3 (2013), p. 449.

[23] McQueen, *Joel and the Spirit*.

[24] Baker, 'Pentecostal Bible Reading', pp. 95-108. John Christopher Thomas, *The Apocalypse: A Literary and Theological Commentary* (Cleveland, TN: CPT Press, 2012), pays close attention to the affective language of the Apocalypse. For my own contribution (outside the book of Psalms), see Lee Roy Martin, *Judging the Judges: Pentecostal Theological Perspectives on the Book of Judges* (Cleveland, TN: CPT Press, 2018), especially pp. 9-34, 57-74, 109-34.

we should avoid writing on Pentecostal topics because that is what others expect of us, and it feeds stereotypes. While I agree that Pentecostal topics and methods must not be our only contribution to the academy, we must share our riches with those outside our tradition. As Peter said, 'Silver and gold have I none, but such as I have I give to thee …' (Acts 3.2). Every tradition brings its own gifts to the theological discussion and those gifts must not be abandoned. I am not asking that we be sectarian, and I am not asking that we give our attention *only* to Pentecostal topics. Nevertheless, I am insisting that we must not withhold what God has given to us. God has given us eyes to see in Scripture what other scholars do not see. God has given us ears to hear what other scholars do not hear, and if we fail to testify of what we have seen and heard then we will fall short of our calling as scholars.[25]

Second, we will always face opposition, but so did our Pentecostal founders. We would not be here today if the disciples on the day of Pentecost had withdrawn into the shadows when faced with the criticism, 'these people are drunk' (Acts 2.13). Because the early disciples did not shrink back from sharing their newly found life in the Spirit, the Christian Church was born. We would not be here today if William Seymour had capitulated to the scorn and ridicule that was heaped upon him from nearly every direction. Because Seymour and his contemporaries did not retreat from their Pentecostal passion, they were able to revolutionize the twentieth-century Church. The question of Acts 2.12, 'What meaneth this?', is the question of biblical scholars, and just like in Acts 2, the answer can come only when the interpreters are filled with the Holy Spirit, a filling that generates newness, creativity, revelation, and wisdom.[26] Perhaps Pentecostal scholars will be able to transform the academy in the twenty-first century.

There will always be critics – biblical scholars live to criticize; and no matter what we do, we will be criticized. Therefore, I suggest that if we are to be criticized, let us be criticized for being constructive, engaging, vigorous, and creative rather than for being stale, accommodating, unimaginative, and docile. If Roger Stronstad had feared

---

[25] Cf. the oft-repeated comment of my good friend John Christopher Thomas: 'If we don't do it, who will?'

[26] See my 'Introduction to Pentecostal Biblical Hermeneutics', in Lee Roy Martin (ed.), *Pentecostal Hermeneutics: A Reader* (Leiden: Brill, 2013), pp. 1-10.

criticism, he would never have published his *Charismatic Theology of St. Luke*,[27] and we and the larger academy would have been much poorer.

Third, we must not underestimate the contemporary openness of some biblical scholars to new perspectives and creative approaches. The Society for Pentecostal Studies biblical studies interest group has seen this openness from notable biblical scholars who have engaged in dialogue with us, including Walter Brueggemann, Frederick Gaiser, Craig Koester, Richard Bauckham, Terence Fretheim, Mark Boda, Luke Timothy Johnson, and others. When I presented an earlier version of this chapter at the Annual Meeting of the Society of Biblical Literature, I was met with much agreement. Several of the listeners affirmed my thesis and offered examples where the affective aspect of the text (in both Old and New Testaments) could have an important impact on interpretation.

A few of my critics, however, have suggested to me that affectivity belongs not in biblical studies but in homiletics. I respond firstly to that assertion with a side note: I would to God that contemporary homiletics would include the affective, but I fear that rationalism has taken over most preaching as well. Educated preachers seem to be afraid(!) of affectivity. Most Western sermons focus upon the teaching of right doctrine and right practices to the exclusion of forming right affections, and other sermons are little more than self-help advice.[28] I respond secondly that the concern of biblical studies is the biblical text; and if the biblical text contains affective material, then affectivity must be a necessary part of biblical exegesis.

A Critical Approach to Affective Language

In the earlier chapter on Psalm 63 I described the affective approach in four steps (pp. 28-30). This chapter expands on the first point, which is to identify and acknowledge the affective dimension of the text along with its implications for interpretation. Every text includes an affective dimension, but the level of affective content varies from one text to another, depending upon the genre of the text in

---

[27] Roger Stronstad, *The Charismatic Theology of St. Luke* (Peabody, MA: Hendrickson, 1984).

[28] I realize that I have engaged in a bit of hyperbole for rhetorical effect. Recently, a number of homileticians have given significant attention to the affective dimension of preaching.

question. The highest concentration of affective language will be found, of course, in the poetic literature such as that found in the Psalms, the prophets, and the apocalyptic literature. The lowest concentration of affective language will be found in the narrative texts, but even the most simple narrative creates a certain tone to which the reader responds unconsciously.

The process of identifying the affective content of a text begins with locating any words or phrases whose content is explicitly affective. Words like 'love', 'hate', 'anger', 'desire', 'fear', 'hope', and 'gratitude' are affective by definition and are easily located. In addition to naming the explicitly affective terminology, the passage should be examined for more subtle indicators of affective tone.

Once the affective content of the text has been identified, it should be interpreted with the same care that is afforded to propositional or rational content. The goal is to determine how the tone may contribute to shaping the reader's perceptions of the text; that is, to determine how the implied reader (and/or readers from any specific reading community or context) might be influenced by the affective dimensions of the text. The reader's context will produce a bias (either conscious or unconscious) that also should be acknowledged critically in the interpretive process.

We will turn now to Psalm 107 and attempt to discern its affective dimension. In order to appreciate its impact, we should read the entire Psalm at once.

A Translation of Psalm 107

¹ Oh give thanks to Yahweh, for he is good;
    For his covenant loyalty is everlasting.

² Let the redeemed of Yahweh say so,
    Whom he has redeemed from the hand of the adversary,
³ And gathered from the lands, From the east and from the west,
    From the north and from the south.
⁴ They wandered in the wilderness in a desert region;
    They did not find a way to an inhabited city.
⁵ Hungry and thirsty;
    Their soul fainted within them.
⁶ Then they cried out to Yahweh in their trouble;

He delivered them out of their distresses.
⁷ He led them also by a straight way,
To go to an inhabited city.
⁸ Oh that they would thank Yahweh for his covenant loyalty,
And for his wonders to the children of humanity!
⁹ For he has satisfied the thirsty soul,
And the hungry soul he has filled with what is good.

¹⁰ Those sitting in darkness and in the shadow of death,
Prisoners in misery and chains,
¹¹ Because they had rebelled against the words of God,
And spurned the counsel of the Most High,
¹² He humbled their heart with labor;
They stumbled and there was none to help.
¹³ Then they cried out to Yahweh in their trouble;
He saved them out of their distresses.
¹⁴ He brought them out of darkness and the shadow of death,
And broke their bands apart.
¹⁵ Oh that they would thank Yahweh for his covenant loyalty,
And for his wonders to the children of humanity!
¹⁶ For he has shattered gates of bronze,
And cut bars of iron asunder.

¹⁷ Fools, because of their rebellious way
And because of their iniquities, were afflicted.
¹⁸ Their soul abhorred all kinds of food;
And they drew near to the gates of death.
¹⁹ Then they cried out to Yahweh in their trouble;
He saved them out of their distresses.
²⁰ He sent his word and healed them,
And brought escape from their destructions.
²¹ Oh that they would thank Yahweh for his covenant loyalty,
And for his wonders to the children of humanity!
²² Let them also offer sacrifices of thanksgiving,
And tell of his works with joyful singing.

²³ Those going down to the sea in ships,
Doing business on great waters;
²⁴ They have seen the works of Yahweh,
And his wonders in the deep.
²⁵ He spoke and raised up a stormy wind,

Which lifted up the waves of the sea.
²⁶ They rose up to the heavens, they went down to the depths;
    Their soul melted away in their misery.
²⁷ They reeled and staggered like a drunken man,
    And were at their wits' end.
²⁸ Then they cried to Yahweh in their trouble,
    And he brought them out of their distresses.
²⁹ He caused the storm to be still,
    So that the waves of the sea were hushed.
³⁰ Then they were glad because they were quiet;
    So he guided them to their desired haven.
³¹ Oh that they would thank Yahweh for his covenant loyalty,
    And for his wonders to the children of humanity!
³² Let them exalt him also in the congregation of the people,
    And praise him at the seat of the elders.

³³ He changed rivers into a wilderness,
    And springs of water into a thirsty ground;
³⁴ A fruitful land into a salt waste,
    Because of the wickedness of those who dwell in it.
³⁵ He changed a wilderness into a pool of water,
    And a dry land into springs of water;
³⁶ And there he settled the hungry,
    So that they may establish an inhabited city,
³⁷ And sow fields, and plant vineyards,
    And gather a fruitful harvest.
³⁸ Also he blessed them and they multiply greatly;
    And he did not diminish their cattle.

³⁹ When they were diminished and bowed down
    Through oppression, misery, and sorrow,
⁴⁰ He poured contempt upon princes,
    And made them wander in a pathless waste.
⁴¹ But he set on high the needy securely away from affliction,
    And made *his* families like a flock.

⁴² The upright will see it, and are glad;
    But all unrighteousness shuts its mouth.
⁴³ Who is wise? Let him give heed to these things;
    And consider the covenant kindnesses of Yahweh.

An Overview of Psalm 107

Psalm 107 is the first psalm in Book Five of the Psalter, and its dual nature as a call to worship and a word of instruction makes it a fitting introduction to the final division of the Psalter.[29] As a teaching psalm, it corresponds to Psalm 1, forming something of an inclusio in that Books 1 and 5 both begin with words of instruction.[30] As a call to praise, it serves as a fitting introduction to Book Five, which is weighted heavily toward communal praise. Psalm 107 contains several topical connections to Psalms 105 and 106, and Ps 107.2-3 ('the redeemed ... whom he has gathered from the lands') seems to display the answer to the final prayer of Psalm 106: 'Save us, O LORD our God, And gather us from among the nations' (v. 47).[31] Thus, Psalm 107 moves implicitly from exilic life to post-exilic life.

The Psalm begins like a hymn of praise, with a call to worship, expressed in the imperative plural (הדו): 'Give thanks to Yahweh because he is good and his covenant loyalty (חסד) is forever'.

With v. 2, the exhortation changes to the third person 'let them say' (ויאמרו), and the third person verb forms continue through the second section of the psalm (vv. 2-32), which is made up of a fourfold recital of salvation: 1. the lost are guided by Yahweh (vv. 2-9);[32] 2. the bound are freed by Yahweh (vv. 10-16); 3. the sick are healed by Yahweh (vv. 17-22), and 4. the storm-tossed are protected by Yahweh (vv. 23-32).

The third section of the psalm, a reflection upon Yahweh's covenant loyalty,[33] is dominated by nine statements where God is the subject of the verb: 'he changed', 'he changed', 'he settled', 'he blessed', 'he did not diminish', 'he poured', 'he made to wander', 'he set on high', 'he made'. God's actions to bless and to curse reflect the Deuteronomic and/or wisdom traditions.[34]

---

[29] For Psalm 107 as a psalm of 'instruction based on thanksgiving', see John W. Roffey, 'Beyond Reality: Poetic Discourse and Psalm 107', in E.E. Carpenter (ed.), *Biblical Itinerary* (Sheffield, UK: Sheffield Academic Press, 1997), p. 62.

[30] The five books begin at Psalms 1, 42, 73, 90, and 107. If it were not for Psalm 42 (a lament), each of the five books would begin with a psalm of instruction.

[31] Cf. DeClaissé-Walford, *Introduction to the Psalms,* p. 115.

[32] The phrase 'the redeemed of the LORD' is found in the Hebrew Bible only here and in Isa. 61.12.

[33] Cf. Erich Zenger, 'Psalm 107', in Hossfeld and Zenger, *Psalms 3: A Commentary on Psalms 101-150,* p. 101.

[34] Roffey, 'Beyond Reality: Poetic Discourse and Psalm 107', pp. 70-71.

The fourth and final section, a concluding word of instruction about Yahweh's covenant loyalty (חסד), exhorts the 'upright' and the 'wise' to 'discern the covenant loyalty of Yahweh'. The ending of the psalm suggests that thanksgiving leads to greater understanding (discernment) of Yahweh and Yahweh's ways.[35]

The Structure of Psalm 107

> I. Call to Worship (v. 1)[36]
>
> II. Fourfold Recital of Salvation (vv. 2-32)
>
>> A. Lost are guided by Yahweh (vv. 2-9)
>>
>> B. The bound are freed by Yahweh (vv. 10-16)
>>
>> C. The sick are healed by Yahweh (vv. 17-22)
>>
>> D. The storm-tossed are protected by Yahweh (vv. 23-32)
>
> III. Reflection on Yahweh's *Ḥesed* (vv. 33-41)
>
> IV. Concluding Praise of *Ḥesed* (vv. 42-43)

The psalm is dominated by the four salvation stories in the second section, with each one including the following elements: 1. The sufferers are named, whether it be the redeemed who wander, the imprisoned, the fools, or the seafarers. The sufferers are identified grammatically by means of substantives (nouns or participles, masculine plural) 2. Their distress is described (The distress is described as past tense, including iterative *yiqtols*). 3. Their cry and deliverance is narrated with very little variation, 'They cried unto Yahweh in their trouble, and he saved them from their distresses'. Verses 6 and 28 use the Hebrew צעק to signify 'cry', while vv. 13 and 19 use the synonym זעק. Yahweh's intervention is described using the word ישע ('save') in vv. 13 and 19, v. 6 uses נצל ('deliver') and v. 28 uses יצא ('bring out'). This cry and subsequent deliverance is based upon the paradigm of the exodus, where the Israelites cried out to God from their bondage, and Yahweh 'heard their cry' and came down to deliver them (Exod.

---

[35] Roffey, 'Beyond Reality: Poetic Discourse and Psalm 107', p. 75.

[36] Commentators normally group vv. 1-3 as the introductory unit, but the change from second person plural imperative to third person plural jussive suggests that vv. 2-3 belong with vv. 4-9. Furthermore, v. 3, supplies the subject ('the redeemed') for the verb in v. 4 ('let them give thanks'). Thus, v. 3 stands as a nominative absolute ('The redeemed of the LORD … let them give thanks'). Similarly, in the three other narratives, the subject is stated as the first word of the narrative: 'those sitting …' (v. 10), 'fools' (v. 17), 'those going down …' (v. 23).

3.7-8).[37] The statement of cry and deliverance is followed by an additional description of God's saving act. 4. Those who have been saved are exhorted to praise Yahweh ('O, that they would give thanks to Yahweh for his covenant loyalty (חסד) and for his wonderful works to humanity'). It should be pointed out here that 'wonderful works' (נפלאות) also evokes memories of the exodus (see Exod. 3.20; 15.11; 34.10, and Judg. 6.13). 5. Finally, a further description of the out-working of Yahweh's covenant loyalty (חסד) is offered in vv. 33-43.

The fourfold narrative of salvation is presented in a chiastic struc-ture, suggesting that it functions as one unified paradigmatic story,[38] narrated from four different contexts:

a – dangers of travel (desert)/undeserved suffering/chaos[39]/צעק
  b – threatening condition (prison)/deserved suffering/sin/זעק
  b' – threatening condition (illness)/deserved suffering/sin/זעק
a' – dangers of travel (the sea)/undeserved suffering/chaos/צעק

The psalms of thanksgiving are stylized testimonies of real-life events in which God rescued the psalmist from calamity. They nor-mally include only one narrative, usually narrated by the individual sufferer, and the narrative includes a report of the distress, the prayer of the sufferer, and a description of God's saving intervention. The four narratives of Psalm 107 are modeled after the psalm of thanks-giving, but they differ from the model by presenting the narrative in the third person plural and by including multiple stories within one psalm. The repetition of the jussive verb, 'Let them give thanks …' (הדו) suggests that this psalm is not a testimony; but is, rather, an encouragement to testimony,[40] an exhortation to the giving of thanks for Yahweh's covenant loyalty (חסד).

The four narratives, based upon the four directions of the com-pass (v. 3), are comprehensive and universal in application. Most scholars want to connect the psalm directly to the exodus or to the

[37] Regarding the exodus paradigm of salvation, see Martin, *Judging the Judges*, pp. 3-7, 62-67, 109-33.
[38] Zenger, 'Psalm 107', p. 100.
[39] Both the desert and the sea represent untamed chaos, which threatens human life. Cf. Jorge Mejia, 'Some Observations on Psalm 107', *Biblical Theology Bulletin* 5.1 (1975), p. 57, and Zenger, 'Psalm 107', p. 100.
[40] Goldingay, *Psalms*, III, p. 246.

exile;[41] and while allusions to these events are obvious, there is no specific mention of Egypt, pharaoh, the Red Sea, Babylon, or any other historical data. The Psalm, therefore, alludes both to the exodus and the exile, powerful images in Israel's memory; but it goes beyond the historical events to fill the theological canvas with present and future confidence in 'a sovereign God capable of reversing even the most desperate situation'.[42] J.W. Roffey observes,

> The poet has drawn on four images of distress that we can all understand even if never having experienced them in reality. It is in this sense that they are archetypal and hence, in Jungian typology, collective or universal ... All four images combine to express the whole spectrum of human needs'.[43]

James Mays agrees and adds the following:

> The four cases are really open paradigms of deliverance into which any and all who have benefited from God's saving work can enter. Hunger and thirst, darkness and gloom, sin and affliction, storm and sea all belong to the general symbolic vocabulary with which the redeemed portray the trouble from which they have been saved. The Psalm as a whole is the great summary song of Thanksgiving for salvation by all the redeemed.[44]

This brief overview of Psalm 107 reveals an artfully expressed theological paradigm that is common to the Hebrew Bible. The paradigm begins with a theological emphasis on Yahweh's covenant loyalty (חסד), which is found six times overall (vv. 1, 8, 15, 21, 31, 43)[45] and which forms an inclusio by its presence in the first and last verses of the psalm. Difficult to translate into English because of its complex range of meaning, חסד expresses primarily the concept of covenantal loyalty or 'commitment',[46] but it is often translated 'mercy' (KJV), 'goodness' (KJV), 'love' (NIV), 'steadfast love' (NRSV), 'lovingkindness' (NASB), 'faithful love' (NJB), ἔλεος (LXX), *misericordia* (VUL and RV), or *Güte* (Luther). The Hebrew word *ḥesed* signifies

---

[41] E.g. Dahood, *Psalms*, III, p. 81, DeClaissé-Walford, *Introduction to the Psalms*, p. 113.

[42] Lennox, *Psalms: A Bible Commentary in the Wesleyan Tradition*, p. 329.

[43] Roffey, 'Beyond Reality: Poetic Discourse and Psalm 107', pp. 68-69.

[44] Mays, *Psalms*, p. 346.

[45] Its appearance 130 times makes חסד a significant theme in the Psalter.

[46] Goldingay, *Psalms*, III, pp. 243-60.

'the goodness of Yahweh as Redeemer. It is at once an everlasting attribute of the character of God and occasional in its manifestation in saving actions'.[47] It is Yahweh's 'affective and effective engagement with those linked with him by the covenant'.[48]

The paradigm continues with the practical outworking of Yahweh's *hesed* in the bringing of salvation and deliverance. Yahweh's caring intervention that results from *hesed* is named variously as 'redemption' (גאל, v. 2), 'deliverance' (נצל, v. 6), 'salvation' (ישע, vv. 13, 19), 'bringing out' (יצא, v. 28), and 'wonderful works' (נפלאות, 5 times). It is important to note that while Yahweh's *hesed* is constant, his intervention is initiated by the cries of those who suffer; therefore, *hesed* is responsive to human need. Yahweh's *hesed* is the only hope when the forces of death threaten to leave God's people in despair (or even beyond despair, in utterly hopeless numbness).

The third element in the paradigm is the human response that is required in light of Yahweh's saving mercy. Five times the redeemed are enjoined to 'give thanks' (הדו), vv. 1, 8, 15, 21, 31). They are also encouraged to 'praise' (הלל, v. 32) Yahweh, to 'exalt' Yahweh (רום, v. 32), and to 'offer thanksgiving sacrifices, and recount his deeds with shouts of joy' (v. 22). The Hebrew injunction to 'give thanks' is theologically equivalent to what we might call 'testimony', and the testimony was expected to include a thanksgiving sacrifice (v. 22).[49] Consequently, the human response of thanksgiving may be understood as the confessing of Yahweh's salvific work within the context of community. Those who have experienced Yahweh's redemption must tell it (v. 2) so that those who are presently facing similar life-threatening powers may have hope.[50]

When we are told that the world operates by cause and effect and our lives are ruled by random chance, Psalm 107 tells us that God is sovereign. When we are told that we must resign ourselves to suffer

---

[47] Goldingay, *Psalms*, III, pp. 243-60. The foundational text for Yahweh's *hesed* is Exod. 34.6-7, a text that is central to OT theology and is reaffirmed by the prophets (e.g. Isa. 16.5; 54.8-10; 55.3; 63.7; Jer. 9.24; 32.18; 33.11; Joel 2.13; Jonah 4.2; and Mic. 7.18).

[48] Mejia, 'Some Observations on Psalm 107', p. 58.

[49] Goldingay, *Psalms*, III, p. 254, states that 'the sacrifice makes the alleged gratefulness more than mere words'.

[50] Roffey, 'Beyond Reality: Poetic Discourse and Psalm 107', describes the four-part structure of Psalm 107 as invitation, memory, response, and instruction (pp. 66-67).

and endure those things that are outside of our control, that systemic evil, oppression, and the 'death dealers' have the upper hand, Psalm 107 tells us that we should cry out to Yahweh and he will deliver us from our distress.[51] When we are told that we must be autonomous and make our own future,[52] Psalm 107 tells us that Yahweh holds the future. When we are told that we must resign ourselves to 'live lives of quiet desperation',[53] Psalm 107 tells us to 'give thanks to Yahweh for he is good'.

This brief overview of Psalm 107 demonstrates that it is a psalm of instruction that exhorts the hearer to discern the *hesed* of Yahweh and to give thanks for it. The prominence of thanksgiving within the psalm indicates that the primary affective tone is that of gratitude.[54] Erich Zenger agrees: 'The great leading motif of Psalm 107 is the exhortation to gratitude'.[55] God's gracious and salvific intervention evokes gratitude, and that gratitude generates the desire and will to praise Yahweh and testify of his wondrous works.

Psalm 107 and Pentecostal Spirituality

In his seminal work on Pentecostal spirituality, Steven Jack Land devotes significant attention to the affection of gratitude. He writes, 'gratitude is the initial and continually relevant Christian affection which, through remembrance and thanksgiving, preserves the believer from the mutually conditioning sins of forgetfulness and presumption'.[56] In what could be a reflection on Psalm 107, Land continues, 'gratitude is grounded in and shaped by the gracious righteousness and merciful faithfulness of a holy, compassionate God'.[57] Gratitude, however, is central not only to Pentecostalism but also to other Christian traditions. For example, John Chrysostom declares that 'thanksgiving adds nothing to [God], but it brings us closer to

---

[51] Cf. Ignacio Carbajosa Pérez, 'Salmo 107: Unidad, Organización Y Teología', *Estudios Bíblicos* 59.4 (2001), pp. 462-79.

[52] Colin E. Gunton, *Enlightenment and Alienation: An Essay Towards a Trinitarian Theology* (Grand Rapids, MI: Eerdmans, 1985), argues that the Enlightenment worldview demands that humans affirm their autonomy (pp. 68-69).

[53] Henry David Thoreau and Francis H. Allen, *Walden, or, Life in the Woods* (Boston: Houghton Mifflin Co., 1910), p. 8.

[54] Also, clearly present are the affections of courage and hope.

[55] Zenger, 'Psalm 107', p. 112.

[56] Land, *Pentecostal Spirituality*, p. 135.

[57] Land, *Pentecostal Spirituality*, p. 135.

Him'.[58] Luther's Small Catechism, reflecting on Article 1 of the Creed, states, '[God]… protects me against all danger, and guards and keeps me from all evil; and all this purely out of fatherly, divine mercy, without any merit or worthiness in me; for all which I am in duty bound to thank (*danken*) and praise (*loben*), to serve and obey Him'.[59] Question 2 of the *Heidelberg Catechism* asks, 'How many things are necessary for you to know, that you, enjoying this comfort [of the gospel], may live and die happily?' The answer is 'Three: First, how great is my sin and misery. The second, how I am redeemed from all my sins and misery. And the third, how I am to be grateful (*dankbar*) to God for such redemption'.[60] John Wesley writes, 'True religion … is, in two words, gratitude and benevolence'.[61] Alexander Schmemann illustrates the Greek Orthodox appreciation for gratitude in his last words spoken in the church. He prayed,

Thank You, O Lord!

Everyone capable of thanksgiving is capable of salvation and eternal joy.

Thank You, O Lord, for having accepted this Eucharist, which we offered to the Holy Trinity, Father, Son and Holy Spirit, and which filled our hearts with the joy, peace and righteousness of the Holy Spirit.

Thank You, O Lord, for having revealed Yourself unto us and given us the foretaste of Your Kingdom.

Thank You, O Lord, for having united us to one another in serving You and Your Holy Church.

Thank You, O Lord, for having helped us to overcome all difficulties, tensions, passions, temptations and restored peace, mutual love and joy in sharing the communion of the Holy Spirit.

Thank You, O Lord, for the sufferings You bestowed upon us, for they are purifying us from selfishness and reminding us of the 'one thing needed'; Your eternal Kingdom …

---

[58] St. John Chrysostom, 'Homily on Ephesians, 2', *PG*, 62.129-30.

[59] Martin Luther, *Luther's Small Catechism Developed and Explained* (Philadelphia: United Lutheran Publication House, 1893), p. 8.

[60] *The Heidelberg Catechism, in German, Latin and English: With an Historical Introduction* (New York: Scribner, 1863), p. 132. (translation mine)

[61] John Wesley, *The Works of the Rev. John Wesley* (10 vols.; Philadelphia: D. & S. Neall and W.S. Stockton, 1826), VII, p. 253.

> Great are You, O Lord, and marvelous are Your deeds, and no
> word is sufficient to celebrate Your miracles.
> Lord, it is good to be here! Amen.[62]

Karl Barth argued forcefully for gratitude as the essential character of Christian faith. He wrote, 'To be sanctified, good, Christian,
means to be thankful'.[63] He saw an indivisible link between grace and
gratitude, explaining that 'Χάρις calls for εὐχαριστία';[64] and 'Grace
and gratitude belong together like heaven and earth. Grace evokes
gratitude like the voice of an echo. Gratitude follows grace like thun-
der lightning.'[65] Furthermore, according to Barth, thanksgiving is not
a transaction; it is 'an act of subordination, not of commerce'.[66]

Public testimony, as called for in Psalm 107, was once a prominent
practice in Pentecostal churches. Scott Ellington has suggested that
perhaps the reason for the demise of testimony as a practice is that
many Pentecostals have no liturgical opportunity for testimony.[67]
However, could it also be true that the practice is less common because gratitude has diminished? Gratitude was once a ruling affection
for Pentecostals (and it still is in many parts of the world), but here
in the West, gratitude has been replaced by greed and autonomy.[68] We
are affluent, educated, powerful, and self-righteous. We have become
like the Pharisee who prayed, 'O God, I thank you that I am not like
the rest of humanity … or even like this tax collector' (Lk. 18.11-12).
We now have no gratitude because we have forgotten that we were
slaves in Egypt. Instead of gratitude, we display self-righteousness.
We have no gratitude because we have forgotten that God gave us
the promised land with its cities intact, its houses built, its trees
planted, its vines producing, and its wells already dug. Instead of gratitude, we display self-sufficiency. We have no gratitude because we

---

[62] Alexander Schmemann, 'Thank You, O Lord!', *The Orthodox Church* 20.2
(February 1984), 1.1.

[63] Karl Barth, *The Knowledge of God and the Service of God According to the Teaching
of the Reformation* (trans. J.L. M. Haire and Ian Henderson; London: Hodder and
Stoughton, 1949), p. 123.

[64] Karl Barth, *Church Dogmatics* (trans. T.F. Torrance and G.W. Bromiley; 5 vols.;
Edinburgh: T & T Clark, 1936), 5.1.670.

[65] Barth, *Church Dogmatics*, 4.1.41.

[66] Barth, *Church Dogmatics*, 2.1.217.

[67] See Ellington, 'The Costly Loss of Testimony'; and *idem*, '"Can I Get a
Witness"'.

[68] J. Clinton McCann Jr., 'Greed, Grace, and Gratitude', in Dave Bland and
David Fleer (eds.), *Performing the Psalms* (St. Louis, MO: Chalice Press), pp. 51-66.

have begun to think that God saved us on account of our inherent value. Instead of gratitude, we display superiority.

Psalm 107 disrupts our arrogant certitude that we can control the future and find our own way It subverts our hubristic confidence that we are free and autonomous. It contradicts the belief that the sickness of sin can be ameliorated by will power and/or proper legislation. Psalm 107 rejects the human confidence in technological control and dominance. It teaches us that without gratitude, we will not be saved. The apostle Paul knew this, and his forecast for what he called 'perilous times' includes the following: 'People will be lovers of themselves, lovers of money, boastful, proud … ungrateful (2 Tim. 3.2 NIV).

Psalm 107 'invites the church to face the disparity between the NT's vision of it and the reality of the church as we know it';[69] therefore, it is texts like Psalm 107 that will restore our gratitude. The biblical text and the Church's spirituality have a reciprocal relationship. It is our spirituality that equips us to hear the affective dimension of the text, and it is the text that will shape and form our affect (if we will submit to the Spirit of the text). The canonical role of the Bible in the Church, therefore, is formational in regard to orthopathy (as well as the usually assumed orthodoxy and orthopraxy). If orthopathy (including gratitude) is to be formed in believers, then our liturgy, our preaching, and our teaching should be planned and executed with that formation in mind.

Biblical texts like Psalm 107 help to shape the affection of gratitude in ways that are not triumphalistic, for 'We are the hungry and thirsty who had been fed. We are the bound who have been liberated. We are the sinners deserving death who have been given life. We are the fearful before the terrors of existence who have been given hope.'[70] Psalm 107, therefore, undergirds Barth's insistence that grace

---

[69] Goldingay, *Psalms*, III, p. 261.

[70] Mays, *Psalms*, p. 347. It might be argued that not everyone who calls upon God is delivered, but Psalm 107 does not entertain that view. Nevertheless, I include here a testimony of how Psalm 107 speaks even in death. My wife Karen and I had been married for only one year when her mother, Ruby Luke, was diagnosed with cancer. The prognosis was grim, but we prayed and felt confident that God would not allow this saintly woman to die at such a young age (48). A steady stream of well-meaning Christian friends came to the hospital proclaiming that she would certainly be healed. Ruby's brother-in-law, Rev. S.A. Luke, taking her illness seriously, prayed earnestly with fasting. Uncle Archie, as we call him, had himself been healed of spinal meningitis and his daughter had been healed of leukemia. After

calls for gratitude. The wanderers are led to safety. Those in bondage are liberated. The sick are healed. Those helplessly tossed by the storm are brought home. In all of these blessings, God's grace calls for gratitude.

If I might borrow a phrase from Dr King, I will move to the New Testament[71] and show examples where grace calls for gratitude:

Somewhere I read,
'God so loved the world that he gave his only begotten son …'

Somewhere I read,
'You shall call his name Jesus, for he will save his people from their sins'.

Somewhere I read,
'While we were yet sinners, Christ died for us'.

Somewhere I read,
'Not by silver and gold were we redeemed … but by the precious blood of Christ'.

Somewhere I read
about 'a lamb slain from the foundation of the world'.

This grace calls for our gratitude.

Conclusion

In conclusion, I would add a new stanza to Psalm 107. Just as Israel remembered its heritage and testified, so I encourage us to remember our Pentecostal heritage and testify about it:

Let the redeemed of the Lord say so,
    Whom he has redeemed from the hand of the adversary,

---

three days, the Lord gave him a Scripture, which he read to Ruby. It was Ps. 107.28-30, 'Then they cried to the LORD in their trouble, and He brought them out of their distresses. He caused the storm to be still, so that the waves of the sea were hushed. Then they were glad because they were quiet; so He guided them to their desired haven.' Soon afterwards, she left this troubled sea and arrived at her desired haven.

[71] See Franz Schnider, 'Rettung Aus Seenot: Ps 107,23-32 Und Mk 4,35-41', in Ernst Haag and Frank-Lothar Hossfeld (eds.), *Freude an Der Weisung Des Herrn*, (Stuttgart: Verlag Katholisches Bibelwerk, 1986), pp. 375-93, who connects Psalm 107 to Mk 4.35-41.

The early Pentecostals;
    Hungry and thirsty for God,
They were cast out of their churches;
    Ridiculed and mocked.
Then they cried out to the Lord in their trouble;
    they cried unto the Lord …
        in a decrepit building on Azusa Street
    they cried unto the Lord …
        in the factories of Memphis, TN
    they cried unto the Lord …
        in the cotton fields of Mississippi
    they cried unto the Lord …
        on the sawdust floors of tent revivals
    they cried unto the Lord …
        in the storefronts of crowded cities
    they cried unto the Lord …
        in the villages of Africa
    they cried unto the Lord …
        in the barrios of Latin America
    they cried unto the Lord …
        in prayer meetings in Asia and Europe
they cried unto the Lord in their distress,
        and he delivered them from their troubles.
He poured out his Spirit upon them,
    Making their lives rich with meaning.
He sent his Word and healed them,
    Infusing life and vitality beyond their imaginations.
Oh, that we would give thanks to the Lord
    For his covenant loyalty
    And for his wonders to our ancestors.
For he has satisfied their thirsty souls,
    And he has filled their hungry souls with goodness.

Finally, to those of us who are still in pain, Psalm 107 offers hope.[72] With the hopeful words of Psalm 107 – 'the Lord is good and

---

[72] Although the primary affection underlying Psalm 107 is gratitude, the affection of hope is also expressed quite strongly. Those who face life-depriving challenges are invigorated by the testimonies of the past.

his covenant loyalty is forever' – I urge you to cry out to the Lord from the midst of your pain:

Young women hearing the Spirit's call to ministry –
    Cry out to the Lord.
Old women breaking forth from the chains of past hurts –
    Cry out to the Lord.
Young men seeking lives of significance –
    Cry out to the Lord.
Old men longing to see the promises fulfilled –
    Cry out to the Lord.
Minorities and immigrants yearning for a home –
    Cry out to the Lord.
Let us cry out to the Lord in our trouble,
    and he will hear us and deliver us from our distress.
Amen.

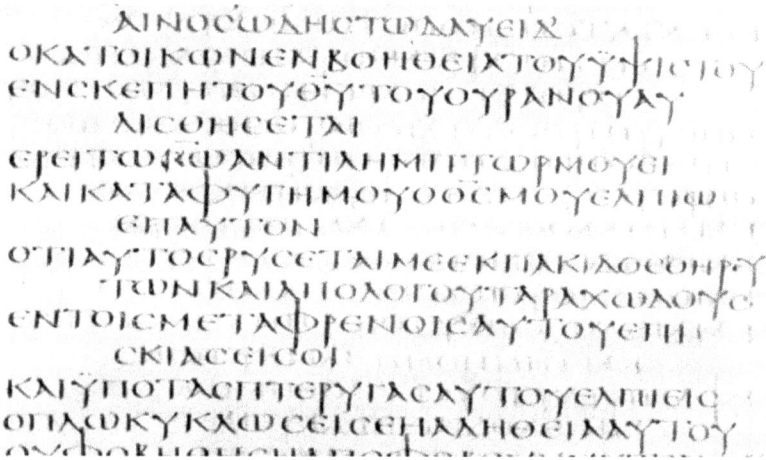

Psalm 91 Codex Sinaiticus

6

PSALM 130: THE HOPEFUL CRY OF LAMENT

We are confronted today with mass despair and the loss of hope, which is being expressed not through passive resignation, but through aggressive and antagonistic monologue. We have become adept at complaining, but we are unable to lament. Biblical lament provides a means to deal with the despair, the fears, the anxieties, and the conflicts that face us today. Psalm 130 demonstrates that lament can forge a way through the deep despair and out into renewed hope.

This chapter examines Psalm 130 and explores its relationship to Pentecostal spirituality. The approach used here is a rhetorical critical analysis that appreciates the nature of the psalm as lyric poetry. As poetry, the psalm expresses its theme and message not only through the straightforward use of words but also through the artistic devices of form (genre and structures), feeling (mood/affective dimension), and figures of speech. These rhetorical devices overlap and intertwine to create theological meaning.[1] Furthermore, this approach values the various contexts of ancient and contemporary hearers of the Psalms. Psalm 130 will be explored from the writer's Pentecostal context; and, given the nature of the psalm as a penitential lament, the study will reflect on the practices of repentance and lament both in early Pentecostalism and in contemporary Pentecostalism.

---

[1] These compositional and semantic devices are found in all types of biblical literature, but they are more pronounced in the poetic sections of Scripture. See, for example, Lee Roy Martin, *Biblical Hermeneutics: Essential Keys for Interpreting the Bible* (Miami, FL: Gospel Press, 2011), and Walter L. Liefeld, *New Testament Exposition: From Text to Sermon* (Grand Rapids, MI: Zondervan, 1984).

Psalm 130

[1] A Song of Ascents
From the depths, I cry to you, LORD.
Lord, hear my voice!
[2] Let your ears be attentive
to the voice of my pleadings for grace.
[3] If you should observe iniquities, LORD,
Lord, who would stand?
[4] But forgiveness is with you,
so that you may be feared.
[5] I wait for the LORD; my whole being waits,
and for his word I hope.
[6] My soul [waits] for the Lord
more than watchmen for the morning;
watchmen for the morning.
[7] Hope, O Israel, in the LORD;
because with the LORD is covenant loyalty,
and abundant with him is redemption.
[8] And he, himself, will redeem Israel
from all their iniquities.

A reading of Psalm 130 immediately reveals three of its characteristics. First, the heading/superscription of the psalm points to its canonical context among the 15 Songs of Ascents (Psalms 120-134), which were sung by the Jewish pilgrims as they journeyed to Jerusalem and as they ascended Mt. Zion to worship at the ancient temple. Second, the fact that the psalm begins with a cry for God's attention suggests that it should be classified as a lament, a request for God's help.[2] Third, the references throughout to sin and forgiveness indicate that this is a particular kind of lament – it is what has been called a penitential psalm.[3] The seven penitential laments, Psalms 6, 32, 38,

---

[2] Psalm 130 is classified as an individual lament by Westermann, *The Psalms: Structure, Content & Message*, p. 53.

[3] According to Orlando di Lasso, *The Seven Penitential Psalms and Laudate Dominium De Caelis* (Madison, WI: A-R Editions, 1990), p. vii, the first person to group together the seven penitential psalms was Cassiodorus in his sixth-century commentary on the Psalms. The earliest edition that I could locate is Flavius Magnus Aurelius Cassiodorus, *Cassiodori Clarissimi Senatoris Romani in Psalterium Expositio* (Venice: Impensa heredum Octaviani Scoti ac sociorum, 1517); see p. 10b. Cassiodorus' reference to the seven penitential psalms is also found in Migne (ed.), *PL*,

51, 102, 130, and 143[4] (and I would include also Psalm 106),[5] are contrite confessions of sin coupled with passionate pleas for God's mercy and forgiveness.

Used in the liturgies of the Synagogue and the Church to voice the contrition and repentance of both the individual and the congregation,[6] Psalm 130 is known in the Latin tradition as 'De Profundis', a title based on the first words of the psalm ('from the depths') as translated in the Latin Vulgate. Because of differences in the numbering of the Psalms, Psalm 130 is number 129 in the Latin, Greek, and Hebrew traditions.

The Structure of Psalm 130

The psalm may be divided into four sections. Verses 1 and 2 express the psalmist's plea for grace, and vv. 3 and 4 describe the Lord's compassionate nature. Verses 5 and 6 declare the psalmist's intent to wait and hope in the Lord, and vv. 7 and 8 challenge the people of Israel to do the same, because the Lord is committed to his covenant with Israel and will redeem them. In addition to these structural characteristics, it should be noted that vv. 1-4 are addressed to God, and vv. 5-6 form a soliloquy that expresses the psalmist's trust in God and assurance of being heard. The last two verses are addressed to the congregation as an encouragement to seek for redemption.

Four-part Structure of Psalm 130
  A. Address to God and plea for pardon (vv. 1-2)
  B. Confession and declaration of God's mercy (vv. 3-4)
  C. Testimony of the psalmist's trust in God (vv. 5-6)
  D. Exhortation for Israel to trust God as redeemer (vv. 7-8)

LXX, p. 60: 'Memento autem quod hic penitentium primus est psalmus, sequitur tricesimus primus, tricesimus septimus, quinquagesimus, centesimus primus, centesimus vicesimus nonus, centesimus quadragesimus secundus'.

[4] These numbers follow the English Bible; the numbering of the Psalms varies in different versions of the canon.

[5] Psalm 106 defies any straightforward form-critical classification. It begins as a song of praise but soon turns into a confession of national sin (v. 6: 'we have sinned'), including requests for forgiveness (vv. 4, 5, 47). Because the structure follows Israel's historical narrative, the psalm could also be grouped with the psalms of historical recital.

[6] In the Roman Catholic tradition, Psalm 130 (129) is read on several occasions throughout the liturgical year. It is also read at funerals as a prayer that the faithful departed may be forgiven of their sins.

Another structural feature of note is the chiasm imbedded in vv. 3-8.

> A Iniquity – 'If you kept a record of iniquities, Yahweh' (v. 3)
> > B Grace – 'But there is forgiveness with you' (v. 4)
> > > C Expectation – 'I wait … I hope' (vv. 5 and 6)
> > > C' Expectation – 'Hope, O Israel, in Yahweh' (v. 7)
> > B' Grace –'with him is abundant redemption' (v. 7)
> A' Iniquity – 'redeem Israel from all his iniquities' (v. 8)

The outer elements of the chiasm point to the work of Yahweh in forgiving iniquity, and the center of the chiasm highlights the role of the supplicant to 'wait' for Yahweh and 'hope' for an answer.

Another way to look at the structure is to compare it to the pattern that is found in many of the psalms of lament. With the exception of the vow of praise, the common elements of the lament can be correlated with Psalm 130.

Elements of Lament	Psalm 130
1. Address to God	v. 1
2. Petition	v. 2
3. Complaint	v. 3
4. Assurance of answer	v. 4-5
5. Statement of trust	vv. 5-7
6. Vow of praise	absent
7. Descriptive praise	vv. 7-8

An Overview of Psalm 130

The Superscription: 'A Song of Ascents'

As mentioned above, Psalm 130 is located among the psalms of ascents. Inasmuch as an approach to the temple is an occasion for rejoicing and celebration, the heading creates a mood of joy and anticipation. While anticipation may continue throughout the psalm, the joy is quickly replaced by sorrow, when the hearer realizes that this is a psalm of lament. At first thought, the psalms of ascents appear to be an inappropriate location for a lament. Nevertheless, Psalms 120, 123, 126, and 130 are all among the psalms of ascents and all of them seem to fit into the category of lament. In an earlier psalm, worshipers are warned about the moral requirements for entering the House of God:

Who may ascend into the hill of Yahweh,
  and who may stand in his holy place?
He who has clean hands and a pure heart,
  who has not lifted up his soul to falsehood,
  and has not sworn deceitfully.
He shall receive a blessing from the Yahweh
  and righteousness from the God of his salvation (Ps. 24.3-5).

Perhaps the repentance that is voiced in these laments prepares the worshipers to enter God's presence with 'clean hands and a pure heart'.

Address to God and Plea for Pardon (vv. 1-2)

Like other psalms of lament, Psalm 130 begins with a direct address to God: 'From the depths I cry[7] to you, Yahweh' (v. 1). Unlike some psalms that speak only *about* God, the laments speak *to* God. All of the agony, all of the pain, all of the guilt, and all of the shame is spoken directly to Yahweh from within the depths of suffering. A powerful figure of speech, 'the depths' brings to mind the feeling of despair and urgency that might overtake a person who is drowning in deep waters with no way of escape (cf. Ps. 69.15). Here, the psalmist is drowning in the guilt and alienation brought on by sin (v. 3); therefore, a desperate cry goes out to Yahweh, the God of Israel, the God who heard the cries of slaves, brought them out of Egypt, and joined himself to them in covenant.

The beginning of v. 2 creates an unusual rhetorical pattern when juxtaposed with the ending of v. 1. The last word of v. 1 is Yahweh, and the first word of v. 2 is Adonai ('Lord'). Therefore, the psalmist states, '...I cry to you Yahweh; Adonai hear my voice ...' The fact

---

[7] This present tense usage of the *qatal* (perfect) is sometimes called 'performative'. See Joüon and Muraoka, *A Grammar of Biblical Hebrew*, §112.f. Cf. Waltke and O'Connor, *An Introduction to Biblical Hebrew Syntax*, who write, 'An instantaneous perfective represents a situation occurring at the very instant the expression is being uttered. This use appears chiefly with *verba dicendi* ("verbs of speaking," swearing, declaring, advising, etc.) or gestures associated with speaking' (§30.5.1.d); and *GKC*, §106.i(b). Present tense is adopted by the CEB, RSV, and by Claus Westermann, *The Psalms: A New Translation* (Philadelphia: The Westminster Press, 1963), p. 225. For further argument in favor of the present tense, see Erich Zenger, 'Psalm 130', in Hossfeld and Zenger (eds.), *Psalms 3: A Commentary on Psalms 101-150*, pp. 421-42, footnote a. On the dagesh in מַעֲמַקִּים, see Joüon and Muraoka, *A Grammar of Biblical Hebrew*, §96.C.

that this pattern is repeated in v. 3 makes it even more remarkable, and the fact that the translations ignore the pattern is disappointing.

Verse two begins as a prayer that God will 'hear' and be 'attentive', essentially highlighting the perceived absence of Yahweh, a feature that is common to the psalms of lament. The psalmist implores God to listen and to hear his prayer. The desire to be heard is emphasized by the repetition of the word 'voice' (קוֹל). At the beginning, the prayer has no specific content; it is a request only that Yahweh hear the psalmist; but at the end of the verse, the content of the prayer is revealed to be an appeal for grace. The word תחנון means 'a plea for grace or favor'[8] and is related to the noun חֵן which means 'grace, favor'. The verb form חנן ('show favor, be gracious')[9] is used in Psalm 51, another Penitential Psalm, when the psalmist prays, 'Be gracious to me, O God' (51.1).[10] The act of pleading for grace is fraught with emotion and reveals the psalmist's deep desire for restoration of the covenant relationship with God.

Confession of Sin and Declaration of God's Mercy (vv. 3-4)
The psalmist, claiming no merit whatever, confesses the universal failure of humanity, and in so doing, confesses his own sinfulness. If God's acceptance of humanity were based upon his observation of iniquities, no one could stand acquitted, including the psalmist.[11] A multitude of iniquities prohibits anyone from standing innocent before God, 'but forgiveness is with' the Lord. The Hebrew כִּי ('but') is used here as a strong adversative,[12] pointing to Yahweh as the only source of hope. The word סְלִיחָה ('forgiveness') signifies 'pardon'[13] and is used in the Hebrew Bible only in reference to the actions of God.[14] Perhaps the psalmist remembers the Lord's forgiveness of Israel when they built and worshiped the golden calf (Exod. 34.9) or when they grumbled at Kadesh Barnea (Num. 14.19-20). The preposition 'with' (עִם) answers the question, 'Where is forgiveness; where

---

[8] Cf. *BDB*, p. 337.

[9] *BDB*, p. 335.

[10] The verb is used in the following Penitential Psalms: 6, 51, 102, and 130. The noun form (תַּחֲנוּן) is found also in Psalm 143, another Penitential Psalm.

[11] For a parallel usage of the verb שָׁמַר, see Job 14.16, 'you do not keep a record of my sin' (CEB).

[12] *DCH*, IV, p. 387. Cf. the same usage in Pss. 44.3 [4]; 115.1; and 118.17.

[13] *HALOT*, p. 757; cf. *NIDOTTE*, III, pp. 259-60; and *TLOT*, II, pp. 797-98.

[14] Walter C. Kaiser, 'סלח', in *TWOT*, II, p. 626.

is it located?' It is 'with' the Lord. Similar language is used later in v. 7, where we learn that 'commitment' is 'with' Yahweh, and 'redemption' is also 'with' him. Because Yahweh is the only source of forgiveness, he is to be 'feared', which means to be revered and held in awe.[15]

Testimony of the Psalmist's Trust in God (vv. 5-6)

The first four verses of Psalm 130 are addressed to God, but vv. 5-6 are a soliloquy, with no explicit addressee: 'I wait for Yahweh; my whole being waits; and I hope for his word'. Having pleaded for God's grace and forgiveness, the psalmist now waits expectantly for the Lord to answer. The theme of vv. 5-6 is communicated through two related terms 'to wait' and 'to hope', and each of these terms is found twice in vv. 5-7. Here it is affirmed that although lament is a statement of suffering and a plea for help, it is also 'an act of hope'.[16]

In modern usage, 'waiting' can be a passive state that is disconnected from the object of waiting. For example, while in the doctor's waiting room, patients may read, watch TV, talk to each other, make phone calls, or even take a nap. However, regarding the biblical word 'wait' (קוה), John Hartley writes, 'This root means to wait or to look for with eager expectation ... It means enduring patiently in confident hope that God will decisively act for the salvation of his people (Gen 49:18). Waiting involves the very essence of a person's being, his soul (*nepeš*; Ps 130:5).'[17] Indeed, the psalmist emphasizes the involvement of his 'whole being' in this intense waiting process.

Waiting for the Lord, the psalmist also 'hopes' for a 'word', an answer from God.[18] The word 'hope' (*hif.* of יחל) overlaps seman-

---

[15] *DCH*, IV, p. 278. Cf. CEB: 'honored'.

[16] Scott A. Ellington, *Risking Truth: Reshaping the World through Prayers of Lament* (Princeton Theological Monograph Series; Eugene, OR: Pickwick Publications, 2008), p. 4. Christoph Barth, 'יחל', *TDOT*, VI, pp. 49-55 (54), writes,

> The formulaic expression 'wait for Yahweh' refers to God as the source of all good for which one can hope: God alone is the source and reality of what is awaited ... Because Israel knows Yahweh to be such a God on the basis of the past, it waits 'for Yahweh'; because it can never possess him as such a God, it 'waits' for Yahweh.

[17] John E. Hartley, 'קוה', in *TWOT*, II, p. 791. Cf. *NIDOTTE*, III, pp. 892-93.

[18] See Raymond Jacques Tournay, *Seeing and Hearing God with the Psalms: The Prophetic Liturgy of the Second Temple in Jerusalem* (JSOTSup 118; Sheffield: JSOT Press, 1991), who provides a list of the Psalms in which 'God is asked to reply and does so' (pp. 162-63).

tically with 'wait' and is used here in parallel to it.[19] The LXX, however, recognizes the difference between the terms and translates קוה with the Greek ὑπομένω, and it renders יחל with ἐλπίζω. Paul Gilchrist argues that the kind of hope signified by יחל 'is not a pacifying wish of the imagination which drowns out troubles, nor is it uncertain ... but rather [it] is the solid ground of expectation for the righteous. As such it is directed towards God.'[20] The psalmist will tarry and persist in prayer until a word of assurance comes forth from God.

The anticipation and longing of the psalmist is symbolized in v. 6 by a comparison with the guards who keep watch upon the city walls each night. Their hope is that they might pass the night successfully without threat or incident. Therefore, they long for the coming of the morning, when they can finally breathe a sigh of relief.[21] The psalmist, however, longs for the Lord even more than the watchmen long for the day. Feeling the burden of iniquity and the guilt that it incurs, the psalmist waits and hopes sorrowfully and apprehensively, unable to claim the joy of forgiveness until the Lord responds with the gift of his word of redemption.[22] The comparison presented in v. 6 does not add new information; rather, its import is to deepen the affective impact of the psalm. The impact is further strengthened by the striking repetition, 'watchmen for the morning, watchmen for the morning'.[23] Consistent with other laments, vv. 5-6 suggest that the psalm is ultimately a psalm of hope.

---

[19] *HALOT*, p. 407.

[20] Paul R. Gilchrist, 'יָחַל', in *TWOT*, I, p. 373. Cf. Pss. 42.5 [6]; 43.5; 131.3; Job 13.15.

[21] The Hebrew text has no verb in v. 6. Translators assume that the verb 'wait' is carried over from v. 5; however, Westermann chooses to insert 'longs for', which is a bit more intense than 'waits for'. See Westermann, *The Psalms: A New Translation*, p. 225. Tournay, *Seeing and Hearing God with the Psalms*, p. 155, remarks that morning is the 'time when YHWH saves the chosen or punishes the guilty'.

[22] The comparison between the lament of Ps. 130.6 and the lament of Habakkuk is striking: 'I will stand on my watchtower and station myself upon the rampart; I will look to see what he will say to me' (Hab. 2.1). Moore, *The Spirit of the Old Testament*, p. 116, writes, 'Habakkuk stages his wait for God on the watchtower, the place from which one would watch for an approaching enemy! The lamenter, who has been moved to see others and himself differently, is now opened to see God in a new way too.'

[23] 'Watchmen' is a substantive participle of the verb שׁמר, 'to keep, guard, watch, observe'. See *BDB* p. 1036.

Exhortation to Trust in God's Redemption (vv. 7-8)

The psalms of lament often make a transition from prayer to praise, but in Psalm 130 the transition is from lament to exhortation. The last two verses of the psalm are addressed to 'Israel', the community of faith, which is encouraged to follow the example of the psalmist and 'hope' in the Lord.[24] Although the last two verses do not constitute praise, they produce a change of tone that is similar to that which would occur with a transition to praise. The first part of the psalm is plaintive and sorrowful, but the psalm concludes on the hopeful and positive note that Yahweh is faithful and will redeem Israel.

In light of the earlier thrice-repeated alternation from 'Yahweh' to 'Adonai' (vv. 1-2, 3, and 5-6), we might expect the same alternation here in v. 7. Instead, 'Yahweh' is repeated, as a kind of poetic climax that emphasizes the importance of the name 'Yahweh'.

Israel's hope in Yahweh is not without sound justification. The psalmist supplies two important reasons for that hope. First, Israel has grounds to hope in Yahweh, because 'with Yahweh is commitment', a theological conviction that is rooted in Yahweh's self-revelation to Moses in Exod. 34.6 and which is a crucial concept in the Psalter.[25] The term 'covenant loyalty' (חסד) refers to Yahweh's faithfulness to his covenant commitment. The Hebrew term has no exact equivalent in English, which has led to a variety of translations: 'faithful love' (CEB), 'mercy' (JPS, NKJV), 'lovingkindness' (NASB), 'steadfast love' (RSV), 'ἔλεος' (LXX), 'misericordia' (VUL and RV), 'Gnade' (Luther). The difficulty in translation results from the fact that in contexts like Psalm 130, חסד expresses a combination of love, mercy, and covenant loyalty.[26] Goldingay translates חסד with the English 'commitment', a word that seems to capture both the loyalty and covenant loyalty that are essential to חסד.[27] On its deep significance, Zenger writes that חסד

> underscores that there is a fundamental relationship between YHWH and Israel on which Israel can rely: It is a loving relationship that determines YHWH's actions toward Israel and drives him

---

[24] Tournay, *Seeing and Hearing God with the Psalms*, p. 209, understands v. 7 as an expression of Jewish messianic hope during the Persian period.

[25] In its various forms, חסד is found 130 times in the book of Psalms. See especially, Psalm 136.

[26] *DCH*, III, pp. 277-78. Cf. *HALOT*, I, p. 336.

[27] Goldingay, *Psalms*, III, p. 530.

to act out of love, which not only yields more than one would 'normally expect but cares lovingly for Israel – unconditionally and 'for nothing', the very love that is not only supportive but in fact constitutive of Israel's life.[28]

Israel's second reason for hope is that God's redemption is 'abundant' (v. 7b). The adjective 'abundant' is stressed by the unusual word order of v. 7b. It is a verbless clause in which 'abundant' is often translated as an attributive adjective: 'With him is abundant redemption' (NASB, NKJV).[29] The placement of the adjective in first position, however, dictates that it be understood as a predicate adjective rather than an attributive adjective. Attributive adjectives follow the nouns they modify, which is not the case in v. 7. Translating 'abundant' as a predicate adjective yields the following meaning in English: 'with him, redemption is abundant'. As is often the case, using normal English word order would obscure the rhetorical impact of the Hebrew text; therefore, a better translation results by retaining the Hebrew word order – 'abundant with him is redemption'.[30] After all, this is poetry; and even in English poetry, word order is fluid.

Another rhetorical feature of v. 7 is its emphasis on relationality, as expressed through the word 'with' (עִם), a preposition that is found three times in vv. 4-7. We read that forgiveness is 'with' Yahweh (v. 4), covenant loyalty is 'with' Yahweh (v. 7a), and redemption is 'with' Yahweh (v. 7b). Perhaps the use of 'with' produces only a minor rhetorical effect, but that effect is suggestive of the personal and qualitative nature of forgiveness, commitment, and redemption. Apart from Yahweh, these salvific benefits are neither possible, nor are they available to anyone. It is only in relation to Yahweh that a believer can be forgiven, made righteous, and made holy.

The word order in v. 8 is equally emphatic, inasmuch as the verse begins with the redundant pronoun 'he', which suggests the translation 'he, himself, will redeem' (he, and no one else!) or more loosely

---

[28] Zenger, 'Psalm 130', p. 438.
[29] JPS and RSV read, 'With him is abundant redemption'.
[30] Cf. Briggs and Briggs, *Psalms*, II, p. 465. The Hebrew הַרְבֵּה was originally a *hifil* infinitive construct, with the meaning 'to increase, to make numerous, to make great', but its grammatical function was expanded to include adjectival and adverbial uses. See *HALOT*, p. 1177.

as 'he is the one who will redeem' (CEB).[31] Once again, repetition adds to the impact of the psalm. The noun 'redemption', found in v. 7, takes a verbal form in v. 8: 'will redeem'. The root of both the noun and the verb (פדה) means 'to buy out',[32] to 'ransom for a price',[33] to 'liberate'.[34] It is used in reference to Israel's redemption from Egyptian bondage (Deut. 15.15) and the redemption from Babylonian exile (Isa. 35.10), but Ps. 13.7-8 is the only Old Testament text where the word פדה is used with reference to redemption from sin.[35] The words 'commitment' and 'redemption' appeal to Israel's communal memory as the covenant people of God, and those memories generate deep affective responses of love, gratitude, and hope.

The ending of Psalm 130 points back to v. 3, where the psalmist asked the sobering rhetorical question: 'If you should observe iniquities, LORD, Lord, who would stand?' This final verse answers v. 3 with the buoyant declaration that the Lord 'himself will redeem Israel from all their iniquities'! Psalm 130 confirms the assertion of Brueggemann that 'when YHWH is rightly understood, sin from the outset is penultimate at best. What is ultimate is the mercy of YHWH that outflanks human failure.'[36]

Psalm 130 and Pentecostal Spirituality[37]

Repentance in Pentecostal Spirituality

Psalm 130 is a plea for grace, forgiveness, and redemption; therefore, it has been characterized as a psalm of repentance. In the Pentecostal tradition, repentance has been associated first with the experience of conversion and justification by faith and second with the lifelong

---

[31] The LXX follows the Hebrew: καὶ αὐτὸς λυτρώσεται τὸν Ισραηλ ἐκ πασῶν τῶν ἀνομιῶν αὐτοῦ. The noun פדות is found in the Psalter only here and in 111.9, and the related noun פדיון occurs once (Ps. 49.9). The verb פדה is found 14 times.

[32] *HALOT*, II, p. 912.

[33] *DCH*, VI, p. 651.

[34] *TLOT*, II, p. 964.

[35] W.B. Coker, 'פָּדָה', in *TWOT*, II, p. 716.

[36] Brueggemann, *From Whom No Secrets Are Hid*, p. 108.

[37] This third section offers brief reflections on the intersection between Psalm 130 and the Pentecostal practices of repentance and lament. Readers should consult the footnotes for resources that address these practices more fully.

pursuit of holiness.[38] The repentance found in Psalm 130 is not the repentance of an unbeliever who is turning to God for the first time; it is the repentance of a believer, and it concludes with a promise of redemption for the believing community (Israel). The Psalm, therefore, informs the Pentecostal theology of post-conversion repentance.

Pentecostal theologian R. Hollis Gause writes that repentance is 'a work/gift of divine grace' that includes an admission of 'guilt' and a 'reversal of the sinner's attitude and behavior'. It involves the 'entire nature of human personality: mind, emotions and will'.[39] In the New Testament, the call to repentance is addressed to the unbeliever (Acts 17.30), to the Jew (Acts 2.38), and to the Christian alike (Rev. 2.5); and for each group, the Greek word is the same (μετανοέω). True repentance includes the act of confessing one's sins (ἐξομολογέω),[40] whether one is an unbeliever (Mk 1.5 vis-à-vis Lk. 3.14), a Jew (Mt. 3.2-7), or a Christian (1 Jn 1.9).[41] Therefore, Gause can say, 'there is only one kind of repentance – repentance from sin'.[42]

The Pentecostal tradition is diverse, and the pursuit of holiness takes on a variety of shapes; but, for the most part, Pentecostal believers are expected to resist sin and to practice a lifestyle of obedience. However, in some sectors of Pentecostalism, post-conversion repentance is not encouraged. Cheryl Bridges Johns warns that 'the vision of penitence that is inherent in the movement is in danger of being discarded for a more socially acceptable "positive" self-

---

[38] For example, the Church of God Declaration of Faith states, 'We believe that ... repentance is commanded of God for all and is necessary for the forgiveness of sins' (http://www.churchofgod.org/beliefs/declaration-of-faith).

[39] R.H. Gause, *Living in the Spirit: The Way of Salvation* (Cleveland, TN: CPT Press, Rev. and expanded edn, 2009), p. 8.

[40] Cf. Gause, *Living in the Spirit: The Way of Salvation*, p. 24.

[41] In light of the consistency of the biblical text, I have chosen to use the word 'repentance' rather than the words 'penance' and 'penitence'. I also want to avoid confusing the Pentecostal view of repentance with the Roman Catholic view of penance, which is a sacrament that grants 'forgiveness of sins committed after baptism' and which, to be valid, must include confession to a priest followed by appropriate penitent acts. See *Catholic Encyclopedia*, accessed online: http://www.catholic.org/encyclopedia/view.php?id=9880. Where Protestant Bibles have the word 'repentance', the Roman Catholic Douay-Rheims Version (1899) has 'penance' 69 times.

[42] Gause, *Living in the Spirit: The Way of Salvation*, p. 27.

image'.[43] Also, the recent hyper-grace movement has downplayed the need for repentance, teaching that all sins were forgiven by Christ at the cross; and, therefore, repentance is a redundant act of works righteousness.[44] Furthermore, some Pentecostal preaching sounds more like lessons in self-help and positive thinking. If these sermons are to be believed, Christians have the power to make themselves better through their own efforts. Hollis Gause, however, warns of the impotence of such an approach. He declares, 'To habituate oneself to an external pattern of life that is behaviorally acceptable to our society is not repentance'.[45]

These contemporary obstacles suggest the need for a renewed focus on the theology of repentance. Foundational work has been provided already by Hollis Gause in his book, *Living in the Spirit* and by Cheryl Bridges Johns in her essay entitled, 'Yielding to the Spirit: A Pentecostal Understanding of Penitence'.[46] Hollis Gause provides a key insight upon which to build:

> In addition to initial repentance [at conversion], repentance is a grace which is to be practiced throughout one's life in Christ. This is necessitated by two conditions. The first is the growing enlightenment of the believer. As the believer becomes more and more mature, he/she realizes patterns of thought and conduct that are not conducive to growing in grace and Christian perfection. As the believer becomes aware of these shortcomings, it is necessary for him/her to repent, turning from these practices and seeking perfection in love. The second is the occasion of known sin in the life of the believer ... Such an occasion requires the confession of sin.[47]

Gause's view of repentance represents the perspective of many in the Pentecostal tradition. Despite the problems that I have named above, the global Pentecostal movement has been animated and

---

[43] Cheryl Bridges Johns, 'Yielding to the Spirit: A Pentecostal Understanding of Penitence', in Mark J. Boda and Gordon T. Smith (eds.), *Repentance in Christian Theology* (Collegeville, MN: Liturgical Press, 2006), p. 306.

[44] See for example, Michael L. Brown, *Hyper-Grace: Exposing the Dangers of the Modern Grace Movement* (Lake Mary, FL: Charisma House, 2014).

[45] Gause, *Living in the Spirit: The Way of Salvation*, p. 29.

[46] Johns, 'Yielding to the Spirit ... Penitence', pp. 287-306. Larry McQueen also discusses Pentecostal repentance as a subset of lament, in his *Joel and the Spirit*, pp. 66-95.

[47] Gause, *Living in the Spirit: The Way of Salvation*, pp. 8-9.

fueled by a spirituality that includes a deep passion for God and for the pursuit of godliness. 'All around the world', writes Cheryl Bridges Johns, 'the floors and prayer altars of Pentecostal churches are often awash with the tears of both sinners and saints'.[48] Pentecostal repentance is more than a simple confession; it intensely involves the affections. 'Though we must not codify particular visceral reactions to repentance, we must understand that repentance is a radical emotional upheaval'.[49]

Rather than a one-time event, Pentecostal salvation is understood to be a journey that involves both 'crisis and development',[50] and Gause argues that as they mature on their journey, believers repent of perceived 'shortcomings'. The 'journey of the believer is therefore marked by a continual submission to God in confession and repentance'.[51] Similarly, Steven Land describes the Pentecostal pursuit of holiness in language reminiscent of Psalm 130:

> There is little peace and rest for the double-minded person who regards iniquity or resistance in his or her heart. The awareness of this struggle, the vigilance, consecration, and the travail of praying through to peace, all contribute to the compassionate drive of Pentecostals toward the world.[52]

Gause insists that repentance is an essential element of the Christian life. He writes, 'To those who already know Christ, the call to repentance is a perpetual call and demand. It is a way of living in Christ. It is an essential for renewal, and life that is not in continual renewal will die.'[53] Pentecostalism has been influenced, in part, by the holiness teachings of John Wesley, who urged his followers to examine themselves daily and to repent of any sins in commission or omission. This process of confession was aided by a list of questions that

---

[48] Johns, 'Yielding to the Spirit ... Penitence', p. 288.
[49] Gause, *Living in the Spirit: The Way of Salvation*, p. 24.
[50] Johns, 'Yielding to the Spirit ... Penitence', p. 291.
[51] Johns, 'Yielding to the Spirit ... Penitence', p. 292.
[52] Land, *Pentecostal Spirituality*, p. 175.
[53] R.H. Gause, *God, Prayer, Redemption, and Hope: Pastoral and Theological Reflections* (Cleveland, TN: Cherohala Press, 2016), p. 5; cf. Gause, *Living in the Spirit: The Way of Salvation*, pp. 21-44. Cf. Land, *Pentecostal Spirituality*, p. 176, who writes regarding ongoing repentance, 'In the Spirit, the blood, or life given and being given, keeps on cleansing daily as believers submitted themselves to God in confession and repentance'.

could be used either in private prayer or in the context of small accountability groups.[54]

The practice of repentance as a part of continual renewal may be illustrated by entries from the diary of early Pentecostal leader A.J. Tomlinson. On July 9, 1901, Tomlinson writes, 'We had a very special meeting last night, which lasted until 2:00 A. M. today … [we] confessed our sins, begged forgiveness of each other …'; and on Dec. 4, he records the following: 'We have been having some confession meetings and we are having a general sifting. One person has been asked to leave the work. Others are searching their lives.'[55]

Corporate repentance is a significant topic that shows up in early Pentecostal literature and in Ps. 130.7-8 (Cf. Joel 2). Although individual repentance is demanded by Scripture, corporate repentance is called for with equal severity and should be the subject of further study and attention by Pentecostal scholars. After all, in his prophetic messages to the seven churches, Jesus calls for repentance seven times (2.5 [twice], 16, 21, 22; 3.3, 19).[56]

This ongoing life of repentance is facilitated by several Pentecostal practices, including water baptism, footwashing, the Lord's Sup-

---

[54] An early list of Wesley's questions can be found online at https://home.snu.edu/~hculbert/selfexam.htm, accessed Feb. 20, 2018:

1. Am I consciously or unconsciously creating the impression that I am better than I really am? In other words, am I a hypocrite? 2. Do I confidentially pass on to others what has been said to me in confidence? 3. Can I be trusted? 4. Am I a slave to dress, friends, work or habits? 5. Am I self-conscious, self-pitying, or self-justifying? 6. Did the Bible live in me today? 7. Do I give the Bible time to speak to me every day? 8. Am I enjoying prayer? 9. When did I last speak to someone else of my faith? 10. Do I pray about the money I spend? 11. Do I get to bed on time and get up on time? 12. Do I disobey God in anything? 13. Do I insist upon doing something about which my conscience is uneasy? 14. Am I defeated in any part of my life? 15. Am I jealous, impure, critical, irritable, touchy or distrustful? 16. How do I spend my spare time? 17. Am I proud? 18. Do I thank God that I am not as other people, especially as the Pharisees who despised the publican? 19. Is there anyone whom I fear, dislike, disown, criticize, hold a resentment toward or disregard? If so, what am I doing about it? 20. Do I grumble or complain constantly? 21. Is Christ real to me?

[55] A.J. Tomlinson, *The Diary of A.J. Tomlinson 1901-1924* (The Church of God Movement Heritage Series; Cleveland, TN: White Wing Publishing House, 2012), pp. 20, 29.

[56] On the importance of repentance in the Apocalypse, see Thomas, *The Apocalypse*, pp. 118-20.

per, and the altar call that may follow preaching.[57] Water baptism, of course, signifies the initial repentance of conversion. Footwashing, as John Christopher Thomas has shown in his groundbreaking work *Footwashing in John 13 and the Johannine Community*, is the Pentecostal sacrament that speaks most directly to post-conversion sin.[58] The footwashing in John 13, Thomas writes,

> signifies the disciples' spiritual cleansing for a continued relationship with Jesus. As such, the footwashing functions as an extension of the disciples' baptism in that it signifies continual cleansing from the sin acquired (after baptism) through life in a sinful world. This act then is a sign of continued fellowship with Jesus, but also a sign of their continued readiness for participation in his mission.[59]

The Lord's Supper provides the opportunity for believers to 'examine' themselves (1 Cor. 11.28) and to repent of any known sin.[60] Repentance can also be a response to the preaching of the Word, as the minister gives opportunity for the congregation to pray at the altar or to kneel at their seats and seek the face of God. Furthermore, whether hearing it preached or reading it privately, the Word of God 'brings us again and again to moments of repentance, times in which a truth in the Scriptures stands over against us as that word of reproof or correction (2 Tim. 3.16)'.[61]

Finally, Psalm 130 shows that repentance can be generated by the suffering that sin causes. Hollis Gause contends that sin produces a 'deep sorrow of knowing that we have offended God, grieved the

---

[57] Johns, 'Yielding to the Spirit … Penitence', pp. 299-303. On the Pentecostal sacraments, see Daniel Tomberlin, *Pentecostal Sacraments: Encountering God at the Altar* (North Charleston, SC: CreateSpace, revised edn, 2015).

[58] John Christopher Thomas, *Footwashing in John 13 and the Johannine Community* (JSNTSup 61; Sheffield: JSOT Press, 1991). I will cite the 2nd edn, (Cleveland, TN: CPT Press, 2013), p. 194. Thomas' discussion regarding the subject of post-conversion sin in the Johannine literature and in early Christianity (pp. 157-65) is also quite relevant to the theology of repentance.

[59] Thomas, *Footwashing*, p. 152. Moreover, Thomas, in his 'Pentecostal Theology in the Twenty-first Century', *PNEUMA* 20 (1998), pp. 3-19, correlates ecclesiologically the sacrament of footwashing with the understanding of the Church as sanctified community.

[60] See, for example, Green, *Toward a Pentecostal Theology of the Lord's Supper*, p. 320.

[61] Chris E.W. Green, *Sanctifying Interpretation: Vocation, Holiness, and Scripture* (Cleveland, TN: CPT Press, 2015), p. 155.

Holy Spirit, defiled the temple of the Holy Spirit and our own hands and heart. It is sorrow that prevails even when we did not "get caught".'[62] 'From the depths' of sorrow, we grieve over our sins against God. Psalm 130 encourages us to cry out to God for his grace, for his forgiveness, and for his redemption.

Lament in Pentecostal Spirituality

The psalm of lament is the worshiper's cry to God for deliverance from distress. The seven penitential psalms, including Psalm 130, link pain to guilt; but this linkage is rare elsewhere within the Psalter.[63] Most of the psalms of lament are expressions of suffering by those who are innocent; that is, their immediate pain is not caused directly by their own guilt (e.g. Psalms 5, 7, 17, 26).[64] In the more common types of lament, the sufferer's trouble may take the form of sickness (Psalms 6, 31, 38), oppression (Psalm 3, 9, 13), or an accusation (Psalm 7, 17, 26).[65] Underlying the lament is the feeling that God is absent (Psalms 13, 22, 44).[66] Scott Ellington explains a number of important components of the biblical lament:

> Biblical lament, while it does include tears, complaints and pro-tests, is something more. It is the experience of loss suffered within the context of *relatedness*. A relationship of trust, intimacy, and love is a necessary precondition for genuine lament. When the biblical writers lament, they do so from within the context of a foundational relationship that binds together the individual with members of the community of faith and that community with their God. That biblical lament is offered to God is clear, but per-haps less obvious is the essential role that the community plays. The prayer of lament is not a private thing, but is offered 'out loud', 'standing up', and 'in church.' Lament is not the property

---

[62] Gause, *Living in the Spirit: The Way of Salvation*, p. 28.

[63] Walter Brueggemann, 'The Friday Voice of Faith', *CTJ* 36 (2001), p. 19.

[64] Westermann, *The Psalms: Structure, Content & Message*, p. 68. Cf. Brueggemann, 'The Friday Voice of Faith', p. 13.

[65] John H. Hayes, *Understanding the Psalms* (Valley Forge, PA: Judson Press, 1976), pp. 64-84. Cf. Westermann, *The Psalms: Structure, Content & Message*, pp. 60-70.

[66] Leonard P. Maré, 'A Pentecostal Perspective on the Use of Psalms of Lament in Worship', *VE* 29.1 (2008), p. 102.

of the individual but belongs to the community that presents it-self before God.[67]

Walter Brueggemann has been instrumental in calling attention to the value of lament in general and to the psalms of lament in partic-ular. In his 1986 article, 'The Costly Loss of Lament',[68] he argues that despite the great value of the psalms of lament, they are now virtually ignored by Church. This avoidance of the psalms of lament is even more surprising when we note that almost half of the psalms are laments. Moreover, many of the laments can be described as com-munal or corporate laments (including the entire book of Lamenta-tions), which are particularly fitting for liturgical use. Brueggemann observes further that lament itself is absent from both 'life and lit-urgy',[69] in that 'most contemporary prayer is denial, as though our secrets can be hid from God'.[70] He insists that by not using the psalms of lament in the Church, 'we have communicated two mes-sages to people: either you must not feel *that* way (angry with God, for example) or, if you feel *that* way, you must do something about it somewhere else – but not here'.[71] Therefore, lament is consigned to the therapist's office and effusive praise to the sports arena.

Claus Westermann contends that the absence of lament in Chris-tian theology and practice is due in part to a one-sided reading of the

---

[67] Ellington, *Risking Truth*, p. 7 (emphasis original). Ellington's Pentecostal stance is in direct opposition to that of Patrick D. Miller, 'Prayer and Worship', *CTJ* 36.1 (2001), pp. 53-62, who argues that lament is a private prayer that has 'its pri-mary focus outside of worship … not *in* the community' (pp. 53-54, emphasis original). Miller uses the prayer of Hannah as support for his model, but he fails to incorporate the communal laments, the book of Lamentations, the laments found in the prophets, and the psalms of lament that include direct address to the com-munity, as Ps. 130.7-8 does. The contrast between Miller and Ellington highlights the competing visions of worship as either safe, predictable, and orderly (as prac-ticed by liturgical and Evangelical traditions) or as open, surprising, and mysterious (as practiced by Pentecostals).

[68] Walter Brueggemann, 'The Costly Loss of Lament', *JSOT* 36 (1986), pp. 57-71. The article is reprinted in Brueggemann, *The Psalms and the Life of Faith*, pp. 98-111. Brueggemann builds upon the groundbreaking doctoral thesis of Claus Westermann, published in English as *The Praise of God in the Psalms* and reprinted as *Praise and Lament in the Psalms*, which includes an additional section devoted en-tirely to the psalms of lament. Westermann argues convincingly for the value of the psalms of lament for the contemporary Church. The Christian significance of lament is later expanded and clarified in Westermann, *The Living Psalms*.

[69] Brueggemann, 'The Costly Loss of Lament', p. 60.

[70] Brueggemann, *From Whom No Secrets Are Hid*, p. 92.

[71] Brueggemann, 'The Friday Voice of Faith', p. 15 (emphasis original).

New Testament, particularly by the Reformed tradition, that empha-sizes the work of Jesus Christ as redemption from sin but not as re-demption from suffering. He writes, 'Here we see the real reason why the lament has been dropped from Christian prayer. The believing Christian should bear suffering patiently and not complain about it to God. The "sufferings of this world" are unimportant and insignif-icant. What is important is the guilt of sin.'[72] The laments, however, reflect a 'spirituality of vigorous protest'.[73] Westermann observes further that by quoting Psalm 22 on the cross, Jesus demonstrated that he 'had taken up the lament of those people who suffer, that he too had entered into suffering … With his suffering and dying, there-fore, Jesus could not have had only the sinner in mind; he must also have been thinking of those who suffer.'[74] The one-sided view of Christ's death that relates his work to sin alone and excludes human suffering does not represent 'the New Testament as a whole'.[75] Therefore, Westermann asserts that Christian theology must be 'cor-rected by the Old Testament. A correction of this sort would have far-reaching consequences. One of these would be that the lament, as the language of suffering, would receive a legitimate place in Chris-tian worship, as it had in the worship of the Old Testament.'[76]

Some Pentecostals tend to ignore lament because they think it mit-igates against praise. Writing from the context of South African Pen-tecostalism, Leonard Maré states bluntly,

> In the liturgy of Pentecostal churches there is virtually no room for lament. It is a fact that someone might attend a Pentecostal service and leave thinking that Pentecostals' lives are free from any

---

[72] Westermann, *Praise and Lament in the Psalms*, p. 274.

[73] Brueggemann, 'The Friday Voice of Faith', p. 16.

[74] Westermann, *The Living Psalms*, p. 274. The place of lament in the New Tes-tament is explored in more detail by McQueen, *Joel and the Spirit*, pp. 37-62, and by Ellington, *Risking Truth*, pp. 163-83.

[75] Westermann, *The Living Psalms*, p. 275. On lament in the book of Revelation, see Thomas, *The Apocalypse*, pp. 251-54, who compares Rev. 6.10 to the psalms of lament. See also Johnson, *Pneumatic Discernment in the Apocalypse*, pp. 368-78.

[76] Westermann, *The Living Psalms*, p. 275. Cf. Brueggemann, 'The Friday Voice of Faith', p. 13, who writes that lament,

> taken theologically and christologically, correlates with the Friday and Sunday of Christian faith. Therefore, it is precisely this psalm-lament genre that gives Christian faith its liturgical pattern of crucifixion and resurrection. One obvi-ous implication is that the loss of the lament psalm in the worship life of the church is essentially the loss of a theology of the cross.

kind of negativity or disharmony. Pentecostals tend to reject any expression of feelings of negativity, anger, revenge and complaint as a legitimate part of worship.[77]

Maré cites Terry Law and Jack R. Taylor as examples of Pentecostals who reject the practice of lament. Regarding Jesus Christ as the believer's advocate, Law states, 'He will only bring our confession of the Word to the Father. He will not bring our begging and our crying and our pleading.'[78] Taylor, likewise, argues that Christians should approach God with praise only.[79]

While Westermann, Brueggemann, and Maré are accurate in their assessments of the Church in general, they might be surprised to learn that a large segment of the Pentecostal tradition has practiced lament as an essential element of their spirituality and continues to do so. Most global Pentecostals live on the margins of Christianity and of society, and they understand that lament and praise are not contradictory. In fact, they know that the pathos and passion of lament fuels and powers praise. Rickie Moore, agrees, commenting that 'lament is not, as is commonly assumed, a negation of praise, but it is ultimately the deep well from which the highest manifestation of praise springs forth'.[80] Brueggemann, likewise, argues, 'Indeed, the proper setting of praise is as lament resolved. In a sense, doxology and praise are best understood only in response to God's salvific intervention, which in turn is evoked by the lament.'[81] Furthermore, insists Moore, 'lament over oppressive life conditions ... becomes the path that, when followed with tenacious faithfulness to the end, indeed the end of ourselves, leads us to the revelation of God as the true end, highest joy, and lasting praise of our life'.[82] Praise without lament is shallow, superficial, and empty. The denial of pain is unhealthy and unbiblical – attempting to ignore the problem will not

---

[77] Maré, 'A Pentecostal Perspective', p. 95. Maré is associated with the Apostolic Faith Mission of South Africa, the largest Pentecostal denomination in SA.

[78] Terry Law, *Praise Releases Faith: Transforming Power for Your Life* (Tulsa, OK: Victory House Publishers, 1987), p. 83.

[79] Jack R. Taylor, *The Hallelujah Factor: An Adventure into the Principles and Practice of Praise* (Nashville, TN: Broadman Press, 1983), pp. 62-64. Perhaps it should be noted that neither Law nor Taylor is a Classical Pentecostal.

[80] Moore, *The Spirit of the Old Testament*, p. 114.

[81] Brueggemann, *The Psalms and the Life of Faith*, p. 99.

[82] Moore, *The Spirit of the Old Testament*, p. 117.

make it go away. The psalms of lament encourage faithful and legitimate protest to God during times of trouble.

Larry McQueen finds evidence that prayers of lament were common in early Pentecostalism, and he argues that lament continues to contribute to holistic Pentecostal prayer.[83] McQueen cites early Pentecostal periodicals and personal diaries that include testimonies of prayers that closely resemble the laments of the Psalms. Church of God evangelist J.W. Buckalew reports that 'two thousand people stand around until midnight listening at the cries of souls praying through to God';[84] and an anonymous writers tells of a meeting in Pleasant Grove, Florida, where 'Great burdens of prayer fell upon the saints at times, and great suffering would seize them as they were plunged into sympathy for this lost world, and saw the great need of workers and power to win souls for Christ'.[85] A.J. Tomlinson, who would be come a leader in the Church of God (Cleveland, TN), wrote in his diary on Sept. 11, 1901,

> This afternoon I repaired to the woods and poured out my heart to God. I am so wonderfully burdened with a desire to go on to Shiloh, at once. I am now at a place for decision, either to return to our mission or go on to Boston. I have no money for either. I have not heard from home for a week. I confess I am in great distress.[86]

Many other entries in Tomlinson's diary could be cited; for example, on Feb. 24, 1908 he wrote,

> For about two hours at home before I went to the night service I was especially exercised in prayer and weeping and groaning. I preached in tears on eternal punishment and made an altar call, and broke down again in agony and blinding tears. After coming to myself again and on looking up I saw the altar filled with seekers. Some were weeping, others crying to God for mercy.[87]

---

[83] McQueen, *Joel and the Spirit*, pp. 70-95. On the recovery of lament for the contemporary church, see also Stephen C. Torr, *A Dramatic Pentecostal/Charismatic Anti-Theodicy: Improvising on a Divine Performance of Lament* (Eugene, OR: Pickwick Publications, 2013).
[84] COGE, 1.16 (Oct 15, 1910), p. 3.
[85] COGE, 1.18 (Nov 15, 1910), p. 1.
[86] Tomlinson, *The Diary of A.J. Tomlinson 1901-1924*, p. 27.
[87] Tomlinson, *The Diary of A.J. Tomlinson 1901-1924*, p. 82.

Narelle Melton discovered similar types of prayers in her study of early Australian Pentecostals. She concludes that they 'were intuitively utilising the biblical form of lament psalms within their prayers of crisis'.[88] She points out that 'the global roots of Pentecostalism began with the marginalised; as such, frequent lamentation would be expected inside this community'.[89] Melton also suggests that glossolalia may serve as a vehicle for Pentecostal lament.[90] Glossolalia is considered by many Pentecostals to be the language of prayer, and the apostle Paul may be referring to glossolalia when he writes, 'the Spirit also helps our weakness; for we do not know how to pray as we should, but the Spirit himself intercedes for us with groanings too deep for words' (Rom. 8.26).[91]

The practice of lament is not limited to the early days of Pentecostalism. The research of Harvard professor Harvey Cox confirms the continued practice of lament. Cox writes,

> Pentecostal theology is found in the viscera of Pentecostal spirituality. It is emotional, communal, narrational, and radically embodied … The day I visited the regular Sunday worship of the Azusa Christian community in Dorchester the members sang with gusto, shook tambourines, and worshipped with infectious jubilation. But what impressed me most was the intensity of their prayers.[92]

Describing another visit to the Pentecostal church, Cox writes, 'People cried out, called, moaned, and wept. Blacks and whites and men and women knelt together in an unintentional reenactment of what must have both thrilled and upset those astonished visitors at Azusa Street.'[93]

---

[88] Narelle Jane Melton, 'Lessons of Lament: Reflections on the Correspondence between the Lament Psalms and Early Australian Pentecostal Prayer', *JPT* 20.1 (2011), p. 69.

[89] Melton, 'Lessons of Lament', p. 76. Cf. McQueen, *Joel and the Spirit*, p. 76.

[90] Melton, 'Lessons of Lament', p. 78-80. Melton draws heavily upon Frank D. Macchia, 'Sighs Too Deep for Words: Towards a Theology of Glossolalia', *JPT* 1 (1992), pp. 47-73. Melton's suggestion is in keeping with my own observation of the Pentecostal church (beginning in 1971). I have personally witnessed (and experienced) countless examples of glossolalic lament.

[91] See also Stephen C. Torr, 'Lamenting in Tongues: Glossolalia as a Pneumatic Aid to Lament', *JPT* 26.1 (2017), pp. 38-47.

[92] Harvey G. Cox, *Fire from Heaven: The Rise of Pentecostal Spirituality and the Reshaping of Religion in the 21st Century* (London: Cassell, 1996), pp. 319-20.

[93] Cox, *Fire from Heaven*, p. 85.

Among many Pentecostals, the prayer of lament is known as 'praying through'.[94] In his recent volume entitled *Pentecostal Theology*, Wolfgang Vondey explains the process of praying through:

> ... while prayer is of course a central practice throughout the Christian life, praying through requires a focused attention and dedication to a particular request or desire ... Although praying through frequently emerges from an attitude of lament, the perceived absence of God, and emptiness of the human life, it eventually moves from anguish to praise. It is a raw form of prayer, firm and straight to God.[95]

Praying through may be experienced during a time of 'tarrying' in prayer.[96] According to Daniel Castelo, 'tarrying implies travailing, waiting, prostrating, and submitting oneself before the presence of God in hopes that God's presence might break forth in the mundane and profane circumstances of life'.[97] Steven Land argues essentially that tarrying in prayer is a mark of the Spirit-filled church. He writes, 'A church that rejoices, waits, and yields in the Spirit, a church that loves the Word and will tarry as long as it takes to pray through to the will of God, the mind of Christ, and the leading of the Spirit, that church is Spirit filled'.[98] What Land describes is the hopeful cry of lament.

Conclusion

Psalm 130 begins with a cry: 'From the depths, I cry to you, LORD'; and, by beginning in this way, the psalm teaches us to give voice to our suffering and our pain. The laments teach us to come openly and honestly to God with our needs, to tell him our doubts and our fears.

---

[94] On the comparison between biblical lament and the Pentecostal terminology of 'praying through' see Land, *Pentecostal Spirituality*, p. 117. Cf. Cox, *Fire from Heaven*, p. 84; McQueen, *Joel and the Spirit*, pp. 70, 71, 72; Melton, 'Lessons of Lament', p. 76; Johns, 'A Pentecostal Understanding of Penitence', p. 302; and Vondey, *Pentecostal Theology: Living the Full Gospel*, p. 86.

[95] Vondey, *Pentecostal Theology: Living the Full Gospel*, p. 86.

[96] Vondey, *Pentecostal Theology: Living the Full Gospel*, pp. 60-63. Vondey points out that some contemporary Charismatics have a similar practice that they call 'soaking prayer'. See Wilkinson, Michael, and Peter Althouse, *Catch the Fire: Soaking Prayer and Charismatic Renewal* (DeKalb, IL: Northern Illinois University Press, 2014).

[97] Daniel Castelo, 'Tarrying on the Lord: Affections, Virtues and Theological Ethics in Pentecostal Perspective', *JPT* 13.1 (2004), p. 51. Cf. McQueen, *Joel and the Spirit*, p. 72.

[98] Land, *Pentecostal Spirituality*, p. 165.

Jesus declared that God's house should be a house of prayer, but many churches no longer include altar calls, prayer for the sick, and times of seeking the face of God. Worship is turned into entertainment, and the preaching of the Gospel is replaced by pop-psychology. The church should be a place where God's people can weep with those who weep and bind up the brokenhearted. Many of our brothers and sisters arrive at church bearing heavy burdens. During times of prayer, the body of Christ can respond to their pain, so that grieving ones are not alone in that moment. In the words of the psalmist, we must cry out to the Lord from the depths.

God Heals You When You Cry
R.B. Stone
Now I was down to nothing, knocked down to my knees.
It's there I found the answer, and I came to believe.
When this world leaves you broken and tears fall from your eyes,
Let sorrow meet surrender – God heals you when you cry.
When sorrow meets surrender, God heals you when you cry.[99]

This QR code links to a performance of the above song.

---

[99] R.B. Stone, 'God Heals You When You Cry' (*Loosen Up*; Nashville, TN: Middle Mountain Music, 2013), https://youtu.be/IgU_3kO1t4U. This song came to my attention when I heard it performed by Kary 'Goat' Varnell on a Sunday morning at Grace Community Church in Cleveland, Tennessee. Goat suffered greatly from the lingering effects of military combat and drug abuse.

7

PSALM 150: LET EVERY BREATH PRAISE THE LORD!

Introduction

Christian rock pioneer Larry Norman recorded a song entitled, 'Why should the devil have all the good music?'[1] A similar sentiment is expressed by an early Pentecostal writer who asserts, 'Some folks seem to think the devil has a monopoly on all the dancing and joy; but dancing and joy really belong to God'.[2] The writer cites Ps. 150.4, 'Praise him with the tambourine and the dance'; then, quotes lyrics from Fannie Crosby: 'the children of the Lord have a right to shout and sing, for … we are going … to the palace of the King'.[3] Psalm 150, in my view, proclaims that the devil does *not* have all the good music. Furthermore, the final psalm not only *allows* God's people to worship enthusiastically, but *demands* that they do so with 'every breath' (Ps. 150.6).

Enthusiastic praise of God has been a vital characteristic of the Pentecostal movement,[4] but not everyone has approved of Pentecostal fervency. A witness to the Azusa St. revival in 1906 disparaged the worshipers in a newspaper article, declaring that the revival was a

---

[1] Larry Norman, 'Why Should the Devil Have All the Good Music?' (*Only Visiting This Planet*, produced by Rod Edwards, Roger Hand and Jon Miller; London: AIR Studios, 1972). I am indebted to Chris Thomas for reminding me of this song.
[2] *The Bridal Call* 2.11 (Apr 1919), p. 4. *The Bridal Call* was published by Aimee Semple McPherson in Los Angeles, CA.
[3] Fannie J. Crosby, 'Glory to God, Hallelujah' (1885).
[4] Alvarado, 'Worship in the Spirit', p. 139.

… disgraceful intermingling of the races … they cry and make howling noises all day and into the night. They run, jump, shake all over, shout to the top of their voice, spin around in circles, fall out on the sawdust blanketed floor jerking, kicking and rolling all over it. Some of them pass out and do not move for hours as though they were dead. These people appear to be mad, mentally deranged or under a spell. They claim to be filled with the spirit.[5]

Responding to that kind of continuing criticism, Steven Land explains that what was deemed by their critics as 'a cacophony of sound and a pandemonium of celebration was to the Pentecostals a concert of prayer, a stereophonic praise temple and a proleptic dance of the kingdom. Where the Spirit was, there was liberty.'[6] He explains that the exuberant worship of Pentecostals is generated by their apocalyptic spirituality, which Land characterizes as 'a passion for the kingdom', which is 'ultimately a passion for God'.[7]

Inasmuch as Pentecostals have appealed to Psalm 150 as justification for their extravagant worship, I have chosen to examine the biblical text through the lens of Pentecostal spirituality and offer a contemporary appropriation of the psalm in dialogue with early Pentecostal literature. The Psalm will be examined in light of its structure, its content, its theology of worship, its role as the final song in the Psalter, its affective rhetoric, and its function in Pentecostalism.[8] As a hermeneutical circle, my context within the Pentecostal worshiping community contributes to a fresh perspective on the text, and the biblical text contributes to a deepening of Pentecostal theology and spirituality.[9]

---

[5] Christopher Knowles, *The Secret History of Rock 'N' Roll: The Mysterious Roots of Modern Music* (Berkeley, CA: Cleis Press, 2010), p. 83.

[6] Land, *Pentecostal Spirituality*, pp. 106-107.

[7] Land, *Pentecostal Spirituality*, pp. 2, 97, 120, 73-80, 212. Cf. Cartledge, 'Affective Theological Praxis', p. 36.

[8] The Pentecostal movement is a global, diverse, and multifaceted tradition; therefore, I do not claim to speak for all Pentecostals. However, I do have a broad knowledge of global Pentecostalism. I have worshiped in Romanian, Jamaican, Puerto Rican, and African-American churches within the USA, and I have worshiped in Pentecostal congregations outside the USA in the following countries: Haiti, Ecuador, Korea, South Africa, and the Philippines.

[9] On whether the worship practices found in the Psalms should inform contemporary Christian worship, see Lee Roy Martin, 'The Book of Psalms and Pentecostal Worship', in Lee Roy Martin (ed.), *Toward a Pentecostal Theology of Worship* (Cleveland, TN: CPT Press, 2016), where I summarized,

A Translation of Psalm 150

[1] Praise Yah!
   Praise God in his sanctuary;
      Praise him in his strong firmament.
[2] Praise him in his mighty acts;
      Praise him according to his abundant greatness.
[3] Praise him with blast of horn;
      Praise him with harp and lyre.
[4] Praise him with tambourine and dance;
      Praise him with strings and flute.
[5] Praise him with cymbals of attention;
      Praise him with cymbals of acclamation.
[6] Every breath should praise Yah;
   Praise Yah!

The Structure and Genre of Psalm 150

Structure of Psalm 150

The poetic structure of this brief psalm consists of three parts: vv. 1-2, vv. 3-5, and v. 6.[10] The psalm is framed by the repeated imperative 'Praise Yah!'[11] Thematically, the psalm can be outlined as follows:

A.   Initial exhortation to praise (v. 1a)
B.   Places of praise (v. 1b and 1c)
C.   Motives for praise (v. 2)
D.   Means of praise (vv. 3-5)

Given the Old Testament's authority in the Christian tradition generally and in the Pentecostal tradition specifically, I will proceed on the assumption that while the relative value of each specific worship practice in the Psalms may be assessed on its own merits, these practices and the broader and more basic theological concerns of the Psalter can be accepted as valuable for constructing a Pentecostal theology of worship (p. 51).

[10] Pierre Auffret, 'Par le Tambour et la Danse: Étude Structurelle du Psaume 150', *ETR* 77.2 (2002), p. 257. Cf. Dirk J. Human, '"Praise Beyond Words": Psalm 150 as Grand Finale of the Crescendo in the Psalter', *HTS* 67.1 (2011), p. 4.

[11] Fokkelman, *The Psalms in Form*, pp. 154, 172, argues that 'Praise YAH!' in v. 1 is 'outside the poem proper', but 'Praise YAH!' in v. 6 serves as the second colon of the last poetic verse. Cf. Goldingay, *Psalms*, III, p. 749. However, Allen, *Psalms 101-150*, places both appearances of 'Praise YAH!' outside the poetic structure (pp. 501-502). In either case, this inclusion functions as a powerful literary device in each of the five final psalms.

E.   Universality of praise (v. 6a)
F.   Continuing exhortation to praise (v. 6b)

Within this simple structure that answers the questions What?, Who? Where?, Why?, and How?,[12] Pierre Auffret identifies dance as the rhetorical center and, therefore, the 'eminent expression of praise'.[13]

Carroll Stuhlmueller suggests that the ten imperatives in the main body of the poem correspond to the Decalogue, and the 13 total exhortations to praise match the 13 attributes of Yahweh that were revealed to Moses in Exod. 34.6-7 and the 13 times that God spoke in Genesis 1.[14] The number ten can also represent 'totality and perfection'.[15] The ten imperatives would also duplicate the ten occurrences of 'Praise YAH!' that begin and end the five final psalms (146-150). Adding the frame of 'hallelujah', makes a total of 12 imperatives, and the number 12 'evokes both the twelve tribes of Israel and the twelve months of the year'.[16]

Genre and Date of Psalm 150

At first glance, Psalm 150 would appear to fit into the form-critical classification of the hymn. A hymn normally consists of three parts, 1. Call to praise, 2. Motive for praise, and 3. Renewed Call to praise. The shortest example of the hymn is Psalm 117.[17]

1. Call to praise	Praise Yahweh, all nations;
	Worship him, all peoples (v. 1)
2. Motive for praise	because (כִּי) his loyalty is strong toward us,
	and his faithfulness is forever! (v. 2a)
3. Renewed call to praise	Praise Yah (v. 2b)

The call to praise serves as only one element of the hymnic form, appearing at the beginning (and often at the end as well). In Psalm 150, however, this one element is creatively expanded into an entire

---

[12] Mays, *Psalms*, p. 450.

[13] Auffret, 'Par Le Tambour et La Danse', p. 257.

[14] Carroll Stuhlmueller, 'Psalms', in *Harper's Bible Commentary* (San Francisco: Harper and Row, 1988), p. 433, cited by Crenshaw, *The Psalms: An Introduction*, p. 9. See also Hans-Peter Mathys, 'Psalm Cl', *VT* 50.3 (2000), who notes that the Psalter names ten authors of the Psalms (p. 332).

[15] Zenger, 'Psalm 150', in Hossfeld and Zenger, *Psalms 3: A Commentary on Psalms 101-150*, p. 657.

[16] Zenger, 'Psalm 150', p. 657.

[17] The following Psalms (among others) also exhibit the three-part hymnic structure: 29, 47, 98, 113, 145, 146, 147, 148, and 149. See Mays, *Psalms*, p. 27.

psalm.[18] While the hymns of praise include a section that details the motive for praising God (e.g. Pss. 47.2-5; 96.4-6; 98.1-3), Psalm 150 is 'only a SUMMONS TO PRAISE'.[19] Motives for praise are included in v. 2, but they are presented as prepositional phrases connected to the imperative. The entire psalm, therefore, is 'just one richly varied introit'.[20]

The mention of the 'sanctuary' (v. 1), the plural form of the imperative, and the use of the ram's horn (often used for gathering the people) combine to indicate that 'The Psalm was not composed for individual reading or meditation, but for communal use in worship performances'.[21]

The date of Psalm 150 is uncertain. Its position at the end of the Psalter does not necessarily indicate a late date. Therefore, it could have been written either before or after the exile, but Goldingay argues that the references to the ram's horn and the cymbals point to a pre-exilic date for its composition. The Hebrew words for 'trumpet' and 'cymbals' that are used in Psalm 150 are different from those found in the book of Chronicles, which is known to be postexilic.[22]

---

[18] See Goldingay, *Psalms*, III, p. 746-47, and Mays, *Psalms*, p. 449. Compare the way in which the statement of trust that is found in the lament (e.g. Ps. 4.5 [6]) was expanded into a new type of psalm, the psalm of trust (cf. Psalms 23, 27, 91, 125).

[19] Gerstenberger, *Psalms, Part 2*, p. 458 (emphasis original). The motives for praise are often (but not always) introduced with the Hebrew כִּי, translated 'because' (e.g. Psalms 47, 96, 98, 100, 103, 117, 147, 148, 149). Hymns that do not utilize the word כִּי include Psalms 29, 81, 111, 113, 134, 146, and 150.

[20] Sigmund Mowinckel, *The Psalms in Israel's Worship* (New York: Abingdon Press, 1967), p. 83. Cf. Zenger, 'Psalm 150', p. 656. After analyzing the rhetorical purposes found in the Psalms, Robert L. Foster, '*Topoi* of Praise in the Call to Praise Psalms: Toward a *Theo*logy of the Book of Psalms', in R.L. Foster and D.M. Howard Jr (eds.), '*My Words Are Lovely': Studies in the Rhetoric of the Psalms* (London: T&T Clark, 2008), alters the form-critical category of hymn to include Psalm 150 and names his revised category the 'Call to Praise' psalms. Other Call to Praise psalms are 29, 47, 81, 96, 98, 100, 103, 111, 113, 117, 134, 146, 147, 148, 149 (p. 76).

[21] Gerstenberger, *Psalms, Part 2*, p. 460. Cf. Dahood, *Psalms*, III, p. 359, and R.G. Bratcher and W.D. Reyburn, *A Handbook on Psalms* (UBS Handbook Series; New York: United Bible Societies, 1993), p. 1188.

[22] Goldingay, *Psalms*, III, p. 747. Psalm 150 uses שׁוֹפָר and צְלְצַל, but Chronicles has הַצֹוצְרָה and מְחֵלֹת.

Overview of Psalm 150

Initial Exhortation to Praise (v. 1a)

Like the four hymns that precede it, this psalm begins with the imperative, 'Praise Yah!' (הללו יה). In the ANE languages, הלל carries the suggestion of loud cheering, voicing of admiration, or speaking well of someone; therefore, it is translated 'praise'. It signifies the showing of approval or the lauding of someone.[23] 'This root connotes being sincerely and deeply thankful for and/or satisfied in lauding a superior quality(ies) or great, great act(s) of the object'.[24] The imperative, therefore, is a call or exhortation to praise.

The book of Psalms teaches us that praise is fundamental to life. 'Praise is [humanity's] most characteristic mode of existence: praising and not praising stand over against one another like life and death: praise becomes the most elementary "token of being alive" that exists'.[25] Moreover, praise is the basic human obligation. Karl Barth argues, 'We misunderstand the Old Testament if we do not realise that this element of praise or doxology is the basic note'.[26]

Regarding the significance of this call to praise, Claus Westermann writes, 'the call issues forth unrelentingly, untiringly, ever anew, because that for which it calls is recognized as absolutely necessary, sustaining, supportive of the community ... Through God's praise, the congregation expresses its self-understanding, its being vis-a-vis God'.[27]

Who is to be praised? The object of praise is Yah, which is a short form of Yahweh, the personal name of the God of Israel. He is God of Abraham, Isaac, and Jacob; and he is the God who met Moses at the burning bush in Exodus 3. He is the God who spoke to the Israelites from Mt. Sinai and said to them, 'I am Yahweh your God, who brought you out of the land of Egypt, out of the house of bondage' (Exod. 20.2). He graciously offered his covenant to the Israelites and claimed them as his own special possession. Praise flows out of the covenant relationship between Yahweh and Israel. It is an expression

---

[23] See *HALOT*, I, p. 249. *DCH*, II, p. 561.
[24] Leonard J. Coppes, 'הלל' in *TWOT*, I, p. 217.
[25] Gerhard von Rad, *Old Testament Theology* (2 vols.; New York: Harper, 1962), I, pp. 369-70, cited by Kraus, *Theology of the Psalms*, p. 69.
[26] Karl Barth, *Church Dogmatics: The Doctrine of Reconciliation, Part 3.1* (ed. G.W. Bromiley and T.F. Torrance; London: T&T Clark, 2004), I, pp. 471-72.
[27] *TLOT*, I, p. 372.

of Israel's covenant commitment to Yahweh, and Israel's praises are in direct response to Yahweh's faithfulness as embodied in Yahweh's חסד ('covenant commitment').[28]

Places of Praise (v. 1b)

'Praise God in his sanctuary'. Praise is directed to 'God' (אֵל), the divine name that is 'used to indicate God in all his might',[29] his powerful sovereignty',[30] or to stress the 'universality of God/Yahweh'.[31] The change in divine name may be connected to the reference to the 'firmament' at the end of the verse. It was El who created the firmament in Gen. 1.6. Also, the name 'El' would also contribute to the alliterative repetition of the letter 'l' (*hallelu El*'). Anthony Ceresko argues that the naming of God as 'El' in v. 1 is an alphabetic compositional device. He suggests that successive letters of the alphabet are stressed as the psalm moves forward, beginning with the letter *alef* (א) in the word אֵל ('God') and concluding with the letter *tav* (ת) in the word תהלל, ('praise'), found in v. 6. Ceresko's proposal explains both the presence of the name 'El' in v. 1, when 'Yahweh' might be expected, as well as the grammatical change from imperative to jussive in v. 6.[32]

Where should praise take place? Worship should take place in God's 'sanctuary', and it should take place in God's 'strong firmament'. The Hebrew קדְשׁוֹ can be translated 'his holiness' (as Amos 4.2) or 'his holy place', i.e. 'sanctuary'. The LXX reads, 'holy ones' (ἁγίοις), which is unlikely, given that the Hebrew word is singular. In Pss. 60.8 and 108.8, קדשׁוֹ is translated 'his holiness' by the NKJV, ESV, and NASB; but it is rendered 'his sanctuary' by the NRSV, CEB, NIV, NJB, and TNK. In Psalm 150, the parallel with 'firmament' suggests a location for God rather than a characteristic of God. Still, the sanctuary can be either the heavenly or the earthly temple. Goldingay, Dahood, Calvin, and Limburg argue that the parallel with 'firmament'

---

28 Walter Brueggemann, *Worship in Ancient Israel: An Essential Guide* (Nashville, TN: Abingdon Press, 2005), pp. 7-9.

29 S.E. Tesh and W.D. Zorn, *Psalms* (Joplin, MO: College Press, 1999), p. 537.

30 Ross, *A Commentary on the Psalms*, III, pp. 964-65.

31 Zenger, 'Psalm 150', p. 659.

32 Anthony R. Ceresko, 'Endings and Beginnings: Alphabetic Thinking and the Shaping of Psalms 106 and 150', *CBQ* 68.1 (2006), pp. 42-44. His proposal is rejected as 'rather improbable' by Zenger, 'Psalm 150', p. 658.

suggests the heavenly temple.[33] Calvin writes that God is located in heaven, but the worshipers are located on earth, and they are exhorted to 'lift their eyes towards the heavenly sanctuary'.[34] 'Yahweh is in his sanctuary; Yahweh – his throne is in heaven' (Ps. 11.4). Samuel Terrien, however, understands the 'holy place' to be 'the temple of Zion' which served in tradition as the 'navel of the earth', where heaven and earth were joined together.[35] Zenger agrees that the earthly temple is 'more probable in this passage, because our psalm is especially concerned with bringing together the earthly (v. 1b) and heavenly (v. 1c) praise of YHWH and filling the whole cosmos with it'.[36] Derek Kidner remarks, 'So the call is to God's worshippers on earth, meeting at his chosen place, but also to his heavenly host … to mingle their praises with ours. Earth and heaven can be utterly at one in this. His glory fills the universe; his praise must do no less.'[37] The ambiguity of this verse could have been removed by substituting for 'sanctuary' either 'heaven' (as in Ps. 148.1, 'praise him in heaven') or 'the assembly/congregation' (as in Ps. 149.1, 'praise him in the congregation). Therefore, I understand the ambiguity to be suggestive of

---

[33] Dahood argues on the basis of the parallelism that the heavenly sanctuary must be in view. Dahood, *Psalms*, III, p. 359. Cf. Goldingay, *Psalms*, III, p. 747; Limburg, *Psalms*, p. 505; and Calvin, *Psalms*, V, p. 319. However, the contrast between heaven and earth is sometimes expressed through parallelism (i.e. Pss. 69.35; 73.9, 25; 76.8; 79.2; 89.6; 102.25). Therefore, Lennox, *Psalms: A Bible Commentary in the Wesleyan Tradition*, p. 433, understands 'sanctuary' to refer to the Jerusalem temple.

[34] Calvin, *Psalms*, V, p. 320. Contra Ross, *A Commentary on the Psalms*, III, p. 966.

[35] Terrien, *The Psalms*, p. 928. Cf. Brueggemann and Bellinger, *Psalms*, p. 618. Cf. Daniel Carro, José Tomás Poe, and Rubén O. Zorzoli, *Comentario Bíblico Mundo Hispano: Salmos* (El Paso, TX: Editorial Munto Hispano, 1993), who write, '*Santuario podría ser el universo como su santuario, pero es mejor tomarlo como el templo. Se empieza en el templo pero Dios recibe alabanza de todo el universo*' (p. 443). Cf. Matthew Henry, *Matthew Henry's Commentary on the Whole Bible: Complete and Unabridged in One Volume* (Peabody, MA: Hendrickson Publishers, 1994). Henry writes 'Let his priests, let his people, that attend there, attend him with their praises. Where should he be praised, but there where he does, in a special manner, both manifest his glory and communicate his grace? (p. 953).

[36] Zenger, 'Psalm 150', p. 658. Cf. Adele Berlin and Marc Zvi Brettler, 'Psalms', in A. Berlin and M.Z. Brettler (eds.), *The Jewish Study Bible* (Oxford: Oxford University Press, 2004), who interpret v. 1 to mean that the 'site of praise is enlarged to include the whole world' (p. 1446).

[37] Derek Kidner, *Psalms 73-150: A Commentary on Books III-V of the Psalms* (London: Inter-Varsity Press, 1975), p. 528. Cf. Kraus, *Psalms 60-150*, who writes, 'At the holy place heaven and earth touch each other. For that reason the heavenly world is repeatedly drawn into the hymns. In v. 1 the appeal makes its way into the heavenly sphere' (p. 570).

both the heavenly and the earthly temples. After all, God has a throne in heaven and in the Jerusalem temple.[38] In any case, the emphasis is upon the 'quality of holiness'.[39] God is holy, and his presence creates holy space.

The Hebrew word רָקִיעַ ('firmament') is exceedingly difficult to translate into a single English word because of the differences between ancient and modern cosmologies. The firmament is 'the firm vault of heaven';[40] it is the dome or arch of the sky, 'considered fixed above the earth'.[41] 'The 'firmament' is often used as a synonym to 'heaven' (e.g. Ps. 19.1), but, as Goldingay points out, 'the psalm is thinking of the solid dome in the heavens, above which Yhwh's throne sits, securely established by Yhwh'.[42] It is God's 'divine residence'.[43] By itself, the firmament would represent God's power, especially the power of creation; but here we have the 'firmament of strength'. The Hebrew עֹז means 'might, strength';[44] therefore, the adjectival construct phrase should be translated 'his strong firmament'.[45] Matthew Henry explains the significance of praising God in his strong firmament:

> *Praise him* because of his power and glory which appear in the firmament, its vastness, its brightness, and its splendid furniture; and because of the powerful influences it has upon this earth. Let

---

[38] Cf. Ross, *A Commentary on the Psalms*, III, p. 965, who suggests that the terminology may be 'deliberately ambiguous, including both the heavenly and earthly sanctuaries in the expression'.

[39] Auffret, 'Par le Tambour et la Danse', p. 259.

[40] *HALOT*, II, p. 1290.

[41] *DCH*, VII, p. 552.

[42] Goldingay, *Psalms*, III, p. 747.

[43] Allen, *Psalms 101-150*, p. 403.

[44] *HALOT*, II, p. 805. *DCH*, VI, p. 322. Dahood's translation of עֹז as 'his fortress' is doubtful (*Psalms*, III, p. 360), given that it is not rendered 'fortress' in other Old Testament texts. Ross, *A Commentary on the Psalms*, III, p. 966, translates the entire phrase, 'in the firmament where his power is displayed'. Against other interpreters, Schaefer, *Psalms*, understands 'in his strong firmament' to refer to human worship that takes place on earth 'under the mighty dome of the sky' (p. 345).

[45] The Hebrew רְקִיעַ is not in apposition but is in construct; contra NJB, NEB, and Bratcher and Reyburn, *A Handbook on Psalms*, p. 1188. The appositional form would be בָּרְקִיעַ (cf. Gen. 1.8). See Joüon and Muraoka, *A Grammar of Biblical Hebrew*, who describe this kind of construction as a genitive of 'quality' (§129.f), and provide the following examples: Exod. 5.9; 29.29; Lev. 10.17; Prov. 1.10.

those that have their dwelling *in the firmament of his power,* even the holy angels, lead in this good work.[46]

Psalm 150.1 'states the obvious truth that [the firmament] belongs to God, and that God is to be praised on account of it'.[47]

Motives for Praise (v. 2)

Why should God be praised? After examination of the hymns, which he describes as the 'Call to Praise' psalms, Robert Foster concludes that the motives for praise can be organized under two categories; 1. 'attributes of YHWH', and 2. 'deeds ascribed to YHWH'.[48] Although in Psalm 150 the motives for praise do not constitute a separate section (see discussion above), they are present in the psalm in the form of prepositional phrases. The general attribute to be praised is God's 'abundant greatness', and the deeds to be praised are 'his mighty acts'. Therefore, Psalm 150 encompasses and summarizes all of the hymns of praise, without supplying a detailed list of God's attributes and actions. After all, the works of God have been recited repeatedly in the Psalter, and God's character has been celebrated throughout the book. The following list is but a brief reminder of God's works and greatness as found in the Psalter: the Lord is our shepherd (23.1); he is our rock and our fortress (18.2); the earth is the Lord's and the fullness thereof (24.1); the Lord is our light and our salvation (27.1), he brought us up out of a horrible pit (40.2); he is our refuge and strength (46.1); the Lord is good (34.8), his covenant loyalty is everlasting (106.1), and his truth endures to all generations (117.2); he forgives all of our sins (86.5); he heals all of our diseases (103.3); his greatness is unsearchable (145.3); the Lord created the heavens and the earth (96.5); he cares for the widow, the orphan, and the stranger (94.6); the Lord reigns forever (97.1). Goldingay asserts, therefore, 'To attempt to say something final about Yhwh would inevitably be anticlimactic'.[49]

Worshipers are commanded to praise God for 'his mighty acts'. The extremely concise wording of Psalm 150 results in several ambiguous words and phrases. In the clause 'praise him for his mighty acts' (הללוהו בגבורתיו), the preposition בּ creates an awkward and

---

[46] Henry, *Matthew Henry's Commentary,* p. 954 (emphasis original).
[47] Barth, *Church Dogmatics: The Doctrine of the Word of Creation, Part 1,* III, p. 137.
[48] Foster, '*Topoi* of Praise in the Call to Praise Psalms', p. 84.
[49] Goldingay, *Psalms,* III, p. 747.

unique construction. Elsewhere in the Hebrew Bible, whenever the verb הלל is followed by a motive for praise, that motive is normally introduced by כי and a verbal clause.[50] When הלל is followed by ב, the ב signifies location or means.[51] Therefore, the preposition ב in v. 2a would most naturally be translated 'with', as it is in vv. 3-5 below. The resulting translation would be 'Praise him with [recital of] his mighty acts', indicating that the recitation of God's mighty acts is one means of expressing praise.[52] Thus, Ps. 150.2a would be a restate-ment of Ps. 145.4, 'One generation shall praise your works to an-other, and shall declare your mighty acts'. However, the preposition ב can also mean 'because' (Gen. 18.28; Zech. 9.11; Lam. 2.29; Neh. 10.1; Dan. 10.2).[53] Therefore, the clause can be translated 'Praise him because of his mighty acts', a meaning that fits thematically into the hymnic genre and is parallel to the following line: 'Praise him accord-ing to his abundant greatness'.

In Hebrew, 'mighty acts' (גבורת) is the plural of גבורה 'strength, might'. The plural means 'feats of strength' and is used many times in reference to God's mighty deeds (e.g. Deut. 3.24; Pss. 20.7, 71.16, 106.2, 145.4, 145.12, Isa. 63.15).[54] Schaefer names God's mighty acts as 'creation, deliverance from Egypt, the crossing of the Red Sea, the giving of the law at Sinai, the entrance to the Promised Land, the choice of Mount Zion as God's residence on earth – God's historical actions on behalf of Israel and every human'.[55]

Other biblical texts glorify God for his 'mighty acts'. Moses speaks to God and says, 'O Yahweh God … what god is there in heaven or on earth who can do anything like your works and your mighty deeds? (Deut. 3.24). The psalmist writes, 'I come with praise of your mighty acts, O Yahweh God (Ps. 71.16); 'Who can express the mighty acts of Yahweh? Who can declare all his praise?' (Ps. 106.2); 'One

---

[50] E.g. 'because (כי) he is good' (Pss. 106.1; 135.3); 'because (כי) it is good to sing praise' (Ps. 147.1); 'because (כי) he delivered the poor' (Jer. 20.13). I was able to find one exception, where the motive is expressed through the preposition על: 'I praise you for (על) your righteous judgments' (הללתיך על משפטי צדקך – Ps. 119.164).

[51] E.g. 'in the assembly' (Pss. 22.23; 35.18; 107.32); 'in the gates' (Prov. 31.31); 'in the heights' (Ps. 148.1); 'Praise him with …' (Ps. 150.3, 4, 5).

[52] Berlin and Brettler, 'Psalms', p. 1446, take this position.

[53] *HALOT*, I, p. 105.

[54] *BDB*, p. 150. *DCH*, II, p. 305. *HALOT*, I, p. 173.

[55] Schaefer, *Psalms*, pp. 345-46.

generation shall praise your works to another, and shall declare your mighty acts' (Ps. 145.4); and 'make known to all people your mighty deeds, and the glorious splendor of your kingdom' (Ps. 145.12). The Jews in exile pray to God, 'Look down from heaven, and see from your holy and glorious dwelling; Where are your zeal and your mighty deeds?' (Isa. 63.15).

Worshipers are also commanded to praise God commensurate with 'his abundant greatness'. God's 'greatness' (גֹּדְלוֹ)[56] is his majesty, his 'magnificence'.[57] His greatness is proven by his 'great works and mighty acts' (Deut. 3.24) and by his redeeming of Israel from Egypt (Deut. 9.26). The adjectival form, 'great', is used of God more frequently than the noun form. The power of Yahweh is great (Exod. 32.11). God is greater than all other gods (2 Chron. 2.4). He is 'great and awesome' (Neh. 4.8). God is great (Neh. 8.6, Pss. 99.2, 135.5; Isa. 12.6; Jer. 10.6). He is great and 'does wonders' (Ps. 86.10). God 'is great and abundant in power' (Ps. 147.5). He is the 'great God' (גָּדוֹל אֵל – Deut. 7.21; 10.17; Neh. 1.5; 9.32; Pss. 77.14; 95.3; Jer. 32.18; Dan. 9.4). God's works are great (Deut. 11.7; Judg. 2.7; Ps. 111.2). His glory is great (Pss. 21.6; 138.5), and his name is great (Josh. 7.9; 1 Sam. 12.22; 1 Kgs 8.42; 2 Chron. 6.32, Pss. 76.2; 99.3; Jer. 10.6; 44.26; Ezek. 36.23; Mal. 1.11). His mercy is great (1 Kgs 3.6; 2 Chron. 1.8; Pss. 57.11; 86.13; 108.5); his goodness is great (Neh. 9.25); and his compassion is great (Isa. 54.7). God has done great acts of salvation and judgment (Deut. 10.21; Job 5.9; 9.10; 37.5; Pss. 71.19; 106.21). A slightly different form of the noun 'greatness' (גְּדוּלָּה) is also applied to God as an attribute (1 Chron. 29.11; Pss. 145.3; 145.6).

As if it were not enough to acknowledge the greatness of God, Ps. 150.2 commands the hearers to praise God in accordance with his *abundant* greatness (גֻדְלוֹ כְּרֹב). The Hebrew רֹב can mean many in number (a multitude), but it can also mean a large 'quantity, abundance'.[58] God's greatness is abundant.

Means of Praise (vv. 3-5)

How should God be praised? God should be praised with every kind of musical instrument, with every kind of jubilant expression, and

---

[56] *DCH*, II, p. 324. *HALOT*, I, p. 179.
[57] *BDB*, p. 152.
[58] *BDB*, p. 913. Cf. e.g. Gen. 27.28 'abundance of grain'; Ps. 145.7 'abundant goodness'.

with every breath. 'Music provides the singing with a special power which is appropriate for the majestic greatness of the God of Israel'.[59] The psalmist insists that every musical instrument should be used in praising the Lord. All humans have preferences for certain musical instruments; but, apparently, Psalm 150 invites us to use all sorts of instruments in praising God. Those of us who cannot play musical instruments can dance unto the Lord. Other physical modes of worship are mentioned in earlier psalms, such as the clapping of hands and shouting.

A variety of musical instruments are attested in ANE iconography.[60] The exact identification of each instrument continues to be debated, but 'what is clear is that this praise is not timid. It is to be done with enthusiasm.'[61] Psalm 150 is 'a witness to the power of music, its amazing potential for evoking beauty and feeling and for carrying vision beyond the range of words'.[62] Psalm 150 calls upon God's people to apply themselves 'diligently to the praises of God' and 'to bring to this service all their powers, and devote themselves wholly to it'.[63]

Ram's horn

The ram's horn (שׁוֹפָר)[64] was an

> unfinished, twisted animal horn, originally without a special mouthpiece (one was created by cutting off the tip of the horn). Given the technique for blowing it, this was not a melodic instrument but one used for signaling; by blowing breath (תָּקַע, 'push, strike') into it one can produce a long-held sound or rhythmic series of sounds.[65]

---

[59] Kraus, *Psalms 60-150*, p. 571.
[60] Crenshaw, *Psalms*, p. 76. See Appendix A for depictions of musical instruments from the ANE.
[61] Limburg, *Psalms*, p. 505.
[62] Mays, *Psalms*, p. 450.
[63] Calvin, *Psalms*, V, p. 320.
[64] DCH, VIII, p. 309; HALOT, II, p. 1447; Gerstenberger, *Psalms, Part 2*, p. 460; Edo Škulj, 'Musical Instruments in Psalm 150', in Jože Krašovec (ed.), *Interpretation of the Bible: The International Symposium in Slovenia* (Sheffield, UK: Sheffield Academic Press, 1998), p. 1120. Ross, *A Commentary on the Psalms*, III, p. 967, states that שׁוֹפָר could mean 'trumpet', but he does not supply any evidence. H.J. Austel, 'שׁוֹפָר', in *TWOT*, II, p. 951, insists, 'In the Old Testament [שׁוֹפָר] is always used of the curved musical instrument made of the horn of a ram'.
[65] Zenger, 'Psalm 150', p. 659.

It was sounded on ceremonial occasions (Lev. 25.9; Ps. 81.4; Joel 2.15; 2 Sam. 15.10), during battle (Judg. 3.27; Jer. 4.5; Hosea 5.8), and to signal a theophany, 'And Yahweh will appear over them … and the Lord Yahweh will sound the shofar' (Zech. 9.14; cf. Exod. 19.16-19; 20.8). The shofar announces Yahweh's presence before his joyful worshipers, 'With trumpets and the sound of the shofar, shout joyfully before the king, Yahweh' (Ps. 98.6; cf. Ps. 47.5; 1 Chron. 15.28; 2 Chron. 15.14). We read that David brought up the ark of Yahweh 'with jubilation and the sound of the trumpet' (2 Sam. 6.15). The sounding of the shofar 'often signaled the start of a special occasion',[66] and here it may signal the beginning of worship.

Harp and lyre

These are stringed instruments, but their exact nature is disputed by scholars.[67] They are mentioned in connection with a liturgical setting.[68] The נבל was a stringed instrument in the harp family. Škulj asserts that it was one of the 'bow harps without a front support and with a sounding box clad in leather in the upper part. It was the second most important musical instrument of the Temple liturgy.'[69] The כנור was also a stringed instrument, probably with two arms and a yoke upon which the strings were stretched.[70]

Tambourine and dance

Nancy DeClaissé-Walford points out that 'Music and dancing were an integral part of worship' in ancient Israel.[71] The tambourine and dance were utilized in celebrations such as the one that is recounted in Exodus 15, after the Israelites escaped from Egypt and passed

---

[66] Lennox, *Psalms: A Bible Commentary in the Wesleyan Tradition*, p. 433.

[67] Zenger, 'Psalm 150', p. 660.

[68] Lennox, *Psalms: A Bible Commentary in the Wesleyan Tradition*, p. 433. According to Mathys, 'Psalm CL', we know relatively little about the Israelite temple service; therefore, caution should be exercised when making assertions about the instruments and their uses (pp. 330-31).

[69] Škulj, 'Musical Instruments in Psalm 150', p. 1121. Translated 'harp' by *DCH*, V, p. 595; and by *HALOT*, I, p. 664.

[70] Škulj, 'Musical Instruments in Psalm 150', p. 1122. Translated 'lyre' by *BDB*, p. 490; and by *DCH*, IV, p. 435. *HALOT* translates it as a 'zither', I, p. 484.

[71] Nancy L. DeClaissé-Walford, 'Psalm 150', in DeClaissé-Walford, Jacobson, and Tanner (eds.), *The Book of Psalms*, p. 1009. Cf. Donatus Udoette, 'Sacred Music and Dance in Israel and in Psalm 150: Biblical-Theological Foundations for African Liturgical Music and Dance', in K. Bisong and M. Kadavil (eds.), *Celebrating the Sacramental World: Essays in Honour of Emeritus Professor Lambert J. Leijssen* (Leuven: Peeters, 2010), p. 258.

through the Red Sea. They began to sing and rejoice, and 'Then the prophet Miriam, Aaron's sister, took a tambourine in her hand, and all the women went out after her with tambourines and dancing' (Exod. 15.20). The narratives about David include similar celebrations. Following David's first great victory, 'it happened as they were coming, when David returned from killing the Philistine, that the women came out of all the cities of Israel, singing and dancing, to meet King Saul, with tambourines, with joy and with musical instruments (1 Sam. 18.6). Later in David's story, he returned the Ark of the Covenant to its rightful place inside the Tabernacle. As he entered Jerusalem, 'David danced before the LORD with all his might … So David and all the house of Israel brought up the ark of the Lord with jubilation and with the sound of the ram's horn' (2 Sam. 6.14-15).

The תֹף was a percussion instrument, often called a tambour or tambourine.[72] The tambourine had a round wooden frame with a skin stretched over it like a drum.[73] The dance (מָחוֹל) was 'usually a group round dance with musical, instrumental or vocal accompaniment', closely associated with the use of the tambourine (cf. Ps. 149.3).[74] As was mentioned above, Auffret argues that dance, though not an instrument, occupies the central position in the psalm's structure; and, therefore, is the most important expression of worship.[75]

In many parts of the world, dance continues to be a common element in worship. For example, Donatus Udoette explains that 'any meaningful worship in Africa has to be accompanied with vibrant singing, dancing to the tunes of musical instruments, and clapping of hands'.[76] However, persons from the west 'have sometimes frowned at music and dancing within liturgical contexts in Africa. Such people tend to think that it is improper and indecent to sing and dance the way Africans do within liturgical contexts'.[77]

Dancing has been a part of Pentecostal worship from the beginning of the movement. In 1919, the subject of dancing is addressed

---

[72] *DCH*, VIII, p. 662; *HALOT*, II, p. 1772; *BDB*, p. 852.

[73] Škulj, 'Musical Instruments in Psalm 150', p. 1123.

[74] Škulj, 'Musical Instruments in Psalm 150', p. 1124. Cf. Kraus, *Psalms 60-150*, p. 571; HALOT, I, p. 568.

[75] Auffret, 'Par le Tambour et la Danse', p. 260. He writes, '*Ainsi la danse, expression muette de la louange, jouit-elle d'une position centrale au beau milieu de l'orchestre pourrait-on dire, position qui à elle seule exprime l'importance que le texte entend lui donner*'.

[76] Udoette, 'Sacred Music and Dance in Israel and in Psalm 150', p. 269.

[77] Udoette, 'Sacred Music and Dance in Israel and in Psalm 150', p. 257.

in *The Bridal Call*, a periodical published by Aimee Semple McPherson. Citing Ps. 150.4 along with Pss. 14.3 and 20.11, the writer insists that 'dancing and joy really belong to God'. Christians should dance because 'Within the heart of him whose hopes are built upon the solid foundation of Christ and His righteousness, there is joy unspeakable and full of glory'.[78] A few years later, R.L. Stewart, encourages the readers of the *Pentecostal Holiness Advocate* to worship in the dance. He writes, 'how many of our folks have praised the Lord in the dance since 1917. We praise Him with the organs all right. Well, why not in the dance. There are a lot of folks that never did praise God in the dance. Say, brother, try it once and see how it goes.'[79]

Strings and flute

It is unclear which instruments are indicated by the Hebrew words מנים and עוגב. Zenger suggests that they may be 'generic designations for stringed instruments and wind instruments'.[80] Edo Škulj insists that the Hebrew מנים is a 'completely unclear expression ... probably a stringed instrument',[81] and the lexicons translate the plural form as 'stringed instrument'.[82] The עוגב may have been 'a wind instrument from the nomadic period ... a folk instrument ... a pipe'.[83] The Targums translate it into Aramaic as an אבובא, which is a reed-pipe or flute.[84] If it does refer to some kind of flute, it would be a reed or pipe with holes. Ancient Near Eastern depictions include both the single flute and the double flute, which had two reeds played simultaneously.

Cymbals

The Hebrew צלצלים signifies a percussion instrument that we call cymbals.[85] According to Škulj, the 'cymbals found in excavations were made of bronze ... The average diameter of the finds is about

---

[78] *BC* 2.11 (Apr 1919), p. 4.
[79] R.L. Steward, 'Have You the Joy of Pentecost as in 1914?', *PHA* 6.38 (Jan 18, 1923), p. 6.
[80] Zenger, 'Psalm 150', p. 661.
[81] Škulj, 'Musical Instruments in Psalm 150', p. 1124.
[82] *BDB*, p. 577; *DCH*, V, pp. 336-37; and *HALOT*, I, p. 597.
[83] Škulj, 'Musical Instruments in Psalm 150', p. 1125.
[84] *BDB*, p. 721. *DCH*, VI, p. 287, and *HALOT*, I, p. 795, also define it as a flute or pipe.
[85] *DCH*, VII, p. 127. *HALOT*, II, p. 1031.

12 cm'.[86] Two types of cymbals are named in Ps. 150.5. Ivor H. Jones calls the first type 'cymbals of attention'. He argues that שׁמע 'has cultic associations' and may suggest 'attention of the congregation to the word of God'.[87] The Hebrew phrase בצלצלי־שׁמע could be translated simply 'with cymbals of sound', apparently signifying loud or noisy cymbals.[88] The second type are 'cymbals of acclamation' or 'cymbals of clashing'.[89] The Hebrew תרועה 'is a cultic word used of cultic acclamation (cf. Ps 33.3; 47.6; 89.16)', hence the Vulgate *jubilationis*.[90] It signifies a loud shout or noise. Context determines whether the shout is generated by surprise, defeat, victory, or joy.[91] As a shout of joy, it can mean 'jubilation' or 'joyful shout' (see e.g. Ps. 100.1, 'shout to the LORD'). The two categories of cymbals may specify two different kinds of cymbals, two different manner of striking the cymbals,[92] or, as Goldingay suggests, 'two different functions fulfilled by the same instrument at different times'.[93]

The full orchestra

If the cymbals are only one instrument that is used in different ways, then seven instruments are named in Psalm 150.[94] The number seven has the symbolic meaning of 'perfection'.[95] This list of instruments 'along with dance encompasses all the ways by which people express God's praise with the body, the hands, and the throat'.[96] The list

---

[86] Škulj, 'Musical Instruments in Psalm 150', p. 1126.

[87] Ivor H. Jones, 'Musical Instruments in the Bible, Pt 1', *The Bible Translator* 37.1 (1986), p. 111. My translation ('cymbals of attention' and 'cymbals of acclamation') follows Jones.

[88] *HALOT*, II, p. 1574. *DCH*, VII, p. 127.

[89] *DCH*, VIII, p. 678 (emphasis original). On the Day of Atonement, the shofar is to be a שׁופר תרועה, 'blaring ram's horn' (Lev. 25.9).

[90] Jones, 'Musical Instruments in the Bible, Pt 1', p. 111. Jones observes that the pairing of the words 'attention' and 'acclamation' also 'provides a resonant alliteration … suited to psalm translation work'.

[91] Tremper Longman III, 'רוע', in *NIDOTTE*, III, pp. 1082-48.

[92] Zenger, 'Psalm 150', p. 662.

[93] Goldingay, *Psalms*, III, p. 749.

[94] Schaefer, *Psalms*, p. 345.

[95] Joachim Vette, 'Psalm 150', in Oeming and Vette, *Das Buch Der Psalmen: Psalm 90-151*, p. 254. Cf. Zenger, 'Psalm 150', p. 657. Gerstenberger, *Psalms, Part 2*, p. 459, however, argues for two different kinds of cymbals, which results in eight instruments.

[96] Schaefer, *Psalms*, p. 345.

includes 'instruments that would be played by priests (horn), by Levites (harp, lyre, cymbals), and by laypeople (tambourine, strings, pipe)'.[97]

This listing of different instruments played by separate groups (priest, Levite, laity) suggests full congregational participation in worship. 'Everybody, with all known instruments, was invited to praise God in this final poem of the Psalter.'[98] 'The tambourine, strings, and flute were instruments which enlivened secular festivities ... Thus, the praise embraces liturgical and secular settings and everybody participates.'[99] The presence of so-called 'secular' instruments would call into question the common Evangelical, Roman Catholic, and Greek orthodox prohibition of such instruments.[100]

The use of a variety of instruments has been a long-standing practice within Pentecostalism. The plethora of instruments was noted on one occasion at the Angelus Temple in Los Angeles, where Aimee Semple McPherson served as pastor. The writer names 'dozens of instruments', including the harmonica, the organ, xylophone, marimba, the golden harp, triangle, auto-harp, the 'Silver Band ... and instruments too numerous to mention'.[101]

James Mays explains the value of the music that is created by a multitude of instruments:

> This emphasis on music in the final psalm ... is a witness to the power of music, its amazing potential for evoking beauty and feeling and for carrying vision beyond the range of words into the realm of imagination. That we sing the praise of God is no accidental custom. Music performed, sung, enacted is so much a dimension of praise that words of praise without music need to be musical in rhythm and elegance if they are to serve as praise.[102]

In his book that claims to be a 'Biblical Theology of Worship', Evangelical scholar Daniel Block complains about the movement away from the pipe organ (which is not found in Scripture) as the

---

[97] Goldingay, *Psalms*, III, p. 748.
[98] Gerstenberger, *Psalms, Part 2*, p. 460.
[99] Schaefer, *Psalms*, p. 345.
[100] As noted earlier, see e.g. *'Musicam Sacram'* (#63).
[101] *BC* 9.6 (Nov 1925), p. 22.
[102] Mays, *Psalms*, p. 450.

primary source of worship music.[103] Like many others in the West, Block is guilty of the colonial sin of imposing his preferences upon others. He is highly selective, ignoring the biblical texts that do not support his own preferences in worship style.[104]

To repeat what I stated above, the Pentecostal tradition has been open to a variety of instruments. Harvey Cox, in his celebrated study of Pentecostalism, devotes an entire chapter to the importance of music; and regarding Pentecostalism's openness to a broad variety of musical styles, Cox observes,

> Most pentecostals gladly welcome any instrument you can blow, pluck, bow, bang, scrape, or rattle in the praise of God. I have seen photos of saxophones being played at pentecostal revivals as early as 1910 ... I have heard congregations sing to the beat of salsa, bossa nova, country western, and a dozen other tempos.[105]

While I applaud Cox's observation and could testify of my own experiences as confirmation, I must also confront the ugly truth that Pentecostals have, at times, been just as biased and unkind as anyone else in their unwarranted restrictions on musical instruments and styles. In various Pentecostal contexts, I have witnessed bans on Christian rock music, drums, electric guitars, and liturgical dance. Moreover, Pentecostal missionaries have imposed artificial prohibitions on native peoples.[106] While personal preference and parochial

---

[103] Daniel I. Block, *For the Glory of God: Recovering a Biblical Theology of Worship* (Grand Rapids, MI: Baker Academic, 2014), p. 228.

[104] Block does not comment on the variety of instruments found in Psalm 150. Regarding the final psalm, he makes only the following observations: verse 3 shows that the shofar was used to praise Yahweh (p. 227, n. 21); verse 6 states the 'inclusive nature' of worship (p. 1, n. 2); and Psalm 150 serves as conclusion to the Psalter, a 'final exclamation of praise' (p. 230). The Roman Catholic position regarding musical instruments in worship is stated in '*Musicam Sacram*: Instruction on Music in the Liturgy' (Second Vatican Ecumenical Council, March 5, 1967). Three points are worth noting here. 1. The 'pipe organ' is the preferred instrument (#62). 2. Cultural preferences for certain instruments should be taken into consideration (#63). 3. 'Secular' instruments are 'altogether prohibited' (#63). (But who gets to decide which instruments are 'secular'?)

[105] Cox, *Fire from Heaven*, pp. 142-43.

[106] See Corky Alexander, *Native American Pentecost: Praxis, Contextualization, Transformation* (NNACMS; Cleveland, TN: Cherohala Press, 2012), p. 63. Alexander's work is an attempt to give voice to indigenous peoples. For further discussion of musical instruments within the Native American/First Nations contextual movement, see also Cheryl Bear-Barnetson, *Introduction to First Nations Ministry* (NNACMS; Cleveland, TN: Cherohala Press, 2013), and Casey Church, *Holy*

traditions deem certain instruments to be more sacred than others and, therefore, more appropriate for worship, the book of Psalms seems to suggest that all musical instruments can be adapted as vehicles of worship.

Universality of Praise (v. 6)

Who should praise Yahweh? The hymns often name their audiences near the beginning of the psalm.[107] 'All the earth' is called upon to praise the Lord in Ps. 96.1. In Psalm 97, it is the 'earth' and the 'isles' who offer praise (v. 1). Other psalms name the addressees as 'the peoples' (99.1), 'all lands' (100.1), 'my soul' (103.1; 104.1), 'seed of Abraham' (105.5), 'the redeemed' (107.2), 'servants of the LORD' (113.1; 134.1; 135.1)), 'all nations' (117.1), 'all his angels' (147.2), and 'Israel' (149.2). Here in Psalm 150, however, 'The expected vocative identifying those to whom the summons is addressed is delayed until the final line (v. 6), where the transition from imperative to jussive mode gives the vocative a special emphasis'.[108] Only in the final verse, following the climactic clashing of cymbals,[109] is it revealed that it is 'every breath' who should praise the Lord.

The series of imperatives is broken in v. 6 by the *yiqtol* (jussive in function), a change that 'gives emphasis to the concluding verse'.[110] With the jussive the verse reads, 'Every breath *should* praise the Lord'. Although jussive *yiqtol* normally occupies the first position in the sentence, it can also occupy the second position, particularly when it follows an imperative, as it does here.[111]

'Every breath should praise YAH'. Whereas the object of praise at v. 1b is 'El', the object in v. 6a is 'YAH'. Therefore, inside the outer

---

Smoke: The Contextual Use of Native American Ritual and Ceremony (NNACMS; Cleveland, TN: Cherohala Press, 2017).

[107] Tesh and Zorn, *Psalms*, p. 540.

[108] Mays, *Psalms*, pp. 449-50.

[109] Zenger, 'Psalm 150', p. 663.

[110] Brueggemann and Bellinger, *Psalms*, p. 619.

[111] Alviero Niccacci, 'A Neglected Point of Hebrew Syntax: Yiqtol and Position in the Sentence', *LA* 37 (1987), pp. 7-9. Alviero Niccacci, *The Syntax of the Verb in Classical Hebrew Prose* (trans. W.G.E. Watson; JSOTSup 86; Sheffield: JSOT Press, 1990), pp. 76-80. The verb 'praise' (תהלל) is singular because when the subject is modified by 'all' (כל), it is normal for the verb to agree with the genitive which, in this case, is singular ('breath', הנשמה). See Joüon and Muraoka, *A Grammar of Biblical Hebrew*, §150.o.

frames of 'hallelujah', the divine names 'El' and 'YAH' are 'noteworthy as framing devices'.[112]

The fact that the verse does not begin with the verb draws attention to the subject, 'every breath'. Adina Moshavi calls this construction 'preposing' and argues that it is a 'descriptive focusing' technique. It is used here to add further description to the previous commands (2nd person plural) that are addressed to 'you'. In answer to the hypothetical question, 'Who are the subjects that being told to praise the Lord?', the answer is 'every breath'.[113]

The noun נשמה ('breath') is used of God and of human beings (cf. Deut. 20.16; Josh. 10.40; 11.11, 14; 1 Kgs 15.24). The word 'breath' is found only one other place in the Psalter: 'the breath of the spirit from your nostrils' (18.16). Zenger argues that the 'focus on human beings here is not an anthropocentric narrowness but corresponds to the dynamic of the psalm's structure'.[114] The mention of 'breath' recalls the creation of the first human and his animation by God, who 'blew into his nostrils the breath of life' (Gen. 2.7). From John Calvin to James Limburg, a number of interpreters have understood the phrase 'every breath' to indicate both humans and animals,[115] a view that is based partly upon Gen. 7.21-22, 'And all flesh died that moved on the earth: birds and cattle and beasts and every creeping thing that creeps on the earth, and every man. All which was on the dry land in whose nostrils was the breath of life died.' The word 'all' in v. 22 may be taken to include animals, but it more likely refers to the humans who are mentioned at the end of the previous verse. The effort to include animals may be fueled by Rev. 5.13, where 'every creature in heaven and on earth and under the earth and in the sea' is heard giving praise to the Lamb, but perhaps Ps. 150.6 is a concise restatement of Ps. 148.10-14, which reads, 'Beasts and all cattle, creeping things and flying birds! Kings of the earth and all peoples, princes and all rulers of the earth! Young men and maidens

---

[112] Brueggemann and Bellinger, *Psalms*, p. 618.

[113] Adina Moshavi, *Word Order in the Biblical Hebrew Finite Clause: A Syntactic and Pragmatic Analysis of Preposing* (Winona Lake, IN: Eisenbrauns, 2010), pp. 130-31.

[114] Zenger, 'Psalm 150', p. 663.

[115] *DCH*, V, p. 779. Cf. Schaefer, *Psalms*, p. 345; Limburg, *Psalms*, p. 506; Kidner, *Psalms 73-150: A Commentary on Books III-V of the Psalms*, p. 529; and Calvin, *Psalms*, V, p. 321, who also include animals in number of those who have breath. The corresponding verb form נשם ('to gasp'), is found only in Isa. 42.14, 'like a woman in labor ... I will gasp'.

together, old men and children! Let them praise the name of the Lord.'[116]

Karl Barth comments on the human obligation to give one's breath back to God in praise. Barth states that the breath that is in every creature 'puts it under obligation to praise the Lord because according to Ps. 104:29f. it is His, the Lord's breath, by which the creature is created and without which it would inevitably vanish away at once'.[117] John Wesley concurs, and in his sermon, 'The Circumcision of the Heart', he exhorts,

> Let the spirit return to God that gave it, with the whole train of its affections ... Other sacrifices from us he would not; but the living sacrifice of the heart he hath chosen. Let it be continually offered up to God through Christ, in flames of holy love ... Let all your thoughts, words, and works, tend to his glory. Set your heart firm on him, and on other things only as they are in and from him. Let your soul be filled with so entire a love of him, that you may love nothing but for his sake.[118]

The invitation for 'every breath' to praise the Lord is extended to worshipers of all ages, even to the 'babes and infants' of Ps. 8.2. From the beginning of the Pentecostal movement, children have enjoyed offering their praises to God. We read of one Pentecostal worship service in 1925 in which the musicians ranged from 'tiny five-year-old Barbara Bell, ... playing her triangle, up, up, up in age to the

---

[116] Cf. Barth, *Church Dogmatics: The Doctrine of God, Part 1*, II, p. 107, who writes,
An audible call is made to all things to praise God: to all lands (Ps. 100:1), to all the earth (Ps. 66:4), to all people (Ps. 67:5), even to the congregation of the gods (Ps. 82:1), to everything that hath breath (Ps. 150:6), to all things that are (Ps. 148). We hear continually that the earth as such is God's (Ps. 24:1–2, 50:10, 95:4f.), and therefore that all the blessings of creation come from God (Ps. 36:6–10, 65:7–14); but also that the lordship and the judgment over all and upon the whole world is God's (Ps. 96, 97, 99). Again and again the heavens, the sea, the storm, the mountains, the earthquake, the world of plants and beasts, the nations and their rulers, and in the height the angels, are all appealed to as the creatures, the servants and instruments and therefore the loudly speaking witnesses of God.

[117] Barth, *Church Dogmatics: The Doctrine of the Word of God, Part 1*, IV, pp. 60-62. See also Barth, *Church Dogmatics: The Doctrine of Creation, Part 2*, III, pp. 361-62. Barth argues, 'the fact that God has breathed into' us the breath of life leads to the conclusion that to 'praise God is in fact our natural office'.

[118] John Wesley, *The Works of the Rev. John Wesley* (10 vols.; London: Wesleyan Methodist Book Room, 3rd edn, 1872), V, pp. 211-12.

snowy haired old lady of ninety years who sang and played her auto-harp'.[119] In an article regarding ministry to orphans in India, Max Wood Moorhead reported that many of the children were confessing their sins and were receiving the gospel of Jesus Christ. At one point during a time of worship, the head of the school dismissed the children, 'but they would not be dismissed … They shouted and praised God victoriously for an hour, for He had put a new song in their mouths … they danced and sang God's praises for some little time.'[120]

'Every breath' also includes persons with disabilities. Many of God's children suffer from physical or mental limitations, but those limitations should not separate them from the believing community. Persons with disabilities should be integrated into the life of the local church the same as anyone else. In an earlier work, I described a significant encounter with an elderly woman in Wynne, Arkansas, who was confined to a wheelchair and crippled by a stroke:

> Whenever I would conduct worship services in the nursing home in which she lived, I would ask the people to share a testimony of God's goodness. This precious sister would lift her right hand (the left was paralyzed), and she would attempt to utter praises to God as tears flowed down her cheeks. The stroke made her praises unintelligible to onlookers, but they were music to the ear of God.[121]

Psalm 150 as Conclusion of the Psalter

Positioned at the end of the canonical Psalter, Psalm 150 has been understood as the closing doxology that summarizes and character-izes the entire collection.[122] Its singular message is the exhortation to praise God (הלל); thus, the Hebrew name of the Psalter is תהלים – 'Praises'.

The Psalter concludes with five 'Hallelujah' psalms, each one beginning and ending with הללו יה – 'Praise YAH'. The five final

---

[119] *BC* 9.6 (Nov 1925), p. 21.

[120] *Confidence* 3.5, p. 114.

[121] Lee Roy Martin, 'Introduction to Pentecostal Worship', in Lee Roy Martin (ed.), *Toward a Pentecostal Theology of Worship* (Cleveland, TN: CPT Press, 2016), p. 2.

[122] Cf. Ross, *A Commentary on the Psalms*, III, p. 962. O. Palmer Robertson, 'The Strategic Placement of the "Hallelu-Yah" Psalms within the Psalter', *JETS* 58.2 (2015), argues for 'deliberate placement' of all the hallelujah psalms, including Psalm 150 (p. 265).

Hallelujah psalms echo the fivefold structure of the Psalter itself.[123] Robertson writes, 'The final grouping of *"Hallelu-YAH"* psalms (Psalms 146-150) clearly intends to serve as the climactic conclusion of the whole of the Psalter'.[124] Books I through IV of the Psalter each end with a doxology, and Psalm 150 is often viewed as the doxology for Book V.[125] A more recent proposal, however, suggests that Psalm 145.21 is the closing doxology for Book V, and Psalms 146-150 form a fivefold conclusion to the Psalter that echoes the fivefold structure of the whole.[126] Psalm 150.6 ('Let every breath praise the LORD'.) is a restatement of the closing wish of Ps. 145.21b, which reads, 'let all flesh bless his holy name forever and ever'.[127]

Wilson argues that Psalm 150 brings closure to the Psalter in a fashion that complements its beginning in Psalm 1. He writes that Psalm 1 'is the entry point to the way of life that issues forth ultimately in praise'.[128] Terrien proposes further that Psalms 149 and 150 stand in reverse parallel to Psalms 1 and 2.[129]

Although the Psalter is 'dominated by prayer',[130] as expressed in the psalms of lament, there is a movement, a progression, a

---

[123] For an evaluation of the proposed fivefold structure of the Psalter, see Wilson, 'The Shape of the Book of Psalms'. He concludes that the fivefold division is a 'real, editorially induced structure' (p. 131).

[124] Robertson, 'The Strategic Placement of the "Hallelu-Yah" Psalms', p. 267.

[125] E.g. Bratcher and Reyburn, *A Handbook on Psalms*, p. 1188.

[126] Donatella Scaiola, 'The End of the Psalter', in E. Zenger (ed.), *Composition of the Book of Psalms* (Leuven: Uitgeverij Peeters, 2010), p. 702; cf. Brueggemann and Bellinger, *Psalms*, p. 618. Thomas McElwain links the sections of the Psalms to different feasts in Israel, and he argues that the five final psalms were associated with the Feast of Tabernacles. Thomas McElwain, 'A Structural Approach to the Biblical Psalms: The Songs of Degrees as a Year-End Pilgrimage Motif', *Temenos* 30 (1994), pp. 119-20.

[127] Cf. Wilson, 'The Shape of the Book of Psalms', pp. 131-32, and Scaiola, 'The End of the Psalter', p. 703.

[128] Wilson, 'The Shape of the Book of Psalms', p. 137. Cf. Scaiola, 'The End of the Psalter', p. 710, who writes,

> The praise of God, the finishing line and goal of the book, is not only reserved to a special people, but becomes a perspective, a lifestyle offered to all those who are willing to accept it, agreeing with the values the Psalter has progressively indicated, starting with that 'man' who in Ps 1 whispered the tôrāh of YHWH and rejoiced in it 'day and night'.

[129] Terrien, *The Psalms*, p. 930. Cf. Scaiola, 'The End of the Psalter', p. 704.

[130] Goldingay, *Psalms*, III, p. 749.

'trajectory of complaint to thanksgiving and praise'.[131] The following chart has 150 sections, and the black sections are hymns of praise. Psalm 1 is at the left and Psalm 150 is at the right. Moving from left to right, the chart illustrates the general movement from prayer to praise in the Psalter. The first major concentration of hymns begins at Psalm 95. Along with the movement towards praise, the Psalter also moves from the individual psalms towards communal psalms.

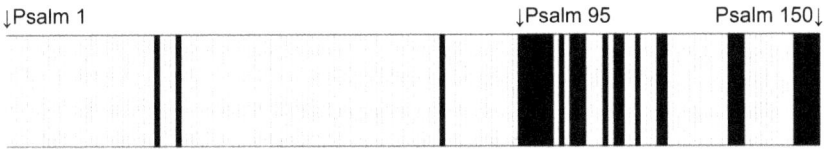

↓Psalm 1   ↓Psalm 95   Psalm 150↓

Although the movement of a reader through the text of the Psalter is a linear one, from lament toward praise, the corresponding movement in real life, according to Brueggemann, consists of a repeated cycle that moves from orientation to disorientation to new orientation. John Goldingay describes the movement through life 'as not simply circular' but as an upward spiral.[132] Psalm 150 is placed as the final psalm because its unrestrained worship would be presumptuous if it did not come after the psalms of lament, psalms of trust, and psalms of historical recital. Scott Ellington writes, 'Often lament

---

[131] Gerstenberger, *Psalms, Part 2*, p. 460. Cf. Ellington, *Risking Truth*, pp. 62-63. This movement is described by Robertson, 'The Strategic Placement of the "Hallelu-Yah" Psalms', who writes,

> The final editor(s) of the Psalter lifts the eyes of *Yahweh's* worshipping people above the strife and struggle of the first two Books of the Psalter (Psalms 1–72), above the painful experience of the exile as vividly depicted in Book III (Psalms 73–89; cf. Psalms 74, 79, 80, 89), and even beyond the repeated declaration of '*Yahweh Malak*' ('The LORD reigns') in a context of national exile as affirmed in Book IV (Psalms 90–106). By the ten-fold '*Hallelu-YAH*' concluding Book V, the celebrative consummation of the Psalter has come' (p. 267).

See also Foster, '*Topoi* of Praise in the Call to Praise Psalms', pp. 87-88, who argues that after reading the closing hymns of the psalter, the act of re-reading of earlier laments is transformed, so that the reader who 'prays the psalms of supplication and lament does so with a new expectation that not only will YHWH answer these prayers and laments, but also she/he will join the psalmists in confidence at the end, calling others to the praise of YHWH' (p. 88).

[132] Brueggemann and Goldingay are cited by Ellington, *Risking Truth*, p. 65. See John Goldingay, 'The Dynamic Cycle of Praise and Prayer in the Psalms', *JSOT* 6.20 (1981), pp. 85-90; and Brueggemann's appreciative response: Walter Brueggemann, 'Response to John Goldingay's "the Dynamic Cycle of Praise and Prayer" (*JSOT* 20 [1981] 85-90)', *JSOT* 7.22 (1982), pp. 141-42.

precedes praise, energizing it and giving it content'.[133] The highest praise is preceded by the deepest struggles.

This final psalm might be called a psalm of absolute praise. In Psalm 150, the focus of the attention is no longer on our prayers and how God answered us; but the emphasis is upon God, his nature, his holiness, his power, his majesty, his love, and his grace. The praise is focused entirely upon God, his glorious character, and his works.

Erich Zenger proposes that Psalm 150 'presents a miniature "theology" of the Psalter'. This theology includes four points:

> (1) the psalms are 'court music for YHWH the king'. They are the expression of joy at his presence (even when they are 'complaints') ... (2) The individual psalms are a practice for and an anticipation of the cosmic feast at the perfection of the world. They keep alive the hope that YHWH's universal royal rule is inevitably coming. (3) In singing/praying the psalms, 'all breath', that is, human beings, realize their specific divine competence and kinship to God, to the extent that they give the divine gift of their 'breath' its highest possible form of expression ... (4) Human happiness, which the Psalter at its beginning in Psalm 1 presents as the 'way of righteousness', is perfected in the praise of YHWH ... Psalm 1 and Psalm 150 establish the arc of tension: from *torah* to *Tehillah*.[134]

Furthermore, by ending with an imperative, Psalm 150 is not the end. Instead it 'provides an open ending to the Psalter and sets the question for faith communities of whether they will fulfill the summons'.[135] The praise of God, therefore, must 'continue, and on coming to an end begin anew'.[136]

The Affective Impact of Psalm 150

Thomas G. Long proposes that the Psalms, because of their poetic multi-layered character, may be approached in at least four ways: 1. One may 'follow the structure'. 2. One may 'focus on the main image or images'. 3. One may 'experience the mood of the psalm'. 4. One

---

[133] Ellington, *Risking Truth*, p. 62.
[134] Zenger, 'Psalm 150', p. 663.
[135] Brueggemann and Bellinger, *Psalms*, p. 619.
[136] Gerstenberger, *Psalms, Part 2*, p. 460.

may 'listen for the theological testimony of the psalm'.[137] It should be clear by now that my Pentecostal approach includes all four of Long's proposed methods. However, I have highlighted Long's third pathway – experiencing the mood of the psalm – but have described it as the affective component or affective dimension. The affective dimension of a psalm includes the mood, but it also includes the effect of the psalm upon the hearer. When I speak of the affections, I mean more than 'emotions'. Emotions are temporary responses to surrounding stimuli, but affections are lasting dispositions, our deepest desires. While the 'theological testimony' of a psalm tells the hearer what to believe, the affective component tells the hearer what to desire and how to feel. As poetry, the Psalms move the hearer toward certain emotive responses and inner dispositions.[138] The psalms are not afraid of human affections and emotions. In fact, the Psalms encourage emotional response; they generate an emotive environment; and they help to shape the hearers' affections. In this section, I will examine the affective dimension of Psalm 150, especially as it relates to the Pentecostal affections.

In most cases, the first step in analyzing the affective impact of a text would be to identify the affective terminology (words like 'love', 'joy', 'fear', etc.) and the emotive images (such as mention of enemies, family, troubles, and metaphors for God). The affective dimension of Psalm 150, however, is indirect rather overt, and implicit rather than explicit. Therefore, it may be profitable to describe the most prominent of the Pentecostal affections and then show how they

---

[137] Thomas G. Long, 'Four Ways to Preach a Psalm', *Journal for Preachers* 37.2 (2014), pp. 31-42. As an example of how to experience the mood of the psalm, Long points to Psalm 150 and to the 'sheer exuberance' expressed in it. He writes that Psalm 150 'is an eschatological breakthrough, an anticipation of those rare moments of ecstatic experience in which the superabundance of God's glory overflows and floods the hearts of worshipers who are "lost in wonder, love, and praise"' (p. 29). Cf. Crenshaw, *Psalms*, p. 37, who speaks of the 'emotional fervor' of the Psalter's piety, and he applauds the appropriateness of Psalm 150 as a conclusion to the book:

> This rousing crescendo resulting from the union of musical instruments and songs of worshippers brings the collection to a fitting close. Voices raised in praise of Yahweh, musical instruments in the divine service, children of God in sacred space – all these appropriately come to rest in Yahweh and create a resounding echo: hallelujah.

[138] On the affections, see my earlier arguments above, especially pages 12-13, 25-30, and 100-104, and in Lee Roy Martin, 'Rhetorical Criticism and the Affective Dimension of the Biblical Text', *JSem* 23.2 (2014), pp. 339-53.

intersect with Psalm 150. Steven Jack Land argues that the Pentecostal experiences of regeneration, sanctification, and Spirit baptism generate the three affections of 'gratitude as praise-thanksgiving, compassion as love-longing, and courage as confidence-hope'.[139] Building on Land's approach, John Christopher Thomas names five affections that connect broadly to the elements of the Fivefold Gospel. The belief in and experience of Jesus as Savior, Sanctifier, Spirit Baptizer, Healer, and Soon Coming King produce the corresponding affections of gratitude, compassion, courage, joy, and hope.[140] These affections/dispositions form the 'integrating center' of Pentecostal spirituality;[141] therefore, I will briefly discuss each of them in relation to Psalm 150.

Gratitude

Inasmuch as gratitude is expressed as thanksgiving and praise, it obviously intersects with Psalm 150. Gratitude is the necessary ground and origin of praise; therefore, if the hearer is exhorted to praise God, it is assumed that gratitude is present. The praises of Psalm 150 are an expression of gratitude for God's 'mighty acts' and God's 'abundant greatness' (v. 2). The connection between salvation and gratitude is apparent when we consider the content of God's 'mighty acts', which would include the exodus and other works of salvation. The call to praise God in his 'sanctuary' and 'strong firmament' also implies gratitude for God's power and sovereignty. The repeated call to praise God and the recounting of musical instruments creates in the hearer a feeling of awe and anticipation that concludes with an explosion of gratitude at the end, when 'every breath' is urged to praise Yahweh.

Compassion

Sanctification produces compassion, which is expressed through love and longing. The love is twofold: love for God and love for neighbor. Although the love of neighbor is not explicit in Psalm 150, Joachim Vette argues that the implications of v. 6 reach beyond the liturgical setting and find fulfillment in the worshipers' active 'confession of

---

[139] Land, *Pentecostal Spirituality*, pp. 47, 135-59.

[140] Thomas, "'What the Spirit Is Saying to the Church'", p. 117. For more on a theological approach to the affections, see Clapper, *John Wesley on Religious Affections*, and Castelo, 'Tarrying on the Lord', pp. 31-56.

[141] Land, *Pentecostal Spirituality*, pp. 50, 52, 63 See also, Land, 'A Passion for the Kingdom', pp. 34-35.

God as king' through service to and solidarity with the poor, widows, orphans, and strangers.[142]

Love for God is expressed throughout the psalm in every utterance of praise because praise is an act of love. Conrad Schaefer observes,

> Everybody wants to love someone, but the question is, whom to love? The Psalter offers the best option. Here we discover that we can choose because we were first chosen. We love because someone first loved us. The inspiration of these poems is just this, that God loved us first and is dedicated to being the object of our love, so that at every turn he is revealed as the font and the goal of life. Inspired by love, the poet invites the believer to praise and pray to God with the divinely inspired words. The poet invites us, praise God and you will come to know your first lover, for you could not praise had God not first chosen you, loved you, lived in you.[143]

Courage

In both Old and New Testaments, the Holy Spirit bestows courage upon God's people, courage to overcome adversity, to sacrifice self-interest, to defend the community of faith, and to speak God's word. Praise is an act of courage, and praise produces courage because praise acknowledges the active role of God in the world. The praise of God is liberating because it trusts in the power of God and minimizes all other powers. The people of God have nothing to fear because God is on his throne, which stands above his 'strong firmament'. Walter Brueggemann asserts that this courage, this trust

> enacted in worship arises because the singer-speaker of praise has found the one praised to be completely available. That is, the basic trust necessary to full praise arises out of intimate, genuinely covenantal communion in which the one praised has been put at risk, placed under test, and has been found … wholly reliable.[144]

---

[142] Vette, 'Psalm 150', p. 245.

[143] Schaefer, *Psalms*, p. 346.

[144] Walter Brueggemann, 'Praise and the Psalms: A Politics of Glad Abandonment', *The Hymn* 43 (1992), p. 14.

Joy

Praise is an expression of gratitude, but it is also an expression of joy.[145] In fact, claims Westermann, 'this praise of God can take place only in joy, that it is an expression of joy addressed to God. One cannot, therefore, hear the call to praise God in the OT without hearing the encompassed call to joy.'[146] The hearing of Psalm 150 generates feelings of joy. From the blast of the shofar (v. 3) to the sound of the harp, the lyre, and the cymbals joy flows forth. At the center of it all we witness the joyful dance, accompanied by the expressive tambourines. In fact, joy may be the affection that is most powerfully displayed and formed by Psalm 150. The worshipers are completely taken up into 'lyrical self-abandonment'[147] as they shout the praises of God and dance in his presence. It is what Pentecostals describe as 'joy unspeakable and full of glory' (1 Pet. 1.8). The Pentecostal outbursts of joy have been criticized as escapist enthusiasm, but I would point to John Goldingay's comments as a defense of joyful praise. Goldingay writes that Psalm 150 'ignores the possible anti-intellectual or escapist implications of its enthusiasm in order to fulfill this function. It is prepared to take that risk in order to remind us that sharp thinking and social function are not the only important things in the world.'[148]

Hope

The language of Psalm 150 evokes wonder, awe, humility, faith, and hope.[149] It demonstrates that 'theology, when chanted, receives the power of hope'.[150] Pentecostal hope is associated with the return of Jesus. Jesus Christ is our soon coming king. This eschatological hope is imbedded in praise, and praise 'is essential to' the continuation of

---

[145] Zenger, 'Psalm 150', p. 663.

[146] *TLOT*, I, p. 372. Schaefer, *Psalms*, p. 346, writes, 'Praise is the joyful recognition that greater than us is someone who loves without limit and on whom we depend for life'. Cf. Kraus, who declares, 'Joy and rejoicing accompany the praise of God' (*Theology of the Psalms*, p. 69).

[147] Brueggemann, 'Bounded by Obedience and Praise, p. 67.

[148] Goldingay, *Psalms*, III, p. 750. Cf. Westermann, who writes, 'In short, the intellect cannot praise God – only the breathing, rejoicing, singing person. An existence relative to God is intended that absolutely cannot come about through reason' (*TLOT*, I, p. 373).

[149] Zenger, 'Psalm 150', p. 663.

[150] Terrien, *The Psalms*, p. 930.

hope.[151] Kraus recognizes this hope-filled anticipation emerging from Psalm 150. He writes,

> Worship in Israel, because it concerns the God who is to come, possessed an unmistakable orientation to the future. Waiting for Yahweh, hoping in him, and above all the expectation of the universal fulfillment of the divine election and destiny of Israel in the world of the nations – these are the things that determined the nature of worship in Jerusalem.[152]

Most of the psalms intersect with only one or two of the Christian affections, but this brief survey of the five prominent Pentecostal affections reveals that Psalm 150 connects in at least a small way with each of them. Matthew Henry's comments on Psalm 150 illustrate the psalm's diverse impact:

> Praise God with a strong faith; praise him with holy **love and delight**; praise him with an entire **confidence** in Christ; praise him with a believing triumph over the powers of darkness; praise him with an earnest **desire** towards him and a full **satisfaction** in him; praise him by a universal **respect** to all his commands; praise him by a **cheerful submission** to all his disposals; praise him by **rejoicing** in his love and solacing yourselves in his great goodness; praise him by promoting the interests of the kingdom of his grace; praise him by a lively **hope** and **expectation** of the kingdom of his glory.[153]

The Life of Praise

I have already cited a number of early Pentecostal writers who referred to Psalm 150. However, I discovered one piece that was longer than all others, and I decided that its argument merited extended treatment. John S. Little, writing from Johannesburg, South Africa,

---

[151] Brueggemann and Bellinger, *Psalms*, p. 619.

[152] Kraus, *Theology of the Psalms*, p. 102. Kraus continues, 'Israel's hope is ultimately directed toward the visible and fully real appearance and triumph of Yahweh's royal authority over all the world' (p. 71). Kraus' statement is consistent with Pentecostal eschatology. Cf. Calvin, *Psalms*, V, p. 321, who writes, 'a time was coming when the same songs, which were then heard only in Judea, would resound in every quarter of the globe ... until being gathered into the kingdom of heaven, we sing with elect angels an eternal hallelujah'.

[153] Henry, *Matthew Henry's Commentary*, p. 954 (emphasis added).

contributed an article entitled 'The Praise Life' to *The Bridegroom's Messenger* in 1917. His article, based upon Ps. 150.6, begins by observing the lack of praise in the churches of his day. Little writes,

> Praise is a lost art of the church – the note that is missing in our worship of God today. There are no 'hallelujahs', 'amens', or 'praise the Lord' to be heard in the apostate churches of Christendom. All the joy seems to have died out in their worship of dear father – they are choked to death with respectability – and if we are not careful, that is what will happen in our Pentecostal assemblies. We are in danger of forgetting that praise played a very important part in the life of Old Testament saints. Turn to the 107th Psalm: 'Oh that men would praise the Lord for his goodness and for his wonderful works to the children of men'. Listen to David: 'I will praise the name of God with a song and will magnify him with thanksgiving' … These Old Testament saints said: 'It is a good thing to give thanks unto the Lord and to sing praises unto your name, Oh, Most High'. They considered thanksgiving and praise a duty; and failure in this is disobedience. But praise was the very essence of Old Testament worship.[154]

Little goes on to say that 'with the New Testament saints it was the same. It is recorded of them that they were continually in the temple praising and blessing God'.[155] He then offers seven reasons that praise is essential for the Church.

Praise 'glorifies God'.[156]
Little cites the following verse from the book of Psalms: 'Whoso offers praise glorifies me'.[157] It should be self-evident that praise glorifies God, but Little thought the point was worth emphasizing. He stressed that worship should be directed toward the Lord as a sacrifice of praise.[158]

---

[154] John S. Little, 'The Praise Life', *TBM* 10.202 (Sept 1, 1917), p. 4. Many early Pentecostal periodicals have been digitized and are available online at https://pentecostalarchives.org/index.cfm? and https://ifphc.org/index.cfm?.

[155] Little, 'The Praise Life', p. 4.

[156] Little, 'The Praise Life', p. 4. Cf. Brueggemann, 'Praise and the Psalms', p. 16.

[157] Little, 'The Praise Life', p. 4.

[158] Little, 'The Praise Life', p. 4. Cf. Brueggemann and Bellinger, *Psalms*, p. 619.

Little argues that praise is the goal of human existence.[159] He writes, 'I have never forgotten the very first question [of the catechism]. What is the chief end of man? The answer was – man's chief end was to glorify God and to enjoy him forever. Beloved one of the ways in which you can glorify God is by praising his holy name'.[160] Kraus would agree; he states,

> In praise and adoration the cultic community is fully committed to Yahweh, looks away from itself, and fulfills its destiny as the 'people of Yahweh' ... The praise of God is the highest joy, the fulfillment of life ... Because those who praise God are 'beside themselves', enjoying the happiness of God's presence.[161]

Moreover, Gerstenberger insists that 'praise of God is the fundament of all human existence'.[162] Karl Barth also describes praise as the goal of the Church. He writes,

> To praise God, as a function in the ministry of the Christian community, is to affirm, acknowledge, approve, extol and laud both the being of God as the One who in His eternal majesty has become human, and the action in which God has taken all humanity to Himself in His omnipotent mercy. [the ministry of the church] is to magnify the God who in this being and action of His is our God, Emmanuel, with us and for us. It is to confess Him publicly as the only true God.[163]

---

[159] Little, 'The Praise Life', p. 4.

[160] Little, 'The Praise Life', p. 4. Cf. Brueggemann and Bellinger, *Psalms*, p. 619, who also make the connection between Psalm 150 and the statement of the catechism.

[161] Kraus, *Theology of the Psalms*, p. 69.

[162] Gerstenberger, *Psalms, Part 2*, p. 460.

[163] Barth, *Church Dogmatics: The Doctrine of Reconciliation, Part 3.2*, IV, p. 867. On the effectiveness of the Old Testament witness of praise and how it is fulfilled in the New Testament, see Barth, *Church Dogmatics: The Doctrine of the Word of Reconciliation, Part 3.1*, I, pp. 58-59. Cf. Carro, Poe, and Zorzoli, *Comentario Bíblico Mundo Hispano: Salmos*, p. 444, who declare regarding Ps. 150.6,

> es el motivo misionero que se declara a menudo; es el clímax a que se dirige todo el plan redentor de Dios. Es lo que fue profetizado: Por mí mismo lo he jurado ... que delante de mí se doblará toda rodilla, y jurará todo lengua (Isa. 45:23). Es la médula de nuestro servicio a Dios; es la meta de la gran comisión, que toda lengua confiese para gloria de Dios Padre que Jesucristo es Señor (Fil. 2:11).

The glorifying of God through praise is a witness to the world inasmuch as effusive praise of God is counter-cultural. In contemporary culture, the norm is to ignore God and to praise one another for our accomplishments in business, sports, politics, art, music, and academics. The focal point of our praise is human achievement, but there is little praise of God. However, the praise of God relativizes human achievement and recognizes the infinitely greater achievements of almighty God.

Praise 'is the outcome of faith'.[164]

Moving in the same direction as the discussion of 'courage' above, Little writes,

> 'Then they believed his words, they sang his praise'. The moment we believe God's word we begin to praise we do not wait to see the fulfillment no, faith deepens into praise there is a point where prayer ceases and praise begins. Faith becomes active you are sick and you ask God for healing, the Holy Spirit brings the word to you, by his stripes we are healed. If you believe the word of God you will cease praying and begin to praise and as you praise, God will manifest his healing power in you. I have yet to see the person who has received their baptism that is in the Holy Spirit, that was not in an attitude of praise either praising inwardly or outwardly.[165]

The praise of God is a bold statement of faith that confronts the all-to-common agnosticism and apathy that are present in contemporary society at large and in the Church.

Praise 'is the inevitable result of being filled with the Spirit'.[166]

Arguing that when a person receives the Holy Spirit they will praise God, Little appeals to Eph. 5.18:

> Listen to what Paul says to the Ephesians, 'be filled with the spirit, speaking to yourselves in Psalms, hymns, spiritual songs, singing and making melody in your heart to the Lord, giving thanks always for all things unto God and the Father in the name of the Lord

[164] Little, 'The Praise Life', p. 4.
[165] Little, 'The Praise Life', p. 4. Cf. Brueggemann and Bellinger, *Psalms*, p. 619.
[166] Little, 'The Praise Life', p. 4.

Jesus Christ' ... You need to drink deeply of the spirit of God and then the praise life will begin again.[167]

Glossolalia is commonly cited by Pentecostals as evidence of Spirit baptism. The fruit of the Spirit are also credited as evidence of Spirit fullness. Little, however, stands in contrast to those who emphasize glossolalia and to those who stress the fruit. According to Little, a person who is filled with the Spirit will praise God extravagantly. His point is illustrated by the testimony of Miss Antoinette Moomean of Eustice, Nebraska, who narrates her journey from the mission field of China to the Azusa Street Revival. She states that when she was baptized in the Holy Spirit, 'The Spirit sang through [her] praises unto God'.[168]

Praise lies 'parallel' to prayer. [169]
Little cites Philippians 4, and connects v. 4 with v. 6:

'Rejoice in the Lord, again I say rejoice! ... Be anxious for nothing, but in everything by prayer and supplication let your requests be known unto God' ... Prayer and praise are the lines along which your engine will run to glory. They are the oars that propel your boat through the stormy seas of life.

Little's point is well-taken. Thirty years later, Old Testament scholar Claus Westermann would write his famous book 'Praise and Lament in the Psalms', which was built upon an argument similar to Little's. As stated above, the book of Psalms includes both prayer and praise, and praise is more than a category within the Psalter; the praise of God can be found even in the laments. Gerstenberger argues that 'Praise does not obliterate suffering, but it may erupt in the middle of suffering'.[170] Explaining the interaction between prayer and praise, Scott Ellington writes, 'while the dominant current in the Psalms is from lament toward praise, in true active tension there is a persistent back eddy in which praise also moves toward lament'.[171]

---

[167] Little, 'The Praise Life', p. 4.
[168] *AF* 1.11 (Oct 1907-Jan 1908), p. 3.
[169] Little, 'The Praise Life', p. 4.
[170] Gerstenberger, *Psalms, Part 2*, p. 460.
[171] Ellington, *Risking Truth*, p. 62. Cf. Wilson, 'The Shape of the Book of Psalms', p. 139, who argues that the earlier parts of the Psalter recognize the presence of pain, suffering, doubt, and evil, but 'Praise constitutes another reality in

Praise makes the worshiper receptive to 'fresh revelations of God's will and power'.[172]

Little quotes from earlier in the Psalms: 'Whoever offers praise glorifies Me; And to him … I will show the salvation of God' (Ps. 50.23). Thus, when praising God, believers are enabled to hear the voice of God more clearly. Aimee Semple McPherson agreed. She wrote in *The Bridal Call*, 'If you would see the Lord, begin to praise Him … Would you see the Lord? Would you behold His beautiful face? Would you know the glory of His presence and catch a vision of Him? Then praise the Lord.'[173] It is when we praise God that we are most open to the transforming work of the Holy Spirit. It is when we praise God that we are most likely to recognize the voice of God. It is when we praise God that perceive the perfections of God and those perfections are fulfilled in us.

Praise leads to 'a life of victory'.[174]

Little points to the story of Jehoshaphat to show that the praise of God will result in victory, even when the size of the enemy is overwhelming. He writes,

> Turn to second Chronicles chapter 20, 22nd verse. You will notice that Jehoshaphat and the children of Judah are in a tight corner. The Moabites and the Ammonites have come against them – a great multitude. But Judah sought God and when the battle was arrayed the singers went out before the Army praising the Lord. That's where God puts the shouters, the praising people in the front rank, hallelujah! Hallelujah to God and the Lamb forever and ever! The doubters and grumblers and slackers are sent home … Now what happened 'when they began to sing and to praise'? The Lord set ambushments against the children of Ammon and they were smitten. Things did not go right with you this morning, the enemy came against you and it has been a stiff fight and there is been no victory yet. Beloved, begin to praise and thank dear

which the presence of God has become so real that anger has no point, pain has no hold, and death lacks all power to sting' (p. 139).
   [172] Little, 'The Praise Life', p. 4.
   [173] *BC* 9.6 (Nov 1925), p. 21.
   [174] Little, 'The Praise Life', p. 4. Cf. 'The Power of Praise', *PE* (Jan 27, 1934), p. 3, which cites Ps. 150.6 and which exhorts: 'Praise toward God is one of God's appointed means for victory over spiritual wickednesses in heavenly places … Praise is still effective. God's ear is still attuned to praise'.

father. Remember the walls of Jericho fell flat before a shout of praise, and the ground trembled and prison doors flew open when Paul and Silas sang praises unto God. Dearly beloved, leave the army of doubters and join the shouters today, right here and now, and the victory is yours to the precious blood of Jesus.[175]

'The praise life is a glory-filled life'.[176]

Little argues here that praise creates a sacred space in which worshipers are able to encounter God's presence freely and unreservedly. Moreover, God responds to praise by making himself known to the worshipers. He points to the dedication of Solomon's temple, citing 2 Chron. 5.13,

> indeed it came to pass, when the trumpeters and singers were as one, to make one sound to be heard in praising and thanking the Lord, and when they lifted up their voice with the trumpets and cymbals and instruments of music, and praised the Lord, … that the house, the house of the Lord, was filled with a cloud … Nothing brings the glory down like praise and thanksgiving. How exceedingly pleased is the dear father with these two offerings.[177]

In my study of Psalm 63, I pointed out the Pentecostal desire to encounter God. This experiential element of Pentecostal spirituality, Daniel Castelo argues, places Pentecostalism within the Christian mystical tradition.[178] The life of praise opens the door to God's presence.

Little's seven reasons for living the praise life lead to his concluding exhortation in which he restates the value of praise and invites the reader to participate with him in praising God forever:

> The Bible is filled with praises, from the creation when the morning stars sang for joy right on to the song of Moses, the song of deliverance by the Red Sea, the psalms of David, the choruses of the Levites, the singers, the shouts of praise from the exiles marching home from Babylon, right on to the early church, the praises of Paul and Silas, right through the revelation to the

---

[175] Little, 'The Praise Life', p. 4. Pentecostal believers were encouraged to praise God as the means to receiving Spirit baptism, healing, and revival; cf. *BC* 9.6 (Nov 1925), p. 22; and F.T. Aikins, 'Confessing "One Another"', *LRE* (Nov 1935), p. 10.

[176] Little, 'The Praise Life', p. 4.

[177] Little, 'The Praise Life', p. 4.

[178] Castelo, *Pentecostalism as a Christian Mystical Tradition*.

hallelujah chorus … [T]he waves of music will roll until they dash against the throne of the Almighty God, the Father of our blessed Lord Jesus Christ! Praise is the very atmosphere of heaven, dearly beloved, breathe it in, breathe it in now, and all praise and glory and honor and power and dominion be unto our blessed triune Godhead, for ever and ever.[179]

Conclusions and Implications for Pentecostalism

If the Pentecostal movement is to maintain its vitality from generation to generation, it must periodically reclaim the passion for the praise of God that we find demonstrated in Psalm 150. The biblical text functions as a vehicle of spiritual formation that can inform Pentecostal spirituality and practice in the following ways.

First, Psalm 150 stresses the importance of genuine praise as a response to God's character and God's works. The verb for 'praise' (הלל) is found 13 times within the six short verses of this powerful psalm. Only Psalm 136, with its 26 occurrences of the phrase 'his covenant loyalty is everlasting', contains more repetition than Psalm 150. The Psalter concludes with repeated injunctions to praise God; therefore, the significance of wholehearted praise for God cannot be overstated.

Second, the practice of praise in Psalm 150 is focused upon God alone. Pentecostals face the danger of seeking out experiences rather than seeking God for God's sake. In the past, Pentecostals called this kind of shallow emotionalism 'wild fire'. On the one hand, it is all too easy for worship to become no more than entertainment or self-gratification. On the other hand, genuine encounter with God results in a dramatic and emotional experiences.

Third, the wide variety of musical instruments named in Psalm 150 suggest that any and all kinds of instruments can be used in worship. Colonialistic restrictions on instruments should be avoided. The choice of instruments depends in part upon local cultural considerations, but efforts should be made to expand the number of instruments in order to reflect the spirit of Psalm 150.

Fourth, Psalm 150 calls for participative praise from the entire congregation (and from the entire world). The praise of Psalm 150

---

[179] Little, 'The Praise Life', p. 4.

is communal, as indicated by the imperatives in the grammatical plural: 'you all praise the Lord'. Wilson writes, 'It is within the community of faith that the isolated individual finds identity, affirmation, renewal, restoration, and a hope for the future. That is the reason to praise – now as well as then'.[180] Unfortunately, many contemporary Pentecostal congregations have adopted a concert-like approach, in which everyone's attention is directed toward the stage, where professional musicians enact a performance of praise. The instruments found in Psalm 150, however, include those that are played by the non-professionals, whom we would call the laity. Furthermore, community is implied in the invitation for 'every breath' to praise the Lord. Psalm 150 invites an egalitarian approach to praise, a democratization of praise – the kind of praise that characterized early Pentecostalism universally and continues to characterize many Pentecostal churches today. This participative praise includes praise offered by both women and men, by children and adults, by every social class and economic strata, by people of every educational level, and by people with disabilities. Early Pentecostal preacher Aimee Semple McPherson writes, 'if we would praise Him together as one great people, I believe everyone would catch the vision of Him high and lifted up'.[181]

Psalm 150 is a model for the Pentecostal tradition's life of praise. It is the greatest example of absolute praise, and its placement at the end of the Psalter points to the fact that our goal as God's people is to worship God completely. As we journey with God, we live before him, pray unto him, and give thanks unto him. We experience the ups and downs of life and sometimes seem to be going nowhere. However, Psalm 150 teaches us that we have one goal and we are headed in one direction – our goal is the place of absolute praise. One day, every knee will bow before him, and every tongue will confess that Jesus Christ is Lord, to the glory of God the Father (Phil. 2.10-11). We are moving towards the day when everything in heaven will praise God, everything in the earth will praise God, and everything under the earth will praise the name of the Lord. Every part of creation will give praise and glory to God (Rev. 5.11-14). Our goal is a time and a place where there will be no more sun because the Son of God

---

[180] Wilson, 'The Shape of the Book of Psalms', p. 139.
[181] *BC* 9.6 (Nov 1925), p. 21.

will be the light. And God's city, the holy city, new Jerusalem, will come down from God out of heaven, and God will dwell there and will be the temple. We will live and remain in God's presence to glorify and praise him for ever and ever.

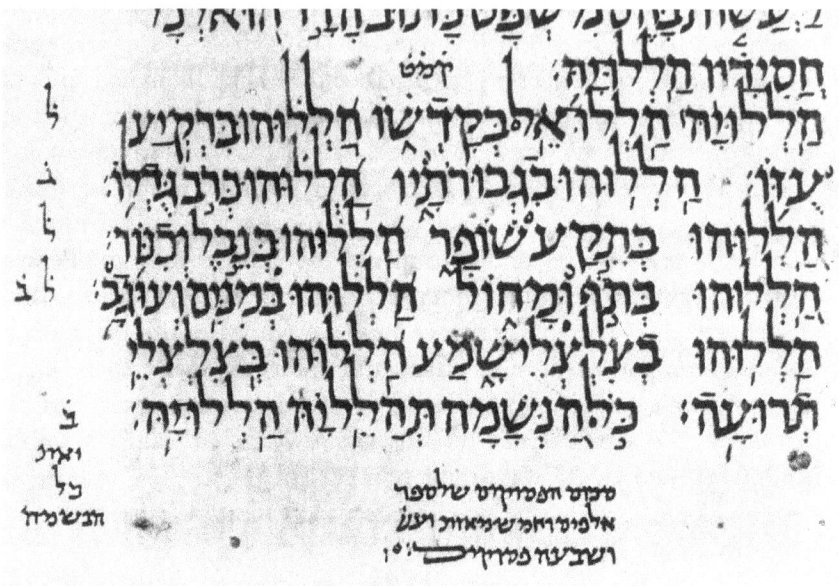

Psalm 150 Codex Leningrad

8

THE PSALMS IN EARLY PENTECOSTAL PERIODICAL LITERATURE

Introduction

While this monograph concentrates on several individual Psalms, it seems altogether proper that I should include a chapter on the function and interpretation of the Psalms in early Pentecostalism. The examination of Pentecostal testimonies, sermons, songs, and essays contributes to the overall project in a number of ways. First, this *Wirkungsgeschichtliche* study of the early Pentecostal literature should correct any previously held misconceptions about the Pentecostal interpretation of the Psalms. Second, the act of engaging with the early literature furthers the researcher's formation as a Pentecostal interpreter as it instills the Pentecostal affections.[1] Third, early Pentecostal approaches to the Psalms can contribute to the ongoing construction of contemporary Pentecostal hermeneutics. Following the lead of recent works in constructive Pentecostal theology, I will focus on the early Pentecostal periodical literature from the beginning of 1906

---

[1] See Land, *Pentecostal Spirituality*, pp. 47, 50, 52, 63, who argues that Pentecostal spirituality consists of orthodoxy (right belief/worship) and orthopraxy (right actions) integrated in the affections (orthopathy). The key Pentecostal affections, according to Land, are gratitude (thanks/praise), compassion (love/longing), and courage (confidence/hope). Thomas, "'What the Spirit Is Saying to the Church'", p. 117, names five affections that correspond broadly to the elements of the Five-fold Gospel: Salvation/Gratitude, Sanctification/Compassion, Spirit Baptism/Courage, Healing/Joy, Return of Jesus/Hope. For more on a theological approach to the affections, see Clapper, *John Wesley on Religious Affections*, and Castelo, 'Tarrying on the Lord', pp. 31-56.

(the start of the Azusa St. revival) to the end of 1915.[2] According to
Steven J. Land, who takes his cue from Walter J. Hollenweger, the
first decade of the movement is crucial for establishing the 'heart' of
the Pentecostal tradition.[3] As with any renewal movement, Pentecostalism's core values and beliefs were generated in the heart and minds
of its founders. That is not to say that contemporary constructive
theology must follow the exact lines of the early tradition. However,
if Pentecostal theology is to remain genuinely Pentecostal (rather
than Evangelical plus glossolalia), any new paths that are constructed
must remain faithful to the heart of the Pentecostal tradition.[4]

Periodical literature is the focus of my investigation for two reasons. First, the early Pentecostals produced few book-length works
on theology. Most of the early theological discussions were carried
on within the pages of numerous periodicals. Second, the Pentecostal
movement had no central authority that was tasked with formulating
guidelines for Pentecostal theology and practice. The periodicals,
published by Pentecostal leaders and often representing the various
newly formed denominations, were the nearest things to authoritative
theological voices.

Like Alexander, McQueen, Green, and Archer, I have divided the
periodicals into two categories, based upon the two major streams of
the Pentecostal tradition: Wesleyan–Holiness and Finished Work.
The Wesleyan–Holiness periodicals that I examined are *The Apostolic
Faith* (*AF* and the Portland, OR edition *AFO*), *The Bridegroom's Messenger* (*TBM*), *The Church of God Evangel* (*CGE*), and *The Whole Truth*
(*TWT*). The Finished Work periodicals are *The Latter Rain Evangel*
(*LRE*), *The Pentecost* (*TP*), *The Pentecostal Testimony* (*PT*), *Word and Wit-
ness* (*WW*), and *The Pentecostal Evangel* (*PE*).[5] In these periodicals, I

[2] This method was pioneered by Kimberly Ervin Alexander, *Pentecostal Healing:
Models in Theology and Practice* (JPTSup 29; Blandford Forum, UK: Deo Publishing,
2006), and was followed by Larry R. McQueen, *Toward a Pentecostal Eschatology:
Discerning the Way Forward* (JPTSup 39; Blandford Forum, UK: Deo Publishing,
2012); Green, *Toward a Pentecostal Theology of the Lord's Supper*; Archer, *'I Was in the
Spirit on the Lord's Day'*, and Johnson, *Pneumatic Discernment in the Apocalypse*.
[3] Land, *Pentecostal Spirituality*, p. 1; Hollenweger, *The Pentecostals*, p. 551.
[4] See Green, *Toward a Pentecostal Theology of the Lord's Supper*, pp. 74-76.
[5] My research was conducted online through the Flower Pentecostal Heritage
Center (https://ifphc.org/) and through the Consortium of Pentecostal Archives
(https://pentecostalarchives.org/). From these sites, I searched the early periodicals for the words 'Psalms', 'Psa', and 'Ps'. The two sites produced different search
results; therefore, I would encourage researchers to utilize both sites when

located 576 references to the Psalms in the ten-year period, 1906-1915. The most popular Psalms were as follows (with number of occurrences in parentheses): 103 (30x), 119 (24x), 91 (23x), 51(20x), 34 (18x), 45 (16x), 9 (14x), 23 (14x), 37 (14x), and 107 (12x). The most popular Psalms in the Wesleyan-Holiness periodicals were 103, 91, 9, 34, 37, 45, and 126; and in the Finished-Work periodicals, 119, 51, 18, 23, 34, 45, 91, and 103. The most commonly cited verses were Ps. 103.3 (20x) 'he healeth all thy diseases';[6] 9.17 (9x) 'the wicked shall be turned into hell'; 45.14-15 (5x) 'she shall be brought unto the king …'; 46.10 (5x) 'Be still, and know that I am God: I will be exalted …'; 107.20 (5x) 'He sent his word, and healed them'; 2.8 (4x) 'I will give thee the heathen for thine inheritance'; 8.4 (4x) 'What is man … and the son of man …?'; 42.11 (4x) 'Why art thou cast down …?'; 51.17 (4x) 'The sacrifices of God are a broken spirit …'; 91.10 (4x) 'He shall cover thee with his feathers, and under his wings thou shalt trust …'; 110.3 (4x) '… in the day of thy power, in the beauties of holiness …'; and 119.105 (4x) 'Thy word is a lamp unto my feet …'[7]

Time and space does not allow for the examination of all 576 references to the Psalms. Therefore, I will limit my detailed study to the citations found in *The Apostolic Faith*. By examining every reference in one periodical, I hope to be freed from the accusation of choosing only those texts that fit my presuppositions. I will supplement this study with an appendix that lists the citations from the other journals.

---

searching for specific words. Full-text searches are incomplete, however, because some of the original texts were in poor condition when scanned and because writers sometimes omitted the Scriptural reference. Therefore, a close reading of the entire corpus would reveal a number of quotations that were not discovered through text searches.

[6] In this chapter, quotations of Scripture are from the KJV because Pentecostal interpretations were sometimes tied to its specific words. It should be noted, however, that the *AF* sometimes used the Revised Version.

[7] Complete indexes for the years 1906-1915 are provided in appendices at the end of the book. Extending the search to 1940 reveals these Psalms as the most frequently cited: 119 (235x), 103 (224x), 37 (149x), 91 (140x), 34 (134x), 2 (133x), 23 (127x), 107 (124x), (120x), 1 (110x), 46 (107x), 27 (104x), 100 (69x), 22 (85x), and 150 (29x). Psalms 103, 119, 91, and 34 remain in the top five, but Psalm 51 drops out, and Psalm 2 moves up to number 6. Psalms 23, 34, 37, and 91 can be called psalms of trust/confidence. Psalm 119 is a torah hymn that invites faithfulness to the 'law of the Lord'. Psalm 2 is highly Christological, and Psalms 103 and 107 are songs of thanksgiving/testimony that contain references to healing. While every Psalm is cited at least once, the following psalms are cited the fewest number of times: 54 (1x), 140 (3x), 59 (4x), 114 (4x), 123 (4x), 135 (4x).

The Apostolic Faith was published from 1906 to 1908 by William J. Seymour at The Apostolic Faith Mission. The four-page newspaper reported on the Azusa Street revival in Los Angeles and included other news, testimonies, articles, and letters from the Pentecostal movement worldwide. The articles focused on distinctive Pentecostal doctrines, and the testimonies recounted dramatic Pentecostal experiences such as healings, miracles, sanctifications, and Spirit Baptisms. Florence Crawford began a version of *The Apostolic Faith* in Portland, OR in 1908 that continued until 1929. I discovered 18 references to the Psalms in *The Apostolic Faith* (1906 to 1908) and seven more in the Portland, OR edition between 1909 and 1915. I have classified these 25 references into five categories based upon the hermeneutical function of the biblical citation.[8]

The Psalms as Affirmations of Doctrine

The first category consists of biblical citations that are used to support the beliefs of the early Pentecostals. In the *Apostolic Faith*, we find the Psalms undergirding four doctrines: divine healing, hell, creation, and sanctification.

Divine Healing

Divine healing was a key element of the early Pentecostal movement, and Jesus as healer was one of the five points of what was called the

---

[8] I am addressing all 25 references in *AF* except for the two cases in which the biblical text itself is not discussed or interpreted at all. First, in an example of glossographia, a man who calls himself 'Bro. Junk' testifies that he wrote Ps. 46.3 in Hebrew while 'under the power of God'. *AF* 1.4 (Dec 1906), p. 1. Second, is a statement that a woman preached from Psalm 103. *AF* 1.6 (Feb-Mar 1907), p. 8. Although not found in the first ten years of *AF*, a sixth prominent use of the Psalms in the early literature is the appropriation of the words of a psalm to express the writer's own praise. See, for example, the use of Ps. 105.1-2 in *TBM* 6.140 (Sept 15, 1913), p. 3; Ps. 79.13 in *TBM* 7.141 (Oct 1, 1913), p. 1; Ps. 107.22 in *TBM* 7.145 (Dec 1, 1913), p. 2; Ps. 34.2 in *CGE* 6.31 (July 31, 1915), p. 3; Psalm 117 in *TBM* 2.44 (Aug 15, 1909), p. 3; Ps. 31.19 in *TBM* 3.63 (June 1, 1910), p. 3; and Ps. 9.1 and 104.24 in *TBM* 4.72 (Oct 15, 1910), p. 2. A seventh category might be added in which the citations from the Psalms are used as exhortations to belief, action, or behavior. See Ps. 110.3, 62.1, and 50.17 in *TBM* 1.7 (Feb 1, 1908), p. 2; Ps. 141.5 in *TBM* 2.29 (Jan 1, 1909), p. 4; Ps. 37.7 and 143.8, 10 in *TBM* 2.36 (Apr 15, 1909), p. 4; Ps. 92.12 in *TBM* 2.43 (Aug 1, 1909), p. 1; Ps. 66.18 in *TBM* 3.57 (Mar 1, 1910), p. 4; and Ps. 119.66 in *TBM* 3.60 (Apr 15, 1910), p. 4.

'full gospel' or the 'fivefold gospel'.[9] The Pentecostal belief in divine healing is based upon many biblical texts, and among them is Ps. 103.3: 'He healeth all thy diseases'.[10] Psalm 103 is *The Apostolic Faith*'s most commonly referenced Psalm by far (nine references), and it occurs in the Apostolic Faith Movement's statement of faith that is printed in the first issue of *The Apostolic Faith*:

> Seeking Healing. – He must believe that God is able to heal. – Ex. 15:26: 'I am the Lord that healeth thee'. James 5:14; Psa. 103:3; 2 Kings 20:5; Matt. 8:16, 17; Mark 16:16, 17, 18.[11]

This statement is repeated in *The Apostolic Faith* 1.2, 1.3, 1.10, 1.12, and 2.13. It is also published in the first issue of *The Apostolic Faith* (Oregon)[12] and in issues 16 and 18; but the statement was rewritten and expanded without explanation in 1909, omitting both Exod. 15.26 and Ps. 103.3 (but adding Isa. 53.4, 5).

Psalm 107.20 is also used to support the teaching on healing. It appears along with Jam. 5.13; Prov. 4.20; Exod. 15.26; and Jn 3.14 under the heading 'Healing'. The writer states, 'We read in Ps. 107.20, "He sent his Word and healed them, and delivered them from their distresses"'.[13]

Hell

Psalm 9.17 is cited three times as support for the doctrine of hell. Under the title 'Awful Realities of Hell', the author asks rhetorically, 'Do you believe in hell?'. The writer continues, noting Ps. 9.17,

> Brother, it makes no difference what you or I believe, that does not do away with God's word. Hell exists in its awful reality, whether you believe it or not, and multitudes are plunging

---

[9] The fivefold gospel holds that Jesus is savior, sanctifier, baptizer in the Holy Spirit, healer, and soon-coming king. See Donald W. Dayton, *The Theological Roots of Pentecostalism* (Studies in Evangelicalism 5; Metuchen, NJ: Scarecrow Press, 1987), p. 20; Land, *Pentecostal Spirituality*, pp. 38, 57, 89-90; and Thomas, '"What the Spirit Is Saying to the Church"', p. 117.

[10] Pentecostals inherited the use of Ps. 103.3 as support for the doctrine of divine healing from the nineteenth-century healing movement. See, for example, A.B. Simpson, *The Fourfold Gospel* (New York: Christian Alliance Publishing Co., 4th edn, 1890), p. 14.

[11] *AF* 1.1 (Sept) 1906, p. 2.

[12] *AFO* 19 (Feb-Mar 1909), p. 2.

[13] *AF* 1.6 (Feb-Mar 1907), p. 6. Other Psalms cited in support of divine healing include Ps. 30.2 in *TBM* 2.35 (Apr 1, 1909), p. 1 and Ps. 105.37 in *TBM* 3.60 (Apr 15, 1910), p. 4.

headlong into it. 'The wicked shall be turned into hell, and all the nations that forget God'.

Further support for the doctrine of hell is then given by Scriptural quotations from the gospels and the book of Revelation.[14] A few months later, William Seymour addresses the question of whether hell is a place of annihilation or a place of eternal punishment. He begins by stating, 'Many people today do not believe in an everlasting hell'.[15] Seymour's article is a direct refutation of Charles Parham's belief in the annihilation of the wicked, a doctrine that Parham had promoted as early as March 1899 in the first issue of his periodical.[16] Apparently, Parham had been convinced by his wife's grandfather that the wicked do not suffer eternally.[17] After citing Lk. 16.19, Rev. 20.10, and Mt. 18.8, Seymour turns to the Psalter:

> Dear loved ones, there is an awful hell. God teaches us in Ps. 9, 17, 'The wicked shall be turned into hell, and all the nations that forget God'. We find the punishment of the wicked taught us from the closed gates of Eden all the way down ... May God help men everywhere to repent of their sins and accept the precious blood of Jesus Christ that cleanses from all sin.

Seymour apparently interprets Ps. 9.17 in light of the New Testament teaching on hell. While it is true that Ps. 9.17 asserts 'the punishment of the wicked', the punishment described in Psalm 9 comes in the form of defeat and death. When the enemy 'turns' to attack (v. 3) they will be 'turned' (v. 17) to *Sheol*, meaning that they will be killed (cf. Pss. 31.17; 55.15; 63.9). Moreover, their 'name' will be 'blotted out' (v. 5), but the poor will not 'be forgotten' (v. 18). It should be pointed out, however, that although Ps. 9.17 does not directly engage the question of eternal punishment, it may be taken as legitimate

---

[14] *AF* 1.2 (Oct 1906), p. 2.

[15] *AF* 1.5 (Jan 1907), p. 2.

[16] Seymour had been a student in Parham's Bible school and would be aware of Parham's teaching.

[17] See Iain MacRobert, *The Black Roots and White Racism of Early Pentecostalism in the USA* (New York, NY: St. Martin's Press, 1988), p. 43. Annihilationism was growing in popularity partly because of the *Seventh-Day Adventist Church*. Ellen G. White had affirmed the doctrine of total annihilation, one aspect of the teaching that the Adventists call 'conditional immortality', as early as 1843. See Gary Land, *Historical Dictionary of the Seventh-Day Adventists* (Lanham: Rowman & Littlefield, 2015), pp. 77-78.

support for Seymour's position, given the fact that *Sheol* is represented in some Old Testament texts as an ongoing state of existence.

In addition to his use of Ps. 9.17 as doctrinal support, Seymour employs the text as an emotional appeal: 'Dear loved ones, there is an awful hell. God teaches us in Ps. 9.17 …' What begins as doctrinal affirmation concludes with a plea for unbelievers to repent and turn to Jesus Christ. He urges, 'May God help men everywhere to repent …' Seymour's hermeneutic is always missional – his theology and his ministry are integrated.

The third reference to Ps. 9.17 appears in an article that is partly personal testimony and partly an evangelistic appeal to unbelievers.[18] After beginning with Lk. 19.10, 'The Son of Man is come to seek and to save that which was lost', the writer testifies to having been a sinner who went to church but 'did not know Jesus' and who did not want to end up in hell. The writer goes on,

> Then we read in Psalms 9:17, 'the wicked shall be turned into hell and all the nations that forget God'. O sinner, where will you spend eternity? Will you spend it with the devil and his angels, or will you spend it with God and his angels?

The emotional appeal continues to the end of the article with support from other biblical texts and affirmations of Jesus' ability to satisfy the hunger and thirst of those who will call upon him. Even in this doctrinal essay, the writer takes advantage of the affective dimension of the text.

Creation of Adam in the Image of God
In December of 1906, after 'Seven Months of Pentecostal Showers', an article appeared in *The Apostolic Faith* that functioned as a testimony, apology, and doctrinal explanation of the new revival movement on Azusa Street. After sharing the origins of the revival and a defense of William Seymour as 'simply a humble pastor of the flock', the writer states the theological position of the movement:

> We believe in old time repentance, old time conversion, old time sanctification, healing of our bodies and the baptism with the Holy Ghost. We believe that God made Adam in His own image, according to Gen. 5.1; Ps. 8.4; and Matt. 19.4. We do not believe

---

[18] *AF* 1.12 (Jan 1908), p. 4.

in any eighth day creation, as some have taught, and we do not believe in the annihilation of the wicked. We stand on Bible truth without compromise. We recognize every man that honors the blood of Jesus Christ to be our brother, regardless of denomination, creed, or doctrine. But we are not willing to accept any errors, it matters not how charming or sweet they may seem to be.[19]

The citations of Gen. 5.1, Ps. 8.4, Mt. 19.4 are apparently intended to counter the divisive 'eighth day creation' theory that was taught by Charles Parham (among others).[20] Although there are variations on the teaching, the eighth-day creation theory proposes that there were two separate human creations, one on the sixth day (Gen. 1.27) and another on the eighth day (Gen. 2.7), resulting in two different species of humans. On the one hand, the sixth-day humans were a race created in the image of God; but, unlike Adam, they were not infused with the breath of God (Gen. 2.7). On the other hand, the eighth-day Adamic race was not 'created' (Gen. 1.27) but was 'formed from the ground' (Gen. 2.7); therefore, Adam was not made in the image of God. Moreover, the sixth-day race had no promise of a redeemer because the redeemer would be from the seed of Eve (Gen. 3.15) who was made on the eighth day. When Cain went to the land of Nod, he married a sixth-day woman and thus defiled the Adamic race with the first interracial marriage.[21] The illicit practice of interracial marriage was made widespread in Gen. 6.1-4 when the 'sons of God' (eighth-day Adamic race) intermarried with the 'daughters of men' (sixth-day race). The statement from *The Apostolic Faith* counters the eighth-day creation by citing Gen. 5.1, which states that Adam was made in 'the image of God' (as in Gen. 1.27). Matthew 19.4 also undermines the eighth-day creation because it portrays all humans as descended from the sixth day of creation where humans were made 'male and female'. While Gen. 5.1 and Mt. 19.4 contain explicit parallels to Gen. 1.26-27, Psalm 8.4 does not. Therefore, its application to the *imago Dei* requires a further hermeneutical step. The verse reads, 'What is man that you are mindful of him? And the son of man, that you visit him?' Creation is obviously in view in Psalm 8, as

[19] *AF* 1.4 (Dec 1906), p. 1.
[20] Douglas G. Jacobsen, *Thinking in the Spirit: Theologies of the Early Pentecostal Movement* (Bloomington, IN: Indiana University Press, 2003), pp. 28-31.
[21] Jacobson, *Thinking in the Spirit*, p. 30. See also *PE* 54 (Aug 1914), which includes a detailed refutation of the doctrine of two creations (p. 3).

it speaks of 'the work of [God's] fingers' (v. 3), but the key is in the phrase 'son of man'. Early Pentecostals, like other Christian interpreters before them, would recognize Ps. 8.4 as a Messianic reference; but, according to the eighth-day creation theory, a son of 'man' would be of the sixth-day race (Gen. 6.1-2) and could not function as the redeemer. As stated above, the redeemer descends from Eve, who was created on the eighth day. Inasmuch as Jesus is both 'son of man' and redeemer, the eighth-day creation theory must be invalid.

Sanctification

Sanctification is the fourth and final doctrine that is supported by references to the Psalms. Under the heading 'Important Questions – Bible Answers', we find questions about the 'witness of the Spirit', the 'immortality of the soul', second chances after death, conditions for divine healing, 'worldly dress', and sanctification. The question about sanctification reads, 'Does the Word teach that after you are saved you should seek sanctification as a second work of grace?' The answer (in the affirmative) is proven by a string of biblical quotations: Jn 17.17, 1 Jn 1.7, 1 Jn 1.9, Eph. 5.25-27, Rom. 6.6, 2 Cor. 7.1, Heb. 13.12, and Ps. 51.7, which states, 'Purge me with hyssop, and I shall be clean: wash me, and I shall be whiter than snow'.[22] The connection between Ps. 51.7 and the other texts on sanctification is found in the shared language of cleansing. 'The blood of Jesus … cleanses us from all sin' (1 Jn 1.7). 'He is faithful to … cleanse us from all unrighteousness' (1 Jn 1.9). 'Christ also loved the church … that he might sanctify and cleanse it' (Eph. 5.25). 'Let us cleanse ourselves … perfecting holiness' (2 Cor. 7.1). The emphasis on cleansing language suggests that the writer views sanctification as more than a declarative and positional setting apart for God's use. The biblical texts chosen by the writer emphasize the purifying effect of sanctification; therefore, like John Wesley, the writer views sanctification as a cleansing from all sin; and like Wesley, a text from the Old Testament is just as relevant as one from the New Testament.[23]

---

[22] *AFO* 30 (Feb 1915), p. 2.

[23] Cf. Wesley's use of Ezek. 36.25 'I will sprinkle clean water upon you and you shall be clean'. See, for example, Wesley, *The Works of the Rev. John Wesley*, V, p. 166; VI, pp. 19, 287; VIII, p. 294; X, p. 191; XI, p. 389; XII, p. 416. Regarding sanctification language, see also the discussion below regarding Psalm 66.10. The doctrine of sanctification is also supported by appealing to Psalm 1 (*TBM* 6.138 [Aug 15, 1913], p. 4); Ps. 4.3 (*CGE* 6.47 [Nov 20, 1915], p. 2); Psalm 24 (*CGE* 6.49 [Dec 4 1915], p. 3; and Psalm 91 (*TBM* 2.29 [Jan 1, 1909], p. 4). Other doctrines supported

The Psalms as Allegories

Like other Christian interpreters at the turn of the twentieth century, Pentecostals were aware of allegorical methods. My search of the periodicals reveals that allegory was an accepted practice in the early Pentecostal movement; but, unlike the Church Fathers, Pentecostals do not appear to have considered allegory as a method that was applicable to any and all texts. The allegorical method was mostly restricted to the Royal Psalms and other Psalms that were deemed 'Messianic' (e.g. Psalm 22).[24] The Wesleyan-Holiness periodicals 1906 and 1915 have 16 references to Psalm 45, a text that was interpreted as an allegory of the Church, the Bride of Christ. In a substantial article entitled 'The Bride of Christ', we read the following:

> The Psalmist in speaking of the Bride of Christ, says, 'Upon Thy right hand did stand the queen in gold of Ophir' [Ps. 45.9]. Gold of Ophir was the finest gold. The Bride will stand before Him in the purest gold, the holiness of Christ. He says, 'Forget also thine own people and thy father's house, so shall the King greatly desire thy beauty' [Ps. 45.10-11]. You must turn your back on everything of the world, and follow after Jesus with all of your heart, soul, mind and strength. And the day will come when you will stand beside the King robed in the finest of gold … The Bride of Christ may have no place to lay her head except as God provides for her, yet she can say that her merchandise is good. It is not worldly goods or houses and lands but souls redeemed. She holds the truth of this wonderful and mighty Gospel, the most pure and glorious gift that ever came into this world. 'She maketh herself coverings of tapestry, her clothing is silk and purple' [Prov. 31.22]. She is arrayed in Royal garments, the holiness of the bride of

---

by the Psalms include total depravity, discerned from Ps. 51.5 (*CGE* 6.31 [July 31, 1915], p. 3. See also the support for general revelation found in Ps. 8.1 and 19.1 (*TBM* 3.52 [Dec 15, 1909], p. 1) and the return of Jesus in Ps. 102.16 (*TBM* 3.55 [Feb 1, 1910], p. 1. The following citations were used to defend the exuberance of Pentecostal worship: Ps. 47.1 in *TBM* 1.9 (Mar 1, 1908), p. 1; Ps. 126.1-3 in *TBM* 3.49 (Nov 1, 1909), p. 4; Ps. 119.120 in *CGE* 1.2 (Mar 15, 1910), p. 6 and *CGE* 5.24 (June13, 1914), p. 5.

[24] However, even Psalm 22 was not always used in the allegorical/typological sense. Cf. *TBM* 7.145 (Dec 1, 1913), p. 4; *CGE* 6.25 (June 19, 1915), p. 1; *CGE* 6.47 (Nov 20, 1915), p. 4. Other allegorical uses of the Psalms include Psalm 45 in *TBM* 2.31 (Feb 1, 1909), p. 2; Ps. 20.5 and 60.4 in *TBM* 2.40 (June 15, 1909), p. 4; and Ps. 29.9 in *TBM* 3.68 (Aug 15, 1910), p.4.

Christ. 'The King's daughter is all glorious within; her clothing is of wrought gold'. Psalm 45:13.[25]

Psalm 45 is a Royal Psalm that praises the king: 'You are fairer than the children of men: grace is poured into your lips: therefore God has blessed you forever' (v. 1). The king is praised for his glory, might, majesty, and righteousness. The Psalm continues, 'Your throne, O God, is forever and ever: the scepter of your kingdom is a right scepter. You love righteousness, and hate wickedness: therefore God, your God, has anointed you with the oil of gladness above your companions' (vv. 6-7). The second half of the psalm celebrates the king in relation to his wife, his daughters, and his children.

Any Psalm that mentions the king is automatically connected to Jesus Christ, and Psalm 45 is no exception to the rule. Beyond the common allegorical concept of Messianic Psalms, however, Ps. 45.6-7 has the further distinction of being cited in the New Testament (Heb. 1.8-9) where it is interpreted as a reference to Jesus. It follows that if the 'king' signifies Jesus then the 'queen' must signify the Church, the Bride of Christ. The figure of the queen is expanded by comparing the queen's golden garment to the believer's garment, which is the 'holiness of Christ'. Inasmuch as the 'daughter' must forget her 'own people' (Ps. 45.10), the believer must turn away from 'everything of the world and follow after Jesus'. Apparently, both the queen and the king's daughter (Ps. 45.13) represent the Bride of Christ that is 'arrayed in Royal garments'.

The quotations from Psalm 45 evoke an emotive response from the writer, who appeals to the reader to 'turn your back on everything of the world, and follow after Jesus with all of your heart, soul, mind and strength'. Moreover, the Bride holds the 'most pure and glorious gift that ever came into the world'. The language of Psalm 45 and subsequent interpretation by the Pentecostal writer evoke deep and powerful feelings.

The Psalms as Analogous to Pentecostal Experience

The third category of citations consists of testimonies in which the experience of the writer is believed to be analogous to the experience of the psalmist. Analogical interpretation is a narrative, theological

---

[25] *AFO* 32 (June-Aug 1915), p. 2.

approach, but it is not the same as typological, spiritual, or allegorical methods, which take an Old Testament text and bring it forward to a New Testament context. The analogical approach takes the reader's present experience and carries it backward into the Old Testament narrative context.[26] The analogy often consists in a shared spirituality that includes a perceived access to God's presence. Two biblical texts are cited in this fashion: Ps. 66.10 and Psalm 23.

Psalm 66.10

A woman who identifies herself as Sister Watts offers a personal testimony in which she recounts her various experiences at the Azusa St. revival. She writes that on her very first visit to the meeting she was wonderfully baptized in the Holy Spirit and spoke in tongues. However, the glory of her spiritual experiences did not prevent her from suffering severe tests and trials. She continues:

> My Jesus is more real to me than ever, the Holy Spirit is more jealous of my life and heart. I had suffered much in the purifying process, as gold in the fire or silver in the fire, Zech. 13:9 and Malachi 3:3, Psalm 66:10 [For thou, O God, hast proved us: thou hast tried us, as silver is tried]. We are tried and molded and purged and chastened and cleansed by the Holy Ghost, through the blood of Jesus Christ, the Author and Finisher of our Faith.[27]

---

[26] What I am calling the analogical approach had its beginning in my mind when I preached a series of sermons from the book of Hebrews; and, at the same time, I became aware of the views of John Bright, *The Authority of the Old Testament* (Nashville: Abingdon, 1967), who suggests that 'The Old Testament rightly heard, places me in my B.C. dilemma' (pp. 208-209). On the one hand, he argues that 'we must not impose Christian meanings' on the Old Testament (p. 184). On the other hand, he insists, 'Every Old Testament text, if rightly heard, has its word for us today' (p. 212). My hermeneutic, forged in the praxis of pastoral ministry, has been refined also by engagement with Walter Brueggemann's rhetorical-theological hermeneutic. See Walter Brueggemann, *The Bible Makes Sense* (Cincinnati, OH: St. Anthony Messenger Press, 2nd edn, 2003); Walter Brueggemann, *A Pathway of Interpretation: The Old Testament for Pastors and Students* (Eugene, OR: Cascade Books, 2008). Other solutions to the dilemma of how to make the OT Relevant to a NT audience have been offered by Rudolph Bultmann, 'Prophecy and Fulfillment', in Claus Westermann (ed.), *Essays on Old Testament Hermeneutics* (Richmond, VA: John Knox, 1963), pp. 50-75, and Friedrich Baumgartel, 'The Hermeneutical Problem of the Old Testament', in Westermann (ed.) *Essays on Old Testament Hermeneutics*, pp. 134-59. See also the more recent approach of Elizabeth Achtemeier, *Preaching from the Old Testament* (Louisville, KY: John Knox Press, 1989), pp. 56-59.

[27] *AF* 1.8 (May 1907), p. 4. See a similar use of Ps. 2.4 in *TBM* 3.66 (July 15, 1910), p. 3.

She goes on to say that, at first, she 'did not understand the sanctifying fire', and she thought that God had left her and had removed the Holy Spirit from her. After she had 'prayed and cried to the Lord', she received assurance that God was forming and shaping her. She continued to 'suffer over three weeks'; and, finally, she experienced a breakthrough in which she 'rejoiced in a double portion of God's love and mercy'.[28] Her testimony is framed in such a way that it demonstrates the Pentecostal affections of gratitude, love, joy, and courage.[29]

Although Sister Watts affirms the connection between Ps. 66.10 and the doctrine of sanctification, her primary purpose is not to argue a doctrinal point. Her focus is on her experience of testing, which is analogous to the refining process described in Zech. 13.9, Mal. 3.3, and Ps. 66.10. The Psalms text, in particular, uses the first-person language of testimony: 'thou [hast] proved us: thou hast tried us'. Just as the Israelites were tested and tried, so also 'we' (i.e. Christians) must be 'tried and molded and purged and chastened and cleansed'. The Old Testament texts are chosen here because of their common reference to the refining of gold and/or silver. The New Testament, while it describes testing as a normal part of Christian experience, does not use refining language.[30]

Another important implication of Sister Watts' testimony is the similarity between her experience and the biblical prayers of lament. Although Watts' article is a statement of praise rather than lament, her testimony displays the elements of lament that preceded her praise. Note the following comparison between the elements of the psalms of lament and Watt's experience:

---

[28] *AF* 1.8 (May 1907), p. 4.

[29] See again Land, *Pentecostal Spirituality*, pp. 47, 50, 52, 63.

[30] An exception, of course, is 1 Cor. 3.12-15. However, the Corinthian text speaks not of fire as a present purifying experience but of fire as a component of future judgment. Paul states that the nature of our 'work ... shall be revealed by fire' (v. 13). The use of the Psalms analogically is quite common in the literature. See, for example, the use of Ps. 73.2 in *TBM* 6.137 (Aug 1, 1913), p. 1; Ps. 22.11 in *TBM* 7.145 (Dec 1, 1913), p. 4; Ps. 42.8 and Ps. 34.7 in *CGE* 6.18 (May 1, 1915), pp. 1, 4; 4; Ps. 25.14 in *CGE* 6.22 (May 26, 1915), p. 1; Psalm 34 in *TBM* 2.43 (Aug 1, 1909), p. 3; Ps. 33.1 in *TBM* 2.46 (Sept 15, 1909), p. 2; Ps. 36.9 in *TBM* 3.49 (Nov 1, 1909), p. 4; Ps. 23.1 in *TBM* 3.52 (Dec 15, 1909), p. 4; Psalm 91 in *TBM* 3.63 (June 1, 1910), p. 4; Ps. 3.3 in *TBM* 3.65 (July 1, 1910), p. 1 and *TBM* 3.66 (July 15, 1910), p. 2; Ps. 19.11 in *TBM* 4.81 (Mar 1, 1911), p. 3; and Ps. 125.6 in *PH* 1.4 (July 1915), p. 3.

Lament Form	*Watts' Testimony*
1. address to God	'Jesus is more real to me than ever'
2. complaint	'I thought God had left me … I suffered much … I read my Bible, but none of the promises seemed for me, only judgment. Thus I suffered over 3 weeks'
3. petition	'I prayed and cried unto the Lord'
4. confession of trust	'We shall stand and come out more than conquerors … [I] knew I loved Jesus'
5. assurance	'One morning I suddenly awoke by Jesus talking to me … I clung to that promise'
6. vow of praise	'I rejoiced … Oh such joy unspeakable'
7. descriptive praise	'Glory to Jesus … Praise his name forever'

Watts' testimony reveals her preceding lament in a fashion similar to the narrative portion of a Thanksgiving Psalm that fulfills the same function. The testimonies published in the early periodicals were mostly framed as statements of thanksgiving and praise; therefore, citations from the psalms of lament are infrequent. However, as Larry McQueen has documented, the Pentecostal practice of lament can be found throughout the early periodicals.[31] The experience of lament often shows up, as it does here, in the writers' descriptions of their sufferings and prayers that led up to their deliverances.[32]

Psalm 23

Mrs. Daisy A. Wilkins, of Littleton, NC, cites Psalm 23 in the following testimony regarding her recent illness:

> I have been quite sick since I wrote you all last … I am praising God for His keeping power that keeps me through health and sickness. Even through my darkest hours, the room was filled with angels singing sweet songs to cheer and strengthen me in faith. Many nights when everybody else would be asleep, the Holy

---

[31] See McQueen, *Joel and the Spirit*, pp. 70-76, who provides a helpful overview and introduction to prayers of lament in early Pentecostalism.

[32] Cf. the implied laments in *AF* 1.4 (Dec 1906), p. 1; *AF* 1.8 (May 1907), p. 4; *AF* 1.11 (Oct 1907-Jan 1908), p. 1; *AF* 1.12 (Jan 1908), p. 2; *AFO* 15 (July-Aug 1908), p. 4; *TBM* 6.137 (Aug 1, 1913), p. 1; *TBM* 6.139 (Sept 1, 1913), p. 2; *TBM* 7.143 (Nov 1, 1913), p. 4; *TBM* 3.65 (July 1, 1910), p. 1; Ps. 65.22 *TBM* 5.112 (June 15, 1912), p. 4; *TBM* 8.174 (Sept 1, 1915), p. 3; *LRE* 1.7 (Apr 1909), p. 2; *LRE* 1.7 (Apr 1909), pp. 5-6.

Ghost would come in mighty power and fill my heart so I could only say what good old David did in the 23rd Psalm. Praise the Lord![33]

Wilkins' testimony is quite unusual in that she does not reveal anything about her healing. Her use of past tense language suggests, however, that she was well at the time of writing; but she does not offer any praise to God for her healing. Instead of the common practice of giving thanks for an answer to prayer, Wilkins praises God for keeping her 'through health and sickness' and through her 'darkest hours'. Like David, when she passed through 'the valley of the shadow of death' (Ps. 23.4), she found comfort in God's presence and in the songs of angels. The Holy Spirit cheered and strengthened her so that she could say with David, 'thy rod and thy staff, they comfort me' (Ps. 23.4). The affections of joy and gratitude are evident in the testimony.

Psalm 23 might be categorized as a psalm of trust,[34] and Wilkins' letter to *The Apostolic Faith* is certainly an unapologetic statement of trust and confidence in God. Her experience and her spirituality, therefore, mirror those of David as expressed in Psalm 23. She has chosen to live in the world of the psalm and to claim its confession of trust as her own. Unlike some other early Pentecostals, Wilkins does not view faith and sickness as mutually exclusive; instead, she understands that a Christian can possess true faith and, at the same time, suffer illness.

The Psalms as Affective Argument

Psalm 72.6-7 is quoted in an article entitled 'The Baptism with the Holy Ghost'. The article begins by explaining the distinction between justification, sanctification, and Spirit baptism. It goes on to describe the effects of Spirit baptism, which include tongues, signs, power to witness, love, praise, and personal communion with God. We read, 'This Holy Ghost is love, power, joy, blessing, wisdom and holiness. He will guide you and open the Scriptures to you'. The article also argues that sanctification is a prerequisite to Spirit baptism; the writer

---

[33] *AF* 1.12 (Jan 1908), p. 4.
[34] Goldingay, *Psalms*, I, p. 345. Other scholars prefer to use the term 'Psalm of confidence', e.g. Brueggemann, *Message of the Psalms*, p. 154.

asserts, 'The baptism of the Holy Ghost comes on the sanctified, cleansed life'.

Consisting mostly of logical theological argument, the article changes direction and tone at the end and concludes with a declaration of the wonderful benefits of Spirit baptism. The final paragraph, which features the quotation from Ps. 72.6-7, constitutes an appeal to the affect:

> The most wonderful thing a man or woman can receive after being sanctified is the outpouring of the Holy Ghost in their heart. He is fire and rivers of salvation in you [*sic*] inmost being. Isaiah prophesied, speaking of the Holy Ghost as floods of water: 'I will pour water upon him that is thirsty, and floods upon the dry ground; I will pour out My Spirit upon thy seed, and My blessing upon thine offspring'. (Isaiah 44, 3.) 'Until the Spirit be poured upon us from on high, and the wilderness be a fruitful field … (Isaiah, 32, 15.) Hallelujah! O it is so sweet and precious to receive this almighty baptism with the Holy Ghost in our souls. 'He shall come down like rain upon the mown grass: as showers that water the earth. In His days shall the righteous flourish; and abundance of peace so long as the moon endureth'. (Ps. 72, 6, 7.)[35]

The quotations from Isaiah and the Psalms demonstrate the writer's ability to utilize the affective dimension of the biblical text. The figurative language in this concluding paragraph creates in the reader a desire to receive the baptism in the Holy Spirit. Through the use of emotive metaphor, the writer shows that Spirit baptism is not only theologically orthodox, but it is 'the most wonderful thing' a person can receive. Furthermore, it satisfies the 'thirsty'; it makes the wilderness fruitful; it is 'sweet and precious'; it is 'like rain'; and it produces flourishing and 'abundance of peace'. The vivid images spark the imagination and generate possibilities. The promise of 'rain', which satiates the thirsty ground, causes the reader to hunger and thirst for the Holy Spirit. The hope of 'peace' – in 'abundance' no less – creates a longing in the hearts of those who suffer in the midst of conflict.[36]

---

[35] *AF* 1.11 (Oct 1907-Jan 1908), p. 4.
[36] Other examples of Psalms texts used in affective argument include Ps. 100.4 in *TBM* 1.3 (Dec 1, 1907), p. 4, and Ps. 104.4 in *TBM* 3.55 (Feb 1, 1910), p. 4. These writers would commonly begin with logical argument and conclude with affective appeal.

It seems clear that the quotation of Ps. 72.6-7 functions rhetorically as an affective argument, but the interpretation of the text as a reference to Spirit baptism requires further comment. On one level, the choice of texts is based upon the well-known metaphor of the Holy Spirit as water. For example, Jesus compares the Holy Spirit to 'rivers of living water' (Jn 7.38), a metaphor that would have influenced the interpretation of early Pentecostals. The texts cited here (Isa. 44.3 and 32.25) present the Spirit metaphorically as life-giving water. Pentecostal writers would be familiar also with the image of the Spirit as 'early' and 'latter rain' (e.g. Hos. 6.3; Zech. 10.1). After Joel promises a 'latter rain' that will generate abundance (2.23-27), he declares next (v. 28) that the Lord will 'pour out' his Spirit, and 'sons and daughters shall prophesy'. Many early Pentecostals even believed that the Pentecostal movement was the last-day fulfillment of these 'latter rain' prophecies.[37] Therefore, the psalmist's assertion that 'He shall come down like rain …' is easily connected to the other passages where Spirit and water/rain are joined.

Another hermeneutical key to the writer's interpretation is the fact that Psalm 72, attributed to Solomon, is a Royal Psalm that praises the attributes of God's righteous king. The king is said to have dominion 'unto the ends of the earth' (v. 8). 'All nations shall serve him' (v. 11), and 'he will save the souls of the needy. He shall redeem their soul …' (vv. 13-14). The descriptions are so extravagant that the psalm is traditionally viewed by Christian interpreters as a Messianic prophecy. The king is said to be so great that 'His name shall endure forever: his name shall be continued as long as the sun: and men shall be blessed in him: all nations shall call him blessed' (v. 17). The references to blessing recall the promise to Abraham (Gen. 12.3; 22.18) that in his 'seed' all the nations would be blessed, a promise that, according to Paul (Gal. 3.8), is fulfilled in Jesus Christ. If the psalm describes the reign of Jesus Christ, then the references to life-giving rain, fruitfulness, and peace (which, after all, is a fruit of the Spirit) could be interpreted legitimately as allusions to the gift of the Holy Spirit.

---

[37] Cf. Archer, *A Pentecostal Hermeneutic*, pp. 136-49. See also the reference to Ps. 65.9 in *TBM* 3.63 (June 1, 1910), p. 4.

The Psalms as Assurance and Comfort

The fifth category consists of citations from the Psalms that serve as encouragement to believers. Within what Brueggemann calls 'the life of faith', these texts would function similarly to the Psalms that he classifies as 'psalms of orientation'. This type of Psalm provides a grounding, a worldview, an orientation for the believer and for the community. Psalms of orientation tell us that God is sovereign, God is good, and God is faithful to his covenant people. Regarding the psalms of orientation, Brueggemann writes, 'Some things are settled and beyond doubt, so that one does not live and believe in the midst of overwhelming anxiety … God is known to be reliable and trustworthy. This community has decided to trust in this particular God'.[38] These Psalms insist that evil is punished and good is rewarded. When life gets messy, the psalms of orientation remind us to trust in God because he will make things right. Like the Israelites, early Pentecostals used the psalms of orientation to create a world of 'no fear'.[39] They encountered a great deal of opposition; and because they were mostly poor, they suffered many deprivations and hardships. It is not surprising that they would look to the Psalms for comfort and assurance in their times of great need.

Psalm 91
Psalm 91 is a psalm of trust that promises protection for anyone who will dwell 'in the secret place of the Most High' (Ps. 91.1). Because the Lord is a 'refuge' (vv. 2, 4, 9) and a 'fortress' (v. 2), those who 'trust' in him (v. 2) will not 'be afraid' (v. 5) of the 'snare' and 'pestilence' (v. 3), the 'terror by night' or 'arrow that flies by day' (v. 5), the 'destruction' (v. 6), the 'plague' (v. 10), the 'lion and adder' (v. 13), or any other peril. Moreover, 'A thousand shall fall at your side, and ten thousand at your right hand; but it will not come near you' (v. 7), 'No harm will come to you, and no plague will come near your tent (v. 10). Thus, Brueggemann asserts that Psalm 91 is 'an intense acknowledgment of trust … [that] has reckoned with real life threats, looking them straight in the face. But none will prevail against this God … [these] are words of trusting people'.[40]

---

38 Brueggemann, *Message of the Psalms*, p. 25.
39 Brueggemann, *Message of the Psalms*, p. 25.
40 Brueggemann, *Message of the Psalms*, p. 157.

John Goldingay observes what we all know – that the promises of Psalm 91 'do not work out' in real life.[41] Faithful children of God get sick and die; churches are burned; missionaries are murdered; and enemies sometimes prevail. The Israelites were also fully aware of life's unpleasant side, but they chose to confess an unwavering faith in God through texts like Psalm 91.[42] The dark side of human life is addressed in the psalms of lament, which stand in the Psalter side-by-side with the psalms of trust. For example, Psalm 22 begins with the cry, 'My God, my God, why have you forsaken me?', but in the very next Psalm we hear this confession of trust: 'The Lord is my shepherd, I shall not want'. Commenting on the confident tone of Psalm 91, Goldingay adds, 'there is something profoundly authentic about maintaining such a conviction, even though experience can clash with it'.[43]

Psalm 91 is quoted frequently in the early Pentecostal periodicals. I located 16 references to Psalm 91 in the Wesleyan-Holiness literature and 7 in the Finished-Work periodicals for a total of 23 references (1906-1915). These quotations functioned in most cases as encouragement to believers who were exposed to some kind of danger, such as contagious disease or contexts of violence.[44] I found two citations of Psalm 91 in *The Apostolic Faith* between 1906 and 1915, both referring to outbreaks of 'the plague'. A report entitled 'The Revival in Portland' features descriptions of healings, miracles, and mighty outpourings of the Holy Spirit. Near the middle of the report, we find a brief narrative about a deadly epidemic. It reads:

> When the plague in Portland was taking the children off at a fearful rate, the Lord healed all the Pentecostal flock as soon as it put in its appearance. Not one of them lost one of their family. The people were told to read the 91st Psalm, stand on the Word, and keep under the Blood, and fear nothing.[45]

---

[41] Goldingay, *Psalms*, II, p. 50.

[42] The decision to assert an uncompromising approach to faith comes early in the Psalter. The First Psalm declares that the wicked are condemned, but the righteous person is 'like a tree planted by the rivers of water, that bringeth forth his fruit in his season; his leaf also shall not wither; and whatsoever he doeth shall prosper' (Ps. 1.3). However, we learn as soon as Psalm 3 that life is not fair – the righteous often suffer.

[43] Goldingay, *Psalms*, II, p. 50.

[44] See Chapter 3, above.

[45] *AF* 1.9 (June-Sept 1907), p. 1.

The Psalm uses hyperbole to emphasize God's power to protect those who trust in God. Although some early Pentecostals may have used Psalm 91 as a 'magical' text that guaranteed both physical and spiritual protection from all harmful forces, the writer from Portland recognizes that Psalm 91 cannot be taken literally. Although the psalm states that the pestilence 'will not come near you … and no plague will come near your tent' (vv. 6-7), in Portland the plague had come 'nigh'. None were lost, but that does not mean none became sick. Some of the Pentecostals became ill and 'the Lord healed all'. In the context of a dreadful plague, the church was encouraged to trust God and 'fear nothing'. Psalm 91 is believed to be just as valid for the Christian as it was for the Israelite. I would suggest that the Pentecostal reliance on Psalm 91 is fully consistent with the Psalm's rhetorical character and corresponds with Israel's stubborn confession of trust in God, even in the face of impossibilities.

The second citation of Psalm 91 comes in a letter from China. The heading reads, 'A Chinese brother writes of the plague', and the letter states,

> The plague is raging in Hong Kong, but we have the lintel and two side posts of our doors covered with the Blood of the Lamb. Ex. 12:23 [For the Lord will pass through to smite the Egyptians; and when he seeth the blood upon the lintel, and on the two side posts, the Lord will pass over the door, and will not suffer the destroyer to come in unto your houses to smite you.]. As yet none of us have caught the plague, not a single soul, but please look at Deut. 7:15 [the Lord will take away from thee all sickness, and will put none of the evil diseases of Egypt, which thou knowest, upon thee]. May the Lord have mercy. The total number of cases of the plague here have been near a thousand, and all fatal, except about 50. Not one of us are a bit afraid. Praise the Lord. Psa. 91:7 [A thousand shall fall at thy side, and ten thousand at thy right hand; but it shall not come nigh thee].[46]

Once again, the God of the Old Testament is believed to be the God of the Pentecostals. If the Israelites were saved by the blood of the lamb; then, in the same way, the Pentecostal believers could be saved by their faith in the blood of Jesus (the Lamb of God). If God

---

[46] *AFO* 15 (July-Aug 1908), p. 4.

would put no diseases upon faithful Israel, then neither would God put any diseases upon faithful Christians. The promises of Psalm 91 were efficacious for the psalmist and for the twentieth-century believer.

Just as in the previous citation of Psalm 91, this writer betrays the possibility that the psalmist's promises are not absolute. We read, 'As yet none of us have caught the plague'. Note the words, 'As yet', which indicate the writer's clear understanding of the dangers that persist. Furthermore, notice the poignant petition: 'May the Lord have mercy'. Apparently, it is not enough to quote the biblical promise and claim it; one must also appeal to the Lord's mercy through petition. In the psalm and in this letter from China, there remains an unresolved tension between complete trust in God and the ambiguities of life's dangers. One thing is resolved, however: the people of God should not be afraid. Therefore, in this letter to *The Apostolic Faith* (and in the earlier one as well) the use of Psalm 91 is related to the Pentecostal affections of gratitude and courage.

Psalm 37.7

In 'The Testimony of a Sunday School Teacher', we read a narrative regarding the writer's experience of Spirit Baptism:

> I claimed my Pentecost through that precious Blood, and stood firm on the blessed promises of Luke xi., 13, and Luke xxiv., 49, and I praised Him for it until Friday, September 13th. Oh, that glorious night when Christ came into my heart in all His fulness. It was about twenty minutes to nine when I went into the meeting and they were singing 'Rest in the Lord', the message He gave me on Thursday, Psalm xxxvii., 7 ['Rest in the Lord, and wait patiently for him'] … oh, the unspeakable joy that flooded my soul … the Spirit fell mightily upon me and I spoke in a strange language.[47]

During the process of seeking God for the baptism in the Spirit, this teacher leaned heavily upon Jesus' promises as recorded in the Gospel of Luke. First, Jesus promises that the Father will give the Holy Spirit to those who ask him. Jesus declares, 'If you then, being evil, know how to give good gifts unto your children: how much more shall your heavenly Father give the Holy Spirit to them that ask him?' (Lk. 11.13) Second, Jesus assures his disciples that if they will wait in

---

[47] *AF* 1.11 (Oct 1907-Jan 1908), p. 1.

Jerusalem, the Holy Spirit will clothe them: 'And, behold, I send the promise of my Father upon you: but tarry in the city of Jerusalem, until you are clothed with power from on high' (Lk. 24.49). These two texts explicitly mention the Holy Spirit. Apparently, while the writer was praying for the Spirit and trusting the promises of Lk. 11.13 and 24.49, God 'gave' Ps. 37.7 as a word of assurance: 'Rest in the Lord, and wait patiently for him'. We are not told the manner or mode of the revelation, only that God 'gave' the Scripture.[48] In this circumstance, the biblical text functioned as a word of assurance that the hearer would receive the Holy Spirit by resting in the Lord and 'waiting patiently'. The seeker's faith was strengthened even further when the very words of the psalm were heard ringing forth in the song of the congregation: 'Rest in the Lord'. Although Ps. 37.7 makes no mention of the Holy Spirit, the rhetoric of the text is broad enough to encompass any situation in which the hearer is awaiting God's action. The implication of the writer's use of Ps. 37.7 is that Spirit baptism is a work of God that cannot be forced or attained by human effort; the seeker must rest from personal effort and surrender to the Spirit.[49]

Conclusion: Implications for Pentecostal Hermeneutics

Although this study of the function of the Psalms in *The Apostolic Faith* (1906-1915) explores only 25 of the 576 references to the Psalms in the early periodicals, it has shown that the function and interpretation of the Psalms in Pentecostalism was neither monolithic nor simple. The early writers utilized a variety of methods and approaches, depending upon their purpose for writing. On the one hand, the language of the Psalter was taken quite literally for the purposes of establishing doctrine; but, on the other hand, the language

---

[48] Another example of God's 'giving' a Scripture to someone is found in *TBM* 7.141 (Oct 1, 1913), p. 3. The writer tells about taking in a group of orphans in Nicaragua: 'The day before these children were put in our care the Lord gave us the 127th Psalm'. See also a reference to Lord's giving of Psalm 107 in *TBM* 7.150 (Feb 15, 1914), p. 3.

[49] Other biblical texts used as words of encouragement and assurance include Ps. 18.2 (*TBM* 6.134 [June 1, 1913], p. 4); Ps. 23.4 (*TBM* 2.34 [Mar 15, 1909], p. 3); Psalm 27 (*TBM* 6.126 [Feb 1, 1913], p. 3); Ps. 34.2 (*TBM* 1.9 [Mar 1, 1908], p. 2); Ps. 34.19 (*TBM* 3.67 [Aug 1, 1910], p. 2); Ps. 50.10 (*TBM* 3.67 [Aug 1, 1910], p. 3); Ps. 118.6 (*TBM* 7.143 [Nov 1, 1913], p. 3); and 118.17-18 (*TBM* 2.34 [Mar 15, 1909], p. 3).

could also be taken allegorically, especially in relation to the Royal Psalms and others that are commonly known as Messianic Psalms. The practice of listing a number of biblical texts as support for doctrines – often without commentary – is consistent with Kenneth Archer's argument that early Pentecostals used the 'Bible reading method'.[50] The allegorical interpretation of the Messianic Psalms confirms Chris Green's argument that, for early Pentecostals, the Old Testament speaks of Christ.[51] However, the other interpretive approaches suggest that Green's point should be tweaked – the Old Testament speaks of Christ, but that is not all it does. In addition to speaking of Christ, the Old Testament speaks of the Father and of the Spirit; it speaks of the patriarchs and prophets; it speaks of Israel's long and tumultuous covenant relationship with God. Therefore, in many respects, the Old Testament speaks with its own voice.

Through the analogical use of the Psalms, the early Pentecostal understanding of reality was shaped by the biblical text, and Pentecostals saw themselves as living within the world of the text. The past, the present, and even the future were fused together by the Holy Spirit.[52] The placing of ourselves in an Old Testament context can appear strange to those of us who have been trained in the historical-critical methods, but the early Pentecostals were following a model

---

[50] Archer, *A Pentecostal Hermeneutic*, pp. 99-102. It might be noted that most of the texts examined in this study consist of brief references to individual verses rather than to detailed expositions of entire Psalms. Expositions of biblical passages are rare in the early Pentecostal periodicals, but see e.g. Psalm 29, *LRE* 1.4-1.5 (Jan 1909); Psalm 93, *LRE* 2.3 (Dec 1909); Psalm 23, *PE* 85 (Apr 1915); Psalm 32, *PE* 93 (June 1915); Psalm 141, *PE* (June 1915).

[51] Chris E.W. Green, '"Treasures Old and New": Reading the Old Testament with Early Pentecostal Mothers and Fathers' (Annual Meeting of the Society for Pentecostal Studies, Virginia Beach, VA, 2012). Green's very helpful proposal requires further explanation as it relates to the practice of Old Testament interpretation. Without any clear hermeneutical direction, the open door into allegory can lead to a devaluing of the Old Testament, inasmuch as the Old Testament has no value in its own context. It is one thing to acknowledge (1) that the Old Testament points to Christ and is ultimately fulfilled in Christ, and (2) that Christ in present everywhere in the Bible because, as part of the trinity, Christ is present whenever 'God' is present; but it is another thing to require that every Old Testament text have an allegorical meaning. Even in the New Testament, not every text is a direct comment on Jesus Christ. See Lee Roy Martin, 'Pre-Critical Exegesis of the Book of Judges and the Construction of a Post-Critical Hermeneutic', *EP* 88 (2006), pp. 338-53, where I argue that the allegorical method is not appropriate for today's context.

[52] Cf. Land, *Pentecostal Spirituality*, pp. 55, 66-67.

of interpretation that is not uncommon in the New Testament. The writer of Hebrews, for example, compares the experience of the Hebrew Christians to that of the Israelites who, in Numbers 13-15, heard God's command to go forward. Those Israelites allowed fear and unbelief to cloud their judgment; and, therefore, they disobeyed God's command and subsequently died in the wilderness. The analogy is stated clearly: 'Beware, brothers, lest there be in any of you an evil heart of unbelief, in departing from the living God' (Heb. 3.12); and 'Therefore, let us labor to enter into that rest, lest any man fall after the same example of unbelief' (Heb. 4.11). The Hebrew Christians faced the same questions of faith and challenges from the enemy as the biblical Israelites.[53] Early Pentecostals were deeply infused with biblical ways of thinking and acting; therefore, it is not surprising that they would imitate the hermeneutical patterns of the New Testament writers. Their use of the Old Testament as analogous to Christian experience is based upon a theological interpretation of Scripture that recognizes the commonality of all human lives that are lived by faith in the presence of God, no matter the location in time or geographical space.[54]

A number of conclusions can be reached from this exploration of *The Apostolic Faith*. First, it is clear that early Pentecostals relied on both Old and New Testament as the Word of God. Second, they emphasized the overall unity of Scripture and downplayed the diversity of Scripture.[55] Third, they utilized intertextuality without reservation.[56] Fourth, their interpretations sometimes followed a rationalist, proof-texting approach; but, at other times, they followed a more literary, narrative, theological approach. Fifth, they appreciated the

---

[53] Cf. Paul's use of the wilderness narrative (1 Cor. 10.1-13). Other texts where New Testament writers use the Old Testament analogically might include Mt. 4.4; 9.13; 13.14-15; 15.8-9; 24.15; 27.46; Mk. 4.12; 7.6-7; 8.18; 13.14; 14.27; 15.34; Lk. 4.4; 4.18-19; 8.10; 12.53; 20.17; 22.37; 23.46; Jn 2.17; 6.45; 12.40; 13.18; 15.25; Acts 1.20; 2.31; 4.25-26; 28.26-27; Rom. 1.17; 2.24; 3.13-18; 4.3, 22; 8.36; 9.25; 10.8, 11, 15-18, 20-21; 11.8-10; 1 Cor. 1.31; 10.7; 14.21; 2 Cor. 4.13; 6.2, 17; Gal. 3.6, 11; 4.27; 1 Tim. 5.18; Hebrews 11; 12.6; 12.25; 13.5-6; Jam. 2.23; 1 Pet. 1.24-25; 2.3, 9, 25; 3.14.

[54] Cf. the similar, though more sophisticated, method of Brueggemann, 'Psalms and the Life of Faith, pp. 3-32, later expanded in his *Message of the Psalms*.

[55] Pentecostals would agree with the statement of John Bright that 'the Testaments are inseparably bound to each other within the unity of a single redemptive history' (*The Authority of the Old Testament*, p. 199).

[56] Cf. Green, '"Treasures Old and New"', p. 15.

affective dimension of the Psalter and made wide use of it. Sixth, the early Pentecostal hermeneutic was thoroughly confessional.

Finally, I would suggest that the early Pentecostal approaches and contemporary scholarship might mutually inform one another to produce a genuinely Pentecostal approach to the Psalms. First, the use of the Psalms as support for doctrine can be refined through critical engagement with exegetical and theological methods. Second, the use of the Psalms as allegory/typology can be enhanced by a greater concern for consistency of application and by comparing the New Testament's appropriation of texts from the Psalter. Third, the use of the Psalms as analogies and as words of encouragement can be improved by giving attention to the theology, context, genre, and purpose of the Psalms and by more thorough exegesis of our own situation, particularly in the area of Pentecostal spirituality and the affections. Fourth, the use of the Psalms as affective argument can be expanded by a broader appreciation of the rhetorical function of the affective language in the Psalter. It is hoped that this kind of approach can benefit the Pentecostal movement by integrating the study of the Psalms with Pentecostal spirituality.

THE EVENING LIGHT

"And when the day of Pentecost was fully come they were all with one accord in one place." Acts 2:1.

And

Church *of* God Evangel.

"And they were all filled with the Holy Ghost, and began to speak with other tongues, as the Spirit gave them utterance." Acts 2:4.

"*For they heard them speak with tongues, and magnify God.*" Acts 10: 46.

Entered as second-class matter March 1, 1910, at the Postoffice at Cleveland, Tenn., under the act of March 3, 1879.

VOLUME 1.
NUMBER 10.

CLEVELAND, TENN., DECEMBER 1, 1910.

3c PER COPY
50c PER YEAR

Healing in the Atonement.

Healing for Our Bodies the Same as Salvation for Our Souls.

"By Whose [Jesus] Stripes Ye Were Healed." 1 Peter 2:24

There are a number of good people who believe God is able to heal their bodies in answer to prayer who do not see healing in the atonement the same as the forgiveness of sins.

It is not our purpose to give a lengthy discussion of this subject at this time, but to make a few statements and give some Scriptures bearing on the subject for the consideration of those who may be interested, with a desire to encourage the faith of all who may read the "Evangel."

In the 103rd Psalm and the second and third verses we read, "Bless the Lord, O my soul, and forget not all his benefits: Who forgiveth all thine iniquities; whe healeth all thy diseases." The Psalmist indicates here that although we might forget some of the Lord's benefits to us, we should not forget these; that God forgives sins and heals our bodies. The human race have forgotten these two benefits largely, and even many professed christians have forgotten both, yet more, probably, have forgotten the latter than the former. The reason why people are so forgetful of things pertaining to their own interests is not to be discussed, but the fact remains just the same. The Bible is, or could be, in every home in America, and yet people are so occupied with the things of this world that they are unmindful of the good things in their Bibles that ought to be remembered for the good of themselves.

In the atonement chapter, Isaiah 53, the prophet did not speak only of salvation for the soul, but healing for the bodies as well. Verses 4 and 5 should be read and studied carefully. "Surely he hath borne our griefs, and carried our sorrows: yet we did esteem him stricken, smitten of God and afflicted. But he was wounded for our transgressions, he was bruised for our iniquities: the chastisement of our peace was upon him; and with his stripes (bruise—margin) we are healed." This same Scripture is mentioned in Math. 8:16, 17.

"When the even was come, they brought unto him (Jesus) many that were possessed with devils; and he cast out the spirits with his word, and healed all that were sick: That it might be fulfilled which was spoken by Esaias (Isaiah) the prophet, saying, Himself took our infirmities, and bare our sicknesses."

There are many good people to-day who believe God has power to heal, and will and does heal in answer to prayer, that never think of healing being provided for us in the atonement the same as salvation for our souls. When people see this fully it will no doubt inspire more faith for healing. Indeed there is no other way provided in the Bible for salvation except by and through Jesus Christ. I will add here that there is no other plan given between the lids of the Bible for the healing of our bodies except through Jesus. For years, yea and ages, christian people have been using other means for healing contrary to the Bible teaching. Many of these same people would not think of any other way for salvation for the soul except through Jesus, and would say, "to climb up any other way would make them thieves and robbers," and yet when it came to healing they never thought of making themselves of the same class by resorting to physicians and medicine. The true light has once more commenced to shine brilliantly on earth. The last message is going forth. In the "evening time it shall be

Psalm 103 is Mentioned in Column 1

9

THE BOOK OF PSALMS AND PENTECOSTAL WORSHIP

Introduction

Depictions of worship, encouragements to worship, and instructions for worship are scattered throughout the Bible – beginning with the offerings of Cain and Abel in Genesis 4 and concluding with the imperative 'Worship God' in Rev. 22.9.[1] It is the book of Psalms, however, that gives the most sustained attention to the topic of worship. Therefore, while any attempt to develop a theology of worship should include the study of a wide variety of biblical texts from both Old and New Testaments, the book of Psalms must be afforded serious consideration.

Unfortunately, the modern study of the Psalms, emerging primarily from the seminal work of Hermann Gunkel, has focused on historical backgrounds rather than theological construction. Gunkel's form-critical approach produced a classification of Psalm types and sought to understand the ancient function of the Psalter and the various *Sitze im Leben* of the individual psalms.[2] More recent studies in the Psalms have moved beyond the study of the ancient context and

---

[1] Cf. Tom Sterbens, 'Worship: The Journey to Worth', in R. Keith Whitt and French L. Arrington (eds.), *Issues in Contemporary Pentecostalism* (Cleveland, TN: Pathway Press, 2012), pp. 185-210 (85).

[2] See Hermann Gunkel, *The Psalms: A Form-Critical Introduction* (Facet Books Biblical Series, 19; Philadelphia: Fortress Press, 1967). Gunkel's approach was refined by later scholars including, for example, Mowinckel, *The Psalms in Israel's Worship*, and Westermann, *Praise and Lament in the Psalms*.

have demonstrated the Psalter's use throughout history and have offered helpful suggestions regarding the employment of the Psalms in the context of the contemporary liturgy. Therefore, for the most part, scholarship on the Psalms has emphasized their liturgical usage, either in ancient times or in contemporary times. What is missing from biblical scholarship, however, is an investigation into how the book of Psalms may contribute to a biblical theology of worship.

It should be pointed out that not everyone accepts the Old Testament as a valid source for Christian theology and practice. At least two questions arise whenever the Old Testament is appealed to in support of particular worship practices: 1. Can the Old Testament can be considered authoritative at all? 2. If we accept the authority of the Old Testament, how do we determine which practices are legitimate for Christian worship and which practices should not be included in Christian worship? I would argue that the role of the Old Testament in theological construction is a hermeneutical matter that impacts not just the question of worship but also the broader theological task. Pentecostalism, in agreement with most other Christian traditions, accepts the authority of the Old Testament in matters of theology, ethics, and practice (cf. 2 Tim. 3.16), with the proviso that certain practices (such as temple rituals, sacrifices, and cleanliness codes) have their theological fulfillment in the New Covenant of Jesus Christ. Therefore, Pentecostal scholar Gerald Sheppard can insist, 'The Psalms as scripture constitute a prime territory for our theological reflection, something far more than merely a prayer book among the artifacts of ancient Israelite religion'.[3] Another Pentecostal writer, P.A. Minnaar, in his article on 'Worship', sees Psalm 95 as a 'guideline on the nature of worship and how to practice it'.[4]

Pentecostals are not the only ones who recognize the importance of the Psalms in discussions about Christian worship. Elizabeth Achtemeier argues that the Psalms tell us 'how properly to lament before the Sovereign Lord of the universe and how properly to praise him'. She explains further:

And the hermeneutics behind that consists in the fact that the church is, according to Paul, the 'Israel of God' (Gal. 6:16), the

---

[3] Sheppard, 'Theology and the Book of Psalms', p. 155. Cf. Maré, 'A Pentecostal Perspective', pp. 91-109, who presents a convincing argument for the theological value of the Psalms.

[4] P.A. Minnaar, 'Aanbidding', *Pinksterboodskapper* 8.9 (1983), pp. 2-5 (3).

wild branches grafted into the root of Israel (Rom. 11:7-24), or in Ephesians, those who, through the work of Jesus Christ, have been brought into the commonwealth.[5]

Ernest Gentile proposes that the Psalms were utilized by early Christians. He writes, 'The worship forms found in the book of Psalms provided an ideal way for the lively, Spirit-filled Christians of Bible days to express themselves in personal and corporate worship'.[6] John Lamb extends the paradigmatic function of the Psalms to contemporary worship: 'The Psalter which itself teaches the duty of praise, provides the necessary ideas and expressions'.[7] Renowned Psalms scholar Sigmund Mowinckel agrees that the Psalms have at least some paradigmatic use. He writes, 'The psalms are not only useful for performance in worship, they are useful as models for contemporary hymn writing'.[8] Michael Barrett suggests that the theology of worship is a prominent element in the book of Psalms and 'the psalms are paradigms for worship'.[9] He argues, 'The Psalms give patterns for both individual and corporate worship'.[10]

When I first came into Pentecostalism, I heard the Psalms being used to validate the general loudness, exuberance, and bodily involvement in Pentecostal worship, as well as more specific Pentecostal practices like shouting, leaping, dancing, clapping, lifting the hands, and the use of musical instruments like the tambourine. For example, Pentecostals have justified their energetic worship by pointing to the following texts in Psalms:

'Shout for joy, all you upright in heart!' (32.11)[11]

---

[5] Elizabeth Achtemeier, 'Preaching the Praises and Laments', *CTJ* 36.1 (2001), p. 104.

[6] Ernest B. Gentile, *Worship God!: Exploring the Dynamics of Psalmic Worship* (Portland, OR: City Bible Pub., 1994), pp. 3-4.

[7] John Alexander Lamb, *The Psalms in Christian Worship* (London: Faith Press, 1962), p. 163.

[8] Mowinckel, *The Psalms in Israel's Worship*, p. v.

[9] Michael P.V. Barrett, *The Beauty of Holiness: A Guide to Biblical Worship* (Belfast: Ambassador Publications, 2006), pp. 159-61.

[10] Barrett, *The Beauty of Holiness*, p. 160.

[11] In regard to shouting, see also Pss. 47.2; 65.14; 66.1; 81.1; 95.1, 2; 98.4, 6; 100.1 (רוע); 5.11; 20.6; 32.11; 17.1; 30.6; 33.1; 35.27; 42.5; 51.16; 59.17; 61.2; 63.8; 65.9; 67.5; 71.23; 81.1; 84.3; 88.3; 89.13; 90.14; 92.5; 95.1; 96.12; 98.4; 98.8; 105.43; 106.44; 107.22; 118.15; 119.169; 126.2, 5; 132.9; 132.16; 142.7; 145.7; 149.5 (רנן). Verse numbering follows the Hebrew text.

'Clap your hands all people' (47.2).[12]
'Praise him with the ... dance' (150.4).[13]
'Lift up your hands in the sanctuary and bless Yahweh' (134.2).[14]
'Make a loud noise, and rejoice' (98.4).[15]
'Take up a song and bring the tambourine' (81.3).[16]
'Those who sow in tears will reap shouts of joy' (126.6).[17]

These examples demonstrate Pentecostalism's appreciation for and imitation of the worship practices found in the Psalter.[18] Furthermore, Pentecostals have adopted certain psalms as models of genuine biblical worship. Psalm 100, for example, is employed often as a paradigm for contemporary Pentecostal worship.[19]

Psalm 100
A Psalm of thanksgiving
[1] Shout to Yahweh, all the earth.
[2] Worship Yahweh with gladness;
    Come before him with a loud cry.
[3] Know that Yahweh himself is God.
    It is he that made us, and we are his;
    We are his people, and the sheep of his pasture.
[4] Enter his gates with thanksgiving, and his courts with praise.
    Give thanks to him, bless his name.
[5] For Yahweh is good;
    His covenant loyalty is forever,

---

[12] Cf. Ps. 98.8. Concerning Pentecostal hand clapping, see David D. Daniels, III, '"Gotta Moan Sometime": A Sonic Exploration of Earwitnesses to Early Pentecostal Sound in North America', *Pneuma* 30.1 (2008), p. 18, who writes, 'The rhythmic pulse of Pentecostal musicality was sustained by clapping. For some early Pentecostals the sound of clapping communicated praise to God. Sometimes this is called praising God with Psalm 47 ("O clap your hands together"), a doxological form of clapping.'

[13] Cf. Pss. 30.11; 149.3.

[14] Cf. Pss. 28.2; 63.5; 119.48.

[15] Concerning loudness, see also Pss. 33.3; 150.5.

[16] Cf. Pss. 149.3; 150.4.

[17] Concerning weeping, see also Pss. 6.7; 30.6; 39.13; 56.9; 69.11.

[18] In the face of the Psalter's consistent call for expressive and passionate worship, I am quite astounded by Block, *For the Glory of God*, who associates enthusiastic worship with idolatry (p. 226).

[19] I inserted my translation of Psalm 100 early on a Sunday morning while my family was getting ready for church. Imagine my astonishment when we arrived later at church and heard the worship leader reading this very Psalm and encouraging the congregation to worship according to its commands.

And his faithfulness endures to all generations.

The Psalm utilizes an impressive series of seven imperatives:

'shout joyfully' (הריעו);
'worship with gladness' (עבדו בשׂמחה);
'come with a loud cry' (באו ברננה);
'know that Yahweh is God' (דעו כי־יהוה הוא אלהים);
'enter with thanksgiving … praise' (באו בתודה בתהלה);
'give thanks to him' (הודו־לו);
'bless his name' (ברכו שׁמו).

These imperatives point to the importance of worship for God's people, to their intense involvement in the act of worship, to the affective dimension of worship, to praise as the indispensable intention of worship, and to God as the exclusive object of worship. It is clear that Pentecostals have used the Psalms as guides to worship, but it remains to be seen how a more comprehensive look at the Psalms might contribute to a Pentecostal theology of worship.

Given the Old Testament's authority in the Christian tradition generally and in the Pentecostal tradition specifically, I will proceed on the assumption that while the relative value of each specific worship practice in the Psalms may be assessed on its own merits, these practices and the broader and more basic theological concerns of the Psalter can be accepted as valuable for constructing a Pentecostal theology of worship. Interpreters will no doubt disagree as to what constitutes the essential concerns of the book of Psalms, but it is hoped that this study will at least generate a helpful discussion about Pentecostal worship and the Psalter.

This chapter will outline a theology of worship derived from the Psalms and suggest ways that the Psalter might contribute more specifically to a Pentecostal theology of worship. I will present my observations according to three categories: 1. observations regarding the book as a whole, 2. observations regarding the various psalm types, and 3. observations regarding the theology expressed in individual psalms.

The Theology of Worship Manifested in the Book of Psalms

The book of Psalms Stresses the Importance of Worship.

We must be careful at the outset that we do not overlook the most obvious point that the Psalter expresses the value of worship both to the individual believer and to the community of faith. The importance of worship is registered in two ways. First, the very presence of the book of Psalms within the canon bears witness to the necessity of worship. It is not insignificant that one of the largest books in the Bible consists of words addressed to God rather than words that come from God. Nahum Sarna writes, 'In the Law and the Prophets, God reaches out to [humanity]. The initiative is His. The message is His ... In the Psalms, human beings reach out to God. The initiative is human. The language is human. We make the effort to communicate.'[20] Although not every psalm addresses God directly, even the indirect praises may be categorized legitimately as words of worship.[21] Therefore, the book of Psalms testifies to the importance of the human covenantal response to God's person and actions. Whenever God acts, the appropriate human response is worship, as may be witnessed not only in the Psalms but also in other texts such as Exodus 15, Deuteronomy 32, Judges 5, 1 Samuel 2, Jonah 2, and Habakkuk 3, where songs of praise and thanksgiving are recorded. However, these human words addressed to God become a word from God as the community participates through joining the dialogue and overhearing the interchange during times of worship.

Second, a multitude of texts in the book of Psalms attest to the importance of worship. Over and over, the Psalms invite and command God's people to sing, to worship, to serve, to pray, to rejoice,

---

[20] Nahum M. Sarna, *On the Book of Psalms: Exploring the Prayers of Ancient Israel* (New York: Schocken Books, 1st paperback edn, 1993), p. 3. Sarna follows the lead of von Rad, *Old Testament Theology*, I, pp. 355-70, who speaks of the Psalms as 'Israel's answer' ('*Antwort*') to Yahweh. Cf. H. Spieckermann, *Heilsgegenwart: eine Theologie der Psalmen* (Göttingen: Vandenhoeck and Ruprecht, 1989), pp. 7-20, and Kraus, *Theology of the Psalms*, pp. 11-14.

[21] By my count, 109 of the 150 psalms include words addressed directly to God while the other 49 offer worship to God in a more indirect fashion (e.g. Psalm 150). Cf. Westermann, *Praise and Lament in the Psalms*, pp. 15-18, who argues that God is praised whenever his actions or attributes are commended either directly or indirectly and that 'praise *occurs*' even in those psalms that lack explicit words of praise (emphasis original).

to call out to God, to dance, to play instruments, to bring offerings, to enter the temple, and so on. For example, we read, 'Sing praises to Yahweh, who dwells in Zion!' (Ps. 9.11); 'Worship Yahweh in the beauty of holiness' (Ps. 29.2); 'Oh come, let us worship and bow down; let us kneel before Yahweh our maker' (Ps. 95.6); 'Oh, give thanks to Yahweh! Call upon his name' (Ps. 105.1); 'Exalt Yahweh our God, and worship at his holy hill' (Ps. 99.9); 'Be glad in Yahweh and rejoice, you righteous; and shout for joy, all you upright in heart!' (Ps. 32.11).[22]

In the Psalms, worship is both individual and communal. The first Psalm opens with a reference to the individual ('Blessed is the man', אִישׁ), but it concludes with statements about the community ('congregation', עֵדָה, and 'righteous ones', צַדִּיקִים). Throughout the Psalter, we find both individual prayers and communal prayers, individual testimonies and communal testimonies, individual praises and communal praises.[23] On the whole, there is a discernable progression from individualistic language at the beginning of the Psalter to communal language at the end of the Psalter. This progression corresponds to the movement from lament at the beginning of the Psalter to praise at the end of the Psalter.

Erhard Gerstenberger argues that the psalms are inherently communal. He writes,

> Modern psalm-research has proved beyond reasonable doubt that Old Testament psalmody in no case was a private, poetic affair of closed-in individuals. There is nothing like our seemingly 'private' poetry in ancient times ... All Old Testament literature is community oriented, destined to be used in groups and congregations.[24]

---

[22] Kraus, *Theology of the Psalms*, p. 12, states that the cult (i.e. worship) was 'the center of the life of the Old Testament people of God'.

[23] Lamb, *The Psalms in Christian Worship*, p. 3, declares, '[S]ome psalms are congregational, that is, that they were meant to be sung in the sanctuary, whether by a priest or a trained soloist ... or by the whole company'.

[24] Erhard S. Gerstenberger, 'Singing a New Song: On Old Testament and Latin American Psalmody', *Word & World* 5.2 (1985), p. 157. Cf. Lamb, *The Psalms in Christian Worship*, p. 162, who writes,

> The worshiper is not merely a human soul alone before his maker and father; he is a member of the family, of the body of Christ, of the communion of saints. He shares in the whole work of the church, whether in worship or in the proclamation of the gospel, or in the social advancement of the kingdom of God. The Psalter witnesses to this solidarity of the church.

Similarly, Teun van der Leer contends that the Psalms 'teach us to believe and pray with and from within the community'. He adds,

> However personal the Psalms can be (Ps. 27:7-14; 77:1-4), they are and remain songs of the faith community. There are quite a few Psalms with an illogical transition from 'I' to 'we', for example Ps. 122:1-2; 123:1-2; or they start with 'me' and conclude within the community, see for example Ps. 22. Many Psalms are even filled with longing for the community: Ps. 42:5.[25]

In anticipation of gathering together with God's people for worship, the psalmist writes, 'I will give you thanks in the great assembly; I will praise you among many people' (Ps. 35.18). Looking back on previous times of worship, the author of Psalm 40 declares, 'I have not concealed your steadfast love and your truth from the great assembly' (Ps. 40.11).

The Book of Psalms Grounds Worship in Covenantal Commitment.

The corporate nature of Old Testament worship is generated by the covenant relationship between Yahweh and Israel,[26] and the book of Psalms testifies to the importance of Israel's worship as a covenantal response to God's person and actions.[27] The worship of the Psalms, therefore, flows out of the covenant relationship between Yahweh and Israel. Worship is an expression of Israel's covenant commitment to Yahweh, and Israel's praises are in direct response to Yahweh's covenant faithfulness as embodied in Yahweh's steadfast love (חסד).[28]

Mutual commitment is the heart of the covenant; and is, therefore, the foundation of genuine worship. Yahweh is fully committed to Israel, and Israel is fully committed to Yahweh. Yahweh promises to be present, 'enthroned on the praises of Israel' (Ps. 22.4), and

---

[25] Teun van der Leer, 'The Psalms as a Source for Spirituality and Worship', *Journal of European Baptist Studies* 13.2 (2013), p. 26.

[26] Walter Brueggemann, *Worship in Ancient Israel: An Essential Guide* (Nashville, TN: Abingdon Press, 2005), pp. 7-9. I would like to express my appreciation to Pastor Guinn Green, whose questions about the commitment of the worshiper helped me to clarify my approach in this section.

[27] Cf. von Rad's above-mentioned characterization of the psalms as Israel's *Antwort* (*Old Testament Theology*, I, pp. 355-70).

[28] Brueggemann, *Worship in Ancient Israel*, pp. 7-9.

every Israelite is required to be present in worship.[29] 'Thus worship in Israel consists in *a dialogic interaction* in which both parties are fully present, both parties are to some extent defined by the other, and both parties are put to some extent at risk by the transaction'.[30]

The covenant is exclusive, which means that Yahweh is the only legitimate object of worship.[31] All other gods are interlopers in the covenant relationship between Yahweh and Israel. The psalmist declares, 'For all the gods of the peoples are idols, but Yahweh made the heavens' (Ps. 96.5).[32] In their worship, the Israelites can affirm, '[W]e have not forgotten you, nor been disloyal to your covenant' (Ps. 44.18).

The importance of the covenant as the foundation of worship is expressed in the Psalter in at least three ways. First and most obvious are the numerous psalms in which the covenant is mentioned.[33] For example, the psalms of historical recital praise Yahweh's faithful remembrance of the covenant. The psalmist exclaims that Yahweh 'remembers his covenant forever, the word which he commanded, for a thousand generations' (Ps. 105.8).[34]

Second, the praises that resound in the hymns are often motivated by Yahweh's covenant loyalty (חסד). Translated as 'lovingkindness', 'mercy', 'faithfulness', or 'steadfast love', חסד is found 130 times in the Psalter.[35] The word חסד indicates the overarching covenantal, relational quality of Yahweh.[36] Therefore, the psalmist enters into worship with Yahweh's steadfast love in mind: 'But I, through the abundance of your steadfast love (חסד), will enter into your house' (Ps.

---

[29] Cf. Brueggemann, *Worship in Ancient Israel*, p. 13, who writes, 'Attendance to worship was not considered optional'.

[30] Brueggemann, *Worship in Ancient Israel*, p. 9 (emphasis original).

[31] Mutual commitment is implied in Exod. 6.7: 'I will take you as my people, and I will be your God'. Israel's commitment to worship Yahweh exclusively is required in the Decalogue: 'You shall have no other gods beside me ... you shall not bow down to them nor serve them. For I, Yahweh your God, am a jealous God' (Exod. 20.3-5).

[32] Cf. Pss. 97.7; 106.36; 115.4; 135.15.

[33] The Hebrew word ברית, which is translated 'covenant', occurs 21 times in the Psalter.

[34] See also Pss. 89.4, 29, 35, 40; 105.10; 106.45; 111.5, 9; 132.12. Moreover, all references to the Torah could be interpreted as references to the covenant.

[35] *BDB*, p. 339; *HALOT*, I, pp. 336-37.

[36] *TLOT*, II, p. 451.

5.8).[37] Psalm 33 encourages the congregation to 'sing to [Yahweh] a new song' (v. 3) because 'the earth is full of the steadfast love (חסד) of Yahweh' (v. 5). Worshipers are encouraged to 'Give thanks to Yahweh, for he is good; his steadfast love (חסד) endures forever' (Ps. 107.1). From beginning to end, Psalm 136 repeatedly calls for the praise of Yahweh because 'his steadfast love (חסד) endures forever' (vv. 1-26).

Third, the pleas voiced in the laments grow out of the psalmist's covenant relationship to Yahweh. The psalmist cries out, 'My God, my God, why have you forsaken me?' (Ps. 22.1). The psalms of lament, therefore, are grounded upon the certainty of the divine–human relationship. John Eaton asserts that 'the emphatic "my God" expresses the covenantal bond with all its assurances'.[38] The phrase 'my God' (or 'Lord') occurs 60 times in the Psalter; and 'our God' (or 'Lord') is found 30 times.[39] The connection between covenant and lament is explored by Scott Ellington, who writes,

> Biblical lament, while it does include tears, pleas, complaints and protests, is something more. It is the experience of loss suffered within the context of *relatedness*. A relationship of trust, intimacy, and love is a necessary precondition for genuine lament. When the biblical writers lament, they do so from within the context of a foundational relationship that binds together the individual with members of the community of faith and that community with their God.[40]

This covenantal foundation of worship includes a number of related elements such as devotion to Mt. Zion (e.g. Psalm 48), the centrality of the Jerusalem temple (e.g. Psalm 84), the role of sacrificial offerings as an expected part of worship (e.g. Ps. 50.5), and the enthronement of the royal Davidic heir (e.g. Psalm 2).[41]

---

[37] Cf. Ps. 100.4-5: 'Enter his gates with thanksgiving and his courts with praise … for Yahweh is good; his steadfast love (חסד) endures forever'.

[38] Eaton, *The Psalms,* p. 235.

[39] Although the phrases 'my God' and 'our God' are connected mostly to Israel's prayers, they can also be associated with Israel's praises. For example, the psalmist proclaims, 'Praise Yahweh. How good it is to sing praises to our God' (Ps. 147.1).

[40] Ellington, *Risking Truth*, p. 7 (emphasis original).

[41] At least 32 different psalms pay tribute to Mt. Zion; 38 refer to the king or the throne; more than 40 psalms mention the temple; and at least 23 psalms include explicit references to sacrificial offerings. Psalm 50.5 views the sacrifices as

The Psalms anticipate and celebrate attendance to the temple. The psalmist writes,

> One thing I have asked from Yahweh;
>   that will I seek:
> that I may dwell in the house of Yahweh all the days of my life,
>   to gaze on the beauty of Yahweh
>   and to seek him in his temple' (Ps. 27.4)

> My soul yearns, even faints, for the courts of Yahweh;
>   my heart and my flesh cry out for the living God' (Ps. 84.2).[42]

Although sacrificial offerings are both assumed and commanded in the Psalter, their efficacy is questioned in a number of texts. Several passages from the Psalter seem to suggest that sacrifice was not sufficient as an expression of worship. Psalm 40.6 reads, 'Sacrifice and offering you did not desire; my ears you have opened. Burnt offerings and sin offerings you did not require.' A similar viewpoint is expressed in Ps. 51.16-17: 'For you do not desire sacrifice, or else I would give it; you do not delight in burnt offerings. The sacrifices of God are a broken spirit; a broken and a contrite heart – these, O God, you will not despise.' Psalm 27 anticipates the New Testament's perspective that some of the sacrifices have been fulfilled in Jesus Christ and others have been transformed into sacrificial praise. The psalmist writes, 'And now my head shall be lifted up above my enemies all around me; therefore I will offer sacrifices of joy in his tabernacle; I will sing, yes, I will sing praises to Yahweh' (Ps. 27.6). In this text, the 'sacrifices of joy' are parallel grammatically to the singing of 'praises' to the Lord, suggesting that singing can be conceived of as a sacrifice offered by the worshiper to the Lord.

Although Israel's theology of worship as found in the book of Psalms assumes the importance of Mt. Zion, the presence of God at the Jerusalem temple, the role of sacrificial offerings, and the continuation of the Davidic dynasty, these elements of worship must be filtered through the New Testament before they can be carried forward into Pentecostal worship. The New Testament shows that each of these Old Testament features has an underlying theology that

---

integrally related to the covenant: 'Gather my holy ones together to me, those who have made a covenant with me by sacrifice' (cf. Ps. 4.6). These central elements of worship are discussed by Kraus, *Theology of the Psalms*, pp. 67-100.

[42] See also Pss. 5.8; 23.6; 26.8; 36.9; 42.5; 52.10; 55.15; 65.5; 66.13; 84.11; etc.

should be part of our theology of worship. Both Mt. Zion and the Jerusalem temple bear witness to the ongoing presence of God in the midst of his people (Cf. Heb. 12.22-24; 1 Cor. 3.16). The sacrifices were fulfilled when Jesus offered himself (Heb. 7.27). However, the costliness of worship is registered through the expected offering of one's body (Rom. 12.1) and one's praises: 'Therefore, through [Jesus] let us continually offer the sacrifice of praise to God, that is, the fruit of our lips, giving thanks to his name' (Heb. 13.15). Finally, the Davidic king continues to reign in the person of Jesus of Nazareth, 'the root and offspring of David, the bright and morning star' (Rev. 22.16). To him we sing a new song, saying, 'You are worthy' (Rev. 5.9).

The Book of Psalms Views Worship as Theological Expression.

The Old Testament is not a book of systematic theology. Instead, Old Testament theology is expressed in story and in song. The Psalms, therefore, are sung theology. Martin Luther declares that the book of Psalms 'might well be called a little Bible. In it is comprehended most beautifully and briefly everything that is in the entire Bible.'[43] Erhard Gerstenberger expresses his amazement at the theological depth and breadth of the Psalms when he writes,

> [T]he Psalter does not contain a summa of theological thought or any kind of theological system ... Still, the Psalter is so vast in its theological dimensions that any systematizing effort must fall short. It will continue to stimulate our life of faith even in this different age, just as it has done for centuries.[44]

Lamb addresses the theological content of the Psalter by recounting a number of important themes that are found in it:

> One cannot read and meditate upon this book without reaching a particular and clear idea of God – a God with a creator's mastery over the universe, with a father's tender pity towards his children, with a judge's interest in righteousness, with a shepherd's care for the erring; a God whose glory is above the heavens, who counts

---

[43] Martin Luther, 'Preface to the Psalter', in Pelikan (ed.), *Luther's Works*, p. 254.
[44] Gerstenberger, *Psalms: Part 1*, p. 36. Cf. Childs, *Introduction to the Old Testament as Scripture*, who writes that the Psalms 'accurately reflect the theology of Israel' (p. 514).

the stars and names them, whose kingdom rules over all, yet whose mercy is from everlasting to everlasting.[45]

Worship, therefore, embodies our theology, celebrates our theology, and communicates our theology. When I first entered Bible college 40 years ago, my teachers complained that too much worship was grounded in bad theology, and I continue to hear similar complaints today. For example, Timothy Pierce observes, 'Music leaders, writers, and performers need to become better versed in theology … Music must be immersed in proper theology precisely because it has a power to instruct and evoke in a manner that few mediums can.'[46] Consequently, the church's liturgy must be planned and executed with theological faithfulness in mind. When evaluating our worship, we should ask what kind of theology our worship conveys.

Moreover, while I agree wholeheartedly that worship must be grounded in good theology, I would also argue for the converse, which is that theology must be grounded in good worship. Samuel Terrien declares, 'Doxology is the key to theology'.[47] Unfortunately, many scholars have severed theology from worship by the creation of an academic version of *theology* that can be practiced apart from the worship of God, which has resulted in *logos* without *Theos*. The book of Psalms is a collection of songs, and these songs are deeply theological, a fact that calls for our intentional integration of worship and theology. Thus, when we consider the book of Psalms as a whole, we conclude that worship should be deeply theological and also that theology should be deeply worshipful.

The Book of Psalms Models the Value of Music in Worship.
The Psalms may be read, recited, or chanted, but they were originally meant to be sung,[48] a fact that testifies to the value of music in worship. The Hebrew word מזמור, translated 'psalm', is 'a song sung to an instrumental accompaniment',[49] and its root word, זמר, encompasses the broad idea of 'making music'.[50] The noun מזמור ('psalm')

---

[45] Lamb, *The Psalms in Christian Worship*, p. 160.
[46] Timothy M. Pierce, *Enthroned on Our Praise: An Old Testament Theology of Worship* (NAC Studies in Bible & Theology; Nashville, TN: B & H Academic, 2008), p. 239.
[47] Terrien, *The Psalms*, p. 60.
[48] Kraus, *Theology of the Psalms*, p. 12.
[49] *HALOT*, I, p. 566.
[50] *BDB*, p. 274.

occurs 57 times in the book of Psalms and the verb זמר ('make music') is found 41 times. The Psalter, therefore, places heavy emphasis upon music as a part of worship. Sigmund Mowinckel observes that in all ancient worship,

> song, music and dance play an important role. So they do in the Psalms … There can be no doubt that the Psalms were meant to be sung. They contain a number of allusions to singing, and they are often described in the titles as songs rendered to music, or as hymns.[51]

In worship we retell our story and share that testimony with our children and with other believers. It is important to note that many of the psalms are directed toward God, but most are directed toward the congregation. Our songs embody our communal memory and transmit our corporate ethos to new believers and to each new generation. The effectiveness of music is confirmed by the fact that I am unable to recall even one sermon that I heard before the age of 16, but I can sing any number of hymns that I had learned by the age of 10.[52]

I infer from the Psalms that worship through song is an end in itself and that singing does not necessarily lead to another, more important part of worship such as preaching or the Eucharist. Evangelical scholar Daniel Block, however, argues that since there is no reference to music in the instructions for the tabernacle (Exodus 25 through Leviticus 16) music is neither 'essential' to worship nor is it the main element in worship. I would point out, however, that music was later added to the sacrificial liturgy by divine command through the prophets Gad and Nathan (2 Chron. 25.29). Because the addition of music to the temple liturgy does not go along with Block's argument, he discounts Chronicles as less important than Exodus and Leviticus to a 'biblical' theology of worship. Block argues, therefore, that music is 'neither indispensable for nor the primary element in biblical worship' (p. 228). As we might expect, Block believes

---

[51] Mowinckel, *The Psalms in Israel's Worship*, p. 8. Cf. Lamb, *The Psalms in Christian Worship*, p. 6, who agrees with Mowinckel that 'the Psalms were intended to be accompanied by musical instruments', though we can say very little about the actual 'rendering of the Psalms in worship' (p. 7), that is, the musical notes etc.

[52] On the value of intergenerational worship, see Bob Bayles, 'Intergenerational Worship', in R. Keith Whitt and French L. Arrington (eds.), *Issues in Contemporary Pentecostalism* (Cleveland, TN: Pathway Press, 2012), pp. 223-40.

preaching to be the central act of worship.[53] If we were to follow Block's logic, we would note as well that there is no reference in the Exodus and Leviticus texts to either preaching or prayer. I also find it interesting that the writer of Hebrews re-envisions the Old Testament sacrifices by referring to Christian worship as 'a sacrifice of praise to God' (Heb. 13.15) not a sacrifice of preaching. Furthermore, as Melissa Archer has shown, the worship of heaven consists entirely of songs and praises to God.[54] If music is as unimportant as Block suggests, then the worship of the Psalms and the heavenly worship of Revelation must be aberrations.

Daniel Block's work purports to be a 'biblical' theology of worship, but he complains about the movement away from the church organ (which is not found in Scripture) as the primary source of worship music. I find it ironic that the instrument deemed by some early Baptists as 'the devil's instrument', should now be preferred over numerous instruments that preceded it in worship.[55] We might also lament the fact that worshipers before the Middle Ages apparently did not have appropriate musical instruments. While Block and others deem certain instruments to be more sacred than others and, therefore, more appropriate for worship, the book of Psalms seems to suggest that all musical instruments can be adapted as vehicles of worship.

The significant role of music in the Pentecostal tradition can hardly be overstated. In their book on global Pentecostalism, Donald E. Miller and Tetsunao Yamamori offer the following insight: 'Whether in a storefront building with bare florescent tubes hanging from the ceiling or in a theater with a sophisticated sound system, the

---

[53] Block, *For the Glory of God: Recovering a Biblical Theology of Worship*, p. 241.

[54] Melissa Archer, 'Worship in the Book of Revelation', in Lee Roy Martin (ed.) *Toward a Pentecostal Theology of Worship* (Cleveland, TN: CPT Press, 2016), pp. 113-38.

[55] Valdis Teraudkains, 'Leaving behind Imagined Uniformity: Changing Identities of Latvian Baptist Churches', in Ian M. Randall, Toivo Pilli, and Anthony R. Cross (eds.), *Baptist Identities: International Studies from the Seventeenth to the Twentieth Century* (Studies in Baptist History and Thought, 19; Eugene, OR: Wipf & Stock, 2006), pp. 109-22 (116). For a thorough analysis of the controversy surrounding the pipe organ, see Randall D. Engle, 'A Devil's Siren or an Angel's Throat? The Pipe Organ Controversy among the Calvinists', in Amy Nelson Burnett (ed.), *John Calvin, Myth and Reality: Images and Impact of Geneva's Reformer, Papers of the 2009 Calvin Studies Society Colloquium* (Eugene, OR: Cascade Books, 2009), pp. 107-25.

heart of Pentecostalism is the music'.[56] Harvey Cox, in his celebrated study of Pentecostalism, devotes an entire chapter to the importance of music; and regarding Pentecostalism's openness to a broad variety of musical styles, Cox observes,

> Most pentecostals gladly welcome any instrument you can blow, pluck, bow, bang, scrape, or rattle in the praise of God. I have seen photos of saxophones being played at pentecostal revivals as early as 1910 … I have heard congregations sing to the beat of salsa, bossa nova, country western, and a dozen other tempos.[57]

Pentecostal historian David Daniels has explored music within the broader context of sound. He argues that a comprehensive approach to Pentecostal history must include more than spatial and temporal data. Daniels proposes that 'historical writing on Pentecostalism should focus on the "sound and sense" that constitute early Pentecostalism between 1906 and 1932'. He writes,

> Silence and noise, chants and shouts, singing in the vernacular and in the spirit, instrumental and non-instrumental music, all were soundmarks of the Azusa Street Revival … Music and music-making become a serious task in the production of early Pentecostal sound, which ranged from sounds described as heavenly to those described as lively.[58]

In his groundbreaking work, *Pentecostal Spirituality: A Passion for the Kingdom*, theologian Steven Land argues that the songs of Pentecostalism are forms of theological reflection, and they contribute to the distinctiveness of Pentecostal worship. Land argues,

> The dance of joy and the celebration of speech were evidence that victims were freed to become participants in salvation history. Music was and is very important in that celebration; it expresses, directs, and deepens that joy. The rhythmic and repetitive nature of much of the singing reflected this joyful celebration or feast of Pentecost in the light of the end, or, to come from the other direction, the marriage supper of the Lamb anticipated in every

---

[56] Donald E. Miller and Tetsunao Yamamori, *Global Pentecostalism: The New Face of Christian Social Engagement* (Berkeley, CA: University of California Press, 2007), pp. 23-24.
[57] Cox, *Fire from Heaven*, pp. 142-43.
[58] Daniels, "'Gotta Moan Sometime'", pp. 8, 17.

Lord's Supper. Hymns of revivalism, of the Holiness movement and of the Wesleyan renewal were sung along with new gospel songs which were usually a testimony, exhortation or chronicle of the journey toward 'home'. The oral-narrative liturgy and witness of Pentecostals was a rehearsal of and for the kingdom of God. They rehearsed for the coming of the Lord, the final event of the historical drama; and the songs, testimonies and so on were a means of grace used to sanctify, encourage, mobilize, and direct them on their journey.[59]

My own experience in the Pentecostal church confirms the research of the scholars cited above. My family was Baptist, and I had been raised in that context. We sang from the hymnal, and the only accompaniment was simple understated piano music. I encountered quite a different approach to music at the Church of God, where we had a large choir that sang high energy gospel songs. Trios, quartets, and soloists were featured in almost every service, and we also had a teenage choir that sang contemporary Christian selections. The singing was accompanied by piano, organ, tambourine, and any other instrument that might be brought in. Our pianist, Carolyn McBrayer, played with such fierce self-abandon that the upright piano would shake and rock. Soon after I joined the Church of God, I invited my mother to attend church with me, and her initial response to the service was, 'I love the music'.

The Pentecostal emphasis upon music is affirmed by the presence of the book of Psalms within the biblical canon – 150 songs (not to mention the other songs scattered throughout Scripture). In light of the Psalms, I would argue that songs can function as the word of God just as surely as preaching can. God speaks to the Church through preaching, but God speaks through music also.

The Book of Psalms Witnesses to Worship as Spiritual Formation.

Worship and discipleship are often separated as two different activities with two different goals, but Jerome Boone argues that worship

---

[59] Land, *Pentecostal Spirituality*, p. 107. See also Josh P.S. Samuel, *The Holy Spirit in Worship Music, Preaching, and the Altar: Renewing Pentecostal Corporate Worship* (Cleveland, TN: CPT Press, 2018), who examines the music of the Azusa Street revival and the contemporary worship music that is in vogue today (pp. 53-134), and Benson Vaughn, *The Influence of Music on the Development of the Church of God (Cleveland, Tennessee)* (Eugene, OR: Wipf & Stock, 2018).

contributes to discipleship. In fact, he insists that within the Pentecostal tradition, worship is the 'primary locus of Christian formation'.[60] According to Boone, all of the elements of Pentecostal worship move toward formation.[61] Marva Dawn agrees, arguing that worship's 'character-forming potential is so subtle and barely noticed, and yet worship creates a great impact on the hearts and minds and lives of a congregation's members'. It follows, therefore, that the worship of Pentecostals 'forms' who they are becoming.[62] We might infer, therefore, that the ultimate purpose and goal of worship is to transform the worshiper into the image of God. The more we worship God, the more we become like God.

The observation that Pentecostal worship is a means to spiritual formation is echoed in the Psalms in at least three ways. First, the overall shape of the book of Psalms portrays the life of faith as dynamic rather than static, and it represents worship as a practice that generates progress toward spiritual growth and maturity.[63] Claus Westermann argues that life is a pendulum that swings back and forth between the extremes of lament and praise and that the Psalms take full advantage of that experiential movement to contribute to the believer's spiritual growth.[64]

Walter Brueggemann, refining and expanding on Westermann's thesis, argues that the psalms can be classified according to their functions as either psalms of orientation, psalms of disorientation, or psalms of reorientation.[65] The psalms of orientation set forth the foundational Hebrew world view. These psalms affirm that God is good and reigns over an orderly world that operates by dependable rules, in which good is rewarded and evil is punished (e.g. Psalm 1). Everything begins with this orientation, but the disruptions of life

---

[60] Boone, 'Community and Worship', p. 135.

[61] Boone, 'Community and Worship', pp. 135-42. Cf. Cheryl Bridges Johns, *Pentecostal Formation: A Pedagogy among the Oppressed* (JPTSup 2; Sheffield: Sheffield Academic Press, 1993), pp. 121-23; and Alvarado, 'Worship in the Spirit', pp. 135-51.

[62] Cf. Marva J. Dawn, *Reaching out without Dumbing Down: A Theology of Worship for This Urgent Time* (Grand Rapids, MI: Eerdmans, 1995), p. 4.

[63] This function of the psalms is explored by Brueggemann, *The Psalms and the Life of Faith*.

[64] Westermann, *The Living Psalms*, p. 14.

[65] Brueggemann, *The Message of the Psalms*. Of course, both Westermann and Brueggemann build upon Hermann Gunkel's groundbreaking form-critical work. See the above-mentioned Gunkel, *The Psalms: A Form-Critical Introduction*.

call into question the goodness of God and the assumption that the world is orderly and just. The psalms of disorientation, therefore, give voice to the complaints that surface when life is thrown into disarray (e.g. Psalm 13). The third category, the psalms of reorientation, are songs of new life that celebrate God's surprising acts of intervention and deliverance (e.g. Psalm 30). Brueggemann explains that the life of faith is a repeated movement through the cycle of orientation to disorientation to reorientation, a movement that should produce spiritual development.

Second, the concern for spiritual formation is reflected not only in the overall shape of the Psalms but also in the psalms of instruction (sometimes called the wisdom psalms).[66] The entire Psalter might be considered instructional, but several psalms are aimed explicitly toward the shaping of world view and the transmitting of the Hebrew faith (e.g. Psalms 1, 32, 37, 49, 73, 78, 112, 119, 127, 128, 133, and 145). Prayer and praise are valuable aspects of worship, but the very first psalm emphasizes worship as a learning experience, and the curriculum for learning is the 'Torah of Yahweh' (Ps. 1.2). Thus, the book of Psalms begins with teaching and includes teaching throughout the book. The wisdom psalms point to the inclusion of instructional songs as a part of the liturgy. Timothy Pierce insists, 'There is little question that the book of Psalms views instruction as an integral part of worship'.[67] According to John Lamb, the Psalms 'might well be used in the worship of the synagogue where so much emphasis was laid on teaching'.[68] Leonard Maré agrees that the Psalms were 'appropriated, conserved, and communicated as instruction to the faithful. The Psalms should therefore also be read as teachings about God, the world, ourselves and the life of faith.'[69]

Third, the function of the Psalms as aids to spiritual formation is implied by the hymns of praise for Torah (e.g. Psalms 1, 19, and 119). The word 'torah' (תורה) itself signifies instruction or teaching. The verbal form of 'torah' is ירה and means 'to point' or 'to show'. James Mays argues that the three major torah psalms outline the way in which the entire book of Psalms should be read:

---

[66] Cf. Kraus, *Theology of the Psalms*, pp. 15-16.
[67] Pierce, *Enthroned on Our Praise*, p. 238.
[68] Lamb, *The Psalms in Christian Worship*, p. 4.
[69] Maré, 'Psalm 63', p. 118.

Psalm 119 is a poetic inventory of the ways in which the instruction of the Lord in all its categories can become the agenda for virtually all the functions of psalmic hymn and prayer. Torah contains the mighty works of the Lord for which he is praised (vv 27, 18) and serves as a basis for and content of praise (vv 7, 62). It is the subject of thanksgiving for deliverance (v 46) and the fashion of sacrifice offered with thanksgiving (v 108). Involvement with torah creates the predicament in which prayer is uttered, excites the opposition of the wicked, and attracts their taunts (vv 22, 39). It is at once the motive for prayer and the answer (vv 28, 29). It is the subject of affirmation of trust (vv 33, 44) and furnishes the terms for the claim of innocence (v 69) and the content of vows (v 117) ... The coherence of the psalter with its introduction becomes clearer. The Psalms are the liturgy for those whose concern and delight is the torah of the Lord. [70]

The Psalter's overall shape, its inclusion of instructional psalms, and its praise of the torah combine to show the power of worship to effect spiritual growth and transformation. One element of this spiritual formation is particularly impacted by the Psalms. As I argue above (pp. 27-30), the book of Psalms is aimed in part at the formation of the affections. Steven Land observes that the Pentecostal experiences of regeneration, sanctification, and Spirit baptism generate the three affections of 'gratitude as praise-thanksgiving, compassion as love-longing, and courage as confidence-hope'.[71] Building on Land's approach, John Christopher Thomas names five affections that correspond broadly to the elements of the Fivefold Gospel: Salvation/Gratitude, Sanctification/Compassion, Spirit Baptism/Courage, Healing/Joy, Return of Jesus/Hope. He writes,

> While it is possible to construe the relationship between the elements of the five-fold and the transformation of the affections differently, these should serve to illustrate the point that the Pentecostal interpreter's formation within the worshipping Pentecostal community, not only opens one up to interpretive possibilities

[70] James L. Mays, 'The Place of the Torah-Psalms in the Psalter', *JBL* 106.1 (1987), pp. 3-12 (p. 9). Mays points also to Psalms 18, 25, 33, 78, 89, 93, 94, 99, 103, 105, 111, 112, 147, 148 as psalms that praise the torah.

[71] Land, *Pentecostal Spirituality*, pp. 47, 135-59.

based on his or her experience, but also has a deeply transforming impact upon the interpreter's affections.[72]

Leonard Maré pushes even farther and suggests that the spiritual formation of the individual will influence the entire community of faith. He writes that Psalm 63, for example, invites the worshiper to 'follow in the footsteps of the poet in the process of spiritual renewal … This will in turn lead to the transformation of the community of the faithful.'[73] It is time that we recognized the potential spiritual growth that can be realized through worship. Gordon McConville agrees: 'Within the context of worship, the psalmists are taking into their thinking the possibility that entire frames of reference may have to be reimagined'.[74]

The Book of Psalms Reveals Worship to be a Prophetic Witness.

The centerpiece of Walter Brueggemann's recent book on the Psalms, *From Whom No Secrets Are Hid*, is his chapter entitled 'The Counter-World of the Psalms', which he delivered at the 2013 Annual Meeting of the Society for Pentecostal Studies. In this essay, which Brueggemann considers to be his clearest formulation of the nature and function of the Psalms, he argues that the Psalms 'voice and mediate to us a counter-world that is at least in tension with our other, closely held world and in fact is often also in direct odds with that closely held world'.[75] Brueggemann identifies 'seven marks of the dominant ideology of our culture',[76] and then suggests contrasting marks that are found in the counter-world of the Psalms. The resulting contrasts are: 1. anxiety that is rooted in scarcity vs. trustful fidelity, 2. greed vs. a world of abundance, 3. self-sufficiency vs. ultimate dependence, 4. denial vs. abrasive truth telling, 5. despair vs. a world of hope, 6. amnesia vs. lively remembering, and 7. a normless world

---

[72] Thomas, "'What the Spirit Is Saying to the Church'", p. 117. For more on a theological approach to the affections, see Clapper, *John Wesley on Religious Affections*, and Castelo, 'Tarrying on the Lord', pp. 31-56.

[73] Maré, 'Psalm 63', p. 227.

[74] J. Gordon McConville, 'Spiritual Formation in the Psalms', in Andrew T. Lincoln, J. Gordon McConville, and Lloyd K. Pietersen (eds.), *The Bible and Spirituality: Exploratory Essays in Reading Scripture Spiritually* (Eugene, OR: Cascade Books, 2013), pp. 56-74 (68).

[75] Walter Brueggemann, *From Whom No Secrets Are Hid: Introducing the Psalms* (Louisville, KY: Westminster John Knox Press, 2014), p. 9.

[76] Brueggemann, *From Whom No Secrets Are Hid*, p. 10.

vs. normed fidelity.[77] Brueggemann then insists that it is the activity of Yahweh that makes this counter-world possible. The truth that we find in the Psalms, but which is absent from our present culture, is that Yahweh 'is a real agent, a lively character, and an agent of firm resolve who brings transformative energy and emancipatory capacity to all our social transactions'.[78]

At this point, Brueggemann inserts references to the Old Testament prophets, making clear a parallel that the reader may have noticed already. That is, Brueggemann's characterization of the theology of the Psalms is in fact quite similar to his description of the fundamental message of the prophets, as we find it described in his book, *The Prophetic Imagination*.[79] The theology of the Psalms, of course, is not structured in the form of judgment speeches and salvation speeches as we find in the prophets, but in the form of songs that imagine what the world is like when the preaching of the prophets is brought to real life.

What Brueggemann's insights bring to this study of worship is that in light of the fact that the psalms are particular examples of worship, they can be a model for our contemporary worship. In many places, Pentecostal worship has begun to imitate the dominant culture of American society when, instead, worship should imagine an alternative community and alternative way of life for God's people. Brueggemann's vision is echoed by Elizabeth Achtemeier:

> I suppose only if a preacher has something of such a worldview – a view of human life and of a world from which God is never absent; a view of a world in which nothing is secular; of a life that is God-haunted and God-accompanied, do the psalms of praise and lament make much sense. For that is the context in which these songs occur.[80]

Furthermore, the prophetic nature of worship is realized in its public quality. The enactment of worship is a form of proclamation, as Patrick Miller has observed:

---

[77] Brueggemann, *From Whom No Secrets Are Hid*, pp. 10-25.
[78] Brueggemann, *From Whom No Secrets Are Hid*, p. 27.
[79] Walter Brueggemann, *The Prophetic Imagination* (Philadelphia: Fortress Press, 1978).
[80] Achtemeier, 'Preaching the Praises and Laments', p. 104.

Praise and thanksgiving, therefore, turn prayer into proclamation. The very heart of the act of giving thanks and praise is a declaration of what I, or we, believe and have come to know about the Lord of life. It is a declaration that thus calls others to a response to that reality, to see, fear, and trust in the Lord who has taken away my fears and helped me.[81]

We find in the Psalms 'the testimony by which those who sing, pray, and speak point beyond themselves, the "kerygmatic intention" of their praise and confession, their prayers and teachings'.[82] Pentecostals have always conceived of their preaching as prophetic speech, and they have practiced the prophetic charismata. I am suggesting, however, that we go even farther and recognize our entire liturgy as a prophetic witness to the transformative presence and power of God in this world.

The Book of Psalms Presents Worship as an Ethical Act.
Theology, ethics, and worship are deeply and inextricably interrelated in the Psalter;[83] but in modern study, these three areas have too often been detached into discrete, exclusive categories.[84] Don Saliers laments this separation of ethical and liturgical studies:

> Questions concerning Christian ethics and the shape of the moral life cannot be adequately understood apart from thinking about

---

[81] Miller, 'Prayer and Worship', p. 62.
[82] Kraus, *Theology of the Psalms*, p. 13. The term 'kerygmatic intention' is borrowed from von Rad, *Old Testament Theology*, I, p. 106. Cf. Don Saliers, 'Liturgy and Ethics: Some New Beginnings', *JRE* 7.2 (1979), pp. 173-89 (183), who asks, '… to what extent ought the church as liturgical community make moral and ethical transformation of persons and society the purpose of worship?'
[83] The following texts from the Psalter suggest a direct link between worship and ethics, addressing, for the most part, either the ethical condition of the worshiper, the ethical requirements of the covenant, or the ethical character of Yahweh: Pss. 1.2; 5.4-6; 7.4-6, 15-17; 9.19; 10.2-11, 14, 17-18; 12.2-9; 14.4-6; 15.1-5; 18.26-28; 24.3-4; 25.8-10; 26.2-3; 31.17-18; 32.6; 33.5; 34.14-15; 37.1-3, 8, 21, 28-29; 39.12; 40.9; 41.2; 49.1-20; 50.5, 16-20; 52.3-7; 53.5; 62.11; 68.6-7; 72.1-14; 73.1-19; 74.21; 82.2-4; 84.11; 92.9, 13; 94.2, 6, 12; 96.9, 13; 97.10; 99.4, 5; 101.5, 7; 107.40-41; 112.5-10; 118.18; 119.9, 19, 29; 125.3; 130.3-8; 141.3-4; 143.2, 10; 146.9; 147.6.
[84] For example, there is no entry for either 'liturgy' or 'worship' in John Macquarrie (ed.), *Dictionary of Christian Ethics* (Philadelphia: Westminster Press, 1967). Cf. Vigen Guroian, 'Seeing Worship as Ethics: An Orthodox Perspective', *JRE* 13.2 (1985), pp. 332-59, who observes the troubling 'separation, if not an outright divorce, of worship, belief, and ethics in much of American religious discourse' (p. 332).

how Christians worship. Communal praise, thanksgiving, remembrance, confession and intercession are part of the matrix which forms intention and action ... But there has to date been a paucity of dialogue between liturgical studies and ethics, even though it seems obvious that there are significant links between liturgical life, the confession of faith, and the concrete works which flow from these. *How* we pray and worship is linked to *how* we live – to our desires, emotions, attitudes, beliefs and actions.[85]

Saliers' perspective on worship and ethics is easily comprehended by Pentecostals, who, according to Daniel Castelo, have instinctively integrated all aspects of human existence into one redeemed and transformed life, which is a 'living sacrifice' offered to God in worship (Rom. 12.1). Castelo writes,

> For early Pentecostals, a conceptual divide did not exist between worship and ethics nor between private and public life; all of these subsequent distinctions and categories that compartmentalize life were incoherent to early Pentecostals, for they saw all of their life within an integrated scheme that originated in the context of God's altering and transforming presence.[86]

It should be clear from the earlier parts of this chapter that the Psalter represents worship as a thoroughly ethical practice.[87] Inasmuch as it flows out of the covenantal relationship between Yahweh and Israel, worship both celebrates and promulgates the covenantal ethical commitments of Israel to Yahweh and to the community. It is in the covenant that Israel finds its origin and purpose for existence. Guroian insists that 'ethics is possible because a new people has come into existence' by God's saving acts and is continually 'nourished' by their liturgical life together before God.[88] This vital connection between worship and covenant is recognized by LaVerdiere, who observes that 'the covenant penetrated and gave significance' to Israel's worship and that 'the covenant is cast in a liturgical context from its very inception'. Liturgy, therefore, 'would always be covenant liturgy,

---

[85] Saliers, 'Liturgy and Ethics' (p. 174) (emphasis original). Cf. Geoffrey Wainwright, 'Eucharist and/as Ethics', *Worship* 62.2 (1988), pp. 123-38.

[86] Castelo, 'Tarrying on the Lord', p. 50.

[87] Cf. Theresa F. Koernke, 'Toward an Ethics of Liturgical Behavior', *Worship* 66.1 (1992), pp. 25-38 (27).

[88] Guroian, 'Seeing Worship as Ethics', p. 335.

flowing from the express will of the Lord of the covenant and offered by the people of God'.[89] In its function as covenant renewal and remembering of Yahweh's acts, worship would 'strengthen their moral life'.[90]

Also, the above-mentioned function of worship in spiritual formation suggests that the moral life is shaped partially through the lifelong participation in the prescribed liturgy. Don Saliers describes the role of worship in forming the affections: *'the relations between liturgy and ethics are most adequately formulated by specifying how certain affections and virtues are formed and expressed in the modalities of communal prayer and ritual action. These modalities of prayer enter into the formation of the self in community'.*[91] Gordon Wenham adds that it is the act of *participation* in prayer, praise, and confession that makes worship so effective in forming the moral life. He argues, for example, that 'if you pray ethically, you commit yourself to a path of action'.[92]

Furthermore, the Psalter's prophetic theology is weighted heavily toward ethical concerns. Therefore, worship in the book of Psalms aims for the 'moral and ethical transformation of persons and society'.[93] To put it another way, the Psalms suggest that worship bears witness to an ethical world view. From the very beginning, the Psalter describes the ethical lives and destinies of the righteous and the wicked, because 'the Lord knows the way of the righteous, but the way of the wicked will perish' (Ps. 1.6). The righteous are like a 'tree planted by the rivers of water' (Ps. 1.3) and they 'flourish like the palm tree and grow like a cedar' (Ps. 92.12). Yahweh hears the 'cry' of the righteous, but Yahweh's face is 'against those who do evil' (Ps. 34.15-16).

Righteousness is more than an abstract quality – it produces ethical actions. Positively, the righteous are generous, lending to their neighbors, and they give 'freely' to 'the poor' (Ps. 112.5-9). Negatively,

---

[89] Eugene A. LaVerdiere, 'Covenant Morality', *Worship* 38.5 (1964), pp. 240-46 (240).

[90] LaVerdiere, 'Covenant Morality', p. 242.

[91] Saliers, 'Liturgy and Ethics', p. 175 (emphasis original). Cf. Castelo, 'Tarrying on the Lord', who writes, 'the inculcation and formation of the affections arise from a context of worship' (37). Cf. Philip J. Rossi, 'Narrative, Worship, and Ethics: Empowering Images for the Shape of Christian Moral Life', *JRE* 7.2 (1979), pp. 239-48 (244).

[92] Gordon J. Wenham, 'Reflections on Singing the Ethos of God', *EJT* 18.2 (2009), pp. 115-24 (121).

[93] Saliers, 'Liturgy and Ethics', p. 183.

the righteous 'turn away from evil' (Ps. 37.27). The wicked person, however, 'plots destruction' and loves 'evil more than good' (Ps. 52.1-5). Therefore, because 'Yahweh loves justice, he will not forsake his saints … but the children of the wicked shall be cut off' (Ps. 37.26-28). The psalmist says to the wicked, 'God will break you down forever; he will snatch and tear you from your tent; he will uproot you from the land of the living' (Ps. 52.4-5).

Within this ethical world view, Yahweh takes up the cause of the oppressed. 'On every side, the wicked prowl', but Yahweh says, 'Because the poor are plundered, because the needy groan, I will now arise … I will place him in the safety for which he longs' (Ps. 12.1-8). Yahweh 'raises up the needy out of affliction and makes their families like flocks' (Ps. 107.41).

Although sometimes overlooked, the concern for justice is a significant theme in the book of Psalms. We find in the book of Psalms 97 references to 'justice' and 130 references to 'righteousness'.[94] Righteousness and justice are attributes of Yahweh, – 'He loves righteousness and justice' (Ps. 33.4-5) – and those attributes are also demanded in society. Israel is commanded, 'Give justice to the weak and the fatherless; maintain the right of the afflicted and the destitute. Rescue the weak and the needy; deliver them from the hand of the wicked' (Ps. 82.1-4). Along with the command comes a promise: 'Blessed is the one who considers the poor! In the day of trouble Yahweh delivers him' (Ps. 41.1). Worship, therefore, 'plays a very special part in telling the story of what we "should be" if we could only see ourselves "truthfully" in its light'.[95] In worship, the believer 'makes a commitment to service of others'.[96]

In this just society envisioned by the Psalms, the weakest and most vulnerable members are afforded special consideration, and worship becomes a shaper of public policy. Therefore, 'We may investigate worship as motivator of moral behavior, or liturgy as political act. Liturgy can be viewed as the promulgator of an ideology, or at least of specific moral and ethical policies.'[97] Just as in other biblical texts,

---

[94] The words 'righteous' and 'righteousness' come from the צדק root, and the words 'justice', 'just', and 'judgment' come from the שפט root.

[95] Jeffrey Bullock, 'Forum: The Ethical Implications in Liturgy', *Worship* 59.3 (1985), pp. 266-70 (269).

[96] Donald P. Gray, 'Liturgy and Morality', *Worship* 39.1 (1965), pp. 28-35 (30).

[97] Saliers, 'Liturgy and Ethics', p. 187.

those weaker members are named as the alien, the fatherless, the widow, and the poor: 'Yahweh watches over the alien; he upholds the widow and the fatherless' (Ps. 146.9, cf. Pss. 39.12; 94.6; 119.19). Regarding Yahweh's concern for the poor, the psalmist writes, 'Oh, Yahweh, who is like you, delivering the poor from him who is too strong for him, the poor and needy from him who robs him?' (Ps. 35.10).

As 'father to the fatherless and protector of widows' (Ps. 68.6), Yahweh not only cares about the weak, he requires that the community care as well. Israel is instructed, 'Give justice to the weak and the fatherless; maintain the right of the afflicted and the destitute' (Ps. 82.3). 'Blessed is the one who considers the poor!' (Ps. 41.1; cf. Pss. 10.2, 9; 37.14; 72.4).

LaVerdiere observes that worship leads to the human 'imitation' of Yahweh's righteousness, justice, goodness, and faithfulness.[98] 'In theological terms, *tsedeq* ("justice") defines how God treats his people within the framework of the covenantal relationship and reveals how God expects humans to treat one another.'[99] In this imitation, the covenant faithfulness of Yahweh is brought together with the requirement for a just society. Yahweh's faithfulness is signified by the Hebrew term חסד, which can be translated 'covenant loyalty' (see pp. 112-13 above). The חסד of Yahweh, therefore, inspires and shapes human חסד (cf. Pss. 18.25-27; 32.5-6; 50.4-5). Don Saliers argues,

> Of God, the Psalmist continually sings: 'for his love endures forever.' From this, intense affectivity may flow; and, upon occasion, from a proleptic experience the dispositions for more enduring love may be laid down in a life. That is, from an overwhelming experience of being mercifully loved and accepted, a person may find new capacities for steadfast love suddenly in place.[100]

---

[98] LaVerdiere, 'Covenant Morality', p. 244.

[99] Elias Brasil de Souza, 'Worship and Ethics: A Reflection on Psalm 15', (accessed 25 Nov. 2015); available from https://www.academia.edu/3089608/Worship_and_Ethics_A_Reflection_on_Psalm_15_A_short_study_on_the_inextricable_relation_between_worship_and_conduct_in_Psalm_15, p. 4.

[100] Saliers, 'Liturgy and Ethics', p. 182. Paul Ramsey, 'Focus on Liturgy and Ethics', *JRE* 7.2 (1979), pp. 139-248, agrees. He writes, 'The notion of steadfast "covenant" love, or agape, in Christian ethics must obviously be constantly nourished by liturgy' (p. 150). It should be noted that Saliers and Ramsey are not without their critics; cf. William W. Everett, 'Liturgy and Ethics: A Response to Saliers and Ramsey', *JRE* 7.2 (1979), pp. 203-14; and Margaret A. Farley, 'Beyond the Formal Principle: A Reply to Ramsey and Saliers', *JRE* 7.2 (1979), pp. 191-202.

The maintenance of a just society is the responsibility of every member of the community, but a greater burden is placed upon those who are in position of authority, namely, the king. The Psalms include prayers that the king may judge righteously, that he may ensure justice for the poor, that he may 'defend the cause of the poor of the people, give deliverance to the children of the needy, and crush the oppressor' (Ps. 72.1-4; cf. Pss. 72.11-14; 99.3-4).

As a relational act, worship cannot be separated from the justice of Yahweh and the covenantal demand for justice within the community. Therefore, the genuineness or validity of worship is judged by ethical criteria that lies outside of the worship act itself. Yahweh accepts only worship that is offered in the context of a just and righteous community. Psalm 15 sets forth the ethical requirements for acceptable worship:

> O Yahweh, who shall sojourn in your tent?
>   Who shall dwell on your holy hill?
> He who walks blamelessly and does what is right
>   And speaks truth in his heart;
> Who does not slander with his tongue
>   And does no evil to his neighbor,
>   Nor takes up a reproach against his friend;
> In whose eyes a vile person is despised,
>   But who honors those who fear Yahweh;
> Who swears to his own hurt and does not change;
>   Who does not put out his money at interest
>   And does not take a bribe against the innocent.
> He who does these things shall never be moved (Ps. 15.1-5).[101]

Elias Brasil de Souza argues that 'Psalm 15 establishes the inextricable relation between worship and conduct and thus highlights important characteristics of the true worshiper'.[102] He adds, 'Such a theology, without denying the value of formal adoration, brings ethics to the foreground of worship and makes appropriate relationships with the neighbor a prerequisite to communion with Yahweh'.[103]

---

[101] Cf. Pss. 5.3-7; 24.2-4; 50.15-20; 101.3-7.

[102] Souza, 'Worship and Ethics: A Reflection on Psalm 15', p. 1.

[103] Souza, 'Worship and Ethics: A Reflection on Psalm 15', p. 4. Cf. Ellen T. Charry, *Psalms 1-50* (Brazos Theological Commentary on the Bible; Grand Rapids, MI: Brazos Press, 2015), who writes that Psalm 50 rebukes those who have failed to practice the covenant's ethical demands for justice.

Further examination of the Psalter would bring to the surface a number of other ethical concerns,[104] but the texts that we have cited thus far are sufficient to illustrate the integration of worship and ethics. The book of Psalms, therefore, would seem to support the assertion of Orthodox theologian Vigen Guroian that 'Christian ethics begins when the people of God gather to worship'.[105]

The Theology of Worship Embodied in the Psalm Types

In addition to the theology of worship that can be discerned from the book of Psalms as a whole, other helpful perspectives emerge from an examination of the various psalm types. Although the book of Psalms is often characterized as a book of praises to the Lord, the very first psalm does not contain a single word of praise to God. It is clear from the outset, therefore, that the book of Psalms contains songs of many different kinds. By employing a variety of psalm types, the Hebrew psalmists were able to respond in worship to the many different situations in their lives. Biblical scholars have identified five basic genres of psalms: the individual lament, the communal lament, the communal hymn, individual thanksgiving psalms, and royal psalms. Other scholars would also suggest categories such as wisdom psalms, psalms of Zion, historical psalms, and psalms of trust. These genres do not exhibit strict, ironclad structures, nor do they explain the nature of every song in the entire collection. Nevertheless, they are helpful guides to the basic forms of biblical psalmic expression.

The Laments Call for Urgent Prayer.
The most common type of psalm is the prayer psalm, which Bible scholars call 'the lament'. The lament is the worshiper's cry to God for deliverance from distress. The sufferer's trouble may take the form of sickness (Psalm 6), personal or corporate sin (Psalm 51), oppression (Psalm 10), or an accusation (Psalm 17). The lament usually begins with an address to God, followed by the specific complaint or need. The worshiper may then confess trust in God and offer up a petition to God. The lament may include a declaration of assurance

---

[104] For example, prayers for sanctification (Pss. 7.2-5; 26.1-3; 119.28-29; 141.2-4; 143.9-10), God's forgiveness of sin (Pss. 130.2-4; 143.1-2), God's ethical teaching (Pss. 25.7-10; 94.11-12; 119.8-9), and worship by those outside of Israel (Pss. 67.4; 72.17; 117.1).

[105] Guroian, 'Seeing Worship as Ethics', p. 349.

that God has heard the prayer and conclude with a promise to praise God with a thanksgiving offering.

The laments suggest that worship is an opportunity for believers to express their deepest needs to God openly and honestly. We have learned in our religious circles to mask our true feelings, but the Psalms teach us that we are permitted to reveal everything to God. According to Walter Brueggemann, 'The church at worship remains an uncommon and peculiar venue where deep secrets of exuberance and dismay can be voiced, a voicing that is indispensable for the social and economic health of the body of faith and the body politic.'[106] Similarly, Elizabeth Achtemeier argues cogently that both praise and lament ought to be part of the believer's worship:

> That genuine life before God includes lament can be surprising to some, of course. But those are the two poles of worship that we find in the Psalter – praise and lament – and indeed, lament makes up two-thirds of the Psalms. That fact … gives the lie to the characterization of worship as only celebration … We make little room in our worship services for sobbing, either inward or outward. But the psalmists sob, as did our Lord.[107]

Therefore, the psalms of lament teach us that we should make a place for prayer in our worship services. Many churches have turned worship into nothing but celebration, and they have relegated prayer to the back rooms. Leonard Maré observes:

> In the liturgy of Pentecostal churches there is virtually no room for lament. It is a fact that someone might attend a Pentecostal service and leave thinking that Pentecostals' lives are free from any kind of negativity or disharmony. Pentecostals tend to reject any expression of feelings of negativity, anger, revenge and complaint as a legitimate part of worship. This situation, to my mind, is an impoverishment of the full spectrum of human worship before God.[108]

---

[106] Brueggemann, *Message of the Psalms*, p. xi. Cf. Samuel, *The Holy Spirit in Worship Music*, pp. 77-130, who argues for the value of lament songs in Pentecostal worship.

[107] Achtemeier, 'Preaching the Praises and Laments', p. 105.

[108] Maré, 'A Pentecostal Perspective', p. 95. Cf. Ellington, *Risking Truth*, pp. 4-14.

In the Psalms, however, worship provides a time and place for passionate prayer, for crying out to God.[109]

Walter Brueggemann argues for the theological importance of the lament:

> [T]he structure of plea and/or praise, when taken theologically and christologically, correlates with the Friday and Sunday of Christian faith. Therefore, it is precisely this psalm of lament genre that gives Christian faith its liturgical pattern of crucifixion and resurrection. One obvious implication is that the loss of the lament psalm in the worship life of the church is essentially the loss of a theology of the cross.[110]

We tend to ignore lament because we think it mitigates against praise. On the contrary, the pathos and passion of lament fuels and powers praise. Praise without lament is shallow, superficial, empty. Also, praise provides the foundation for lament. We are free to lament because we know the reality of a wonderful God. Having known praise, we feel free to lament. We know our pain will pass.

The practice of lament was commonplace in early Pentecostalism, taking the form of 'praying through' and 'tarrying'. However, this form of lament, which refers almost exclusively to seeking for salvation, has largely disappeared from present-day Pentecostalism.[111]

The lament psalms teach us that prayer is a vital component of genuine worship. Steven Land insists that 'it must be acknowledged that prayer – individual and corporate, human and "angelic", with sighs and groans, praise and petition – is at the heart of [Pentecostal] spirituality'.[112] On any given Sunday, a large portion of any congregation will consist of people who are hurting severely. The most meaningful and helpful thing we can do for them in the service is to reach out to them. They need more than a sermon. They need more than uplifting songs. They need the prayerful touch of caring brothers and

---

[109] The New Testament instructs us to include times of prayer for people in the congregation (Jas 5.13-18). We are to 'be anxious for nothing, but in everything by prayer and supplication, let [our] requests be made known unto God' (Phil. 4.6). Peter says, 'casting all your care upon him, because he cares for you' (1 Pet. 5.7). The early church prayed together in times of need (Acts 1.14; 2.42; 3.1; 4.31; 6.4, 6; 8.15; 12.5; 13.1-3; 14.23; 16.13, 25; 20.36).

[110] Brueggemann, 'The Friday Voice of Faith', p. 13.

[111] Ellington, 'The Costly Loss of Testimony', pp. 48-59.

[112] Land, *Pentecostal Spirituality*, p. 24.

sisters in Christ. They need a church that will spend time with them in prayer until the Holy Spirit breaks through to victory. Elizabeth Achtemeier writes:

> That opportunity to sob, to cry, to lament is moreover the most realistic of expressions to God. For human life is beset with miseries, fear, anxiety, and futility; with hatred and violence, cruelty and suffering; and with corruption and wasting and death. As one laywoman put it to a group of ministers, 'There's a lot of pain out there.' And it is precisely the pain of all our lives that lament lets us express – the awful, terrible upheavals and distortions caused by human sin. Until that is acknowledged, there is no reason for the gospel. Lament forms the prelude to the praise of the Lord.

The Thanksgiving Psalms Call for Times of Testimony.
The song of testimony, often called the psalm of thanksgiving, is a public celebration of answered prayer (e.g. Psalm 30). It is a testimonial to all who are present that God has intervened in the life of the worshiper. The thanksgiving psalm is based upon the final element of the lament. At the end of the lament, the petitioner promises that when the prayer has been answered, he or she will offer a thanksgiving sacrifice. After God has answered the prayer and brought deliverance, the psalmist comes with his or her family and friends to the temple. At the temple, an offering or sacrifice is made in thanks to God, and a song of testimony is sung to commemorate the occasion in praise to God.[113]

The psalm of testimony teaches us the value of public thanksgiving and the expectation of bringing an offering to God. Patrick Miller writes,

> The prayers of thanksgiving are the primary Old Testament form of testimony. They are declarations to others of what God has done … To the extent that we have abandoned that personal testimony, we have forgotten the very character of thanksgiving as a liturgical act in Scripture. It is in the most profound sort of way a testimony to one person's experience of the power of God to deliver, to be present, to transform from death to life, to lift up from the depths to the heights.[114]

---

[113] Cf. Boone, *Let There Be Praise*, pp. 121-28.
[114] Miller, 'Prayer and Worship', p. 61

Public testimony, as it is called for in the thanksgiving psalms, was once a prominent practice in Pentecostal churches. Scott Ellington has suggested that perhaps the reason for the demise of testimony as a practice is that many Pentecostals have no liturgical opportunity for testimony.[115] However, could it also be true that the practice is less common because gratitude has diminished? Gratitude was once a ruling affection for Pentecostals (and it still is in many parts of the world), but here in the West, gratitude has been replaced by greed and autonomy.[116] We are affluent, educated, powerful, and self-righteous.

The psalm of thankful testimony is meant to encourage the congregation who hear the song. John Goldingay insists that God's purposes in bringing deliverance are incomplete without our testimony. He states that 'if an Israelite sought and received God's deliverance and did not come to stand in the midst of the people of God to give God the glory, at least half of the point of that deliverance disappears'.[117] Our children need to hear that God has answered our prayers. Our friends and family need to hear what God has done in our lives. Some churches have become very impersonal, and the members of the congregation no longer share their lives with each other. These psalms demonstrate the value of sharing our testimonies with one another in the context of worship.

The Hymns Call for Extravagant Praise.
Another common type of psalm is the hymn. The hymn utters praise, glory, and honor to God. Walter Brueggemann writes, 'Israel's most characteristic utterance in worship is *praise*, the exuberant rhetorical act of gladly ceding one's life and the life of the world over to Yahweh in joyous self-abandonment'.[118] In light of the Psalter's emphasis upon praise, Michael Barrett argues, 'Since true worship is all about God, praise and thanksgiving for His person and for His works are always integral elements in biblical worship'.[119]

---

[115] See Ellington, 'The Costly Loss of Testimony', pp. 48-59; Ellington, '"Can I Get a Witness"', pp. 54-67. Cf. Boone, 'Community and Worship', pp. 140-41, and Smith, *Desiring the Kingdom*.

[116] McCann, 'Greed, Grace, and Gratitude', pp. 51-66.

[117] Goldingay, *Psalms*, I, p. 579.

[118] Brueggemann, *Worship in Ancient Israel*, p. 43 (emphasis original).

[119] Barrett, *The Beauty of Holiness*, p. 166.

While the psalm of thanksgiving offers praises to God because of a specific event in the life of the worshiper, the hymn offers praises to God because of his nature and attributes. It is a psalm that is uttered in praise of God's more comprehensive virtues (e.g. 'Praise him for his excellent greatness', Ps. 150.2). The hymns emphasize both God's majesty and his love. His majesty is expressed through affirmations of his sovereignty and his rule over creation. His love is expressed through statements about his works of salvation and provision. These hymns normally begin with an invitation to worship, followed by the reason for praise, and end with a concluding invitation to worship.

God is the God who is majestic and exalted, the King of kings, the Lord of lords, the God of gods; therefore, he is worthy of praise. God created the heaven, the earth, the angels, and all of humanity; therefore, he is worthy of praise. Not only is God majestic in holiness, but God is also loving, kind, and compassionate. God saved Israel from the bondage of Egypt; therefore, he is worthy of praise!

Regarding Psalm 150, Brueggemann writes,

> [T]his Psalm is a determined, enthusiastic, uninterrupted, relentless, unrelieved summons which will not be content until all creatures, all of life, are 'ready and willing' to participate in an unending song of praise that is sung without reserve or qualification. The Psalm expresses a lyrical self-abandonment, an utter yielding of self, without vested interest, calculation, desire, or hidden agenda. This praise is nothing other than a glad offer of self in lyrical surrender made only to the God appropriately addressed in praise. The one who speaks in this Psalm is utterly ceded over to God in praise. Everything focuses on the God to be praised. The Psalter, in correspondence to Israel's life with God when lived faithfully, ends in glad, unconditional praise, completely, and without embarrassment or distraction, focused on God.[120]

The hymns teach us that the goal of worship is praise; therefore, the Psalter concludes with a hymn of praise that declares 'Let everything that has breath praise the Lord!' (Ps. 150.6).

---

[120] Brueggemann, 'Bounded by Obedience and Praise', pp. 68-68.

The Psalms of Trust Call for Hopeful Worship.
One of the most beloved types of psalms is the psalm of trust. The psalm of trust is an expression of faith and trust that God is with his people and that God is their helper. Psalm 23 is a psalm of trust, and so is Psalm 27, which begins with these words:

> The Lord is my light and my salvation.
>   Whom shall I fear?
> The Lord is the strength of my life.
>   Of whom shall I be afraid?
> When my enemies and foes came against me to eat up my flesh,
>   they stumbled and fell.
> Though an army would encamp against me,
>   in this I will be confident (Ps. 27.1-3).

The psalms of trust suggest that through both its content and its atmosphere, worship should encourage believers to trust God. In a world where self-sufficiency is praised, the gospel demands that we admit our dependency upon almighty God. In a world characterized by despair, the worshiping Church proclaims a message of hope.[121] In a world of violence, ethnic conflict, and international power struggles, the worship of God's people should be a witness to the soon return of the Prince of Peace. In the midst of a chaotic world, worship provides a sacred space in which the heavenly voice can be heard saying, 'The Lord God omnipotent reigns!' (Rev. 19.6).

The Historical Psalms Call for Recitals of Communal Memory.
The historical psalms recount a portion of the history of Israel (see Psalms 78, 105, 106, and 136), and some of the historical psalms cover the story of Israel from the days of Abraham all the way up to the time when the psalm was written. Throughout these recitals of Israel's story, the psalms will praise God because he helped the patriarchs and because he brought Israel out of Egypt. Like the psalms of testimony, these psalms teach God's faithfulness and provide encouragement to God's people. Furthermore, the identity and ethos of the people of God are embedded in the songs.

Therefore, the historical psalms teach us that reciting our common story builds community and transmits the ethos of the

---

[121] Brueggemann, *From Whom No Secrets Are Hid*, pp. 10-25.

community to new members and to the next generation. Songs that remind us of God's involvement in our lives serve an important role in today's fast-paced world where we quickly forget our story. Claus Westermann argues that we now experience 'a great measure of *forgetting*, to a degree previously unknown in the history of the world'; therefore, 'the call not to forget' is as important now as it was when the psalms were written.[122]

Many of today's churches, particularly the mega-churches, are little more than a weekly convention of strangers, who sing, pray, and listen to a very generic sermon. Then they go their separate ways, often not even knowing one another's names. It is more vital than ever before that the Church's worship include frequent mention of the larger Christian story as well as the more particular story of the individual congregation and its families. This process of knowing one another will build community identity. It will also strengthen relationships so that everyone is less alone.[123]

The Theology of Worship Expressed in Individual Psalms

In addition to the theology of worship that can be discerned from the book of Psalms as a whole and from the various Psalm types, further insights into worship can be gained through the study of individual psalms. While space does not permit the full exploration of this category of observations, a few examples will be offered.

Psalm 1 Suggests the Centrality of Scripture in Worship.
Psalm 1 serves as an introduction to the entire book of Psalms, and it points to the central place of Scripture in worship. This first Psalm states,

> Blessed is the man
>   who does not walk in the counsel of the wicked,
>   nor stands in the path of sinners,
>   nor sits in the seat of the scorner;

---

[122] Westermann, *The Psalms: Structure, Content & Message*, p. 7 (emphasis original).
[123] My pastor, Kevin Mendel, often remarks that even in the utopian environs of the Garden of Eden, it was 'not good that Adam should be alone' (Gen. 2.18); therefore, God created community.

but his delight is in the torah of Yahweh,
  and in his torah he meditates day and night' (Ps. 1.1-2).

The key phrase of Psalm 1 is found in v. 2: 'but his delight is in the torah of Yahweh, and in his torah he meditates day and night'. The first psalm, therefore, stands as an invitation to take 'delight' in God's Word and to 'meditate' on it. Before entering into the worship of the Psalter, the worshiper is encouraged to orient his or her affections toward the torah. After the heart is attuned to the torah, then the worshiper can sing and worship. Perhaps the singing of psalms (i.e. worship) is not the only way to 'meditate' on God's torah, but it is one way to do so.[124]

Psalm 51 Includes Repentance as an Act of Worship.
For the most part, Pentecostals have emphasized repentance only in relation to conversion. The traditional Pentecostal affirmation that believers can 'live above sin' has resulted in a devaluation of post-conversion repentance. The psalms of repentance, and especially Psalm 51, however, point to the importance of repentance as a means whereby God's people can renew their covenant commitment to Yahweh. The psalmist writes boldly,

> Have mercy upon me, O God, according to your steadfast love; according to the multitude of your tender mercies, blot out my transgressions. Wash me thoroughly from my iniquity, and cleanse me from my sin. For I acknowledge my transgressions, and my sin is always before me … Create in me a clean heart, O God, and renew a steadfast spirit within me. Do not cast me away from your presence, and do not take your Holy Spirit from me. Restore to me the joy of your salvation (Ps. 51.1-12).

In light of the book of Psalms, Barrett argues that 'confession of sin' is an important ingredient in biblical worship.[125]

Psalm 63 Conceives of Worship as a Longing for God's Presence.
A passion for God is evident in from the beginning of Psalm 63:

---

[124] See Chapter 1 above. The centrality of Scripture is also attested in Psalms 19 and 119.
[125] Barrett, *The Beauty of Holiness*, p. 168.

God, you are my God;
　I will seek you earnestly;
my soul is thirsty for you;
　my flesh longs for you in a dry and weary land without water.
Thus in the sanctuary I have seen you,
　beholding your power and your glory' (Ps. 63.2-3).

Here is an articulation of deep spiritual inclinations, an expression of the psalmist's intense desire to encounter God and to experience God's presence.[126]

The longing for God is made more concrete through the metaphorical, yearning cry, 'My soul is thirsty for you; my flesh longs for you'. The language of hunger and thirst 'voices the intensity of emotional intimacy between the psalmist and God'.[127] The combination of 'soul' and 'flesh' signifies that the whole person is involved in the longing. The psalmist longs, body and soul, for his God. He longs deeply and passionately for God's presence, a presence that he has experienced in the past. In God's holy place, recounts the psalmist, 'I have seen you, beholding your power and your glory'.

The longing for God expressed in Psalm 63 brings to mind the affective component of Pentecostal spirituality, a spirituality that Steven Land has characterized as 'a passion for the kingdom', which is 'ultimately a passion for God'.[128] The psalmist's 'hunger' and 'thirst' for God is consistent with Pentecostal spirituality and that the desire to encounter God in the sanctuary is consistent with the goals of Pentecostal worship. Chris Green insists that 'Pentecostal spirituality is nothing if not a *personal* engagement' with God,[129] a 'holy desire for God Himself'.[130] Like the psalmist, the Pentecostal community is hungry and thirsty for God and seeks to behold God's power and glory, to lift up their hands in adoration, to testify of past blessings, to praise God with joyful lips, to shout for joy, to stick close to God, to rejoice in God, and to live in hope of the coming reign of God.

---

[126] See Chapter 2, above.
[127] Crenshaw, *The Psalms: An Introduction*, p. 15.
[128] Land, *Pentecostal Spirituality*, pp. 2, 97, 120, 73-80, 212, 219.
[129] Green, *Toward a Pentecostal Theology of the Lord's Supper*, p. 289 (emphasis original).
[130] Castelo, 'Tarrying on the Lord', p. 53.

Psalm 103 Demands that the Entire Self be Engaged in Worship.

Psalm 103 begins with these extraordinary words:

> Bless Yahweh, O my soul;
>> and all that is within me, bless his holy name!
> Bless Yahweh, O my soul,
>> and forget not all his dealings: (Ps. 103.1-2).

The hymns normally begin with a call to worship – 'Praise the Lord' – which is directed to the congregation. However, in Psalm 63, the exhortation is to the self. The psalmist calls upon himself to worship God. The words 'my soul' (נפשׁי) mean 'my total self'.[131] The words 'all that is within me' confirm that the 'self' includes the inner totality of the person. Therefore, the psalmist is saying, 'Bless the Lord, Oh, my total self – my body, mind, emotions, and will'. In this psalm, therefore, worship is the directing of the entire self toward engagement with God in remembrance and praise. The worship of Psalm 103 is not half-hearted worship.

If we take seriously Psalm 103, then everything that is inside of us – our minds, hearts, feelings, thoughts, and will – should shout the praises of God. This is not shallow worship, outward ceremony, or empty ritual. This is not the kind of worship where we are only observers, while those who are on the stage perform worship. This is worship that is coming from deep inside, with all our hearts, all of our minds, and all of our strength. This is worship 'in Spirit and in Truth' (Jn 4.23-24).

Conclusion

We have seen that, when taken as a whole, the book of Psalms stresses the importance of worship, grounds worship in covenantal commitment, integrates worship and theology, conceives of music as an end in itself, sees worship as a location of spiritual formation, and presents worship as a form of proclamation. The major psalm types suggest that worship should include urgent prayer, frequent testimonies, extravagant praise, hopeful content, and recitals of the Church's story. We have observed four individual psalms that point to the

---

[131] Cf. Goldingay, *Psalms*, III, p. 166.

centrality of Scripture in worship (Psalm 1), the inclusion of repentance as an element of worship (Psalm 51), the goal of worship as divine encounter (Psalm 63), and the call for total engagement of the self in worship (Psalm 103).

Furthermore, this study highlights a number of tensions that are found in the worship of Israel and that should be maintained in the church's worship: exuberant joy over against fearful awe, transcendence over against immanence, past remembrance over against future hope, the address to God over against the address to each other, and liturgy over against liberty.

Obviously, the observations made in this chapter are not comprehensive; nevertheless, they are suggestive for a Pentecostal theology of worship. Many of the elements of worship that I have identified in the Psalms were present in early Pentecostalism, and they remain present in many churches, especially in the majority world. Pentecostal worship in the USA, however, has been influenced by contemporary evangelical currents, including the so-called seeker friendly, emergent, and missional models, which have pushed Pentecostalism closer in worship practices to mainline Protestantism. Unfortunately, if Pentecostalism loses the distinctive heart of its worship practices, it will also lose its distinctive spirituality, theology, and identity. Furthermore, history demonstrates that the growth of the Pentecostal church is linked to its depth of worship. Hopefully, constructive studies like this one will bring renewed attention to the heart of the Pentecostal tradition and will help to strengthen the movement. May Pentecostals continue to affirm with the psalmist:

As the deer pants for brooks of water,
    so pants my soul for you, O God.
My soul thirsts for God,
    for the living God … (Ps. 42.2-3).

Appendix A

Ancient Near Eastern Musical Instruments

Assyrian Harp

Assyrian Harp

Egyptian Harp

Ram's Horn

Double Flute

Double Flute

Flute

Assyrian Cymbals

Cymbals

Seven-Stringed Lyre

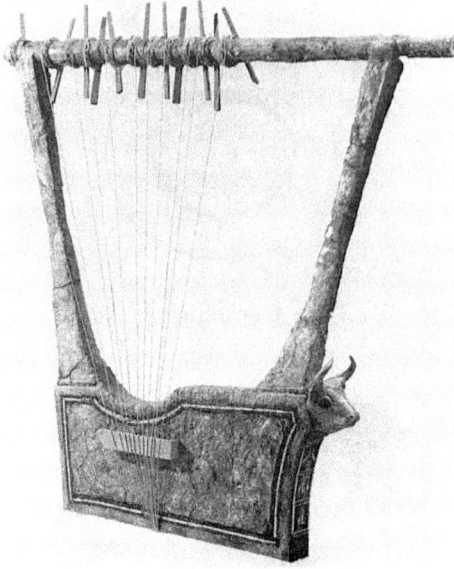

Lyre from Ur

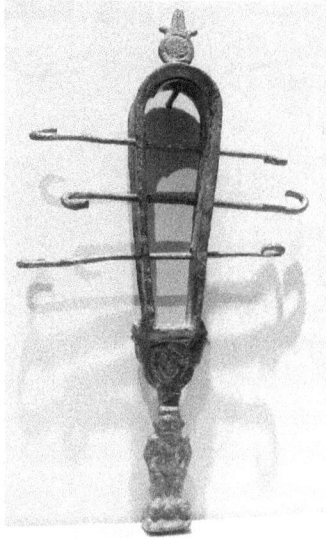

Sistrum

Hittite Musicians and Dancer

Large Hittite Drum

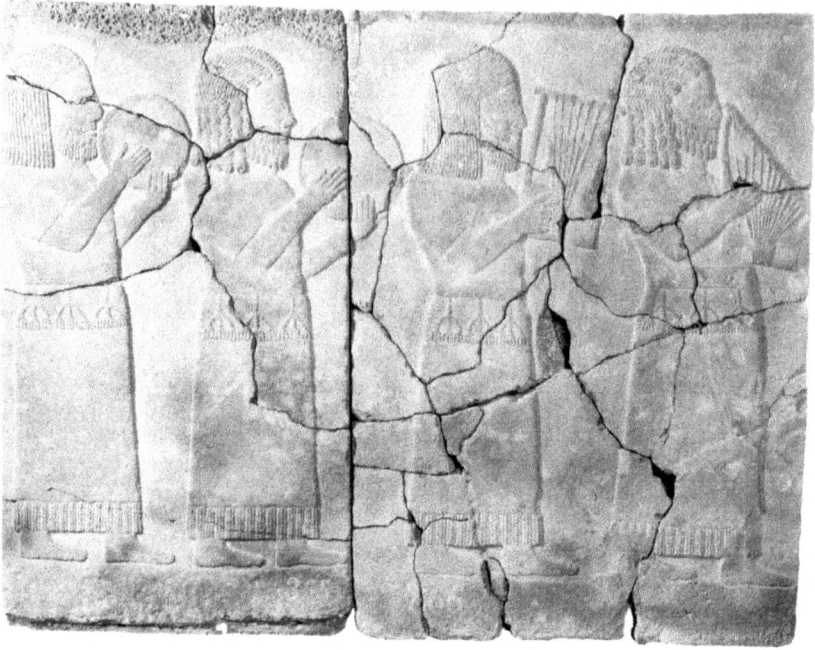

Hittite Tambourine, Lyre, and Harp

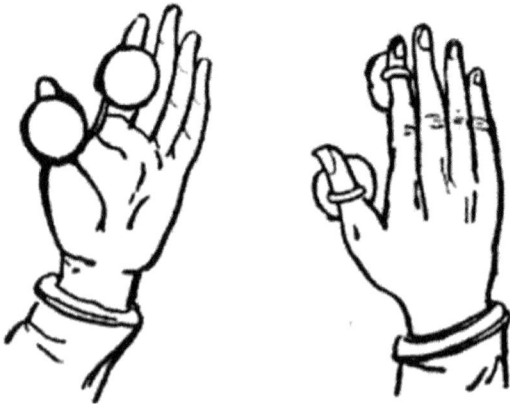

Hand Cymbals

Egyptian Dancers and Musicians

APPENDIX B

Most Frequently Cited Psalms in Early Pentecostal Periodicals (1906-1915)

The following chart lists the most frequently cited Psalms. To be included, a psalm must have been cited at least four times in either Wesleyan-Holiness or Finished Work periodicals, and it must have been cited a total of at least seven times. The Wesleyan-Holiness periodicals are *The Apostolic Faith*, *The Bridegroom's Messenger*, *The Church of God Evangel*, and *The Whole Truth*. The Finished Work periodicals are *Latter Rain Evangel*, *Pentecostal/Christian Evangel*, *The Pentecost*, *Pentecostal Testimony*, and *Word and Witness*.

W-H Most Freq.		F-W Most Freq.		Total Most Freq.	
Psalm	Freq.	Psalm	Freq.	Psalm	Freq.
103	23	119	17	103	30
91	16	51	15	119	24
9	11	18	9	91	23
34	11	23	7	51	20
37	10	34	7	34	18
45	9	45	7	45	16
126	8	91	7	9	14
2	7	103	7	23	14
23	7	32	5	37	14
107	7	66	5	107	12
119	7	71	5	2	11
27	6	107	5	18	11
50	6	139	5	27	9
105	6	2	4	50	9
1	5	24	4	105	9
8	5	37	4	126	9
19	5	42	4	42	8
30	5	78	4	8	7
51	5	122	4	19	7
104	5	149	4	30	7
25	4			32	7
42	4			46	7
46	4			66	7
62	4			78	7
143	4			104	7

All Citations of the Psalms in Early Pentecostal Periodicals (1906-1915)

The following chart lists the Psalms and their frequency of citation in the Wesleyan-Holiness periodicals and the Finished Work periodicals. The Wesleyan-Holiness periodicals are *The Apostolic Faith, The Bridegroom's Messenger, The Church of God Evangel,* and *The Whole Truth.* The Finished Work periodicals are *Latter Rain Evangel, Pentecostal/Christian Evangel, The Pentecost, Pentecostal Testimony,* and *Word and Witness.* Psalms that are missing altogether are left blank.

W-H	Freq.	F-W	Freq.	Total
1	5			5
2	7	2	4	11
3	1			1
4	2	4	1	3
5	2			2
6	2	6	2	4
		7	3	3
8	5	8	2	7
9	11	9	3	14
				0
		11	2	2
12	2	12	2	4
				0
				0
				0
16	1	16	3	4
17	2	17	1	3
18	2	18	9	11
19	5	19	2	7
20	3			3
		21	2	2
22	3	22	3	6
23	7	23	7	14
24	1	24	4	5
25	4	25	2	6
				0
27	6	27	3	9
28	2	28	2	4
29	1	29	3	4
30	5	30	2	7
31	3	31	1	4
32	2	32	5	7
33	3	33	2	5
34	11	34	7	18
35	1			1
36	1	36	1	2

W-H	Freq.	F-W	Freq.	Total
37	10	37	4	14
38	2	38	1	3
39	2			2
40	3	40	1	4
41	2			2
42	4	42	4	8
43	1			1
				0
45	9	45	7	16
46	4	46	3	7
47	3			3
48	1			1
		49	1	1
50	6	50	3	9
51	5	51	15	20
				0
				0
				0
55	2	55	1	3
56	2			2
				0
58	1			1
59	1	59	1	2
60	1			1
				0
62	4	62	2	6
63	1			1
				0
65	2	65	1	3
66	2	66	5	7
				0
68	1	68	3	4
69	2	69	3	5
				0
71	1	71	5	6
72	2	72	3	5
73	2	73	1	3
74	3			3
				0
		76	1	1
		77	3	3
78	3	78	4	7
79	1			1
		80	1	1
81	1	81	2	3
				0
				0
84	2	84	2	4
		85	3	3
		86	1	1
				0

W-H	Freq.	F-W	Freq.	Total
88	1			1
		89	1	1
90	1	90	3	4
91	16	91	7	23
92	3			3
		93	1	1
				0
95	2			2
96	1	96	1	2
		97	1	1
98	2			2
		99	2	2
100	3			3
				0
102	3	102	2	5
103	23	103	7	30
104	5	104	2	7
105	6	105	3	9
106	2	106	1	3
107	7	107	5	12
				0
109	1			1
110	3	110	1	4
111	2	111	1	3
		112	1	1
		113	3	3
		114	1	1
115	2	115	1	3
116	2	116	3	5
117	2			2
118	3	118	3	6
119	7	119	17	24
				0
121	3	121	1	4
		122	4	4
				0
				0
125	1			1
126	8	126	1	9
127	3			3
				0
				0
		130	2	2
				0
		132	1	1
133	2	133	1	3
134	1	134	1	2
135	1			1
		136	1	1
137	1			1
138	1	138	3	4

W-H	Freq.	F-W	Freq.	Total
		139	5	5
		140	1	1
141	2	141	3	5
				0
143	4	143	1	5
144	2			2
145	2			2
146	1	146	1	2
147	1			1
148	1	148	1	2
149	2	149	4	6
150	1			1

BIBLIOGRAPHY

Achtemeier, Elizabeth, *Preaching from the Old Testament* (Philadelphia: John Knox, 1989).

—'Preaching the Praises and Laments', *CTJ* 36.1 (2001), pp. 103-14.

Albrecht, Daniel E., 'Pentecostal Spirituality: Looking through the Lens of Ritual', *PNEUMA* 14.2 (1992), pp. 107-25.

—*Rites in the Spirit: A Ritual Approach to Pentecostal/Charismatic Spirituality* (JPTSup 17; Sheffield, England: Sheffield Academic Press, 1999).

—'Worshiping and the Spirit: Transmuting Liturgy Pentecostally', in T. Berger and B.D. Spinks (eds.), *Spirit in Worship–Worship in the Spirit* (Collegeville, MN: Liturgical Press, 2009), pp. 223-44.

Alden, Robert L., 'Chiastic Psalms (III): A Study in the Mechanics of Semitic Poetry in Psalms 101-150', *JETS* 21.3 (1978), pp. 199-210.

Alexander, Corky, *Native American Pentecost: Praxis, Contextualization, Transformation* (NNACMS; Cleveland, TN: Cherohala Press, 2012).

Alexander, Kimberly E., *Pentecostal Healing: Models in Theology and Practice* (JPTSup 29; Blandford Forum, UK: Deo Publishing, 2006).

Allen, Leslie C., *Psalms 101-150* (WBC, vol. 21; Waco, TX: Word Books, rev. edn, 2002).

Alvarado, Johnathan E., 'Worship in the Spirit: Pentecostal Perspectives on Liturgical Theology and Praxis', *JPT* 21.1 (2012), pp. 135-51.

Anderson, A.A., *The Book of Psalms: Based on the Revised Standard Version* (New Century Bible Commentary; 2 vols.; Grand Rapids, MI: Eerdmans, 1981).

Apostolic Faith, The (Los Angeles, California).

Apostolic Faith, The (Portland, Oregon).

Archer, Kenneth J., *A Pentecostal Hermeneutic: Spirit, Scripture and Community* (Cleveland, TN: CPT Press, 2009). First published (JPTSup 28; London: T&T Clark, 2004).

Archer, Melissa L., *'I Was in the Spirit on the Lord's Day": A Pentecostal Engagement with Worship in the Apocalypse* (Cleveland, TN: CPT Press, 2014).

—'Worship in the Book of Revelation', in Lee Roy Martin (ed.) *Toward a Pentecostal Theology of Worship* (Cleveland, TN: CPT Press, 2016), pp. 113-38.

Aristotle and J.E.C. Welldon, *The Rhetoric of Aristotle*. London: Macmillan, 1886.

Auffret, Pierre. '"Afin que nous rendions grâce à ton nom": Étude Structurelle du Psaume 106', *Studi Epigrafici e Linguitici* 11 (1994), pp. 75-96.

—'L' Étude Structurelle des Psaumes Réponses et Compléments I (Pss. 51, 57, 63, 64, 65, 86, 90, 91, 95)', *Science et Esprit* 48.1 (1996), pp. 45-60.

—'Comme un Arbre ... Étude Structurelle du Psaume 1', *BZ* 45.2 (2001), pp. 256-64.

—'Par le Tambour et la Danse: Étude Structurelle du Psaume 150', *Études Théologiques et Religieuses* 77.2 (2002), pp. 257-61.

Austel, H.J., 'שָׁפַר' in R.L. Harris, G.L. Archer and B.K. Waltke (eds.), *TWOT* (Chicago: Moody Press, 1999), II, pp. 951-52.

Baker, Robert O., 'Pentecostal Bible Reading: Toward a Model of Reading for the Formation of the Affections', in Lee Roy Martin (ed.) *Pentecostal Hermeneutics: A Reader* (Leiden: Brill, 2013), pp. 95-108.

Bayles, Bob, 'Intergenerational Worship', in R.K. Whitt and F.L. Arrington (eds.), *Issues in Contemporary Pentecostalism* (Cleveland, TN: Pathway Press, 2012), pp. 223-40.

Barrett, Michael P.V., *The Beauty of Holiness: A Guide to Biblical Worship* (Belfast: Ambassador Publications, 2006).

Barth, Christoph, 'יהל', in G.J. Botterweck and H. Ringgren (eds.), *TDOT* (trans. D.E. Green; 15 vols.; Grand Rapids, MI: Eerdmans, 1990), VI, pp. 49-55.

Barth, Karl, *Church Dogmatics* (trans. T.F. Torrance and G.W. Bromiley; 5 vols.; Edinburgh: T & T Clark, 1936).

—*The Knowledge of God and the Service of God According to the Teaching of the Reformation* (trans. J.L. M. Haire and Ian Henderson; London: Hodder and Stoughton, 1949).

Bartholomew, Ecumenical Patriarch, *Encountering the Mystery: Understanding Orthodox Christianity Today* (New York: Doubleday, 1st edn, 2008).

Baumgartel, Friedrich, 'The Hermeneutical Problem of the Old Testament', in Claus Westermann (ed.) *Essays on Old Testament Hermeneutics* (Richmond, VA: John Knox, 1963), pp. 134-59.

Bear-Barnetson, Cheryl, *Introduction to First Nations Ministry* (NNACMS; Cleveland, TN: Cherohala Press, 2013).

Berger, Teresa, and Bryan D. Spinks (eds.), *The Spirit in Worship – Worship in the Spirit* (Collegeville, MN: Liturgical Press, 2009).

Berlin, Adele, and Marc Zvi Brettler, 'Psalms', in A. Berlin and M.Z. Brettler (eds.), *The Jewish Study Bible* (Oxford: Oxford University Press, 2004), pp. 1280-446.

Beyerlin, Walter, 'Der nervus rerum in Psalm 106', *ZAW* 86.1 (1974), pp. 50-64.

Block, Daniel I., *For the Glory of God: Recovering a Biblical Theology of Worship* (Grand Rapids, MI: Baker Academic, 2014).

Blumhofer, Edith Waldvogel, *'Pentecost in My Soul': Explorations in the Meaning of Pentecostal Experience in the Assemblies of God* (Springfield, MO: Gospel Pub. House, 1989).

Boone, R. Jerome, *Let There Be Praise* (Bible Study Series; Cleveland, TN: Pathway Press, 1985).

—'Community and Worship: The Key Components of Pentecostal Christian Formation', *JPT* 8 (1996), pp. 129-42.

Booth, Wayne C., *Modern Dogma and the Rhetoric of Assent* (Notre Dame, IN: University of Notre Dame Press, 1974).

Botterweck, G. Johannes, 'חָפֵץ', in H. Ringgren (ed.), *TDOT* (trans. D.E. Green; 15 vols.; Grand Rapids, MI: Eerdmans, 1986), V, pp. 92-106.

Bratcher, R.G., and W.D. Reyburn, *A Handbook on Psalms* (UBS Handbook Series; New York: United Bible Societies, 1993).

Bridegroom's Messenger, The (Atlanta, Georgia).

Briggs, Charles A., and Emilie Grace Briggs, *A Critical and Exegetical Commentary on the Book of Psalms* (ICC; 2 vols.; Edinburgh: T. & T. Clark, 1969).

Bright, John, *The Authority of the Old Testament* (Nashville: Abingdon, 1967).

Brown, Francis, *et al.*, *The New Brown, Driver, Briggs, Gesenius Hebrew and English Lexicon: With an Appendix Containing the Biblical Aramaic* (trans. Edward Robinson; Peabody, MA: Hendrickson, 1979).

Brown, Michael L., *Hyper-Grace: Exposing the Dangers of the Modern Grace Movement* (Lake Mary, FL: Charisma House, 2014).

Broyles, Craig C., *Psalms* (New International Biblical Commentary; Peabody, MA: Hendrickson, 1999).

Brueggemann, Walter, *The Prophetic Imagination* (Philadelphia: Fortress Press, 1978).

—'Psalms and the Life of Faith: A Suggested Typology of Function', *JSOT* 17 (1980), pp. 3-32.

—*The Creative Word: Canon as a Model for Biblical Education* (Philadelphia: Fortress Press, 1982).

—'Response to John Goldingay's "the Dynamic Cycle of Praise and Prayer" (JSOT 20 [1981] 85-90)', *JSOT* 7.22 (1982), pp. 141-42.

—*The Message of the Psalms: A Theological Commentary* (Minneapolis, MN: Augsburg, 1984).

—*Hopeful Imagination: Prophetic Voices in Exile* (Philadelphia: Fortress Press, 1986).

—'The Costly Loss of Lament', *JSOT* 36 (1986), pp. 57-71.

—*Abiding Astonishment : Psalms, Modernity, and the Making of History* (Louisville, KY: Westminster/John Knox Press, 1st edn, 1991).

—'Bounded by Obedience and Praise: The Psalms as Canon', *JSOT* 50 (1991), pp. 63-92.

—'Praise and the Psalms: A Politics of Glad Abandonment', *The Hymn* 43 (1992), pp. 14-18.

—*The Psalms and the Life of Faith* (ed. Patrick D. Miller; Minneapolis, MN: Fortress Press, 1995).

—*Theology of the Old Testament: Testimony, Dispute, Advocacy* (Minneapolis, MN: Fortress Press, 1997).

—'The Friday Voice of Faith', *CTJ* 36.1 (2001), pp. 12-21.

—*The Bible Makes Sense* (Cincinnati: St. Anthony Messenger Press, 2nd edn, 2003).

—*Worship in Ancient Israel: An Essential Guide* (Nashville, TN: Abingdon Press, 2005).

—*A Pathway of Interpretation: The Old Testament for Pastors and Students* (Eugene, OR: Cascade Books, 2008).

—'A Grateful Response among Pentecostals', *JPT* 22.2, (2013), pp. 182-86.

—*From Whom No Secrets Are Hid: Introducing the Psalms* (Louisville, KY: Westminster John Knox Press, 2014).

Brueggemann, Walter, and W.H. Bellinger, *Psalms* (New Cambridge Bible Commentary; New York: Cambridge University Press, 2014).

Brueggemann, Walter and Patrick D. Miller, *Old Testament Theology: Essays on Structure, Theme, and Text* (Minneapolis, MN: Fortress Press, 1992).

—'Psalm 73 as a Canonical Marker', *JSOT* 72 (1996), pp. 45-56.

Bullock, C. Hassell, *Encountering the Book of Psalms: A Literary and Theological Introduction* (Encountering Biblical Studies; Grand Rapids, MI: Baker Academic, 2001).

Bullock, Jeffrey, 'Forum: The Ethical Implications in Liturgy', *Worship* 59.3 (1985), pp. 266-70.

Bultmann, Rudolph, 'Prophecy and Fulfillment', in Claus Westermann (ed.) *Essays on Old Testament Hermeneutics* (Richmond, VA: John Knox, 1963), pp. 50-75.

Calvin, John, *Commentary on the Book of Psalms* (trans. James Anderson; 5 vols.; Edinburgh: Calvin Translation Society, 1849).

Campbell, Iain D., 'Jonathan Edwards' Religious Affections as a Paradigm for Evangelical Spirituality', *SBET* 21.2 (2003), pp. 166-86.

Carro, Daniel, José Tomás Poe, and Rubén O. Zorzoli, *Comentario Bíblico Mundo Hispano: Salmos* (El Paso, TX: Editorial Munto Hispano, 1993).

Cartledge, Mark J., 'Affective Theological Praxis: Understanding the Direct Object of Practical Theology', *IJPT* 8.1 (2004), pp. 34-52.

Cassiodorus, Flavius Magnus Aurelius, *Cassiodori Clarissimi Senatoris Romani in Psalterium Expositio* (Venice: Impensa heredum Octaviani Scoti ac sociorum, 1517).

Castelo, Daniel, 'Tarrying on the Lord: Affections, Virtues and Theological Ethics in Pentecostal Perspective', *JPT* 13.1 (2004), pp. 31-56.

—*Pentecostalism as a Christian Mystical Tradition* (Grand Rapids, MI: Eerdmans, 2017).

Cate, Robert L., 'Psalm 105: The Mighty Acts of God', *The Theological Educator* 29 (1984), pp. 45-50.

Ceresko, Anthony R., 'Endings and Beginnings: Alphabetic Thinking and the Shaping of Psalms 106 and 150', *CBQ* 68.1 (2006), pp. 32-46.

Charry, Ellen T., *Psalms 1-50* (Brazos Theological Commentary on the Bible; Grand Rapids, MI: Brazos Press, 2015).

Childs, Brevard S., *Introduction to the Old Testament as Scripture* (Philadelphia: Fortress Press, 1st American edn, 1979).

Chrysostom, John, 'Homily on Ephesians, 2', *PG*, 62.129-30.

Church of God Evangel, The (Cleveland, Tennessee).

Church, Casey, *Holy Smoke: The Contextual Use of Native American Ritual and Ceremony* (NNACMS; Cleveland, TN: Cherohala Press, 2017).

Clapper, Gregory S., *John Wesley on Religious Affections: His Views on Experience and Emotion and Their Role in the Christian Life and Theology* (Pietist and Wesleyan Studies; Metuchen, NJ: Scarecrow Press, 1989).

—'John Wesley's Abridgement of Isaac Watts' the Doctrine of the Passions Explained and Improved', *WTJ* 43.2 (2008), pp. 28-32.

—'Affections', in Joel B. Green (ed.), *Dictionary of Scripture and Ethics* (Grand Rapids, MI: Baker Academic, 2011), pp. 44-45.

Clarke, Adam, *The Holy Bible Containing the Old and New Testaments: ... With a Commentary and Critical Notes* (6 vols.; New York: Abingdon-Cokesbury, A new edn, 1883).

Clifford, Richard J., *Psalms 73-150* (Abingdon Old Testament Commentaries; Nashville: Abingdon, 2003).

Clines, David J.A., *Dictionary of Classical Hebrew* (8 vols.; Sheffield: Sheffield Academic Press, 1993).

—*The Concise Dictionary of Classical Hebrew* (Sheffield, UK: Sheffield Phoenix Press, 2009).

Coker, W.B., 'פדה', in R.L. Harris, G.L. Archer, and B.K. Waltke (eds.), *TWOT* (2 vols.; Chicago: Moody Press, 1980), II, p. 716.

Collins, C. John, 'Psalm 1: Structure and Rhetoric', *Presbyterion* 31.1 (2005), pp. 37-48.

Collins, Kenneth J., 'John Wesley's Topography of the Heart: Dispositions, Tempers, and Affections', *Methodist History* 36.3 (1998), pp. 162-75.

Conley, Thomas M., 'The Enthymeme in Perspective'. *QJS* 70, no. 2 (1984), pp. 168-87.

Coppes, Leonard J., 'הלל', in R.L. Harris, G.L. Archer and B.K. Waltke (eds.), *TWOT* (Chicago: Moody Press, 1999), I, pp. 217-18.

Coulter, Dale M., 'Pentecostals and Monasticism: A Common Spirituality?', *AGH* 30 (2010), pp. 43-49.

—'The Spirit and the Bride Revisited: Pentecostalism, Renewal, and the Sense of History', *JPT* 21.2 (2012), pp. 298-319.

—'The Whole Gospel for the Whole Person: Ontology, Affectivity, and Sacramentality', *PNEUMA* 35.2 (2013), pp. 157-61.

Cox, Harvey G., *Fire from Heaven: The Rise of Pentecostal Spirituality and the Reshaping of Religion in the 21st Century* (London: Cassell, 1996).

Craigie, Peter C., *Psalms 1-50* (WBC, 19; Waco, TX: Word, 1983).

Creach, Jerome F.D., *Yahweh as Refuge and the Editing of the Hebrew Psalter* (JSOTSup 217; Sheffield, UK: Sheffield Academic Press, 1996).

—'The Shape of Book Four of the Psalter and the Shape of Second Isaiah', *JSOT* 80 (1998), pp. 63-76.

Crenshaw, James L., *The Psalms: An Introduction* (Grand Rapids, MI: Eerdmans, 2001).

Dahood, Mitchell J., *Psalms* (AB; 3 vols.; Garden City, NY: Doubleday, 1966).

Daniels, David D., III, '"Gotta Moan Sometime": A Sonic Exploration of Earwitnesses to Early Pentecostal Sound in North America', *PNEUMA* 30.1 (2008), pp. 5-32.

Davies, Eryl W. *Biblical Criticism* (Guides for the Perplexed; London: T & T Clark, 2013).

Dawn, Marva J., *Reaching out without Dumbing Down: A Theology of Worship for This Urgent Time* (Grand Rapids, MI: Eerdmans, 1995).

Dayton, Donald W., *The Theological Roots of Pentecostalism* (Studies in Evangelicalism, 5; Metuchen, NJ: Scarecrow Press, 1987).

DeClaissé-Walford, Nancy L., *Reading from the Beginning: The Shaping of the Hebrew Psalter* (Macon, GA: Mercer University Press, 1997).

—*Introduction to the Psalms: A Song from Ancient Israel* (St. Louis, MO: Chalice Press, 2004).

DeClaissé-Walford, Nancy L., Rolf A. Jacobson and Beth LaNeel Tanner (eds.), *The Book of Psalms* (NICOT; Grand Rapids, MI: Eerdmans, 2014), pp. 1009-10.

Delitzsch, Franz, *Biblical Commentary on the Psalms* (trans. Francis Bolton; 3 vols.; Grand Rapids, MI: Eerdmans, 1867).

DiCicco, Mario M. *Paul's Use of Ethos, Pathos, and Logos in 2 Corinthians 10-13* (Mellen Biblical Press Series; Lewiston: Mellen Biblical Press, 1995).

Dixon, Thomas, *From Passions to Emotions: The Creation of a Secular Psychological Category* (Cambridge: Cambridge University Press, 2003).

Eaton, John, *The Psalms: A Historical and Spiritual Commentary with an Introduction and New Translation* (London: T & T Clark International, 2003).

Edgerton, W. Dow, *The Passion of Interpretation* (Literary Currents in Biblical Interpretation; Louisville, KY: Westminster/John Knox Press, 1992).

Edwards, Brian, *Shall We Dance?: Dance and Drama in Worship* (Welwyn, Herts, England: Evangelical Press, 1984).

Edwards, Jonathan, *Religious Affections* (Works of Jonathan Edwards; New Haven: Yale University Press, 1959).

Ellington, Scott A., 'The Costly Loss of Testimony', *JPT* 16 (2000), pp. 48-59.

—'The Reciprocal Reshaping of History and Experience in the Psalms: Interactions with Pentecostal Testimony', *JPT* 16.1 (2007), pp. 18-31.

—*Risking Truth: Reshaping the World through Prayers of Lament* (Princeton Theological Monograph Series; Eugene, OR: Pickwick Publications, 2008).

—'"Can I Get a Witness": The Myth of Pentecostal Orality and the Process of Traditioning in the Psalms', *JPT* 20.1 (2011), pp. 54-67.

Engle, Randall D., 'A Devil's Siren or an Angel's Throat? The Pipe Organ Controversy among the Calvinists', in Amy Nelson Burnett (ed.), *John Calvin, Myth and Reality: Images and Impact of Geneva's Reformer, Papers of the 2009 Calvin Studies Society Colloquium* (Eugene, OR: Cascade Books, 2009), pp. 107-25.

Eriksson, Anders, Thomas H. Olbricht and Walter G. Übelacker, *Rhetorical Argumentation in Biblical Texts: Essays from the Lund 2000 Conference* (Emory Studies in Early Christianity; Harrisburg, PA: Trinity Press, 2002).

Everett, William W., 'Liturgy and Ethics: A Response to Saliers and Ramsey', *JRE* 7.2 (1979), pp. 203-14.

Farley, Margaret A., 'Beyond the Formal Principle: A Reply to Ramsey and Saliers', *JRE* 7.2 (1979), pp. 191-202.

Flint, Peter W., *et al.*, *The Book of Psalms: Composition and Reception* (VTSup 99; Boston: Brill, 2005).

Fokkelman, J.P., *Major Poems of the Hebrew Bible: At the Interface of Hermeneutics and Structural Analysis* (Studia Semitica Neerlandica 37; Assen, The Netherlands: Van Gorcum, 1998).

—*The Psalms in Form: The Hebrew Psalter in Its Poetic Shape* (Tools for Biblical Study 4; Leiden: Deo Publishing, 2002).

Foster, Robert L., '*Topoi* of Praise in the Call to Praise Psalms: Toward a *The*ology of the Book of Psalms', in R.L. Foster and D.M. Howard Jr (eds.), *'My Words Are Lovely': Studies in the Rhetoric of the Psalms* (Library of Hebrew Bible/Old Testament Studies 467; London: T&T Clark, 2008), pp. 75-88.

Fraine, J. de, 'Le Démon du Midi: Ps 91', *Biblica* 40.2 (1959), pp. 372-83.

Fullerton, Kemper, 'Studies in the Hebrew Psalter', *BW* 36 (1910), pp. 323-28.

Gaiser, Frederick J., '"It Shall Not Reach You": Talisman or Vocation? Reading Psalm 91 in Time of War', *Word & World* 25.2 (2005), pp. 191-202.

Garrett, Mary M., 'Pathos Reconsidered from the Perspective of Classical Chinese Rhetorical Theories', *QJS* 79.1 (1993), p. 19.

Gärtner, Judith, 'The Torah in Psalm 106: Interpretations of JHWH's Saving Act at the Red Sea', in E. Zenger (ed.), *Composition of the Book of Psalms* (Bibliotheca Ephemeridum Theologicarum Lovaniensium 238; Leuven: Uitgeverij Peeters, 2010), pp. 479-88.

Garver, Eugene, *Aristotle's Rhetoric: An Art of Character* (Chicago: University of Chicago Press, 1994).

Gause, R.H., *Living in the Spirit: The Way of Salvation* (Cleveland, TN: CPT Press, Rev. and expanded edn, 2009).

—*God, Prayer, Redemption, and Hope: Pastoral and Theological Reflections* (Cleveland, TN: Cherohala Press, 2016).

Gentile, Ernest B., *Worship God!: Exploring the Dynamics of Psalmic Worship* (Portland, OR: City Bible Pub., 1994).

Gerstenberger, Erhard S., 'Singing a New Song: On Old Testament and Latin American Psalmody', *Word & World* 5.2 (1985), pp. 155-67.

—*Psalms: Part 1, with an Introduction to Cultic Poetry* (FOTL 14; Grand Rapids, MI: Eerdmans, 1988).

—*Psalms, Part 2, and Lamentations* (FOTL 15; Grand Rapids, MI: Eerdmans, 2001).

Gesenius, Wilhelm, E. Kautzsch, and A.E. Cowley, *Gesenius' Hebrew Grammar* (Oxford: The Clarendon Press, 2d English edn, 1910).

Gilchrist, Paul R., 'יָחַל', in R.L. Harris, G.L. Archer, and B.K. Waltke (eds.), *TWOT* (2 vols.; Chicago: Moody Press, 1980), I, p. 373.

Gillmayr-Bucher, Susanne, 'David, Ich und der König: Fortschreibung und Relecture in Psalm 63', in Josef M. Oesch, Andreas Vonach and Georg Fischer (eds.), *Horizonte biblischer Texte: Festschrift für Josef M. Oesch zum 60. Geburtstag* (Göttingen: Vandenhoeck & Ruprecht, 2003), pp. 71-89.

Golden, James L., *The Rhetoric of Western Thought: From the Mediteranean World to the Global Setting* (Dubuque, Iowa: Kendall/Hunt Pub. Co., 8th edn, 2003).

Goldingay, John, 'The Dynamic Cycle of Praise and Prayer in the Psalms', *JSOT* 6.20 (1981), pp. 85-90.

—*Psalms* (Baker Commentary on the Old Testament Wisdom and Psalms; 3 vols.; Grand Rapids, MI: Baker Academic, 2006).

Gray, Donald P., 'Liturgy and Morality', *Worship* 39.1 (1965), pp. 28-35.

Greco, Monica, and Paul Stenner, *Emotions: A Social Science Reader* (New York: Routledge, 2008).

Green, Chris E.W., *Toward a Pentecostal Theology of the Lord's Supper: Foretasting the Kingdom* (Cleveland, TN: CPT Press, 2012).

—'"Treasures Old and New": Reading the Old Testament with Early Pentecostal Mothers and Fathers', Presented at the Annual Meeting of the Society for Pentecostal Studies, February 29-March 3 (Virginia Beach, Virginia, 2012).

—*Sanctifying Interpretation: Vocation, Holiness, and Scripture* (Cleveland, TN: CPT Press, 2015).

Grogan, Geoffrey, *Psalms* (The Two Horizons Old Testament Commentary; Grand Rapids, MI: Eerdmans, 2008).

Gros, Jeffrey, 'Ecumenical Connections across Time: Medieval Franciscans as a Proto-Pentecostal Movement?', *PNEUMA* 34.1 (2012), pp. 75-93.

Gunkel, Hermann, *The Psalms: A Form-Critical Introduction* (Facet Books Biblical Series, 19; Philadelphia: Fortress Press, 1967).

Gunton, Colin E., *Enlightenment and Alienation: An Essay Towards a Trinitarian Theology* (Grand Rapids, MI: Eerdmans, 1985).

Guroian, Vigen, 'Seeing Worship as Ethics: An Orthodox Perspective', *JRE* 13.2 (1985), pp. 332-59.

Haidt, Jonathan, *The Righteous Mind: Why Good People Are Divided by Politics and Religion* (New York: Pantheon Books, 2012).

Harris, R. Laird, Gleason Leonard Archer, and Bruce K. Waltke (eds.), *TWOT* (2 vols.; Chicago: Moody Press, 1980).

Hartley, John E., 'קוה', in R.L. Harris, G.L. Archer, and B.K. Waltke (eds.), *TWOT* (2 vols.; Chicago: Moody Press, 1980), II, p. 791.

Hasel, G.F., 'יעף', in G.J. Botterweck and H. Ringgren (eds.), *TDOT* (trans. D.E. Green; 15 vols.; Grand Rapids, MI: Eerdmans, 1990), VI, pp. 148-54.

Hayes, John H., *Understanding the Psalms* (Valley Forge, PA: Judson Press, 1976).

Heidelberg Catechism, in German, Latin and English: With an Historical Introduction, The (New York: Scribner, tercentenary edn, 1863).

Hengstenberg, E.W., *Commentary on the Psalms* (3 vols.; Cherry Hill, NJ: Mack Publishing, 4th edn, 1972).

Henry, Matthew, *Matthew Henry's Commentary on the Whole Bible: Complete and Unabridged in One Volume* (Peabody, MA: Hendrickson Publishers, 1994).

Heschel, Abraham Joshua, *The Prophets* (2 vols.; New York: Harper & Row, 1962).

Hessel-Robinson, Timothy, 'Jonathan Edwards (1703-1758): A Treatise Concerning Religious Affections', in *Christian Spirituality* (London: Routledge, 2010), pp. 269-80.

Hill, A. Rebecca Basdeo, *Visions of God in Ezekiel: Pentecostal Explorations of the Glory and Holiness of Yahweh* (Cleveland, TN: CPT Press, 2018).

Hollenweger, Walter J., *The Pentecostals* (trans. R.A. Wilson; Minneapolis, MN: Augsburg Pub. House, 1st U.S. edn, 1972).

Hopkins, Denise Dombkowski, *Journey through the Psalms: A Path to Wholeness* (New York: United Church Press, 1990).

Hossfeld, Frank-Lothar, and Erich Zenger, *Die Psalmen I, Psalm 1-50* (Die Neue Echter Bibel Kommentar Zum Alten Testament Mit Der Einheitsübersetzung; Würzburg: Echter Verlag, 1993).

Hossfeld, Frank-Lothar, and Erich Zenger, *Psalms 2: A Commentary on Psalms 51-100* (ed. K. Baltzer; trans. L.M. Maloney; Hermeneia; Minneapolis, MN: Fortress Press, 2005).

Hossfeld, Frank-Lothar, and Erich Zenger, *Psalms 3: A Commentary on Psalms 101-150* (ed. K. Baltzer; trans. L.M. Maloney; Hermeneia; Minneapolis, MN: Fortress Press, 2011).

Human, Dirk J., '"Praise Beyond Words": Psalm 150 as Grand Finale of the Crescendo in the Psalter', *HTS* 67.1 (2011), pp. 1-10.

Hyde, Michael J., 'Emotion and Human Communication: A Rhetorical, Scientific, and Philosophical Picture', *CQ* 32.2 (1984), pp. 120-32.

Israel, Richard D., 'Rickie D. Moore, *The Spirit of the Old Testament* (JPTSup 35; Blandford Forum, Uk: Deo Publishing, 2011)', *PNEUMA* 35.3 (2013), pp. 449-50.

Jacobson, Douglas, *Thinking in the Spirit: Theologies of the Early Pentecostal Movement* (Bloomington, IN: Indiana University Press, 2003).

Jaichandran, Rebecca, and B.D. Madhav, 'Pentecostal Spirituality in a Postmodern World', *AJPS* 6.1 (2003), pp. 39-61.

Janowski, Bernd, 'Wie Ein Baum an Wasserkanälen: Psalm 1 Als Tor Zum Psalter', in Friedhelm Hartenstein and Michael Pietsch (eds.), *'Sieben Augen Auf Einem Stein' (Sach 3,9)* (Neukirchen-Vluyn: Neukirchener Verlag, 2007), pp. 121-40.

Jenkins, Philip, 'The Travels of Psalm 91', *CC* 135.2 (2018), pp. 36-37.

Jenni, Ernst, and Claus Westermann (eds.), *TLOT* (3 vols.; Peabody, MA: Hendrickson Publishers, 1997).

Jerome, *The Homilies of Saint Jerome: I, Homilies 1-59* (FC 48; Washington, DC: Catholic University of America, 1964).

—*The Homilies of Saint Jerome: II, Homilies 60-96* (FC 57; Washington, DC: Catholic University of America, 1966).

Jobs, Steve and George W. Beahm, *I, Steve: Steve Jobs, in His Own Words* (Chicago, IL: Agate, 2011).

Johns, Cheryl Bridges, *Pentecostal Formation: A Pedagogy among the Oppressed* (JPTSup 2; Sheffield: Sheffield Academic Press, 1993).

—'Yielding to the Spirit: A Pentecostal Understanding of Penitence', in Mark J. Boda and Gordon T. Smith (eds.), *Repentance in Christian Theology* (Collegeville, MN: Liturgical Press, 2006), pp. 287-306.

Johnson, David R., *Pneumatic Discernment in the Apocalypse: An Intertextual and Pentecostal Exploration* (Cleveland, TN: CPT Press, 2018).

Jones, Ivor H., 'Musical Instruments in the Bible, Pt 1', *The Bible Translator* 37.1 (1986), pp. 101-16.

Joüon, Paul, and T. Muraoka, *A Grammar of Biblical Hebrew* (Subsidia Biblica 14.1-14.2.; 2 vols.; Rome: Editrice Pontificio Istituto Biblio, corrected edn, 1993).

Kärkkäinen, Veli-Matti, '"Encountering Christ in the Full Gospel Way": An Incarnational Pentecostal Spirituality', *JEPTA* 27.1 (2007), pp. 9-23.

Kennedy, George Alexander, *Classical Rhetoric & Its Christian & Secular Tradition from Ancient to Modern Times* (Chapel Hill: University of North Carolina Press, 2nd edn, 1999).

Kidner, Derek, *Psalms 73-150: A Commentary on Books III-V of the Psalms* (London: Inter-Varsity Press, 1975).

Kimbrough, S.T., *Orthodox and Wesleyan Spirituality* (Crestwood, NY: St. Vladimir's Seminary Press, 2002).

King, Martin Luther, Jr, 'Letter from Birmingham Jail', *Liberation: An Independent Monthly*, (1963), pp. 10-16, 23.

—*Why We Can't Wait* (New York: Harper & Row, 1964).

Klein, Anja, 'Fathers and Sons: Family Ties in the Historical Psalms', in M.S. Pajunen and J. Penner (eds.), *Functions of the Psalms and Prayers in the Late Second Temple Period* (Berlin: Walter de Gruyter, 2017), pp. 320-38.

Knight, Leonard C., 'I Will Show Him My Salvation: The Experience of Anxiety in the Meaning of Psalm 91', *ResQ* 43.4 (2001), pp. 280-92.

Knowles, Christopher, *The Secret History of Rock 'N' Roll: The Mysterious Roots of Modern Music* (Berkeley, CA: Cleis Press, 2010).

Koernke, Theresa F., 'Toward an Ethics of Liturgical Behavior', *Worship* 66.1 (1992), pp. 25-38.

Köhler, Ludwig, *The Hebrew and Aramaic Lexicon of the Old Testament* (2 vols.; Leiden: E. J. Brill, Study edn, 2001).

Kourie, Celia, 'Reading Scripture through a Mystical Lens', *Acta Theologica* 15/Suppl. (2011), pp. 132-53.

Kraus, Hans-Joachim, *Theology of the Psalms* (trans. K.R. Crim; Continental Commentaries; Minneapolis, MN: Augsburg Pub. House, 1986).

—*Psalms 1-59* (trans. H.C. Oswald; Continental Commentaries; Minneapolis, MN: Augsburg Pub. House, 1988).

—*Psalms 60-150* (trans. H.C. Oswald; Continental Commentaries; Minneapolis, MN: Augsburg, 1989).

Kugler, Gili, 'The Dual Role of Historiography in Psalm 106: Justifying the Present Distress and Demonstrating the Individual's Potential Contribution', *ZAW* 126.4 (2014), pp. 546-53.

Kuizenga, John E., 'The Shadow of the Almighty', *ThT* 4.1 (1947), pp. 17-18.

Kuntz, J. Kenneth, 'Wisdom Psalms and the Shaping of the Hebrew Psalter', in Randal A. Argall, Beverly A. Bow and Rodney A. Werline (eds.), *For a Later Generation* (Harrisburg, PA: Trinity Press International, 2000), pp. 144-60.

Lack, Remi, 'Le Psaume 1 – Une Analyse Structurale', *Biblica* 57 (1976), pp. 154-67.

Lamb, John Alexander, *The Psalms in Christian Worship* (London: Faith Press, 1962).

Land, Gary, *Historical Dictionary of the Seventh-day Adventists* (New York: Rowman & Littlefield, 2nd edn, 2015).

Land, Steven J., 'A Passion for the Kingdom: Revisioning Pentecostal Spirituality', *JPT* 1 (1992), pp. 19-46.

—*Pentecostal Spirituality: A Passion for the Kingdom* (Cleveland, TN: CPT Press, 2010). First published (JPTSup 1; Sheffield: Sheffield Academic Press, 1993).

Lasso, Orlando di, *The Seven Penitential Psalms and Laudate Dominium De Caelis* (Madison, WI: A-R Editions, 1990).

Latter Rain Evangel (Chicago, Illinois).

LaVerdiere, Eugene A., 'Covenant Morality', *Worship* 38.5 (1964), pp. 240-46.

Law, Terry, *Praise Releases Faith: Transforming Power for Your Life* (Tulsa, OK: Victory House Publishers, 1987).

Leer, Teun van der, 'The Psalms as a Source for Spirituality and Worship', *Journal of European Baptist Studies* 13.2 (2013), pp. 22-28.

LeFebvre, Michael, 'Torah-Meditation and the Psalms: The Invitation of Psalm 1', in Philip S. Johnston and David Firth (eds.), *Interpreting the Psalms: Issues and Approaches* (Downers Grove, IL: IVP Academic, 2005), pp. 213-25.

Lennox, Stephen J., *Psalms: A Bible Commentary in the Wesleyan Tradition* (Indianapolis, IN: Wesleyan Pub. House, 1999).

Lewis, C.S. *Reflections on the Psalms*. [1st American ed. New York,: Harcourt, 1958.

Liefeld, Walter L., *New Testament Exposition: From Text to Sermon* (Grand Rapids, MI: Zondervan, 1984).

Limburg, James, *Psalms* (Westminster Bible Companion; Louisville, KY: Westminister John Knox Press, 2000).

Little, John S., 'The Praise Life', *TBM* 10.202 (Sept 1, 1917), p. 4.

Loewenstamm, Samuel E., 'Number of Plagues in Psalm 105', *Biblica* 52.1 (1971), pp. 34-38.

Long, Thomas G., 'Four Ways to Preach a Psalm', *Journal for Preachers* 37.2 (2014), pp. 21-32.

Lossky, Vladimir, *The Mystical Theology of the Eastern Church* (London: J. Clarke, 1957).

Luther, Martin, *Luther's Small Catechism Developed and Explained* (Philadelphia: United Lutheran Publication House, General Synod edn, 1893).

—'Preface to the Psalter', in *Luther's Works* (Philadelphia: Fortress Press, 1960), pp. 253-57.

Ma, Julie C., 'Korean Pentecostal Spirituality: A Case Study of Jashil Choi', *AJPS* 5.2 (2002), pp. 235-54.

Macchia, Frank D., 'Sighs Too Deep for Words: Towards a Theology of Glosso-lalia', *JPT* 1 (1992), pp. 47-73.

Macquarrie, John (ed.), *Dictionary of Christian Ethics* (Philadelphia: Westminster Press, 1967).

MacRobert, Iain, *The Black Roots and White Racism of Early Pentecostalism in the USA* (New York: St. Martin's Press, 1988).

Maddox, Randy L., 'A Change of Affections: The Development, Dynamics, and Dethronement of John Wesley's Heart Religion', in *'Heart Religion' in the Methodist Tradition and Related Movements* (Lanham, MD: Scarecrow Press, 2001), pp. 3-31.

Maguire, Daniel C., '*Ratio Practica* and the Intellectualistic Fallacy', *JRE* 10.1 (1982), pp. 22-39.

Maré, Leonard P., 'A Pentecostal Perspective on the Use of Psalms of Lament in Worship', *VE* 29.1 (2008), pp. 91-109.

—'Psalm 63: I Thirst for You, Oh God …', *EP* 95 (2013), pp. 217-27.

Margulis, B., 'Plagues Tradition in Ps 105', *Biblica* 50.4 (1969), pp. 491-96.

Martin, Lee Roy, 'God at Risk: Divine Vulnerability in Judges 10:6-16', *OTE* 18.3 (2005), pp. 722-40.

—'Pre-Critical Exegesis of the Book of Judges and the Construction of a Post-Critical Hermeneutic', *EP* 88 (2006), pp. 338-53.

—*The Unheard Voice of God: A Pentecostal Hearing of the Book of Judges* (JPTSup 32; Blandford Forum, UK: Deo Publishing, 2008).

—'Yahweh Conflicted: Unresolved Theological Tension in the Cycle of Judges', *OTE* 22.2 (2009), pp. 356-72.

—'"Letter from Birmingham Jail" by Martin Luther King, Jr.', in Laurence W. Mazzeno (ed.), *Masterplots II: Christian Literature* (12 Vols., Pasadena, CA: Salem Press, 4th edn, 2010), VI, pp. 3200-202.

—'Delight in the Torah: The Affective Dimension of Psalm 1', *OTE* 23.3 (2010), pp. 708-27.

— '"Where Are the Wonders?": The Exodus Motif in the Book of Judges', *Journal of Biblical and Pneumatological Research* 2 (2010), pp. 87-109.

—*Biblical Hermeneutics: Essential Keys for Interpreting the Bible* (Miami, FL: Gospel Press, 2011).

—'Longing for God: Psalm 63 and Pentecostal Spirituality', *JPT* 22.1 (2013), pp. 54-76. Reprinted as 'Psalm 63 and Pentecostal Spirituality: An Exercise in Affective Hermeneutics', in Lee Roy Martin (ed.), *Pentecostal Hermeneutics: A Reader* (Leiden: Brill, 2013), pp. 263-84.

—'"Oh Give Thanks to the Lord for He Is Good": Affective Hermeneutics, Psalm 107, and Pentecostal Spirituality', *PNEUMA* 36.3 (2014), pp. 355-78.

—'Rhetorical Criticism and the Affective Dimension of the Biblical Text', *JSem* 23.2 (2014), pp. 339-53.

—'Psalm 91 and Pentecostal Spirituality: Dwelling in the Secret Place of the Most High', Presented at the Annual Meeting of the Society of Biblical Literature, November 20-23 (San Antonio, Texas, 2016).

—'The Book of Psalms and Pentecostal Worship', in Lee Roy Martin (ed.) *Toward a Pentecostal Theology of Worship* (Cleveland, TN: CPT Press, 2016), pp. 47-88.

—(ed.), *Pentecostal Hermeneutics: A Reader* (Leiden: Brill, 2013).

—*Judging the Judges: Pentecostal Theological Perspectives on the Book of Judges* (Cleveland, TN: CPT Press, 2018).

Mathys, Hans-Peter, 'Psalm CL, *VT* 50.3 (2000), pp. 329-44.

Mayer, G., 'ידה III. Usage', in G.J. Botterweck and H. Ringgren (eds.), *TDOT* (trans. D.E. Green; 15 vols.; Grand Rapids, MI: Eerdmans, 1986), V, pp. 431-42.

Maxwell, David J., 'The Durawall of Faith: Pentecostal Spirituality in Neo-Liberal Zimbabwe', *JRA* 35.1 (2005), pp. 4-32.

Mays, James L., 'The Place of the Torah-Psalms in the Psalter', *JBL* 106.1 (1987), pp. 3-12.

—'A Question of Identity: The Threefold Hermeneutic of Psalmody', *Asbury Theological Journal* 46.1 (1991), pp. 87-94.

—*Psalms* (Interpretation; Louisville, KY: John Knox Press, 1994).

McCann, J. Clinton, Jr, 'Psalms', in *The New Interpreter's Bible* (Nashville, TN: Abingdon Press, 1996), IV, pp. 639-1280.

—'Greed, Grace, and Gratitude: An Approach to Preaching the Psalms', in David Fleer and Dave Bland (eds.), *Performing the Psalms: With Essays and Sermons by Walter Brueggemann, J. Clinton McCann Jr., Paul Scott Wilson, and Others* (St. Louis, MO: Chalice Press, 2005), pp. 51-66.

McClymond, Michael James, and Gerald R. McDermott, *The Theology of Jonathan Edwards* (New York: Oxford University Press, 2012).

McConville, J. Gordon, 'Spiritual Formation in the Psalms', in Andrew T. Lincoln, J. Gordon McConville and Lloyd K. Pietersen (eds.), *The Bible and Spirituality: Exploratory Essays in Reading Scripture Spiritually* (Eugene, OR: Cascade Books, 2013), pp. 56-74.

McElwain, Thomas, 'A Structural Approach to the Biblical Psalms: The Songs of Degrees as a Year-End Pilgrimage Motif', *Temenos* 30 (1994), pp. 113-23.

McGroarty, Brendan Ignatius, 'Humility, Contemplation and Affect Theory', *Journal of Religion and Health* 45.1 (2006), pp. 57-72.

McKay, John W., 'The Experiences of Dereliction and of God's Presence in the Psalms: An Exercise in Old Testament Exegesis in the Light of Renewal Theology', in Paul Elbert (ed.) *Faces of Renewal: Studies in Honor of Stanley M. Horton Presented on His 70th Birthday* (Peabody, MA: Hendrickson Publishers, 1988), pp. 3-19.

McMillion, Phillip, 'Psalm 105: History with a Purpose', *ResQ* 52.3 (2010), pp. 167-79.

McQueen, Larry R., *Joel and the Spirit: The Cry of a Prophetic Hermeneutic* (Cleveland, TN: CPT Press, 2010). First published (JPTSup 8; Sheffield: Sheffield Academic Press, 1995).

—*Toward a Pentecostal Eschatology: Discerning the Way Forward* (JPTSup 39; Blandford Forum, UK: Deo Publishing, 2012).

Mejia, Jorge, 'Some Observations on Psalm 107', *Biblical Theology Bulletin* 5.1 (1975), pp. 56-66.

Melton, Narelle Jane, 'Lessons of Lament: Reflections on the Correspondence between the Lament Psalms and Early Australian Pentecostal Prayer', *JPT* 20.1 (2011), pp. 68-80.

Migne, J.P., *Patrologiae Cursus Completus ... : Series Latina* (221 vols.; Paris: Apud Garnier Fratres, 1844).

—*Patrologiae Cursus Completus ... : Series Graeca* (161 vols.; Paris: Garnier, 1857).

Miller, Donald E., and Tetsunao Yamamori, *Global Pentecostalism: The New Face of Christian Social Engagement* (Berkeley, CA: University of California Press, 2007).

Miller, Patrick D., *Israelite Religion and Biblical Theology: Collected Essays* (JSOTSup 267; Sheffield, UK: Sheffield Academic Press, 2000).

—'Prayer and Worship', *CTJ* 36.1 (2001), pp. 53-62.

Minnaar, P.A., 'Aanbidding [Worship]', *Pinksterboodskapper [Pentecostal Messenger]* 8.9 (1983), pp. 2-5.

Mittelstadt, Martin W., 'Receiving Luke–Acts: The Rise of Reception History and a Call to Pentecostal Scholars', *PNEUMA* 40.3 (2018), pp. 367-88.

Moore, Rickie D., *The Spirit of the Old Testament* (JPTSup 35; Blandford Forum, UK: Deo Publishing, 2011).

Moshavi, Adina, *Word Order in the Biblical Hebrew Finite Clause: A Syntactic and Pragmatic Analysis of Preposing* (Linguistic Studies in Ancient West Semitic, 4; Winona Lake, IN: Eisenbrauns, 2010).

Mournet, Krista, 'Moses and the Psalms: The Significance of Psalms 90 and 106 within Book IV of the Masoretic Psalter', *Conversations with the Biblical World* 31 (2011), pp. 66-79.

Mowinckel, Sigmund, *The Psalms in Israel's Worship* (2 Vols. in 1; New York: Abingdon Press, 1967).

Muilenburg, James, 'Form Criticism and Beyond', *JBL* 88 (1969), pp. 1-18.

Muraoka, T., 'Foreward', in L.J. de Regt *et al.*, *Literary Structure and Rhetorical Strategies in the Hebrew Bible* (Assen, The Netherlands: Van Gorcum, 1996).

Musy, Meghan D., 'Hearing Voices: Exploring Psalmic Multivocality as Lyric Poetry' (PhD diss., McMaster Divinity College, 2018).

Negoiță, A., and H. Ringgren, 'הגה', in G.J. Botterweck and H. Ringgren (eds.), *TDOT* (trans. J.T. Willis; 13 vols.; Grand Rapids, MI: Eerdmans, 1978), III, pp. 321-24.

Niccacci, Alviero, 'A Neglected Point of Hebrew Syntax: *Yiqtol* and Position in the Sentence', *LA* 37 (1987), pp. 7-19.

—*The Syntax of the Verb in Classical Hebrew Prose* (trans. Wilfred G.E. Watson; JSOTSup 86; Sheffield: JSOT Press, 1990).

—'Analysing Biblical Hebrew Poetry', *JSOT* 74 (1997), pp. 77-93.

Norman, Larry, 'Why Should the Devil Have All the Good Music?' (*Only Visiting This Planet*, produced by Rod Edwards, Roger Hand and Jon Miller; London: AIR Studios, 1972).

Nysse, Richard William, 'Retelling the Exodus', *Word & World* 33.2 (2013), pp. 157-65.

Oeming, Manfred, *Das Buch Der Psalmen: Psalm 1-41* (Nuer Stuttgarter Kommentar Altes Testament; Stuttgart: Verlag Katholisches Bibelwerk, 2000).

Oeming, Manfred and JoachimVette, *Das Buch Der Psalmen: Psalm 42-89* (Nuer Stuttgarter Kommentar Altes Testament; Stuttgart: Verlag Katholisches Bibelwerk, 2010).

—*Das Buch Der Psalmen: Psalm 90-151* (Nuer Stuttgarter Kommentar Altes Testament; 3 vols.; Stuttgart: Verlag Katholisches Bibelwerk, 2016).

Ognibene, Richard, and Richard Penaskovic, 'Teaching Theology: Some Affective Strategies', *Horizons* 8.1 (1981), pp. 97-108.

Oikonomou, E.B., 'לִיץ', in G.J. Botterweck, H. Ringgren and H.-J. Fabry (eds.), *TDOT* (trans. D.E. Green; 15 vols.; Grand Rapids, MI: Eerdmans, 1995), VII, pp. 543-46.

Park, Myung Soo, 'Korean Pentecostal Spirituality as Manifested in the Testimonies of Believers of the Yoido Full Gospel Church', *AJPS* 7.1 (2004), pp. 35-56.

Pelikan, Jaroslav, *et al.* (eds.), *Luther's Works* (55 vols.; Saint Louis, MO: Concordia Pub. House, 1955).

Pentecostal Herald (Chicago, Illinois).

Pérez, Ignacio Carbajosa, 'Salmo 107: Unidad, Organización Y Teología', *Estudios Bíblicos* 59.4 (2001), pp. 462-79.

Pfeiffer, Robert Henry, *Introduction to the Old Testament* (New York: Harper, 1948).

Phillips, Wade H., *Quest to Restore God's House: A Theological History of the Church of God (Cleveland, Tennessee), Vol. I 1886-1923, R.G. Spurling to A.J. Tomlinson, Formation-Transformation-Reformation* (Cleveland, TN: CPT Press, 2015).

Pierce, Timothy M., *Enthroned on Our Praise: An Old Testament Theology of Worship* (Nac Studies in Bible & Theology; Nashville, TN: B & H Academic, 2008).

Poole, Matthew, *A Commentary on the Holy Bible* (3 vols.; London: The Banner of Truth Trust, 1962).

Porter, Stanley E. *Handbook of Classical Rhetoric in the Hellenistic Period : 330 B.C.-A.D. 400* (Boston: Brill, 2001).

Proudfoot, Wayne L., 'From Theology to a Science of Religions: Jonathan Edwards and William James on Religious Affections', *HTR* 82.2 (1989), pp. 149-68.

Rad, Gerhard von, *Old Testament Theology* (2 vols.; New York: Harper, 1962).

Ramsey, Paul, 'Focus on Liturgy and Ethics', *JRE* 7.2 (1979), pp. 139-248.

Regt, L.J. de, Jan de Waard, and J.P. Fokkelman, *Literary Structure and Rhetorical Strategies in the Hebrew Bible* (Winona Lake, IN: Eisenbrauns, 1996).

Robeck, Cecil M., Jr, 'The Nature of Pentecostal Spirituality', *PNEUMA* 14.2 (1992), pp. 103-106.

—*The Azusa Street Mission and Revival: The Birth of the Global Pentecostal Movement* (Nashville, TN: Nelson Reference & Electronic, 2006).

Robertson, O. Palmer, 'The Strategic Placement of the "Hallelu-Yah" Psalms within the Psalter', *JETS* 58.2 (2015), pp. 265-68.

Roffey, John W., 'Beyond Reality: Poetic Discourse and Psalm 107', in E.E. Carpenter (ed.), *Biblical Itinerary* (Sheffield, UK: Sheffield Academic Press, 1997), pp. 60-76.

Rogerson, J.W., and John W. McKay, *Psalms* (3 vols.; Cambridge: Cambridge University Press, 1977).

Rosenblatt, Samuel, 'Notes on the Psalter', *JBL* 50.4 (1931), pp. 308-10.

Ross, Allen P., *A Commentary on the Psalms* (3 vols.; Kregel Exegetical Library; Grand Rapids, MI: Kregel Academic & Professional, 2011).

Rossi, Philip J., 'Narrative, Worship, and Ethics: Empowering Images for the Shape of Christian Moral Life', *JRE* 7.2 (1979), pp. 239-48.

Ryan, Thomas, 'Revisiting Affective Knowledge and Connaturality in Aquinas', *TS* 66.1 (2005), pp. 49-68.

Rybarczyk, Edmund J., 'Spiritualities Old and New: Similarities between Eastern Orthodoxy & Classical Pentecostalism', *PNEUMA* 24.1 (2002), pp. 7-25.

—*Beyond Salvation: Eastern Orthodoxy and Classical Pentecostalism on Becoming Like Christ* (Paternoster Theological Monographs; Carlisle, UK: Paternoster Press, 2004).

Saliers, Don, 'Liturgy and Ethics: Some New Beginnings', *JRE* 7.2 (1979), pp. 173-89

Samuel, Josh P.S., *The Holy Spirit in Worship Music, Preaching, and the Altar: Renewing Pentecostal Corporate Worship* (Cleveland, TN: CPT Press, 2018).

Sarna, Nahum M., *On the Book of Psalms: Exploring the Prayers of Ancient Israel* (New York: Schocken Books, 1st paperback edn, 1993).

Scaiola, Donatella, 'The End of the Psalter', in E. Zenger (ed.) *Composition of the Book of Psalms* (Bibliotheca Ephemeridum Theologicarum Lovaniensium, 238; Leuven: Uitgeverij Peeters, 2010), pp. 701-10.

Schaefer, Konrad, *Psalms* (Berit Olam; Collegeville, MN: Liturgical Press, 2001).

Schmemann, Alexander, *The Historical Road of Eastern Orthodoxy* (Chicago: H. Regnery, 1966).

—'Thank You, O Lord!', *The Orthodox Church* 20.2 (February 1984), 1.1.

Schnider, Franz, 'Rettung Aus Seenot: Ps 107,23-32 Und Mk 4,35-41', in Ernst Haag and Frank-Lothar Hossfeld (eds.), *Freude an Der Weisung Des Herrn* (Stuttgart: Verlag Katholisches Bibelwerk, 1986), pp. 375-93.

Sheppard, Gerald T., 'Theology and the Book of Psalms', *Int* 46 (1992), pp. 143-55.

Simpson, A.B., *The Fourfold Gospel* (New York: Christian Alliance Publishing Co., 4th edn, 1890).

Simpson, John, and Edmund Weiner (eds.), *Oxford English Dictionary* (Oxford: Oxford University Press, 2nd edn, 1989).

Škulj, Edo, 'Musical Instruments in Psalm 150', in Jože Krašovec (ed.) *Interpretation of the Bible: The International Symposium in Slovenia* (JSOTSup 289; Sheffield, UK: Sheffield Academic Press, 1998), pp. 1117-30.

Smith, James K.A. *Desiring the Kingdom: Worship, Worldview, and Cultural Formation.* Vol. 1 Cultural Liturgies, 1. Grand Rapids, MI: Baker Academic, 2009.

Smith, John E., 'Testing the Spirits: Jonathan Edwards and the Religious Affections', *USQR* 37.1-2 (1982), pp. 27-37.

Souza, Elias Brasil de, 'Worship and Ethics: A Reflection on Psalm 15' (accessed 25 Nov. 2015); available from https://www.academia.edu/3089608/Worship_and_Ethics_A_Reflection_on_Psalm_15_A_short_study_on_the_inextricable_relation_between_worship_and_conduct_in_Psalm_15.

Spencer, F. Scott (ed.), *Mixed Feelings and Vexed Passions: Exploring Emotions in Biblical Literature* (Resources for Biblical Study 90; Atlanta: SBL Press, 2017).

Spengel, Leonhard von, *Rhetores Graeci* (3 vols. Lipsiae: Teubner, 1854).

Spieckermann, H., *Heilsgegenwart: eine Theologie der Psalmen* (Göttingen: Vandenhoeck and Ruprecht, 1989).

Staley, Jeffrey Lloyd, *Reading with a Passion: Rhetoric, Autobiography, and the American West in the Gospel of John* (New York: Continuum, 1995).

Steinmetz, David C., 'The Superiority of Pre-Critical Exegesis', *ThT* 37 (1980), pp. 27-38.

Sterbens, Tom, 'Worship: The Journey to Worth', in R. Keith Whitt and French L. Arrington (eds.), *Issues in Contemporary Pentecostalism* (Cleveland, TN: Pathway Press, 2012), pp. 185-210.

Steven, James H.S., 'The Spirit in Contemporary Charismatic Worship', in T. Berger and B.D. Spinks (eds.), *Spirit in Worship – Worship in the Spirit* (Collegeville, MN: Liturgical Press, 2009), pp. 245-59.

Stevens, Marty E., 'Psalm 105', *Int* 57.2 (2003), pp. 187-89.

Stronstad, Roger, *The Charismatic Theology of St. Luke* (Peabody, MA: Hendrickson, 1984).

Stuhlmueller, Carroll, 'Psalms', in *Harper's Bible Commentary* (San Francisco: Harper and Row, 1988).

Tate, Marvin E., *Psalms 51-100* (WBC, 20; Dallas, TX: Word Books, 1990).

Taylor, Jack R., *The Hallelujah Factor: An Adventure into the Principles and Practice of Praise* (Nashville, TN: Broadman Press, 1983).

Teraudkains, Valdis, 'Leaving behind Imagined Uniformity: Changing Identities of Latvian Baptist Churches', in I.M. Randall, T. Pilli, and A.R. Cross (eds.), *Baptist Identities: International Studies from the Seventeenth to the Twentieth Century* (Studies in Baptist History and Thought, 19; Eugene, OR: Wipf & Stock, 2006), pp. 109-22.

Terrien, Samuel L., *The Psalms: Strophic Structure and Theological Commentary* (Eerdmans Critical Commentary; Grand Rapids, MI: Eerdmans, 2003).

Tesh, S. Edward, and Walter D. Zorn, *Psalms* (The College Press NIV Commentary; Joplin, MO: College Press, 1999).

Theodoret and R.C. Hill, *Theodoret of Cyrus: Commentary on the Psalms, 73-150* (Washington, DC: Catholic University of America Press, 2001).

Thomas, John Christopher, 'Pentecostal Theology in the Twenty-first Century', *PNEUMA* 20 (1998), pp. 3-19.

—'"Where the Spirit Leads": The Development of Pentecostal Hermeneutics', *Journal of Beliefs & Values: Studies in Religion & Education* 30.3 (2009), pp. 289-302.

—*The Apocalypse: A Literary and Theological Commentary* (Cleveland, TN: CPT Press, 2012).

—'"What the Spirit Is Saying to the Church": The Testimony of a Pentecostal in New Testament Studies', in Kevin L. Spawn and Archie T. Wright (eds.), *Spirit and Scripture: Exploring a Pneumatic Hermeneutic* (New York: T & T Clark, 2012), pp. 115-29.

—*Footwashing in John 13 and the Johannine Community* (Cleveland, TN: CPT Press, 2nd edn, 2013). First published (JSNTSup 61; Sheffield: JSOT Press, 1991).

—'The Spirit, the Text, and Early Pentecostal Reception' (48th Annual Meeting of the Society for Pentecostal Studies, College Park, MD, 2019).

Thoreau, Henry David and Francis H. Allen, *Walden, or, Life in the Woods* (The Riverside Literature Series; Boston: Houghton Mifflin, 1910).

Tiefenbrun, Susan, 'Semiotics and Martin Luther King's "Letter from Birmingham Jail"', *Cardozo Studies in Law and Literature* 4.2 (1992), pp. 155-87.

Tomberlin, Daniel, *Pentecostal Sacraments: Encountering God at the Altar* (North Charleston, SC: CreateSpace, revised edn, 2015).

Tomlinson, A.J., *The Diary of A.J. Tomlinson 1901-1924* (The Church of God Movement Heritage Series; Cleveland, TN: White Wing Publishing House, 2012).

Torr, Stephen C., *A Dramatic Pentecostal/Charismatic Anti-Theodicy: Improvising on a Divine Performance of Lament* (Eugene, OR: Pickwick Publications, 2013).

—'Lamenting in Tongues: Glossolalia as a Pneumatic Aid to Lament', *JPT* 26.1 (2017), pp. 30-47.

Tournay, Raymond Jacques, *Seeing and Hearing God with the Psalms: The Prophetic Liturgy of the Second Temple in Jerusalem* (JSOTSup 118; Sheffield: JSOT Press, 1991).

Tucker, W. Dennis, Jr, 'Revisiting the Plagues in Psalm CV', *VT* 55.3 (2005), pp. 401-11.

Tuell, Steven Shawn, 'Psalm 1', *Int* 63.3 (2009), pp. 278-80.

Udoette, Donatus, 'Sacred Music and Dance in Israel and in Psalm 150: Biblical-Theological Foundations for African Liturgical Music and Dance', in K. Bisong and M. Kadavil (eds.), *Celebrating the Sacramental World: Essays in Honour of Emeritus Professor Lambert J. Leijssen* (Leuven: Peeters, 2010), pp. 257-71.

Van Gemeren, Willem (ed.), *New International Dictionary of Old Testament Theology and Exegesis* (5 vols.; Grand Rapids, MI: Zondervan, 1997).

Vaughn, Benson, *The Influence of Music on the Development of the Church of God (Cleveland, Tennessee)* (Eugene, OR: Wipf & Stock, 2018).

Vincent, M.A., 'The Shape of the Psalter: An Eschatological Dimension?', in P.J. Harland and C.T.R. Hayward (eds.), *New Heaven and New Earth – Prophecy and the Millennium: Essays in Honour of Anthony Gelston* (VTSup 77; Leiden: Brill, 1999), pp. 61-82.

Vogels, Walter, 'A Structural Analysis of Ps 1', *Biblica* 60 (1979), pp. 410-16.

Vondey, Wolfgang, *Pentecostalism: A Guide for the Perplexed* (New York: T & T Clark, 2013).

—*Pentecostal Theology: Living the Full Gospel* (Systematic Pentecostal and Charismatic Theology; New York: Bloomsbury T&T Clark, 2017).

Waddell, Craig, 'The Role of Pathos in the Decision-Making Process: A Study in the Rhetoric of Science Policy', *QJS* 76.4 (1990), p. 381.

Waltke, Bruce K., 'Preface to the Psalter: Two Ways', *Crux* 43.3 (2007), pp. 2-9.

Waltke, Bruce K., and Michael Patrick O'Connor, *An Introduction to Biblical Hebrew Syntax* (Winona Lake, IN: Eisenbrauns, 1990).

Ward, Roger, 'The Philosophical Structure of Jonathan Edward's Religious Affections', *CSR* 29.4 (2000), pp. 745-68.

Warnick, Barbara, 'Judgment, Probability, and Aristotle's Rhetoric', *QJS* 75.3 (1989), p. 299.

Warrington, Keith, *Pentecostal Theology: A Theology of Encounter* (New York: T & T Clark, 2008).

Weiser, Artur, *The Psalms: A Commentary* (Philadelphia: Westminster, 1962).

Welshman, F.H., 'Psalm 91 in Relation to Malawian Cultural Background', *Journal of Theology for Southern Africa* 8 (Sept 1974), pp. 24-30.

Wenham, Gordon J., 'Reflections on Singing the Ethos of God', *EJT* 18.2 (2009), pp. 115-24.

Wesley, John, *A Plain Account of Christian Perfection* (New York: G. Lane & P.P. Sanford, 1844).

—*The Works of the Rev. John Wesley* (10 vols.; London: Wesleyan Methodist Book Room, 3rd edn, 1872).

Westermann, Claus, *The Psalms: A New Translation* (Philadelphia: The Westminster Press, 1963).

—*The Praise of God in the Psalms* (Richmond: John Knox Press, 1965).

—*The Psalms: Structure, Content & Message* (Minneapolis, MN: Augsburg Pub. House, 1980).

—*Praise and Lament in the Psalms* (Atlanta, GA: John Knox Press, 1981).

—*The Living Psalms* (Grand Rapids, MI: Eerdmans, 1989).

Whybray, R.N., *Reading the Psalms as a Book* (JSOTSup 222; Sheffield: Sheffield Academic Press, 1996).

Wilcock, Michael, *The Message of Psalms 1–72: Songs for the People of God* (Bible Speaks Today; Downers Grove, IL: InterVarsity Press, 2001).

Wilkinson, Michael, and Peter Althouse, *Catch the Fire: Soaking Prayer and Charismatic Renewal* (DeKalb, IL: Northern Illinois University Press, 2014).

Wilson, Gerald H., *The Editing of the Hebrew Psalter* (SBL Dissertation Series 76; Chico, CA: Scholars Press, 1985).

—'The Shape of the Book of Psalms', *Int* 46.2 (1992), pp. 129-42.

—'Shaping the Psalter: A Consideration of Editorial Linkage in the Book of Psalms', in J. Clinton McCann Jr (ed.), *Shape and Shaping of the Psalter* (JSOTSup 159; Sheffield: JSOT Press, 1993), pp. 72-80.

Wilson, Lindsay, 'On Psalms 103-106 as a Closure to Book IV of the Psalter', in E. Zenger (ed.), *Composition of the Book of Psalms* (Bibliotheca Ephemeridum Theologicarum Lovaniensium 238; Leuven: Uitgeverij Peeters, 2010), pp. 755-68.

Wong, Fook Kong, 'Use of Overarching Metaphors in Psalms 91 and 42/43', *Sino-Christian Studies* 9 (2010), pp. 7-27.

Zenger, Erich, 'The God of Israel's Reign over the World (Psalm 90-106)', in Norbert Lohfink and Erich Zenger, *The God of Israel and the Nations: Studies in Isaiah and the Psalms* (trans. E.R. Kalin; Collegeville, MN: Liturgical Press, 2000), pp. 161-90.

Zimmerli, Walther, 'Zwillingspsalmen', in *idem, Studien zur alttestamentlichen Theologie und Prophetie: Gesammelte Aufsätze Band II* (Theologische Bücherei 51; Munich: Kaiser, 1974), pp. 261-71.

Zschech, Darlene, 'The Role of the Holy Spirit in Worship: An Introduction to the Hillsong Church, Sydney, Australia', in T. Berger and B.D. Spinks (eds.), *Spirit in Worship – Worship in the Spirit* (Collegeville, MN: Liturgical Press, 2009), pp. 285-92.

CREDITS

Permission is gratefully acknowledged for republication of material included in the following chapters of this book:

Chapter 1: *Old Testament Essays* 23.3 (2010), pp. 708-27.

Chapter 2: *Journal of Pentecostal Theology* 22.1 (April 2013), pp. 54-76.

Chapter 4: *Journal for Semitics* 28.1 (2019), forthcoming.

Chapter 4: *Old Testament Essays* 31.3 (2018), pp. 507-22.

Chapter 5: *PNEUMA* 36.3 (Fall 2014), pp. 1-24.

Chapter 6: *Pharos Journal of Theology* 100 (2019), online.

Chapter 8: *Old Testament Essays* 30.3 (2017), pp. 725-48.

Chapter 9: Lee Roy Martin (ed.), *Toward a Pentecostal Theology of Worship* (Cleveland, TN: CPT Press, 2016), pp. 47-88.

Index of Biblical References

92.12	188, 235	101.3-7	238	106.21	156
92.13	233	101.5	233	106.31	82
93	207, 230	101.7	233	106.34-44	89
94.2	233	102	123, 126	106.36	219
94.6	154, 233, 237	102.1	17	106.44	213
94.11-12	239	102.10-16	109	106.45	89, 219
94.12	233	102.16	194	106.47	83, 89, 109
95	54, 169, 212	102.17-22	109	107	97-120
95.1	213	102.25	152	107.1	220
95.2	213	103	14, 149, 187,	107.2	113, 164,
95.3	156		188, 189,		187, 189
95.4	165		210, 230,	107.2-32	109
95.6	217		249, 250, 47	107.2-9	109
96	149, 165	103.1-2	249	107.2-3	109
96.1	164	103.1	164	107	xii, xiii, 175,
96.4-6	149	103.3	154, 187, 189		187, 206
96.5	154	104.1	33, 164	107.3	111
96.9	233	104.4	200	107.6	113
96.12	213	104.29	166	107.13	113
96.13	233	105	xii, xiii, 69-	107.19	113
97	164, 165		96, 109, 19,	107.22	188, 213
97.1	154, 233		230, 245	107.23-32	109
97.7	219	105.1-2	188	107.28	113
97.8	11	105.6-11	76	107.32	155
98	149	105.1	217, 219	107.40-41	233
98.1-3	149	105.5	164	107.41	236
98.4, 6	213	105.6	76	108.5	14, 51
98.4	213, 214	105.7	76	110.3	187, 188
98.6	158	105.8-11	76	111	149, 230
98.8	213, 214	105.8-9	76	111.2	156
99	165	105.8	76, 219	111.5	219
99	230	105.9	76	111.9	219
99.1	164	105.23-25	76	112	229, 230
99.2	156	105.37	189	112.1	10
99.3-4	238	105.42	76	112.5-10	233
99.3	156	105.43	76, 213	112.5-9	235
99.4	233	105.44	76	113	81, 149
99.5	233	105.45	76	113.1	164
99.9	217	106	xii, xiii, 69-	114	187
100	149, 187,		96, 109, 123,	115	81
	214, 215		245	115.1	33, 126
100.1	161, 164,	106.1	82, 154	115.4	219
	165, 213	106.2	82, 155	117	81, 148, 149,
100.2	13	106.4-6	83		188
100.4-5	220	106.4-5	81, 83	117.1	164, 239
100.4	200	106.6	83	117.2	14, 51, 154
101.1	33	106.7-46	83	118.6	206

Index of Authors

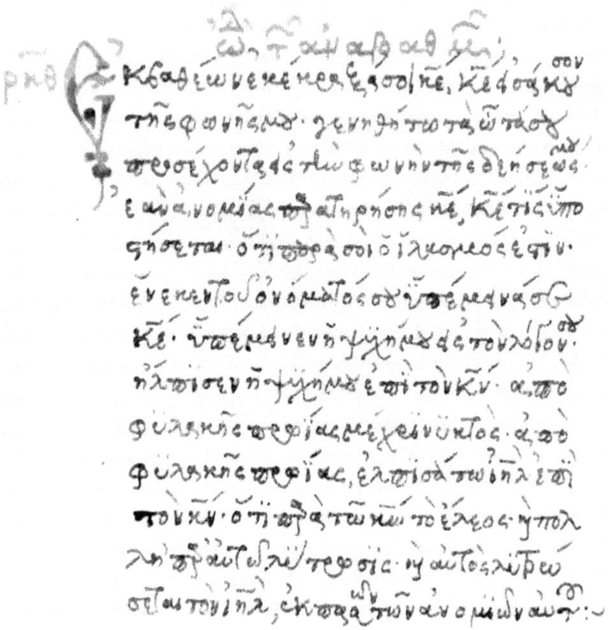

Psalm 130 [129] Codex Vaticanus

www.ingramcontent.com/pod-product-compliance
Lightning Source LLC
Chambersburg PA
CBHW060248100426
42742CB00011B/1683